ROMANIA SINCE THE SECOND
WORLD WAR

ROMANIA SINCE THE SECOND WORLD WAR

A POLITICAL, SOCIAL AND ECONOMIC HISTORY

Florin Abraham

Bloomsbury Academic
An imprint of Bloomsbury Publishing Plc

B L O O M S B U R Y
LONDON · OXFORD · NEW YORK · NEW DELHI · SYDNEY

Bloomsbury Academic

An imprint of Bloomsbury Publishing Plc

50 Bedford Square	1385 Broadway
London	New York
WC1B 3DP	NY 10018
UK	USA

www.bloomsbury.com

BLOOMSBURY and the Diana logo are trademarks of Bloomsbury Publishing Plc

First published 2017

© Florin Abraham, 2017

Florin Abraham has asserted his right under the Copyright, Designs and Patents Act, 1988, to be identified as Author of this work.

British Library Cataloguing-in-Publication Data
A catalogue record for this book is available from the British Library.

ISBN: HB: 978-1-4725-3218-3
PB: 978-1-4725-3418-7
ePDF: 978-1-4725-2992-3
ePub: 978-1-4725-2629-8

Library of Congress Cataloging-in-Publication Data
Names: Abraham, Florin, author.
Title: Romania since the Second World War: a political, social and economic history/Florin Abraham.
Description: New York: Bloomsbury Academic, 2016. | Includes bibliographical references and index.
Identifiers: LCCN 2016010353 (print) | LCCN 2016011492 (ebook) | ISBN 9781472534187 (pbk.) | ISBN 9781472532183 (hardback) | ISBN 9781472529923 (ePDF) | ISBN 9781472526298 (ePub)
Subjects: LCSH: Romania—History—1944–1989. | Romania—History—1989– | Romania—Politics and government—1944–1989. | Romania—Politics and government—1989–
Classification: LCC DR267 .A65 2016 (print) | LCC DR267 (ebook) | DDC 949.803—dc23
LC record available at http://lccn.loc.gov/2016010353

Cover design: Catherine Wood
Cover image © Getty Images, National Museum of Art of Romania

Typeset by RefineCatch Limited, Bungay, Suffolk
Printed and bound in India

To my wife, Adriana, and our children, Marco and Eliza

CONTENTS

Contents

Contents

FIGURES AND TABLES

Figures

Tables

ABBREVIATIONS

ACL	*Alianța Creștin Liberală* (Christian Liberal Alliance)
ADA	*Alianța 'Dreptate și Adevăr'* (Justice and Truth Alliance)
ALD	*Alianța Liberalilor și Democraților* (Alliance of Liberals and Democrats)
ALDE	Alliance of Liberals and Democrats for Europe
ApR	*Alianța pentru România* (Alliance for Romania)
ÁVH	Hungarian secret police
BCR	*Banca Comercială Română* (Romanian Commercial Bank)
BGC	*Biserica Greco-Catolică* (Greek-Catholic Church)
BND	*Blocul Național Democratic* (National Democratic Bloc)
BNR	*Banca Națională a României* (National Bank of Romania)
BOR	*Biserica Ortodoxă Română* (Romanian Orthodox Church)
BPD	*Blocul Partidelor Democratice* (Bloc of Democratic Parties)
BRC	Roman Catholic Church
BRD	*Banca Română de Dezvoltare* (Romanian Development Bank)
CADA	Action Committee for Army Democratization
CAP	*Cooperative Agricole de Producție* (Agricultural Production Cooperatives)
CD	*Convenția Democratică* (Democratic Convention)
CDR	*Convenția Democratică din România* (Romanian Democratic Convention)
CEC	*Casa de Economii și Consemnațiuni* (Home Savings Bank)
CEE	Central and Eastern Europe
CFE	Conventional Forces in Europe
CFSN	*Consiliul Frontului Salvării Naționale* (Council of the National Salvation Front)
CIE	Foreign Intelligence Centre
CME	Central European Media Enterprises
CNA	*Consiliul Național al Audiovizualului* (National Audiovisual Council)
CNAS	National Health Insurance Fund
CNI	National Intelligence Community
CNID	*Convenția Națională pentru Instaurarea Democrației* (National Convention for Establishing Democracy)

CNSAS	*Consiliul Național pentru Studierea Arhivelor Securității* (National Council for the Study of the *Securitate* Archives)
CoE	Council of Europe
COMECON	Council for Mutual Economic Assistance
Cominform	Communist Information Bureau
Comintern	Third International, a communist organization (1919–43)
CPSU	Communist Party of the Soviet Union
CPUN	*Consiliul Provizoriu de Uniune Națională* (the Provisional National Unity Council)
CSAȚ	Supreme Council of National Defence
CSM	*Consiliul Superior al Magistraturii* (Superior Council of Magistracy)
CSP	*Comisia de Stat a Planificării* (State Planning Commission)
CVM	Cooperation and Verification Mechanism
DNA	*Direcția Națională Anticorupție* (National Anticorruption Directorate)
DPMN	Department for the Protection of National Minorities
EADS	European Aeronautic Defence and Space Company
EBRD	European Bank for Reconstruction and Development
ECtHR	European Court of Human Rights
EIB	European Investment Bank
EPP	European People's Party
EU	European Union
FDGR	*Forumul Democrat al Germanilor din România* (Democratic Forum of Germans in Romania)
FDP	Front of Popular Democracy
FDSN	*Frontul Democrat al Salvării Naționale* (Democratic National Salvation Front)
FER	*Federația Ecologistă din România* (Romanian Ecology Federation)
FIDESZ	Hungarian Civic Alliance
FND	*Frontul Național Democrat* (National Democratic Front)
FRN	*Frontul Renașterii Naționale* (National Renaissance Front)
FSN	*Frontul Salvării Naționale* (National Salvation Front)
GAC	*Gospodării Agricole Colective* (Agricultural Collective Farms)
GATT	General Agreement on Tariffs and Trade
GDP	Gross Domestic Product
GEG	German Ethnic Group
GRU	Main Intelligence Directorate (of the Soviet Army intelligence service)

Abbreviations

IAS	*Întreprinderi Agricole de Stat* (State Agricultural Enterprises)
ÎCCJ	*Înalta Curte de Casație și Justiție* (High Court of Cassation and Justice)
ICR	Romanian Cultural Institute
IMF	International Monetary Fund
IRRD	Institute of the Romanian Revolution of December 1989
MADOSZ	Popular Hungarian Union
MAN	*Marea Adunare Națională* (Grand National Assembly)
MEBO	Management Employee Buy Out
MER	*Mișcarea Ecologistă* (Romanian Ecology Movement)
ML	*Mișcarea Legionară* (Legionary Movement)
NAVROM	Romanian maritime transport agency
ND	*Noua Dreaptă* (New Right)
NKVD	People's Commissariat for Internal Affairs
PAC	*Partidul Alianței Civice* (Civic Alliance Party)
PAR	*Partidul Alternativa României* (Alternative for Romania Party)
PC	*Partidul Conservator* (Conservative Party)
PCR	*Partidul Comunist Român* (Romanian Communist Party)
PD	*Partidul Democrat* (Democratic Party)
PDAR	*Partidul Democrat Agrar din România* (Democratic Agrarian Party of Romania)
PDL	*Partidul Democrat Liberal* (Democratic Liberal Party)
PDSR	*Partidul Democrației Sociale din România* (Party of Social Democracy in Romania)
PER	*Partidul Ecologist* (Romanian Ecology Party)
PES	Party of European Socialists
PfP	Partnership for Peace
PLD	*Partidul Liberal-Democrat* (Liberal Democratic Party)
PMR	*Partidul Muncitoresc Român* (Romanian Workers Party)
PNA	National Anticorruption Prosecution Office
PNG	*Partidul Noua Generație* (New Generation Party)
PNG-CD	PNG-'Christian-democratic' identity
PNL	*Partidul Național Liberal* (National Liberal Party)
PNL-AT	PNL-*Aripa Tânără* (PNL-Young Wing)
PNL-CD	PNL-Democratic Convention
PNR	*Partidul Național Român* (Romanian National Party)
PNȚ	*Partidul Național Țărănesc* (National Peasant Party)

PNȚCD	PNȚ Christian Democrat
PP-DD	*Partidul Poporului – Dan Diaconescu* (Dan Diaconescu People's Party)
PRM	*Partidul România Mare* (Greater Romania Party)
PS	*Partidul Socialist* (Socialist Party)
PSAL	Private Sector Adjustment Loan
PSD	*Partidul Social Democrat* (Social Democratic Party)
PSDR	*Partidul Social Democrat Român* (Romanian Social Democratic Party)
PSM	*Partidul Socialist al Muncii* (Socialist Party of Labour)
PUNRT	*Partidul de Uniune Națională a Românilor din Transilvania* (National Union Party of the Romanians of Transylvania) – later PUNR
PUR	*Partidul Umanist Român* (Romanian Humanist Party)
PV	*Partidul Verde* (Green Party)
RFE	Radio Free Europe
SI	Socialist International
SIE	*Serviciul de Informații Externe* (Foreign Intelligence Service)
SIPA	Anticorruption Intelligence and Protection Service
SLOMR	Free Trade Union of the Working People of Romania
SMT	Machines and Tractors Stations
Sovrom	joint Romanian—Soviet companies
SPP	Protection and Guard Service
SRI	*Serviciul Român de Informații* (Romanian Intelligence Service)
STS	Special Telecommunications Service
TOZ	*Întovărășiri* (agricultural associations)
UDMR	*Uniunea Democratică a Maghiarilor din România* (Democratic Alliance of Hungarians in Romania)
UFD	*Uniunea Forțelor de Dreapta* (Union of the Forces of the Right)
UNPR	*Uniunea Națională pentru Progresul României* (National Union for the Progress of Romania)
UPM	*Uniunea Populară Maghiară* (Hungarian Popular Union)
USD	*Uniunea Social Democrată* (Social Democratic Union)
USL	*Uniunea Social Liberală* (Social Liberal Union)
UTC	*Uniunea Tineretului Comunist* (Union of Communist Youth)
UTM	*Uniunea Tineretului Muncitoresc* (Union of Working Youth)
VAT	Value Added Tax
WEU	Western European Union

INTRODUCTION

We live in a world in which the impression of space compression, as a result of global communication, creates the false appearance of dilating time, of a break with the past. But this is the link of superposed plates of our memory. In a cultural context with aspirations to universality, in which the individual seems to have won the fight with his own memory, living only in the present and future, there is a risk that superficial perceptions may substitute themselves for more profound forms of knowledge. In the landscape of the global world, 'Romania' is vaguely, confusedly or conflictingly identified, as are most small and medium-sized countries. Romania is at the same time an imagined reality and a real country, populated by people with qualities and defects. Romania's recent history is not a positive or negative exceptionalism, but is the sum of tragic or fortunate experiences.

The temptation to answer the Great Questions such as 'What is Romania?' (Boia 2001: 7) or 'What are Romanians?' with the methods of social psychology (Drăghicescu 1996) is risky, as it involves the danger of uncertain generalizations. The ambition to find the Great Explanation for long-term processes such as modernization (Vlăsceanu and Hâncean 2014) can prove scientifically imprudent, as factors such as 'time' and 'historical context' are expelled in order to allow generalizations intended to superficially validate grandiose theories. Historians know that facts, or rather their documentary representations, are hard to establish and control in a causal relation. Prudence and gnoseological scepticism are the predominant attributes of the historian. That is why I am not venturing in search of some 'total' or 'ultimate' explanation of Romania's recent history. My purpose is more modest: to answer the question 'What important events happened in Romania after the Second World War?' Of course, following the evaluation of the facts, partial answers also emerge concerning the Great Questions such as 'What is Romania?' and 'What are Romanians?'

My undertaking does not unfold on an empty field. The subject of Romania's history after the Second World War is present in the specialized literature in English. Valuable studies about Romania were published in the West starting in the communist period (Ionescu 1964; King 1980; Shafir 1985; Turnock 1986; Gilberg 1990), but these are inevitably obsolete due to the 'historiography revolution' that resulted from the opening of the archives. After the fall of communism, histories of political life during communism were published (Tismăneanu 2003) as well as several other monographic studies around various issues (Verdery 1995; Kligman 1998; Kligman and Verdery 2011; Stan 2013; Stan and Turcescu 2007; Deletant 1999; Leuştean 2008). The scholarly literature on the 1989 Revolution (Siani-Davies 2005; Roper 2000) and the transition period, especially with regard to political (Gallagher 2005, 2009; Light and Phinnemore 2001) or economic

(Cernat 2006) aspects is vast. This is not the place for an exhaustive bibliographic inventory.

Individual (Georgescu 1990; Fischer-Galati 1991) or collective (Giurescu and Fischer-Galati 1998; Giurescu 2013) efforts to offer works of synthesis on Romania's history are praiseworthy. The most recent synthesis of Romania's history (Hitchins 2014) undoubtedly represents a valuable contribution, but by its conception is limited to general aspects. Another attempt at synthesis in French concerning the transition period (Petre and Durandin 2008) mainly approaches political aspects. Until the present book, a history of Romania including communism and the transition period alike and not limited to political or economic aspects or to particular aspects of socio-cultural life was missing. My undertaking seeks to fill a gap in the historiography concerning Romania, by an individual effort which has the advantage of unity of conception and analysis.

I am not seeking here to demystify Romania's history by excessive emphasis upon negative elements; neither do I wish to mythologize it by inventing fake victories and heroisms. The reader will find a balanced and nuanced analysis of the main events and processes in Romania's recent history, as a basis for understanding the complexity of the Romanian nation's past.

The book is structured chronologically and thematically. The first sequence refers to the period of the Second World War, because the establishment of the communist regime is the result of the world conflagration and cannot be understood outside of the consequences of the Hitler–Stalin Pact (1939). The part dedicated to the communist regime is more reduced than the part dedicated to the post-1989 period, because the history of communism is treated in a rich and accessible historical literature, which can easily be accessed, while for the transition period historical studies in English are only now emerging. I have included a distinct chapter about social and demographic phenomena in order not to fragment information which must be analysed as a whole.

I would like to thank James Christian Brown, Radu Ciuceanu, Remus Pricopie, Octavian Roske, George Tiugea and Marius Turda for their support towards the accomplishment of this project. This book was made possible only as a result of the openness and flexibility of Rhodri Mogford and of the competent support offered by Emma Goode of Bloomsbury. My warm gratitude goes to my wife, Adriana, and to our children, Marco and Eliza, who often did without my presence in order for this book to be ready.

Florin Abraham

Bucharest, January 2016

CHAPTER 1
UNDER THE SIGN OF THREE DICTATORSHIPS (1938–44)

When enemies become allies, and nations prey

Barely one week before Nazi Germany attacked Poland and started the Second World War, the Ribbentrop–Molotov Pact, ironically dubbed a 'non-aggression treaty', was being signed in an eerily happy atmosphere in Moscow. In the secret annex of the Soviet–German document, in the third paragraph, it was stated that: 'With regard to South-eastern Europe attention is called by the Soviet side to its interest in Bessarabia. The German side declares its complete political disinterestedness in these areas' (Bold and Seftiuc 1998: 145).

The broader significance of this seemingly impossible agreement between Stalin and Hitler is the brutal return to manifest spheres of influence, drawn and maintained with the help of military force, which seemed to have disappeared with the conclusion of the First World War. Then, new states had been formed from the ruins of old empires by application of the Wilsonian principle of self-determination of nations. The Hitler–Stalin agreement of 23 August 1939 marks the symbolic entry of Romania into a tunnel of history, along a path set by the interests and geopolitical ploys of the Great Powers.

Prior to the understanding between Hitler and Stalin, the collective security principle enshrined by a system of treaties after the end of the First Wold War had collapsed with the Munich Agreement of 30 September 1938. The partition of Czechoslovakia in favour of Germany, sanctioned by France, Britain and Italy, was also a mighty blow to Romania, since one of its Little Entente allies (the alliance created in 1920–1 between Romania, Czechoslovakia and Yugoslavia) had become unable to defend its borders against the aggression of Great Powers and revisionist states, mainly Hungary (Gardner 1995: 45–68).

While the totalitarian Great Powers went on with their unexpected non-aggression pact, and France and Britain still lived with the illusion of appeasing Hitler, Romania was more unprepared than ever to defend its strategic interests. Through a cunning and undeterred policy, King Carol II had managed to discredit the fragile democracy and political parties and establish his own authoritarian regime in February 1938. The democratic constitution of 1923 was repealed and replaced by a new fundamental law, conferring wide powers on the monarch. The traditional political parties were dissolved, while *Mișcarea Legionară* (ML – the Legionary Movement), inspired by the European far right, gained increased popular support despite its illegal status (Feldman 2008). The abolition of parliamentary democracy was welcomed by street crowds in the main Romanian cities, against a wider European setting in which dictatorships were considered to regenerate nations. The single party created by Carol II, called *Frontul Renașterii*

Naționale (FRN – the National Renaissance Front), was incapable of mobilizing the positive energy of the nation, in spite of its very large formal popular support (more than three and a half million members). The main outcome of Carol II's internal policy was the marginalizing and subsequent dissolution of political elites. The beginning of the Second World War found Romania politically, diplomatically and militarily unprepared, in a sea of geopolitical turmoil.

Dismantling Greater Romania

The invasion of Poland by Germany on 1 September 1939, and subsequently by the Soviet Union on 17 September 1939 confirmed the darkest expectations of Romanian decision-makers. Romania and Poland had been bound by a defensive alliance convention since 1921, which provided for military aid in case of foreign aggression. The convention was not applied, however, since although Britain and France declared war on Germany on 3 September 1939, they did not take any effective action, living with the consequences of illusory appeasement against the brown totalitarianism. The realistic argument of King Carol II and Armand Călinescu's government was that any Romanian intervention in favour of Poland could only be successful if supported by French and British military operations against Germany, otherwise the Romanian army would not stand a chance of defeating the *Wehrmacht*.

On 6 December 1939, Romania declared its neutrality in the new war, following the prudent path it had taken at the beginning of the First World War, when it had remained neutral from 1914 to 1916, before joining the war on the side of France, Britain and their allies. Despite not intervening in the military defence of its Polish ally, it nonetheless allowed the evacuation of the Polish treasury (worth around $45 million) to Britain through the Port of Constanța, while three tons of Polish gold were safely stored in the mountains with the Romanian treasury, and returned to Poland in 1947. The Romanian state allowed the transit of weapons to Poland, provoking the obvious resentment of the Germans. Furthermore, Romania offered asylum to many Polish military and civilian refugees (*Refugiații polonezi* 2013).

The dissolution of Poland confirmed Romania's worst fears. With a Soviet Union whose borders had become even more extensive after the occupation of Poland (the Romanian–Soviet border had increased from 812 kilometres to 1,158.6 kilometres), a Horthy regime in Budapest bent on dismantling the Versailles system in the hope of restoring Greater Hungary, and a Bulgaria seeking to recover the Quadrilateral (southern Dobrogea), which it had lost in the Second Balkan War in 1913, the geopolitical situation of Romania was very fragile.

On the internal political stage, the successes of German militarism in Poland encouraged the ML to become more aggressive. On 21 September 1939, it assassinated Armand Călinescu in plain sight, the second of the three serving or former prime ministers killed by this fascist organization. The murdered prime minister had promoted close relations with Britain and France instead of Nazi Germany and Italy, which brings into question the geopolitical implications of this political assassination. Political life in Bucharest was dominated by uncertainty, as the Anglo-French security guarantees of 1939 proved increasingly delusive.

For the Romanians, the bottom line of the entire Phoney War (September 1939 to April 1940) was that the country sorely needed to review its foreign policy in the search for new guarantors of its unity. The reorientation towards Germany and Italy, decided by King Carol II, was seen as a necessary measure to 'adapt to realities'. On 7 March 1940, Romania signed an oil agreement with Germany, completed on 27 May, whereby the Romanian state undertook to export oil predominantly to Germany, in exchange for weapons and war supplies (the Armament–Oil Pact). On 28 May 1940, Romania abandoned neutrality, but without becoming an actual belligerent. Carol II, as a symbolic gesture of courtesy to Hitler, replaced Foreign Minister Grigore Gafencu, known for his Anglo-French sympathies, with the pro-German Ion Gigurtu (Scurtu and Buzatu 1999: 369). The opportunistic change of Romania's foreign policy vector towards the Axis was the result of despair: increasingly challenged internally by the ML, Carol II was in need of foreign allies. Germany was quickly emerging as the new dominant power in Europe after the invasion of Denmark and Norway, the occupation of the Netherlands, and the less than expected resistance put up by France. The surrender of France, Romania's traditional ally, on 22 June 1940 produced a genuine shockwave in Romanian society, with collective anxiety taking over the country. On the day of France's surrender, Carol II, in an attempt to emulate the totalitarian system of Germany, decided to turn the FRN into a 'single and totalitarian party, under the name of the Party of the Nation'.

However, the greatest threat came from the East. After the end of the 'winter war' with Finland (Edwards 2006), the Soviet Union became increasingly anxious to restore the former Tsarist empire. It had already occupied Latvia, Estonia and Lithuania as early as the autumn of 1939. On 29 March 1940, in a speech to the Supreme Soviet, the Soviet foreign affairs minister, V.M. Molotov, raised the issue of the annexation of Bessarabia in 1918, when the mostly Romanian-populated former Tsarist province decided to reunite with Romania (27 March/9 April 1918). Molotov's statement represents the official onset of the USSR's campaign to annex Bessarabia, thus enforcing the secret agreement of 23 August with Nazi Germany (Constantiniu 2010: 359).

The spectacular military and political failure of France against Hitler bolstered the imperialist disposition of the Soviet Union. In June 1940, pro-Soviet governments were imposed in the three Baltic States, and in August, Estonia, Lithuania and Latvia were annexed by the Soviet Union (Lache 2012: 11).

On 23 June 1940, the Soviet Union informed the German ambassador in Moscow, Count von Schulenburg, that it intended to request Romania to cede Bessarabia and Bukovina, and to use military force if met with resistance. Two days later, with the Red Army amassing at the Romanian border (Văratic 2000: 334–7), Germany informed Bucharest that it did not plan to prevent a Soviet attack. During the German–Russian diplomatic exchanges, Hitler argued that the annexation of Bukovina, which had belonged to Austria between 1775 and 1918, was not acceptable, being 'a new element' in relation to previous understandings (the Ribbentrop–Molotov Pact). Thus, to avoid a premature antagonization of Germany, Stalin limited his demands to northern Bukovina, including the city of Chernivtsi (Corneanu 2007: 78–87).

Having reached a (temporary) agreement with Hitler on how to divide the spoils of war, Stalin decided to perform the public ritual of sacrificing yet another nation: Romanian. On the evening of 26 June, the Romanian plenipotentiary minister to Moscow was summoned to Molotov, and presented with an ultimatum: 'to return Bessarabia to the Soviet Union; to cede northern Bukovina to the Soviet Union, with the frontiers as depicted in the attached map' (Dobrinescu and Constantin 1995: 40). In Bucharest, the first reaction of King Carol II was to resist, or at least negotiate the Soviet demands, but the diplomatic representatives of Germany and Italy advised yielding to the Soviet requests in order to 'maintain peace' in the Balkans. On 27 June, after two meetings of the Crown Council, an advisory body to the king, it was decided to accept the territorial losses without military resistance. Messages from Athens and Belgrade pointed towards giving up the territories without a fight; only Turkey was ready to provide military support to Romania against any Bulgarian aggression. On the night of 27/28 June, the Soviet Union submitted a second ultimatum, requesting Romania to evacuate Bessarabia and northern Bukovina within four days, starting with 28 June, at 14.00 hours. Without even waiting for the four-day deadline, on 28 June, at 13.00 hours, the Red Army crossed the Dniester and occupied Bessarabia and northern Bukovina. On 3 July, the Prut border was closed, and the Soviet Union could begin harsh reprisals against the inhabitants of the reconquered territory. In short, following a genuine political and military diktat, Romania lost 50,762 square kilometres of territory with a population of 3.9 million, of whom more than 2 million were ethnic Romanians (53.49 per cent). The USSR took over Bessarabia, northern Bukovina and the Hertza region (which had not been part of Tsarist Russia), and subsequently, a few small islands of the Danube Delta.

The loss of major territories to the Soviet Union with the manifest consent of the Axis powers generated a tremendous political problem for Romania. Sensing the weakness of the Carol II regime, Hungary and Bulgaria restated their intention to call for an immediate revision of their borders with Romania. The political legitimacy and moral authority of King Carol II had been lost. The result of his policy-making was merely the international isolation of Romania and the loss of important territories. Both in 1940 and later, the question as to why Romania had not resisted the Soviet aggression as had Finland was raised. At the end of June 1940, pragmatic arguments prevailed, focusing on the need to preserve Romania's statehood and avoid the fate of Poland. Subsequently, an increasing number of voices held that the Romanian Army should have resisted the Soviet aggression, with Romania thus earning a moral right to demand reunification at the end of the war. But the die had been cast, and the survival instinct of politicians gained the upper hand over moral arguments and political visions for an uncertain future.

However, the irony of history turns great successes into even larger disasters. Dominating continental Europe, though unable to defeat Britain, Hitler informed his close collaborators on 29 July 1940 of his decision to attack the Soviet Union in May 1941

(Stahel 2009: 33–8). The aim of the 'crusade against Bolshevism' was part of the genetic code of National Socialism to begin with, but attacking the Soviet Union became a strategic priority for Hitler after gaining supremacy over the continent. In the new geostrategic equation, Romania held an important role as both an oil-rich country and a springboard for attacks against the Soviet Union. In Hitler's new strategic vision, Romania would have to relinquish part of its territories to ensure the loyalty of Hungary and Bulgaria. The Romanian state did not have to be wiped out, however, but merely weakened to a large extent, since its resources had to be employed in the fight against 'Bolshevism'.

The Soviet aggression against Romania was received by Hungary as a long-overdue opportunity to reverse the consequences of the Trianon Peace Treaty on 4 June 1920. Concurrently with the occupation of Bessarabia by the Red Army, Hungary asked Germany for permission to attack Romania, in return for free passage of the *Wehrmacht* on Hungarian territory. Hitler did not agree with such unilateral action from Budapest, as he could not dismiss the possibility of Romania fighting to defend itself, thus sparking a war in South-East Europe. Moreover, Germany could not rule out that the Soviet Union might cross the Prut to occupy an even larger share of Romania and send it to Poland's fate. Germany had a vital interest in keeping oil-rich southern Romania secure to ensure the supply of the *Wehrmacht* (Simion 1996: 190–204). However, the Romanian decision-makers did not fathom the importance of Romanian oil to Germany, and in the dramatic summer of 1940, they failed to leverage this in their relations with Berlin.

In a letter of 15 July 1940, Hitler requested King Carol II of Romania to reach a territorial agreement with Hungary and Bulgaria or face the destruction of its statehood (Simion 1996: 205–11). Without any allies, Romania could not withstand the pressure and started negotiations with Hungary (16 August 1940) in Turnu Severin, and with Bulgaria (19 August 1940) in Craiova. Romania handed southern Dobrogea, also called the Quadrilateral, over to Bulgaria on 7 September. This contained Caliacra and Durostor counties, on an area of 6,826 square kilometres with 0.42 million inhabitants, only a minority of them Romanian. However, the negotiations with Hungary proved much more difficult, since Budapest initially demanded 75 per cent of Transylvania, with 2 million ethnic Romanians. Faced with such demands, the strategy of the Romanian government was to procrastinate, and the talks stalled on 24 August. Three days later, von Ribbentrop, the German foreign minister, called his Italian counterpart, Ciano, informing him that 'the *Führer* believed that the Romanians should relinquish 40,000 square kilometres to the Hungarians, who in turn claimed 60,000 square kilometres (actually, 66,000 square kilometres)' (Simion 1996: 316). Germany and Italy invited Hungary and Romania for 'arbitration' in Vienna. Hungary accepted the invitation in the hope of a reconfirmation of its claims. Romania also agreed to arbitration, believing that it would keep its western borders or relinquish no more than 18,000 square kilometres. Both Romania and Hungary were, however, under the threat of a German invasion should they not accept the Berlin 'solution'. The Italian–German 'Arbitration Tribunal', obviously assembled outside of international law, decided the following on 30 August 1940: Romania had to cede 43,492 square kilometres to Hungary (an area larger than that of the Netherlands), with a population of 2.66 million people, of whom 50.1 per cent were Romanians, 37.1 per cent Hungarians and 2.7 per cent Germans (Constantiniu 2010: 368). The new Romanian boundaries were 'guaranteed' by Germany and Italy. As with the relinquishment of Bessarabia, the Vienna awards were the subject of painful debates, with several Crown Council sessions being summoned by King Carol II. Important voices (Nicolae Iorga, Iuliu Maniu, Gheorghe Brătianu) demanded the refusal of any negotiations and armed resistance. The result was the same as with the Soviet threats: Romania agreed to cede significant territories in the hope of maintaining its statehood, waiting for history to change before recovering its lost territories (Case 2009: 199–217).

The dream of Greater Romania, for which hundreds of thousands had sacrificed their lives in the First World War, fell apart in less than seventy days. Romania lost one-third of its territory to the Soviet Union, Hungary and Bulgaria (approximately 100,000 square kilometres, more than the territory of Austria) and an equal share of its population, including 3 million ethnic Romanians, without the Army firing a single shot to defend its land, in total contrast with the stance of the Poles or the Finns. This political and psychological trauma would mark Romanian history in the short, medium and long term. The safeguarding of national borders became the fundamental matrix in defining national interests, with all other interests subordinated to this goal.

The Antonescu regime

The loss of northern Transylvania gave rise to a strong state of revolt, both against Germany, Italy, and Hungary and against King Carol II. Street marches took place in the main cities of the country, expressing support for Transylvania and even for armed defence of its northern part. Scorned internally, isolated externally, Carol II looked for a way to save himself. He called for the support of the democratic parties *Partidul Național Liberal* (PNL – the National Liberal Party) and *Partidul Național Țărănesc* (PNȚ – the National Peasant Party) which he had banned several years before, but their leaders, Iuliu Maniu and Constantin (Dinu) Brătianu, declined any talks, instead seeking his abdication. Carol II then turned to General Ion Antonescu, seen as the rescuing leader, who was appointed prime minister on 4 September 1940, after release from the house arrest previously ordered by the king (Watts 1993: 282–90). The next day, Carol II was forced to grant 'full state powers' to General Antonescu. One day later, on 6 September, Antonescu compelled the king to abdicate and leave Romania. At barely nineteen years old, Michael I became King of Romania, with Antonescu assuming the position of *Conducător al Statului* (state leader), with the authority to initiate and enact legislation.

Berlin did not find the installation of Antonescu unpalatable, for although the state leader was not pro-German by conviction, he could nevertheless ensure order in the country, avoid a military conflict with Hungary during the Romanian Army's withdrawal from northern Transylvania, and ultimately, turn Romania into a valuable ally for the Third Reich. Antonescu's desire was to create a government backed by all the important political forces, hoping to include both the PNL, PNȚ and the ML in the cabinet. The party leaders rejected this project, which would have deprived the country of any political alternative as regards its traditional allies, France and Britain (Deletant 2006: 55). The only option available to Antonescu remained the ML, which frantically supported a speedy and full cooperation with Germany by virtue of its ideological compatibility with National Socialism. On 14 September 1940, Romania was proclaimed a 'National Legionary State' after the entry of the ML into the government. Horia Sima, the Legionary leader, became Deputy Prime Minister, and four important ministries (Internal Affairs, Foreign Affairs, Education, and Work and Health) were run by the fascist organization (Heinen 1999: 414). The ML was the 'only recognized movement in the new state', but the regime was a mixed one: a military dictatorship with the ideological support of a totalitarian-inspired movement.

As regards foreign affairs, Romania fully entered a mechanism of extended cooperation with Germany, which was, in fact, full subordination. Antonescu renewed Carol II's request for a German military mission to Romania for the military training of Romanian troops, and then, on 23 November 1940, signed the Tripartite Pact, concluded between Germany, Italy and Japan, on 27 September 1940.

Relations between Antonescu and the ML became increasingly tense, as the fascist organization sought to take full control of Romania. On 26/27 November 1940, the ML assassinated sixty-four political prisoners at Jilava prison (where they had been held as enemies of the Legionaries), together with other prominent intellectuals and politicians (the historian Nicolae Iorga, the economist Virgil Madgearu) (Veiga 1995: 292–3). The army could not condone assassinations as a means of reprisal against political enemies without running the risk of losing credibility, which overstrained relations with the ML, particularly as Antonescu disbanded the Legionary Police, which had been responsible for murders and repeated unrest, on 2 December 1940.

Similarly to General Francisco Franco of Spain, Antonescu was a staunch conservative and heartfelt anti-Bolshevik, and boasted paternalist views on society. In contrast, the ML sought a 'revolution' to overturn the entire social and political order (Trașcă and Stan 2002: 21). While in Romania the Antonescu government was under constant attack by the ML, 'Directive 21' was being wrapped up on 18 December 1940 in Berlin, preparing for 'Operation Barbarossa', the offensive against the Soviet Union. Without consultation, Romania was identified as the main ally for the southern flank of the attack against the Soviet Union (Stahel 2009: 66–9).

Against a confused backdrop of internal affairs and without a clear-cut German approach to relations with the ML, Antonescu was determined to put an end to the murders and disorders of the Legionaries, while the latter were bent on a full seizure of power. The days of 21 and 22 January 1941 saw the so-called 'Legionary rebellion', in fact a bloody confrontation between the Army and the ML in the pursuit of total political and military control over Romania. Eventually, Hitler chose to support Antonescu, who managed to crush the ML with the help of the Army. The orchestrators of the Legionary rebellion were taken under German political protection, removed from the country and transferred to Germany. Hitler's message became clear: Antonescu was the only person capable of maintaining order and preparing Romania for a war in the East. On 27 January 1941, Antonescu formed a military government and Romania entered the stage of military dictatorship (the National Legionary State was officially abolished on 14 February 1941). The image of the Leader became the main insignia of the Antonescu military regime, which was based on the ideologies of traditional nationalism and conservatism, and bolstered by anti-Semitism (Ciucă et al. 1997–2008; Achim 2013).

In preparation for the launch of 'Operation Barbarossa', Hitler met with Antonescu on 12 June 1941 in Munich and informed him of the decision to attack the Soviet Union, but without specifying an exact date. At this meeting, Hitler cleverly manipulated the hopes of his Romanian counterpart: he did not bluntly request participation in the war, but said that he 'expected Romania to act solely in its own interest, in order to ease the course of this conflict' (Trașcă 2001: 156–60). Antonescu hoped to bring up the issue of northern Transylvania and its reunification with Romania at the end of the war. Hitler hinted that in exchange for her participation in the war, Romania would receive territorial compensation in the East, on the territory of the Soviet Union. This also revealed the Nazi vision of *Lebensraum*: Romania had to transfer the centre of gravity of its statehood towards the East, by taking up territories in the Slavic space.

On 22 June 1941, Romania joined and marched alongside Germany in the war by attacking the Soviet Union in the Army Group 'South', within which the 'General Antonescu Army Group' was formed. Following Antonescu's personal decision, Romania entered the war against the USSR without a formal declaration (Deletant 2006: 80). By 25 July 1941, supported by the German Army's offensive, Romania had recovered the losses it had incurred during the previous year. Romania rejoiced and felt that it had achieved a great victory, albeit not a total one. The fundamental issue of northern Transylvania still lingered. On 26 June 1941, Slovakia, a natural enemy of Hungary given Hungarian revisionism, joined the war on the side of the *Wehrmacht*. The following day, Hungary also declared war on the Soviet Union, joining the same coalition with Romania and Slovakia in the hope of not losing Hitler's support in territorial matters. Hitler's strategy was paying off: Romania, Hungary and Slovakia were committed to the German objectives through the very effective manipulation of ethnic and territorial issues. The decision-makers in Bucharest, Budapest and Bratislava believed that Germany could not be defeated by the Anglo-Soviet coalition, and that they had to pay with military sacrifices for a suitable position in the post-war negotiations.

On 27 July, Hitler requested that Antonescu continue the anti-Soviet operations across the Dniestr, beyond the borders of the Romanian state. The leader of the Romanian state referenced an ideological motivation of the war against the Soviets: 'I shall march to the end in our action in the East against the great enemy of civilization, Europe and my country: Russian Bolshevism' (Constantiniu and Schipor 1995: 97–8). The crossing of the Dniestr was one of the most controversial unilateral decisions made by Antonescu. The leaders of the traditional parties, and particularly the PNȚ president, Maniu, still expecting a Soviet-British victory, branded it as an act of overt aggression. Antonescu had military arguments on his side: once in a war, an alliance should be maintained until complete victory, or all achievements (recovery of lost territories) would be unsustainable. It would also have been political nonsense to abandon the alliance with Germany as long as the latter guaranteed reunification with Bessarabia and northern Bukovina. All Antonescu's political and military designs relied on the assumption that Germany and its allies would be victorious. Instead, the Nazi military failure made Romania responsible for the attack against the Soviet Union.

Romania's participation in the war alongside Germany and its allies provided the opportunity for territorial gains by which the Germans meant to compensate for the loss of northern Transylvania to Hungary. Romania was assigned to manage a territory of 40,000 square kilometres between the rivers Dniestr and Bug, called Transnistria, with Odessa as the largest city. This territory was under Romanian civil administration between 19 February 1941 and 29 January 1944, headed by governor Gheorghe Alexianu (Verenca 2000). Out of a population of more than 2.3 million according to the December 1941 census, ethnic Romanians represented merely 8.5 per cent (Pântea 2008: 176–7). Despite Hitler's repeated urging Antonescu refused to annex Transnistria to Romania and refused to incorporate the conquered territory for several reasons: he wanted a restoration of the *status quo ante* 1940, including the recovery of northern Transylvania; the war against the Soviet Union was defined as defensive by Antonescu, with the civil administration of Transnistria being regarded as a temporary measure until the end of the war; and, in the words of the Antonescu government, Transnistria was 'economic and financial collateral' for the reparations owed by the Soviet Union to Romania (Deletant 2006: 166–7).

As regards the rise to power of communism in Romania, a few important issues between the joining by Antonescu of the war against the Soviet Union and the removal of the military dictatorship on 23 August 1944 have to be considered.

Antonescu was not an ideological follower of Hitler, but thought that the alliance with Nazi Germany and the maintenance thereof were prerequisites for the restoration of the *status quo ante* 1940 (Hillgruber 2007). The Romanian army took part in the war against the Soviet Union, crossing the internationally recognized border on the Dniester, and fighting at Stalingrad and in the battles of the Don bend, the Kalmuk Steppe and the Caucasus (Duţu 1999: 67–124). Despite the unpreparedness of the army for a war against the Soviet Union, Antonescu believed that the Romanian nation should pay for the reunification of Romanian territory in blood, as had happened in the First World War. During more than 20 meetings with Hitler, the Romanian leader raised the issue of winning the competition with Hungary for northern Transylvania, under the illusion that the Nazi leader would be attracted to the Romanian cause by mere loyalty and regard for its sacrifices on the Eastern front. Antonescu had joined Germany in the war without an alliance treaty, in the hope that Romania would benefit from a future *Pax Germanica*. He lived with the irrational and very damaging conviction that he had a personal relationship with Hitler based on mutual trust, rather than on formal state treaties. Both Antonescu and Hitler had built their cult of personality around their being saviours of the people: strong leaders delivering their nations from the 'decadence' and 'corruption' of bourgeois democracies.

Even after the loss of the Battle of Stalingrad (November 1942 to February 1943), which reversed the course of the war (Geoffrey 2002), Antonescu remained confident of a final German victory. However, he became more cautious both with the allocation of food and oil resources for the Reich, and in internal politics, allowing the leaders of the opposition parties to come to contact with representatives of the Western states.

Romania did not condone an alliance with Germany, but the popular feeling of the 1940 to 1942 period was that, according to a traditional Romanian proverb, 'one should make a pact with the devil to cross the bridge'. The Axis's military failures on the Eastern and Mediterranean fronts at the end of 1942 and in 1943 brought a wave of hostility towards Germany, and several channels of negotiations were opened with the United Nations for an early exit from the war. Diplomatic negotiations or mere attempts to probe the United Nations' positions were initiated by the Antonescu government and the leaders of the democratic parties. The essential element influencing armistice negotiations between Romania and the Anglo-Americans was the 'doctrine of unconditional surrender' of the Axis and their allies, established by the Conference of Casablanca (14–24 January 1943). The most important negotiation channels from 1943 to the Romanian exit from the war against the USSR were Stockholm (used by government and opposition alike), for direct contact with the Soviets; Ankara, for talks between Antonescu and the British and Americans; and Cairo, where Barbu Ştirbei represented the government and the opposition parties, together with Constantin Vişoianu in the search for an agreement with the Anglo-Americans (Puşcaş 1995a).

The common theme of the diplomatic talks between the Antonescu government and leaders of the political parties was the preservation of the pre-1940 borders. The dynamics of the negotiations and of the mutual interests of the Great Powers fighting the Axis on all fronts proved that maintaining a greater Romania was not a realistic aim in view of the advance of the USSR. After reversing the tide of the war at Stalingrad and Kursk (5 July to 23 August 1943), Stalin was interested in a speedy advance to Berlin, and Romania's exit from the war would clear the path to the whole of South-Eastern Europe. Before the Allied landing in Normandy on 6 June 1944, and with the Red Army reaching the Dniester on 24 March 1944, the Soviet Union offered Romania the most lenient surrender conditions ever accepted by the Allies: none of the territories lost in 1940 were to be returned, but Transylvania ('or the largest part thereof' – British wording in the hope of removing Hungary from its alliance with Germany) could be recovered, provided the Romanian army took part in the military action for its liberation. Antonescu declined the Soviet conditions. He tested whether Maniu would accept such armistice conditions, in which case he was prepared to relinquish power in his favour. Hoping for better conditions from the Anglo-Americans, Maniu refused to take responsibility for losing such extensive territories. Thus, Antonescu did not accept the Soviet proposal, counting on a spectacular German victory with the help of 'secret weapons'. Maniu made a desperate attempt, on behalf of the democratic Romanian parties, to secure new surrender conditions from the Anglo-Americans. However, tied up with preparations for the western offensive against Germany, the latter were not interested in Romania, and as far as the British were concerned, Eastern Europe could remain, at least for the time being, in the Soviet sphere of influence.

The interesting side of the negotiations for the Romanian exit from the war against the United Nations (Great Britain had declared war on Romania and Finland on 6 December 1941, at the request of the USSR; on 12 December 1941, at the behest of the German and Italian representatives in Bucharest, Romania had declared war on the US, reciprocated only on 5 June 1942, at Russian insistence) was the fact that although the Soviets and the Anglo-Americans carried out separate negotiations with various Romanian emissaries, they all considered Antonescu to be the most capable of achieving an armistice, as he controlled the army. In turn, Antonescu was of the opinion that any Romanian exit from the war had to be agreed in advance by the Germans, which was absolutely naïve. While Hungary was preparing to leave the war, it was occupied by Germany on 19 March 1944, in operation 'Margarethe I'. Germany also had a plan for the military occupation of Romania ('Margarethe II'), but never carried it out, Hitler saw Antonescu as a faithful ally, who was in control of both the country and the army (Traşcă 2013).

23 August 1944: from responsibility to adventure

The military victories of the Red Army and the reoccupation of Bessarabia and northern Bukovina gave rise to new anguish in Romanian society and prompted in the political elite a frantic search for solutions to cope with the new military realities. Iuliu Maniu's hopes for an Anglo-American landing in the Balkans were quashed by the Normandy landings. For anyone with a grasp of the dynamics of the war, it became increasingly obvious that Germany would be clenched between an offensive of the Red Army in the east, and another offensive by the Anglo-Americans and their allies in the west and south. The biggest riddle of the summer of 1944 was how the post-war peace would be shaped by the armies of the United Nations in Europe.

The first step towards a political solution was the formation of *Blocul Naţional Democratic* (BND – the National Democratic Bloc) by *Partidul Comunist Român* (PCR – the Romanian Communist Party), the PNŢ and the PNL, the main objective being a Romanian withdrawal from the war against the United Nations. The acceptance by the democratic leaders of an alliance with the Communist Party, which had been outlawed since 1924, was meant as a gesture of goodwill to provide for a channel of negotiation acceptable to Stalin. The Soviet Union had suggested one way of involving the Communists in post-war public life in the closing lines of the armistice proposal of 12 April 1944: 'Fifth: if Romania also wishes (...) a political representative for political matters, the Soviet government does not have any objections' (Corneanu 2007: 421). That was a concrete sign of the Soviet post-war vision: the spheres of influence would depend on the military positions of the Great Powers, while the political and social systems of the USSR-controlled zones would be aligned as closely as possible to the communist model. The cooperation between the democratic parties and the communists was also proposed by the Anglo-Americans during the negotiations for the Romanian exit from the war, in the spirit of the then cross-ideological mindset of the Great Alliance (Constantiniu 1997: 123).

On 2 April 1944, the Russian offensive on the Romanian front was halted, and calm installed throughout the summer. On 23 June, the Red Army began a strong offensive against the *Wehrmacht's* Army Group Centre of Byelorussia. On 20 August, the Red Army also attacked the Romanian-held territories, hastening the political decisions, as the Prut line was breached and the new front line lay between Chişinău and Iaşi, continually moving westward. Aware of the weakness of the Romanian forces against the Russians, Antonescu requested help from the Germans. The defence of the Romanian front by the Germans was neither welcome in Berlin, nor was it possible in such a short time frame. In the new military situation, Ion Antonescu looked to resume the armistice negotiations with the USSR (Djuvara 2012).

As the military pressure upon Romania grew, an ad hoc coalition between the representatives of the BND parties, the young King Michael I and a few army commanders decided to act in a plot against the state leader. The action against Antonescu was scheduled for 26 August 1944 to avoid the occupation of the country by the Red Army. On 23 August, Antonescu requested an audience with the king to discuss the new situation in the wake of the Russian offensive in Moldavia. Michael I urged Antonescu to sign the armistice with the United Nations. On the afternoon of 23 August 1944, he was arrested and taken into custody by a team of communists led by Emil Bodnăraş. He was in a safe house, transported to the USSR, and was only brought back for his trial in 1946.

This was an undoubtedly bold action on the part of Michael I, taking advantage of the fact that Antonescu had not *de jure* abolished the monarchy. The position of state leader was equivalent to that of prime minister, and thus subordinated to the king. On the evening of 23 August, the king broadcast his 'Proclamation to the Country', announcing Romania's exit from the Axis, the cessation of the war against the United Nations (USSR, Britain and the US) and of 'any hostilities against the Soviet Army'. The king stated that 'the United Nations have guaranteed the independence of our country and non-intervention in our internal affairs. They have recognized the injustice of the Vienna Awards, through which Transylvania was taken away from us' (Scurtu 2005: 102–3). A new government was formed, led by General Constantin Sănătescu, with the political support of the BND parties. PNŢ leader Iuliu Maniu, PNL leader Dinu Brătianu, *Partidul Social Democrat* (PSD – the Social Democratic Party) leader Constantin Titel-Petrescu and Communist leader Lucreţiu Pătrăşcanu became ministers of state to underscore the wide political support for the new government. Pătrăşcanu also took over the Justice portfolio for a short period, to facilitate the release of Communist political prisoners.

The removal of Antonescu from power and the abolition of the military dictatorship came as a stunning surprise. Hitler ordered the arrest of King Michael I – who had already left Bucharest – and his replacement with a pro-Nazi puppet regime. The Germans did not find any volunteers among the Romanian generals, and the *Wehrmacht* attacks were eventually repelled. Moreover, as an amicable agreement for the retreat of the German troops could not be reached, Romania declared war on Germany on 25 August 1944 (Duţu 2000: 220–8).

The removal of the Antonescu regime was also unexpected for the United Nations. Even if armistice negotiations had been carried out on behalf of the major parties and King Michael I, neither Moscow, London nor Washington had anticipated a successful overthrow of the Antonescu government. The entire 23 August operation was a tragic improvisation. The Romanian troops found themselves in an impossible situation: on the one hand, they were supposed to resist German attacks, and on the other, the Red Army began to disarm and deport Romanian military personnel to the USSR. Romanian documents mention 60,000 to 160,000 troops taken into captivity without a fight (Duțu 2000: 234–5) with 100,783 troops going missing in the period between 24 and 31 August 1944. Soviet sources confirm the arrival of 97,000 prisoners of war in NKVD (People's Commissariat for Internal Affairs) detention facilities, having been captured following the liquidation of 'enemy groups encircled in the Chișinău area' (*Prizonieri* 2013: xxi). The Romanian fleet was compelled to surrender to the Soviet fleet.

In fact, King Michael I and the other participants in the coup against the Antonescu regime acted 'blindly': the first steps towards signing an armistice agreement were taken only on 24 August. The Anglo-Americans left the entire political and military responsibility for relations with Romania to the Soviets. A delegation led by the Communist leader Lucrețiu Pătrășcanu was sent to Moscow to negotiate and sign an armistice convention. The choice of Pătrășcanu was not random, as he was expected to attract Soviet sympathy for Romania. The negotiations were delayed by the Soviets and the British (the latter, under the pretext of requesting the agreement of the Dominions for their own proposals) until an important share of Romanian territory was under occupation. The 'Agreement Between the Governments of United States of America, the United Kingdom, and the Union of Soviet Socialist Republics, on the one hand, and the Government of Rumania, on the other hand, concerning an Armistice' was eventually signed in Moscow (Official Journal no. 219 of 22 September 1944). For Romania, this was the end of staking its statehood on the German card. A new historic cycle began, in which communist totalitarianism would generate profound changes throughout Romanian society.

Victims of war and of racial and class hatred

Europe's entry into destruction, caused by national rivalries and exacerbation of racial or class hatred, generated tremendous loss and suffering. War crimes, crimes against humanity, genocide, deportations and mass arrests, rapes and other atrocities were unleashed with the onset of the Second World War. To these victims must be added those dead, wounded and missing on battlefields, losses which took a heavy toll on the Romanian population. The misfortunes of the war and conflicts between various ethnic and racial groups have had a long-lasting effect through the creation of a traumatic collective memory, manifested both during the communist period and after the end of the Cold War. The crimes and horrors of the war are still unhealed wounds in the memory of the nation.

The first to suffer in the aftermath of the Ribbentrop–Molotov Pact were the Bessarabians and Bukovinians, as the Soviet Union began mass deportations just as it had in Poland and the Baltic countries. After the incorporation of Bessarabia and northern Bukovina into the Soviet Union, repressive action began against the civilian population (mainly against 'anti-Soviet elements' and 'counter-revolutionary organizations'), culminating in the deportations of 12–13 June 1941, when 24,360 people were transported to Siberia and Kazakhstan out of a total of 29,839 people removed from their homes. Families were separated, and the long journey to the forced labour camps was completed in inhumane conditions, in cattle wagons (Caşu 2000: 32–3).

The winning of a large share of Transylvania by Hungary following the German–Italian Vienna decision was seen by some ethnic Hungarians as an opportunity for revenge against local Romanian elites. The Hungarian army, together with the Hungarian police, paramilitaries and locals undertook arrests, torture and murders. According to a report by the Bucharest Secretariat for Nationalities, between 30 August 1940 and 1 November 1941, 919 murders, 1,126 cases of torture, 4,126 beatings, and 15,893 arrests were recorded (Fătu et al. 1985: 56–99; Grad 1998: 154–68). Symbols of the crimes against civilians are the villages of Ip and Trăznea in Sălaj County (Puşcaş 1995b: xxii–xxiii).

The redrawing of borders meant waves of refugees fled to Romania. More than 200,000 people fled immediately from Bessarabia and northern Bukovina in the summer of 1940, some of them returning to their homes after the reconquest of those territories by the German and Romanian armies in 1941. By the end of 1943, 218,919 deportations from northern Transylvania were recorded (*Istoria României. Transilvania* Vol. II 1997: 24). To this must be added those people who fled northern Transylvania on their own initiative, bringing the number of Romanians who left their homes following the Vienna Award of 30 August 1940 to nearly half a million. In the same context, more than 100,000 Hungarians from southern Transylvania left Romania to live in Hungary, with approximately half a million ethnic Hungarians remaining in Romania between 1941 and 1944.

The war started in Europe was an opportunity for the supporters of anti-Semitism to attempt to solve the 'Jewish problem'. The broader ideological objective was the achievement of an 'ethnically pure' nation, by assimilation, then, due to war conditions, by the physical elimination of 'undesirable minorities'. These were Jews and Roma. The process was called 'Romanization', becoming ever more extended and violent and acquiring the character of mass crimes during the war (Heinen 2011; Solonari 2009).

Anti-Semitic economic and administrative policies had been applied in Romania as early as 1938, but anti-Semitism became criminally violent after the beginning of the war and Nazi military victories. The Legionary rebellion of January 1941 caused 416 deaths, including 120 Jews in the Bucharest pogrom (*Raport final* 2005: 112; Ioanid 2006).

The loss of Bessarabia and northern Bukovina to the Soviet Union resurrected older 'Jewish-communist' stereotypes. In 1940, rumours of hostile acts by Jews against the retreating Romanian army created the psychological conditions for the incitement of latent anti-Semitism among some Romanians. After the attack of Germany and its allies against the Soviet Union, Antonescu assumed the time had come to apply the plan for the removal of Jews from Moldavia, Bessarabia and northern Bukovina. The Iași pogrom in the summer of 1941 left 14,850 Jews dead. Antonescu's plan was to 'cleanse' Bessarabia and northern Bukovina of the Jewish population by massive deportations to Transnistria. There, measures for the extermination of Jews were carried out by both the Romanian and German armies. In this context, the human condition of Jews witnessed an unimaginable degradation. Many Jews died following executions by *Einsatzgruppe* and units of the Romanian army, but also due to starvation, freezing and disease. The massacre of Odessa Jews (October 1941), accomplished as repressive measure for an attempt against the Romanian military command, was ordered by Antonescu. Twenty-two thousand Jews were shot or burned alive in Odessa and another 65,000 were deported, many of them dying in the process (Ancel 2012: 315–429). The total number of Jews deported from Romania to Transnistria is estimated at between 154,449 and 170,737 people (*Raport final* 2005: 176). In Transnistria, the Romanian authorities found between 150,000 and 200,000 local Jews. An estimated 220,000 died under the Romanian administration in Transnistria during the Holocaust, but the number could be as high as 270,000 (*Raport final* 2005: 178). In addition, the approximately 132,000 Jews deported from northern Transylvania to Auschwitz between May and July 1944 by the Hungarian authorities cannot be ignored.

The Antonescu regime employed a different policy towards the Jews of the Old Kingdom and southern Transylvania. Although an application of the German 'Final Solution' (*Die Endlösung*) was also being envisaged for these Jews, deportations to Transnistria were halted in October 1942, for fear of post-war consequences: the Romanian army was in a fragile situation on the Eastern front, and Hungary had not yet surrendered its Jews for extermination. Antonescu was increasingly mindful of the future, as Germany's final victory was no longer certain anymore. In the Old Kingdom and Transylvania, the 'Jewish problem' could be solved not by deportation, but by emigration. It would resurface again in Romania during the communist regime.

Another ethnic group who suffered during the Antonescu regime was the Roma: 25,000 were deported to Transnistria, where approximately 11,000 died; 14,000 survived and returned to Romania (*Raport final* 2005: 240; Achim 2004a).

The joining of the war by Romania on the German side brought the recovery of the territories lost in 1940, but it also brought high human sacrifice. The Romanian army lost 71,585 dead, 243,622 were wounded and 309,533 were missing (mostly prisoners of war) on the Eastern front (Duțu 1999: 251).

PART I
COMMUNISM

For more than four decades the Romanian nation was led by a political regime which had not been expected or wanted, but which was accepted as an immense but not unique historical tragedy. Caught behind the Iron Curtain, Romania was forced to break relations with Western civilization, to which it had been organically bound since the second half of the nineteenth century. At the beginning of the regime, national sovereignty was drastically limited by the Soviets; though after 1960, Romania enjoyed relative political autonomy within the Soviet bloc. The Communists brutally eliminated old elites in the name of class struggle and brought about a reset of the social elevator according to Marxist-Leninist ideological values. While for some, communism was a collective disaster, due to loss of wealth and freedoms, for others the communist regime represented an opportunity to overcome the condition of marginal individuals and turn into new elites. In the name of the utopia of the New Man and of a society free from social exploitation, a criminally repressive regime was established, which committed abominable abuses, strangled freedom and destroyed destinies. The collectivization of agriculture represented both loss of land and a chance for millions of peasants to escape the trap of subsistence agriculture and to become first-generation townspeople. Following a huge social mobilization, Romania built a broad industrial sector. The rhythm of economic accumulation was quick, but this did not turn into prosperity because the population was deprived of a decent living, especially after 1982. Lies and social hypocrisy became mandatory conditions for survival and success. The regime tried to compensate for tyranny through social stability: safe jobs, affordable housing, universal medical insurance and free education.

Communism failed in the authoritarian modernization of society, although this was its fundamental project. When the economy most needed an opening in order to consolidate the accumulated modernization of previous decades, Nicolae Ceaușescu made the fatal mistake of pursuing an autarkic policy, wasting the dramatic efforts and sacrifices that had been made by the population to develop the country. Started under the flag of a social revolution, Romanian communism ended up under the despotic leadership of the Ceaușescu clan, which exhausted the whole capital of hope in Romanian society with an aberrant personality cult.

The communist regime was not uniform from the beginning. There were two main periods, which may be labelled according to the names of the main political leaders, Gheorghe Gheorghiu-Dej (1948–65) and Nicolae Ceaușescu (1965–89). Between the two eras there are both fundamental elements of continuity and significant differences. In spite of the crimes committed by the state and the terror against society until 1964, the communist regime imposed a new social contract, based on the promise of mobility and rise in the social hierarchy, which was tacitly or sometimes genuinely enthusiastically accepted by a part of the population. Communism created its own legitimacy by a skilful use of national feelings, which collapsed with the humiliation and hunger to which the population was submitted at the end of the Ceauşescu regime. The signal given by Mikhail Gorbachev, that he would not intervene militarily to support the regimes of obsolete dictators such as Erich Honecker, Nicolae Ceauşescu or Todor Zhivkov, resulted in the fall of communism in Europe. The Ceauşescu regime collapsed because it was internationally ostracized, the population no longer supported it, and the repressive apparatus would no longer assume the risk of supporting a leader who had lost contact with reality.

CHAPTER 2
THE ESTABLISHMENT OF THE COMMUNIST REGIME (1944–47)

From the Grand Alliance to the Cold War: the sovietization of Eastern Europe

Romania's entrance into the Soviet Union's sphere of influence and its subsequent communization, as a guarantee of its relation of geopolitical subordination, must be understood as part of a global process of transformation within the international system. The complexity and contradictory character of the transformation concerning relations between the Great Powers in just three years, from an alliance aimed at defeating the Axis Powers to open confrontation between the former partners of the anti-fascist coalition, makes the evaluation of the sovietization of Eastern Europe difficult. In order to understand developments in Romania, some main elements may be recalled.

In the concept of US President F.D. Roosevelt, it was vital that international security was not threatened by another power. Germany, not the Soviet Union, was also considered the main threat in the future. In the international policy vision of the Roosevelt administration, the space between Germany and the Soviet Union did not present a special importance, being a periphery of the West, which only held political significance due to the fact that Polish immigration to the US was a factor that had to be attended to during presidential elections (Kissinger 2008: 348–9). In an unrealistic manner, Americans considered that territorial issues, power balances and the fate of colonial empires had to be solved within a global political framework, ignoring the role of the presence of Soviet military forces in the conquered areas.

Far from illusions of Wilsonian idealism, Britain's Winston Churchill had two strategic objectives: preserving the colonial empire and restoring the European power balance, together with France and, eventually, Germany, in order to counterbalance the rise of the USSR. Eastern Europe was a space of variable geometry; it could be an area of 'compensations' and a future 'buffer' zone against the Soviets. The British Prime Minister considered that London had at best a moral duty towards Poland, to which it had offered security guarantees and in defence of which it had declared war on Hitler. Italy, Greece and Turkey were defined as vital states for the strategic interests of the British Empire, as they allowed the preservation of trade routes towards the East (Anton 2013: 66).

The Soviet Union's expansionist interest in Central and Eastern Europe (CEE) became visible through the Hitler–Stalin Pact in 1939. Finland, the Baltic States, a part of Poland and a part of Romania were incorporated into the USSR, in order to extend the borders of the Soviet state to the west by a few hundred kilometres, under the pretext of either legitimate security needs or an 'historical right' over territories that had at some point been part of the Tsarist Empire. After the Battle of Stalingrad, which marked the turning of the tide in the war, Stalin informed the Anglo-Americans of his wish to keep what he had won after the agreement with Hitler, preserving the USSR's borders as of June 1941 (Gaddis 2009: 25–6). De facto, after the Tehran Conference in 1943, Churchill and Roosevelt considered as desirable Stalin's claim of a return to the borders resulting from the Ribbentrop–Molotov Pact, although such a tacit acceptance was never made public, as it went against the Atlantic Charter of August 1941. Ensuring a 'friendly neighbourhood' for the USSR was considered a legitimate objective for both London and Washington, without meaning, *ab initio*, an acceptance of the region's communization.

In October 1944, Churchill and Stalin met in Moscow. The main result was the so-called 'percentages agreement', which brought with it an insidious return to the politics of spheres of influence. According to the final result of the negotiations, Stalin recognized a 90 per cent British influence in Greece and Churchill accepted a similar Soviet share in Romania. Britain got from Stalin recognition of a 50 per cent influence in Yugoslavia and Hungary, but only 20 per cent in Bulgaria, the rest being attributed to the Soviets (Constantiniu 1997: 96). Thus, the USSR had a free hand in the political and military control of Romania, without fearing a serious response from the Anglo-Americans. Stalin had the strategic advantage of the Red Army presence in the CEE, but turning it into an occupation force in countries 'liberated' from the leadership of 'fascist' regimes could only be legitimized in terms of spheres of influence, which tolerated the right of the fait accompli. After Roosevelt's death, when the US became conscious of the nature and purposes of the USSR's international policies, in light of George F. Kennan's 'Long Telegram', the Cold War began. The Soviet Union had to be 'contained', as stated in the 'Truman Doctrine' of March 1947, because it represented a danger; it was as totalitarian as Nazi Germany. Eastern Europe was already under Soviet military control, but Greece and Turkey had to be helped in order to save them from communization. Thus, the demarcation of antagonistic blocs was achieved.

At the Yalta Conference of 4 to 12 February 1945, relations among the Great Powers were apparently cordial, and understanding about Europe's future seemed complete (Harbutt 2010). Stalin acquired an important advantage from the fact that President Roosevelt died on 12 April 1945, and Churchill lost the parliamentary elections in the UK on 26 July 1945, being forced to give up the leadership of the government to Clement Attlee, a Labour politician lacking international experience. During a crucial period for the post-war setting, Stalin was the most experienced leader within the Grand Alliance. At the Potsdam Conference from 17 July to 2 August 1945, Stalin was the winner at the negotiations: he obtained a modification of Poland's borders, proposed territorial 'compensations' to the USSR in exchange for establishing a new Polish western border, to Germany's detriment and, on the rivers Oder and Neisse; the German populations of Poland, Czechoslovakia and Hungary were relocated, offering Moscow an important advantage in relation to those nations. Peace treaties with Italy, Bulgaria, Finland, Romania and Hungary were considered secondary issues, assigned to the level of the Great Powers' foreign affairs ministers, so the Soviet Union could manoeuvre to impose friendly governments in countries where the Red Army was present. The

Soviets also made political use of the border issues between Romania, Hungary and Bulgaria.

Stalin considered that Eastern Europe's sovietization (by the creation of satellite states and the communization of institutions, society and the economy) would ensure the military and economic security of the USSR. Stalin's plan could be achieved as the Soviets controlled the region militarily and the Anglo-Americans were not psychologically, politically or militarily prepared for a new conflagration with a new superpower. The hypothesis of using the atomic bomb against the USSR, in order to avoid the sovietization of Romania, Poland and Hungary was considered unacceptable in political and military evaluations in Washington (Constantiniu 2010).

Sheltered by the Iron Curtain, Western leaders initially hoped to avoid direct military confrontation with Moscow; they hoped that communist regimes would liberalize. Communism persisted in Eastern Europe longer than was hoped at the end of the world conflagration and less than was anticipated during the 1980s. Beyond this Great Power game, the drama of some nations went on, often in silence: nations whose only 'fault' was being too close to aggressive and greedy neighbours.

The first steps in Romania's sovietization

The Armistice Convention laid the basis of Romania's satellite status towards the USSR. Romania was forced to pay war reparations amounting to $300 million, within a period of six years, which was a significant economic burden. Soviet and Allied troops could move freely over Romania's territory, without assuming their withdrawal until after the end of the war. The Romanian government was subordinated to the Allied (Soviet) Control Council (12 November 1944), with the Romanian authorities being forced to apply capitulation provisions. Within the Commission the Soviets had the first and the last word, as the representatives of the US (Cortland Van R. Schuyler) and the UK (Donald Stevenson) had specific instructions not to generate conflict with them. The Anglo-Americans knew precisely what was happening in Romania, but considered they lacked the necessary instruments to stop communization (Chiper, Constantiniu and Pop 1993).

Immediately after removal of the Antonescu regime, a new government was formed, led by General Sănătescu. Its first political decision was to return to a democratic political regime of constitutional monarchy. The 1923 Constitution was thus reinstated (albeit with the introduction of some limitations on citizens' rights). Multi-party democracy was revived and the minute communist party, together with traditional political groups, had a legal framework for beginning the power struggle through parliamentary elections.

According to the Armistice Convention, Romania went from one war to another, having to provide 'no less than twelve infantry divisions with auxiliary technical services' to fight against Germany and Hungary. Romania participated, together with the Red Army, in the liberation of its own territory from German and Hungarian troops. On

25 October 1944 the last Romanian towns, Carei and Satu Mare, were liberated. Hoping to get better terms during the peace conference, Romania also participated in the liberation of Hungary and Czechoslovakia. Romania's war materialized in participation on the Western front with the deployment of 560,000 military personnel, resulting in the liberation of over 900 villages and towns, at the price of 169,822 dead and wounded. During the Hungarian campaign, the Romanian army lost 42,700 soldiers, and in Czechoslovakia it had 66,995 dead and missing in action (Duțu 1999: 251).

While the Romanian army was participating in the war against Germany, leaving the country without any defences, at the political level, important events were taking place. While any faint hopes of regaining Bessarabia and northern Bukovina from the USSR had been shattered by the Armistice Convention, the fundamental national stake was the recovery of northern Transylvania. The Armistice Convention stipulated: '19. The Allied Governments regard the decision of the Vienna award regarding Transylvania as null and void and are agreed that Transylvania (or the greater part thereof) should be returned to Rumania, subject to confirmation at the peace settlement, and the Soviet Government agrees that Soviet forces shall take part for this purpose in joint military operations with Rumania against Germany and Hungary.' Introduction of the phrase 'or the greater part thereof' was made at the demand of the British, who hoped that the ambiguity of this formula could attract Hungary onto their side. Romania participated in the military effort against the Axis, as it had vowed, but the Soviet Union turned the territorial issue into a blackmail tool for satellization and communization. On 14 November 1944, the whole Romanian administration of northern Transylvania was withdrawn, and replaced by a Soviet military administration. The decision to impose a Soviet military administration in Transylvania was communicated in Bucharest by A.Y. Vyshinski, Deputy People's Commissioner for Foreign Affairs, Soviet chargé d'affaires for the application of the provisions of the Armistice Convention with Romania (Constantiniu 2001: 70). Thus Bucharest decision-makers were influenced by an important blackmail factor, with multiple purposes: continuing war efforts on the Western front; giving up Bessarabia and northern Bukovina indefinitely; and accepting a government controlled by the Soviets (Sălăgean 2002: 39).

Simultaneously, the communists began an intense activity of subversion in order to achieve power. On 24 September 1944, *Frontul Național Democrat* (FND – the National Democratic Front), was formed by the PCR and PSD, joined by other satellite parties. Following political pressure, the communists, with Soviet support, obtained six ministries and secretariats in the second Sănătescu government (4 November 1944). New political tensions caused by the communists followed and a new government was established, led by General Nicolae Rădescu (Giurescu 1996). He was not favourable to the communists and in a harsh radio address, on 12 February 1945, he criticized the agitations they had produced. New street violence followed and the Red Army disarmed the Romanian army in Bucharest. Moscow demanded the resignation of the Rădescu government, which was dismissed by King Michael I on 27 February. A.Y. Vyshinski arrived in Bucharest to pressure Michael I to accept a pro-communist government led by Petru Groza (Ciuceanu et al 1997). The Anglo-Americans present in the Allied Control Commission could not prevent the Soviet undertaking. On 6 March 1945, a government led by Petru Groza was established, made up of communists, social democrats and dissidents from the traditional parties (PNL – Gheorghe Tătărescu, and PNŢ – Anton Alexandrescu). The Soviets tried to create the perception of a grand coalition, which could be presented to the Anglo-Americans as a democratic and representative government. As Romania proved to be docile, on 9 March 1945 the Romanian administration was restored in northern Transylvania. The PCR could thus present to the nation that it wanted to dominate a first success in relations with Moscow. The Communists had made a first important step in their conquest for power, but Hitler was not yet defeated and uncertainty reigned in relations among the Big Three. Achieving power required thorough preparation.

Consolidation of communist power

Immediately after the Soviets imposed the Groza government, the communists went on consolidating power. The first major decision after taking power was the agrarian reform. According to the agrarian reform law of 23 March 1945, the properties of ethnic Germans and Romanians who had collaborated with Nazi Germany were expropriated, as well as the lands of 'war criminals and those guilty of the country's disaster' and individual properties larger than 50 hectares. Great landowners were also dispossessed of agricultural machinery and equipment. Almost 1.46 million hectares were expropriated; 1.1 million hectares were given to 0.91 million people, the rest remained state property. The size of allotment properties could not go above 5 hectares. In order to avoid fragmented properties, as had happened after the 1921 agrarian reform, the beneficiaries of allotments could not sell or mortgage their new property.

The agrarian reform attracted the sympathy of a part of the peasantry for the communists, but this did not guarantee that they could win free elections. For this reason, the communist leaders, supported by the Soviets, undertook systematic action to weaken the democratic parties. First, the Communists hid behind alliances with various obscure political groups, such as *Frontul Plugarilor* (the Ploughmen's Front), in order to create the impression that they were numerous and strong. Second, the PNŢ and PNL were submitted to various administrative chicaneries by the Groza government and the members of these parties began to be eliminated from the administration. Third, dissidences from the traditional parties were encouraged. In December 1944, liberal Gheorghe Tătărescu formed a new liberal party, which was kept in government until November 1947. In February 1945, dissidence emerged in the PNŢ, led by Anton Alexandrescu, who became Minister of Cooperation in the Groza government. He was eliminated from the government after the 19 November 1946 elections. One dissidence which the Communists did not want was that from the PSD (March 1946). At their congress, partisans of an alliance with the communists (Lothar Rădăceanu and Ştefan Voitec) prevailed, and Constantin Titel-Petrescu founded a new party

(PSD-Independent), close to the PNȚ and PNL. Accidental allies of the communists ('fellow travellers'), they were useful both for creating confusion in Romanian society and for gaining international legitimacy for the Groza government by including some non-communist parties.

After the Potsdam Conference the first great political crisis occurred. The USSR recognized the Groza government on 6 August 1945, but the Anglo-Americans refused, as they did not consider it sufficiently representative from a democratic point of view. Encouraged by this situation, on 19 August King Michael I asked Prime Minister Groza to resign, in order to allow the formation of a new government recognized by the Big Three. The latter refused, knowing that he was supported by Stalin. As a reaction, Michael I refused to validate governmental documents and meet with ministers (a 'royal strike'). Following the Moscow Conference in December 1945 of the foreign affairs ministers of the Big Three, the US and the UK agreed to recognize the Groza government on condition that it included some representatives from the PNȚ and PNL. Emil Hațieganu from PNȚ and Mihail Romniceanu from PNL were accepted in minor governmental positions. As a result of this solution endorsed by the Anglo-Americans, Michael I resumed relations with the Groza government, which was recognized by the US and the UK on 5 February 1946.

Meanwhile, political confrontations took place in the country. On 8 November 1945, the PNL and PNȚ organized a support rally for Michael I in Bucharest, on the occasion of his name day. The Groza government, backed by the Soviets, repressed the rally (leaving eleven dead). Winning Romanians' sympathy was difficult for the Groza government, as it had undertaken the application of the Armistice Convention, under the trusteeship of the Allied (Soviet) Control Commission in Bucharest. From May 1945, no less than sixteen joint Romanian-Soviet companies (Sovrom) were set up for the purpose of 'increasing economic cooperation'. Also, the abusive manner in which war reparations payment were made was perceived as a Soviet spoliation helped by their local instrument, the PCR.

Punishment of those guilty of war crimes, according to article 14 of the Armistice Convention, was a difficult issue, as the perception of the victors was different from that of the population. In 1945, legislation was adopted to punish not only war criminals, but also those responsible for 'the country's disaster'. The task of judging was attributed to the People's Court, an ad hoc judicial court. In the beginning, fourteen 'fascist journalists' were judged, although not all of them were Legionaries. In 1946, the so-called 'Great National Betrayal Trial' took place. Brought back from detention in the USSR in order to be judged, Antonescu and other leaders of his regime were either sentenced to death or to long prison terms. The former Leader of the state and three of his collaborators were executed in the Jilava penitentiary on 1 June 1946.

The PCR managed to take over power institutions, subordinate the secret services and dominate the Army by means of political activists from the 'Tudor Vladimirescu' Division, formed in 1943 from among Romanian prisoners in the USSR. The rhythm of power-acquiring actions was dictated from Moscow, which had control over the whole process of Eastern Europe sovietization.

The PCR: from political sect to mass party

Established in 1921, the PCR had been dissolved in 1924 on the grounds that it was a section of the Comintern, which had been involved in violent events in Bessarabia, with the purpose of destabilizing Greater Romania. Mostly made up of ethnic minority members, the Communists considered the Romanian state to be 'artificial' and 'imperialist'. Until 1944, the PCR was just a 'messianic sect' (Tismăneanu 2003), marked by infighting, without any real appeal to society.

At the time of its entry into legality, the PCR only had around 1,000 members. The Communist leaders' main objective was to increase the number of party members. The presence of Soviet troops in Romania and their status as an occupation force was the main element which from the first part of 1945 indicated the entrance of the Romanian state under Soviet hegemony. The PCR was seen as a political opportunity or a protecting shield for people with a past in the ML. PCR leaders (mainly Ana Pauker), assisted by Soviet advisors encouraged massive party registration, without taking into account the political past or the human and political quality of new members. Numerous ML members and sympathizers were accepted within the PCR's ranks. In folklore there was even the saying 'Comrade, don't be sad, the Guard [ML] continues in the Communist Party!' The statistics of PCR members indicate an upward trend: October 1944 – 5,000 members; February 1945 – 15,000; April 1945 – 42,653; June 1945 – 110,041; October 1945 – 256,863; June 1946 – 717,490; December 1947 – 799,351 members (Cătănuş and Neacşu 1998).

The PCR's numerical ascent hid the terrible struggle for power among factions. The logic of the power struggle was merciless: those who lost power could even lose their lives. Within the PCR, there were three factions at the moment of taking power (Tismăneanu et al. 2007: 119–25). The first was the party leadership, whose head, Ştefan Foriş was removed from the helm of the party as early as April 1944, and was killed in 1946. The second group was made up of communist illegalists from prison (mostly ethnic Romanians) whose main leader was the railway worker Gheorghe Gheorghiu-Dej (imprisoned since 1933, he had escaped only ten days before 23 August 1944). The third group was made up of émigré communists from Moscow (most of them ethnic minority members), their undisputed leader being Ana Pauker. She occupied an important position following her activity within the Comintern.

In October 1944 the PCR had a collective leadership, made up of Gheorghiu-Dej, Pauker and Vasile Luca (the latter also from the 'Muscovite' group). Following a visit to Moscow, in September 1945, Gheorghiu-Dej obtained Stalin's agreement to take over the PCR leadership as secretary general, a situation which was formalized on the occasion of the National Conference of October 1945. The imposition of Gheorghiu-Dej at the helm of the PCR (instead of Ana Pauker) can be explained by the fact that he was an ethnic Romanian and had a 'healthy social origin' (he was a worker) while Pauker was a woman of Jewish origin and had not spent time in jail.

During this acquisition of state power there were no significant differences of vision between the three factions. The communist leaders all agreed with Soviet satellization and political and institutional change according to the Soviet model. All displayed a humble fear towards Stalin, as they knew their political and human destiny depended on the decisions of the Soviet leader. All important state and party decisions were taken following orders from Moscow or at least with Soviet approval.

Rigging the 19 November 1946 elections

The promises made to Europeans by the Great Powers in the Yalta 'Declaration on liberated Europe' concerning their right to decide their governments, following free elections, meant that at least an appearance of fairness had to be maintained. Parliamentary elections were thus organized in the countries occupied by the USSR. They were relatively fair in Hungary in 1945 and Czechoslovakia in 1946, but completely rigged in favour of local communists in Bulgaria and Romania in 1946 and Poland in 1947 (Țârău 2005).

After the Anglo-American recognition of the Petru Groza government on 5 February 1946 and the resumption of diplomatic relations, the grounds were created for elections which could be recognized as 'free and fair' by the Great Powers. Conscious of their weak popular support, but also of Soviet backing for their conquest of power, the communists established a political alliance on 17 May 1946, called *Blocul Partidelor Democratice* (BPD – the Bloc of Democratic Parties), which included the PSD, the Ploughmen's Front, the Union of Patriots, the two dissidents from the PNȚ and the PNL, and the Jewish Democratic Committee.

In contradiction with the 1923 Constitution, the Senate was abolished and the Romanian Parliament was left with only one chamber, elections being organized only for the Assembly of Deputies. Simultaneously, a new electoral law was introduced, according to which mandates were attributed following a proportional method. The main novelty was giving the right to vote to women and the military, thus making voting truly universal. However, there were also seven categories of people considered to be 'shameful' who were barred from participating in elections. This blocked the candidacies of some from the democratic parties, who were generically labelled as 'fascists'.

The electoral campaign from July to November outdid in violence the interwar elections, which had also been marked by fraud and confrontations between parties. This time, the communists had to win at any price and the Soviets were massively involved with reaching this objective. The intelligence services (the *Siguranța* and the Special Intelligence Service) monitored opposition parties. The PNȚ, PNL and PSD-Independent were systematically discriminated against by banning rallies, censoring newspapers, destroying electoral materials and arresting their sympathizers. The organization of the elections was such as to allow the communists to proclaim their victory. Electoral abuses and, in fact, a system controlled by the Soviets for the purpose of rigging the elections determined the following official results: BPD 347 seats out of 414 (83.8 per cent); PNȚ only 33 seats, PNL 3 and PNȚ-Dr. Lupu 2. MADOSZ – the popular Hungarian union, allied with the communists, won 29 seats. The PSD-

Independent remained out of parliament. According to later historians, the communists and their allies failed to achieve more than 15–20 per cent of votes, even after using terror.

Following the official results, the PCR achieved the appearance of democratic legitimacy and the PNȚ and PNL leaders desperately tried to save democracy. Maniu demanded that King Michael I should refuse to participate in the opening of the Assembly of Deputies, thus invalidating the elections. The Anglo-Americans were informed about the election rigging, but they lacked any real means to change the situation. Michael I did not follow Maniu's demand, hoping that things would improve. On 1 December 1946, the session of the Assembly of Deputies was opened. The main stake for the country was the signing of the Peace Treaty, which lawfully guaranteed that the whole of Transylvania belonged to Romania (Giurescu 2007). On 20 December 1946, *Banca Națională a României* (BNR – the National Bank of Romania) was nationalized, as a foretaste of the communists' future actions.

The Paris Peace Conference and the Peace Treaty

While in Romania the political situation was tense, with all the political forces preparing for the parliamentary elections, at the same time crucial events were happening outside the country. Stalin convinced the Anglo-Americans that the peace treaties with Italy, Romania, Bulgaria, Hungary and Finland (considered satellite states of Nazi Germany) represented a secondary issue to be solved by foreign affairs ministers. Following the Potsdam Conference, the Foreign Affairs Ministers Council was established (made up of the Big Three, joined by France and China), a permanent body which submitted draft treaties projects with the five 'satellite states' to debate at the Paris Peace Conference (29 July to 15 October 1946). Romania prepared a delegation of 120 people, made up of politicians and experts, who went to Paris to defend its borders and resources. A broad statement was written and presented, concerning essential issues of the Peace Treaty (*România la Conferința de Pace de la Paris* 2007, 2011). Romanian diplomatic representatives, supported by Romanians in exile, tried to get the best possible. All the political and diplomatic effort in Paris depended, however, on the will of the Foreign Affairs Ministers Council's members, as proposals accepted by the Peace Conference had the status of recommendations for the ministers of foreign affairs of countries with the status of UN Security Council permanent members. The peace treaties were finalized at the Conference of Foreign Affairs Ministers in New York (4 November to 12 December 1946). On 10 February 1947, the Romanian government signed the Peace Treaty in Paris, in a context in which the communists' political rise could no longer be stopped, following the rigging of the 19 November 1946 elections.

In the Peace Treaty, Romania was not accorded the status of co-belligerent, although it had joined the United Nations on 23 August 1944, participating in the war effort until the proclamation of victory over Nazi Germany. Stalin did not accept the co-belligerent status as it would have meant he could not justify the seizure of Bessarabia and northern

Bukovina from an allied country. Romania had to accept the loss of Bessarabia and northern Bukovina to the USSR, as well as southern Dobrogea to Bulgaria. The provisions of the 30 August 1940 Vienna Award were declared 'null and void', thus settling the issue of Transylvania, despite Hungary's efforts to get at least a part of this region. War reparations to the USSR remained at the level established by the Armistice Convention: $300 million US dollars, payable in kind ('oil products, cereals, wood, maritime and river vessels, various equipments and other merchandise'). On the basis of these provisions, Romania's economy was rifled; important factories were transferred to the USSR, as well as raw materials (Lache 2013: 242–65).

Omission of the fact that Romania had fought alongside the United Nations as early as 23 August 1944, and not just from the date of signing the Armistice Convention, hid the fact that the Red Army had taken around 100,000 Romanian soldiers prisoner before the clarification of the Romanian army's legal status as allied or enemy. According to the Peace Treaty, Romanian prisoners were to be repatriated as soon as possible. In reality, the repatriation of Romanian prisoners of war from the USSR was a process lasting over a decade. In August and September 1945 almost 40,000 Romanian prisoners of war were liberated from Soviet camps. In 1946, another 12,512 were released. The last prisoners of war were repatriated in 1955; many of them were considered war criminals and re-incarcerated in Romania (*Prizonieri* 2013: xxxii–xxxvi).

Another deficiency of the Peace Treaty was its lack of precision concerning the Soviet troops present in Romania. The Red Army had to withdraw ninety days after the treaty's entering into force (15 September 1947); however the USSR had the right to keep 'on the Romanian territory forces which might be necessary for maintaining communication lines of the Soviet Army with the Soviet occupation area in Austria'. Although the Soviet military administration in Austria ended in 1950, the Red Army remained in Romania until 1958, playing an essential role in the communization process. The Peace Treaty signed by Romania reflects, on the one hand, the Soviet pre-eminence over Eastern Europe, as the provisions of the Armistice Convention were preserved at the end of the war and, on the other hand, the lack of solutions from the Anglo-Americans to prevent a division of Europe.

The dissolution of the PNȚ: 'Operation Tămădău'

The signing of the Peace Treaty and the clarification of the border issue were a new impetus for the anti-communist parties in their desperate attempt to prevent the country's sovietization. Although reduced to a minute size following the 19 November 1946 elections, the PNȚ enjoyed strong support among the population. This was a known fact to the communists and the Soviets and could not be tolerated by them.

Maniu considered that a group of PNȚ leaders had to be sent abroad in order to establish a government-in-exile. The leaders of the democratic parties still hoped for an energetic Anglo-American intervention to force a Soviet retreat from the country. It was a hope often cynically nourished by various Anglo-American diplomats, who could not simply tell Romanians 'It's over, the Russians have you!', but instead ambiguously supported an anti-communist resistance.

A trap was set for the PNȚ leaders, as the communists already knew about the escape plan. Thus, a group of party leaders, headed by Ion Mihalache (vice-president) and Nicolae Penescu (secretary general), were arrested on the Tămădău airfield (near Bucharest) on 14 July 1947 and charged with trying to flee to Turkey. On 29 July, the PNȚ was dissolved by the Groza government. Three months later, the trial of the PNȚ leaders, including Maniu and Mihalache, started in Bucharest. On 11 November 1947 the main leaders were sentenced to life imprisonment and confiscation of property. Maniu died in the Sighet prison (5 February 1953) and Mihalache in the Râmnicu Sărat penitentiary (5 February 1963). The PNL and the PSD-Independent were also eliminated from political life at the end of 1947. The party-state system was ready to be established.

The removal of the monarchy and proclamation of the Republic

Signs were emerging as early as 1946 indicating a new stage in relations among the Allied Powers of the Second World War, as they turned from cooperation to Cold War; these intensified during 1947, with the emergence of the 'Truman Doctrine' on 12 March and the launching of the 'Marshall Plan' on 5 June (Seyom 2015: 28–5). The Soviet reaction was to abandon any pretence concerning respect for the sovereignty of states under Red Army occupation. The 1946 plan regarding the creation of the Communist Information Bureau – Cominform – was implemented during a marathon meeting at Szklarska Poreba in Poland on 22–27 September 1947, attended by seven East European communist parties, including the Romanian one, and two Western parties. The purpose of Cominform was to offer a formal, apparently democratic, framework to Soviet control over communist parties in the satellite states (Procacci 1994). At Szklarska Poreba, the USSR's Andrei Zhdanov launched the theory of confrontation between the two camps: the 'imperialism camp' versus the 'peace camp'. The signal was clear: the waters had to be separated and the satellization of Eastern Europe had to evolve into full sovietization.

In this international policy context and following the takeover of key institutions by the Romanian communists and the dissolution of the PNȚ, constitutional monarchy became out of place in a 'popular democracy'. King Michael's visit to London for the marriage of Princess Elizabeth, heir to the throne in the UK, was received with optimism by the communists; they hoped the monarch would not return to Romania. However, Michael I came back to Bucharest on 21 December, having failed in his attempt to obtain British support for Romania. Moreover, his plan to get married showed that he did not intend to leave. The communists took the initiative through Petru Groza and Gheorghiu-Dej; following an ultimatum meeting with King Michael I and his mother Helen, the king was forced to abdicate on 30 December 1947. The Grand National Assembly was immediately convened, under the chairmanship of Mihail Sadoveanu, and the Republic was proclaimed. It was led by an interim presidential committee made up of five people

(C.I. Parhon, Mihail Sadoveanu, Ştefan Voitec, Gheorghe Stere and Ion Niculi) but without real political influence (Scurtu 2010b).

On 3 January 1948, Michael I was allowed to leave Romania in a small train, going to Switzerland. Following the *coup d'état* of 30 December 1947, the last institution of democratic Romania was eliminated and the way was clear for the communists to turn the country to their ideological project under orders sent from the Kremlin.

CHAPTER 3
THE GHEORGHIU-DEJ ERA (1948-65)

The beginning of the communist regime and its consolidation in Romania are related to the personality of Gheorghiu-Dej, who gradually turned from *primus inter pares* into the undisputed leader. A follower of Stalinism, Gheorghiu-Dej was not only linked with Romania's sovietization, and its accompanying crimes and dramas, but also with the launch of a policy of empowerment of the country within the Soviet bloc.

The new state organization

The fundamental difference brought about by 'popular democracy' was the abolition of the principle of checks and balances among state powers and its replacement by the subordination of all institutions to the party-state. The formal organization of institutions created the appearance of separation of powers, but this was only meant to hide the communist party dictatorship.

During the communist regime there were three constitutions. The first, adopted in April 1948, reflected the transition from representative democracy to a totalitarian system, an interlude euphemistically called 'popular democracy' (*Constituția RPR* 1948). The fundamental law included the ambiguities of an era in which communist power was not fully consolidated, the Cold War had become certitude, but systemic totalitarian change had not yet been achieved. The fundamental law of 1952 was the constitution of victorious Stalinist communism, in which society is dominated and controlled by the party-state and the foundations of 'bourgeois' constitutionalism are replaced by Marxism-Leninism. From being a document stating values and principles, the 1952 Constitution turns into a propaganda document (*Constituția RPR* 1952). Ceaușescu's decision to adopt a new constitution was meant to be a step towards reconciling the Communist nomenklatura with society. Some of the Marxist-Leninist dogmas were eliminated, but the totalitarian state is obvious in the manner of organizing institutions and structuring citizens' liberties and obligations. From 1965, Romania became a 'socialist republic'; it continued to be 'the state of working people in towns and villages', but the state is 'sovereign, independent and unitary' and its 'territory is unalienable and indivisible' (Art.1). Sovereignty belongs to the 'people' and the Communist authorities felt the need to specify that it is 'free and the master of its fate' (Article 2) (*Constituția RSR* 1965).

Formally, the state leadership belonged to *Marea Adunare Națională* (MAN – the Grand National Assembly), which was the 'single legislative body', having the competency to form and control the government. The MAN was elected with a four-year mandate, which was extended to five years from 1969. The MAN met in sessions twice a year until all laws were adopted. The legislative body was led by a Presidium, who exercised the office of a 'collective head of state' until the creation of the *Consiliu de Stat* (State Council, 1961), also a collective body. In 1974, Nicolae Ceaușescu introduced the office of *Președinte al Republicii* (President of the Republic), who headed the State Council. The government (*Consiliul de Miniștri* – the Council of Ministers) was accountable to the MAN. The State Council and the President of the Republic were also accountable to the MAN, who in fact elected them.

The single-party principle did not have an explicit constitutional value. Under the 1952 Constitution, *Partidul Muncitoresc Român* (PMR – the Romanian Workers Party) was the only political formation with the right to submit candidates for election to the MAN (Article 100). The 1965 Constitution stated that the PCR is the 'leading political force of the entire society' (Article 3).

The key to the functioning of the communist system was the manner of the MAN's formation. Though not enshrined in the constitution as such, the single-party principle was the de facto reality of the dictatorial regime. The communist party did not run as itself in MAN elections, but as the Front of Popular Democracy (FDP) and, from 1968, as the Front of Socialist Unity (which changed its name in 1980 into the Front of Socialist Unity and Democracy), both of which were led by the party-state.

During the first MAN elections, in March 1948, the FDP comprised candidates from the PMR, the Ploughmen's Front, the National Popular Party and the Hungarian Popular Party, but seats were also assigned to the PNL-Bejan (7) and the PNȚ-Dr. Lupu (2). After this, in elections from 1952 to 1989, members elected to the MAN on behalf of these umbrella organizations were not only chosen from among party members, but also included various persons from trade unions and other 'mass and non-governmental organizations'. The nine MAN elections (from 1948 to 1985) were only a semblance of electoral competition, as until 1975, only single candidates were allowed and thereafter two candidates but only on the basis of the PCR programme. The so-called 'elections' recorded scores of between 97 and 99.9 per cent for the communists (Giurescu 2013: 522–9).

At local level, administrative leadership ('local bodies of state power') was carried out by *consilii populare* (people's councils), renamed *sfaturi populare* (a synonymous expression, but using a word of Slavic origin) between 1952 and 1968, before returning to their former name. They were elected according to the same rules as the MAN. As far as administrative-territorial structure is concerned, in 1950 Romania abandoned the system of 58 *județe* (counties), divided into 424 *plăși* (places) and 6,276 urban and rural communes, and replaced it with a Soviet-inspired structure of 28 *regiuni* (regions), made up of 177 *raioane* (districts), 4,052 communes and eight cities of republican subordination. In 1952 the number of regions was reduced to sixteen. In 1968 there was a return to organization in *județe* (39 in number) together with the Municipality of Bucharest.

Avatars of the party-state

Internal organization

The transition from a subversive organization to a mass structure after taking power led to changes in the PCR's organization. From 1945 to 1989, the party's organization underwent several changes, but the Leninist principle of democratic centralism remained sacrosanct in order to ensure unity and discipline. The second fundamental principle was that of collective leadership, according to which party members had the right to hold an opinion concerning all issues discussed. In reality, most of the time this principle was a political fiction, as the informal rule of mass organization was to generate apparent unanimities. Communist leaders had every interest in presenting the party's 'monolithic unity' for propaganda purposes, and 'deviationism' was punished by exclusion or even physical elimination.

The PCR became a party-state not only because it imposed its ideology within the state's leadership, but also because it created structures in all institutions and most economic units. The dynamic of party flocks emphasizes the leaders' preoccupation with turning an elitist 'vanguard group' into a mass structure: in May 1948, it had 595,398 members. This had risen to 1,454,727 members by June 1965.

The simplest political structure was the basic organization, which had to have at least three members. These were organized following the 'territorial and production place principle'. Organizations were established according to the territorial criterion (commune, town, district, region – later county). The supreme leading body was the Congress and in the periods between congresses there was the National Conference, which had a more reduced composition. During the period of the Gheorghiu-Dej regime only three congresses took place (in 1948, 1955 and 1960), during which the main projects for Romanian society were established (Buga 2012).

The party was led by the Central Committee, within which an executive structure (the Political Bureau) was elected, and then the Executive Committee. Meetings of Central Committee members were called Plenaries. Nevertheless, the executive structure became increasingly extended, so that within it a more reduced leading formula was established, initially called the Permanent Presidium and, from 1974, the Permanent Bureau. Unipersonal leadership was ensured by a First Secretary of the Central Committee, an office changed by Ceauşescu into that of Secretary General in 1965, to give expression to his supremacy over other communist leaders. The First Secretary was part of the small Secretariat structure, which exercised day-to-day party leadership.

Subordinated to the political bodies of the party-state was the bureaucracy, organized in sections (staff, propaganda, office, foreign affairs, agriculture, industry, etc.). According to the Soviet model, party schools were created both for the wide ideologization of members and for training senior members. The most important institutions were the A.A. Zhdanov Superior School of Social Sciences (1948–58) and the Ştefan Gheorghiu Academy, the latter was transformed into a public higher education institution.

Fratricidal struggles

The year 1948 brought the full sovietization of Eastern Europe and ended the illusion that the Cold War could be avoided, as long as Stalin was leading the USSR. For Romania, this was the year when the most important measures for the communization of its society were taken, and the model of the state-centralized economy was imposed.

At the level of political life, the first important event was the absorption of the PSD by the PCR, announced as early as October 1947, after previously eliminating tens of thousands of social democrats. On 21–23 February 1948 the so-called 'unification congress' took place, resulting in the creation of the PMR.

On the same occasion, the struggle for power between communist factions continued, but this time the state's repressive institutions were used to eliminate opponents. Teohari Georgescu, member of the Political Bureau and Minister of the Interior, accused Lucreţiu Pătrăşcanu, Minister of Justice, of being under the influence of 'bourgeois ideology'. This was followed not only by Pătrăşcanu's removal from the PMR and loss of ministerial office, but also his arrest and a long investigation. Pătrăşcanu was a lawyer who had held communist beliefs since the PCR had been illegal; he had been involved in the signing of the Armistice Convention, then, from the position of Minister of Justice had been instrumental in removing the democratic regime. Pătrăşcanu was an authentic intellectual and all his public activity contrasted with that of the proletarian leaders. He had not managed to build a power base within the party, and the Soviets did not trust him. Pătrăşcanu also had an adversarial relationship with Gheorghiu-Dej; he wanted to eliminate a dangerous competitor who was not from the ethnic minorities and was a senior party member. After the initial accusation of February 1948 others followed: that he was a 'Titoist' and an 'English agent'. His collaborators were also arrested. In March 1954, the PMR Political Bureau validated the trial of the 'Pătrăşcanu batch' and, following a mock trial, Pătrăşcanu was sentenced to death and executed in April 1954 (Betea 2011).

Conflicts at the level of the communist leaders were also transferred within the party. If, immediately after 23 August 1944, the communists were interested in increasing the size of the party, after seizing power in December 1947, they stopped the enrolment of new members. Aware that over a million members had enrolled in the party not so much out of love and belief as from a desire to gain protection from political repression (ML members), the PMR leaders decided in June 1948 to 'check' party members. The purpose of this measure was to eliminate the undesirable: 'exploiting elements', chauvinist and anti-Soviet members and 'right wing' social democrats, for example. According to the statistical data of the PMR, 192,881 members were excluded, 112,901 of them for hostile activities and various serious deviations and the rest for avoiding checking (Ionescu-Gură 2004). Similar actions of communist party homogenization resembling that in Romania were also carried out in Czechoslovakia, Poland and Hungary, and were coordinated by the Soviets.

Although the communist leaders eliminated their 'bourgeois' adversaries, they knew that their political and even biological survival depended on Stalin's goodwill. The fragility of any group's power position was also emphasized by the political trials that took place in an atmosphere dominated by suspicion and conspiracy psychosis: László Rajk, former Minister of the Interior in Hungary, was executed in 1949 under the accusation of being a 'Titoist spy'; Bulgarian Traycho Kostov, initially noted by Soviets for his anti-Titoist attitude, was accused and executed in 1949 for spying; Koci Xoce, Minister of the Interior in Albania, was also executed.

The docility which Gheorghiu-Dej showed towards Stalin, much greater than that of the other East-European leaders, created the premises for winning the trust of 'Daddy'. Starting in 1951, the latter was increasingly convinced of the existence of an imperialist-Zionist conspiracy, not only within the Soviet Union, but also in the satellite states, a situation which had to be fought with repressive instruments (Rees 2004: 221–5).

The struggle for power at the helm of the PMR also affected apparently untouchable leaders. Among these were the Ana Pauker–Vasile Luca–Teohari Georgescu group. They supported Gheorghiu-Dej in eliminating Pătrășcanu, but the merciless logic of power struggles turned former allies into irreducible enemies. The first person who was removed was Vasile Luca, accused during the PMR Central Committee Plenary of 29 February–1 March 1952 of 'right wing deviationism' and blamed for mistakes in leading the Ministry of Finance and the BNR. Vasile Luca was replaced as head of the Ministry of Finance, but Pauker and Georgescu tried to defend him. In April 1952, Gheorghiu-Dej's reaction was to go to Moscow to get Stalin's agreement to the fight against 'deviationists' in the 'anti-party faction'. Stalin seems to have agreed with the elimination of the Muscovite group. The PMR Plenary of 26–27 May 1952 meant imposing a new leadership formula, in which the Pauker–Luca–Georgescu group was removed and key positions were occupied by protégés of Gheorghiu-Dej. It was the beginning of changes in the ethnic composition of the PMR national leadership; minority Hungarian and Jewish leaders were replaced by ethnic Romanians.

Vasile Luca lost all state offices, was excluded from the party, and was arrested and sentenced to death on 10 October 1954. The sentence was then commuted to life imprisonment. Vasile Luca died in the Aiud prison in July 1963. Teohari Georgescu was dismissed from all party and state offices – Minister of the Interior, Deputy Prime Minister, member of the Secretariat and the Political Bureau. He was arrested, but then released after Stalin's death. From 1953 he became the director of a printing enterprise. In her turn, Ana Pauker was excluded from the PMR, lost all state offices and after a short period of arrest was released; she was later hired as a Russian translator at the Political Printing House (Levy 2002).

Stalin's death in March 1953 brought with it continuation of uncertainty, as a result of the Kremlin power struggles between Beria, Malenkov and Khrushchev. The PMR leadership was called to report in Moscow in June 1953. Much to its surprise, it was blamed for its Stalinist economic policy, including works for the Danube–Black Sea Canal, investments in heavy industry, military spending and decreasing agriculture spending. Molotov's accusation – 'You've alienated the people!' – was followed by Soviet demands that the PMR get the support of the population in order to be able to rule without repression. Molotov was explicit: 'You feel alone under the Soviet Union's wing. Without our support, you wouldn't last two weeks. If you aren't bound to the people, we won't be able to help you either. Who will respect your power?' Gheorghiu-Dej's psychological reaction to the new attitude of the Soviet leaders was significant: 'We felt rather awkward when the leaders of the Soviet party and government discussed with us on equal terms' (Buzatu 2003: 598–601). The Romanian leader's confession reveals his mimetic behaviour towards the Soviet Union: he was used to being told everything he had to do and for this to be sufficient to maintain him in power.

Gheorghiu-Dej felt threatened by de-Stalinization, as he was considered a product of the Stalinist age; in order to survive he tried to position himself on the side of the winning faction in the Kremlin. 'Prudence' was the main commandment of the Romanian Communist leader. The PMR Central Committee Plenary of 19–20 August 1953 decided to follow Soviet indications by reducing the rhythm of industrialization and ending mass repression. The principle of the separation of state and party offices was adopted, following the Soviet model. However, Gheorghiu-Dej was in no hurry to give up the office of First Secretary for that of prime minister; he only did so after the execution of Lucreţiu Pătrăşcanu in April 1954 and after he had ensured that Gheorghe Apostol, the new First Secretary, would not remove him from power. In October 1955, profiting from the fact that Khrushchev had managed to remove Malenkov, so that the party leadership had again become more important than the state, Gheorghiu-Dej regained the PMR leadership and Chivu Stoica became prime minister of Romania.

A new challenge for the PMR came on the occasion of the Twentieth Congress of the Communist Party of the Soviet Union (CPSU) in February 1956, during which Khrushchev presented the 'secret report' which criticized the personality cult of Stalin's era. The key concepts of de-Stalinization were 'collective leadership' and 'peaceful coexistence'; the latter formula aimed at abandoning aggressive competition with the capitalist system. Khrushchev was the partisan of flexible satellization, which created the appearance of a 'new course' not only in relations with the West, but even within the communist bloc.

The de-Stalinization message re-launched power competition at the helm of the PMR. Gheorghiu-Dej's authority was questioned in relation to *Securitate* abuses, the personality cult and party democracy. Miron Constantinescu and Iosif Chişinevschi, two old Stalinists, raised the issue of Gheorghiu-Dej's responsibility during a Special Plenary on 25 March 1956, but the PMR leader, as in the case of Titoism, found scapegoats in the past: the Pauker–Luca–Georgescu group were to blame for all Stalinist excesses. The PMR leader, together with his group of protégés, immediately reacted against challengers, criticizing them, but he did not go so far as to eliminate them, as long as the impact of de-Stalinization was difficult to anticipate and any retaliation measures against political leaders demanding application of the 'Twentieth Congress lessons' could be risky (Bosomitu and Burcea 2012: 175–204).

After the defeat of the Budapest revolt, in the context of the active role played by the PMR leaders in 'defending the Soviet bloc's unity', the relation of trust between Khrushchev and Gheorghiu-Dej was strengthened. The failed plan of the Molotov–Kaganovich–Malenkov group to remove Khrushchev, the result of which was the elimination of the three in June 1957, consolidated Gheorghiu-Dej's conviction that decreasing Romania's dependence on the Soviet Union had to become a strategic preoccupation. The Romanian Communist leader used the favourable situation to eliminate his main adversaries, Miron Constantinescu and Iosif Chişinevschi, during the Central Committee Plenary of 28 June–3 July 1957 (Tudor and Cătănuş 2001: 248–55).

In the context of the Soviet troops' withdrawal from Romania in 1958, the party leadership unleashed a new wave of repression outside the PMR and purges within. This time the target of PMR exclusions were people who had previously criticized Gheorghiu-Dej's team. At the PMR Plenary of 9–13 June 1958, a discussion topic was the 'factious and anti-party attitude of some party members led by Constantin Doncea, Pavel Ştefan, Grigore Răceanu and Ovidiu Şandru'. Several thousand people were excluded from the PMR in 1958–9, the most visible group being that of the so-called 'illegalists': people who had been active in the party since the interwar period.

In October 1961, the Twenty-second Congress of the CPSU took place and a second wave of de-Stalinization was launched; conflicts within the socialist camp came into the open. The Albanian communists were criticized for 'schismatic, factious and subversive' activities, being helped by the Chinese communist party. Gheorghiu-Dej was again contemplating a political option: the Soviets or the Chinese. The preservation of solidarity with Khrushchev was confirmed during the PMR Plenary of 30 November–5 December 1961. This time, de-Stalinization theses were well received in Bucharest and the excesses of the Stalinist leader were firmly assigned to the Pauker–Luca–Georgescu and Chişinevschi–Constantinescu groups. Albania, and consequently China, was the object of the Romanian Communists' criticism. Constantin Pârvulescu, a former illegalist and former head of the PMR cadres, was removed from office. Gheorghiu-Dej's domination over the party was complete, as alternative power groups were either marginalized or removed. The 'Carpathian fox', had managed to achieve control over the party-state and his public image was haloed by the fact that in 1958 the Soviets had withdrawn their troops from Romania.

Great transformations

Shortly after achieving power, the communist regime implemented major transformations in Romania, which included the status of property, agriculture collectivization, administrative-territorial organization, the educational system, the organization of religious denominations and the ideological subordination of cultural and artistic life. All these changes were meant to revolutionize bourgeois society, and were considered to be necessary steps for building a society without class, led by the proletariat.

The basis of the socio-economic transformation was a new model of political regime, based on the supremacy of the communist party over state institutions. The most important change was in the government's modus operandi. From being the main decisional factor concerning domestic and international policy, the cabinet of ministers became a body meant only to execute decisions taken by the party. Petru Groza was maintained as President of the Council of Ministers until 1952, precisely because his political role was reduced. Gheorghiu-Dej's takeover of the government's leadership in June 1952, simultaneously with holding the office of PMR First Secretary, was accomplished by eliminating the rival Pauker–Luca–Georgescu group. Gheorghiu-Dej gave up the leadership of the government in 1955, because, according to the Soviet model, party leadership was more important. Chivu Stoica was prime minister until 1961, but he was just a secondary political leader, an executor of Gheorghiu-Dej's decisions. Ion Gheorghe Maurer became President of the Council of Ministers until 1974.

The nationalization of the economy

The decisions which affected society most profoundly in the long term, apart, of course, from the restraining of freedoms, were those aimed at changes in property. For tactical reasons, the PCR did not initially assume the project of property nationalization, although this was a consequence of Marxist-Leninist postulates. The sign of the apocalypse came in August 1947 when, as a result of hyperinflation, the PCR decided upon a measure of monetary stabilization, by which 20,000 *lei* was exchanged for 1 new *leu*, but only to a maximum limit of 5 million old *lei* for peasants and 3 million old *lei* for employees.

This baffling blow to society was enacted on 11 June 1948 (Law no. 119 for the nationalization of industrial, banking, insurance, mining and transport enterprises) when no less than 8,894 enterprises were transferred into state ownership without compensation (Giurescu 2015: 54–9). This was only the beginning of complete state control: by 1950, the medical system, the film industry, pharmacies and, eventually, 'bourgeois-landlord' estates, including hotels had been nationalized. In June 1948, the State Planning Commission was established. This marked the beginning of the command economy.

On 2 March 1949, as a prelude to agricultural collectivization, Decree no. 83 provided for the confiscation of the remaining 'landlord agricultural exploitations' together with the agricultural and semi-industrial equipment which had escaped the agrarian reform of 1945. Confiscation of large agricultural properties was carried out simultaneously with the eviction and establishment of mandatory residence for almost 3,000 'landowners', accounting for a total of 7,804 persons (Oprea 2008). From the position of quasi-absolute owner of the economy, with the exception of small agricultural properties and a part of the estates, the communist state achieved a real revolution with predominantly negative consequences.

Collectivization of agriculture

The 'socialist transformation of agriculture', as the collectivization was called, represented an essential measure for the sovietization of Romania and the political conquest of the rural world by the communists. The beginning of collectivization in Romania was achieved following the 3–5 March 1949 Plenary of the PMR Central Committee, which practically annulled the 1945 agrarian reform. After thirteen years of pressure on the rural world, the collectivization process was officially finalized in 1962. The event was marked by a festive session of the Grand National Assembly on 27 April 1962, attended by 11,000 peasants.

The forms of collective structure used in Romania were entirely copied from the USSR. The first organizational structures were *întovărășiri* (TOZ, agricultural associations), which maintained private property over land; poor and middle peasants, for whom this form of labour organization was intended, worked the land in common and achieved its consolidation for rational exploitation. The classical structure for the Soviet type of collectivization is that of *kolkhozes*, called *Gospodării Agricole Colective* (GAC – Agricultural Collective Farms); these were based on the principle of 'common property in the means of production, collective labour and full property in the resulting production' (Roske, Abraham and Cătănuș 2007: 341).

The collectivization of agriculture was the result of a combination of internal and external factors. The first stage (1949–53) was marked, on the one hand, by Stalin's attempt at sovietizing the space within Moscow's new sphere of influence, and, on the other hand, by the competition for power within the PMR, between the group represented by Gheorghiu-Dej and that led by Ana Pauker. Stalin's death in March 1953 brought some uncertainty about the new direction that the Kremlin intended to take. Confronted with hostility from the rural world, collectivization was making slow progress; by 1953 only 10 per cent of land had been included in collective forms (Kligman and Verdery 2011: 103)

The years 1953–5 marked a 'freezing' of collectivization, with the political emphasis being placed upon blocking the disintegration of the TOZs and GACs that had been created in the first stage and upon their organizational and economic consolidation. Although a political decision to re-launch collectivization was taken at the end of 1955, the unsettled atmosphere in Moscow, and especially the Hungarian Revolution, caused communist leaders to have a more cautious attitude. Starting from 1957, collectivization was resumed by a change of strategy in the direction of a regional approach; the first purpose was the total collectivization of Constanța region, followed by Galați. After the withdrawal of Soviet troops from Romania in 1958, communist authorities doubled their efforts to demonstrate their attachment to the Soviet model, intensifying collectivization campaigns together with a new wave of repression. The finalization of the collectivization process in Hungary and Czechoslovakia was a pressure factor for the communists in Romania, and in 1961, the final push for complete collectivization was launched.

Until 1952, the communist leadership oscillated between establishing more TOZs and going directly to GACs. Between 1952 and 1959, the emphasis was on creating more TOZs, which would be turned into GACs in the final stage. After 1959, GACs were established directly and peasants thus lost ownership over land, animals and agricultural inventory (ploughs, carts, etc.). According to figures presented by Gheorghiu-Dej in April 1962, 96 per cent of the country's arable land and 93.4 per cent of the agricultural surface was nationalized or collectivized. By 1962, over 3.2 million families with over 9 million hectares of agricultural land had entered GACs.

In order to overcome the rural world, the PMR used both persuasion and physical violence. The communists looked for allies in the rural areas and found them among the rural proletariat and middle peasants. TOZs and GACs had to include only these categories, who were induced to associate in order to work the land by some tax exemptions and by technological assistance from the state. The non-violent strategy was a failure, as either the peasants were not convinced of the advantages of jointly working the land or those who were interested had too little land, so that collective were not significant for the economy. Therefore, collectivization was mostly achieved by violent means, such as direct physical aggression, repression through economic tools, or symbolic violence.

As early as 1948, peasants were subjected to an abusive system of mandatory collection quotas, which were conceived in such a way as to mainly affect the category of rich peasants (*chiaburi* in Romanian, equivalent of the Russian *kulaks*). Peasants who had less land could not easily withstand the collection regime concerning agricultural products and animals, so that until their abolition in 1956, the quotas represented a system of constraints supporting collectivization. Peasants who accepted collectivization were offered a preferential system; there was official discrimination concerning taxes between individual households and cooperative forms (TOZ and GAC). *Chiaburi* did not have access to agricultural loans and the Machines and Tractors Stations (SMT), owned by the state, refused to work the land of rich peasants, even if they offered money.

If economic pressures failed, peasants were submitted to systematic persuasion (harassment) actions by teams made up of party activists, *Miliția* and *Securitate* employees, as well as public sector workers such as teachers. Pressure was exerted on families, by blocking access to education or offering access to jobs only on acceptance of the collective system. Social ascension was associated with the acceptance of collectivization.

The whole rural world was submitted to massive propaganda campaigns aimed at demonstrating the 'superiority of the collective system'. Periodic meetings were organized in village halls at which party activists attempted to get collective approval for establishing TOZs and GACs. In order for the superiority of the collective system to be obvious, the Communist regime organized visits of peasant groups to the Soviet Union, to model *kolkhozes*; these delegations were heavily promoted in the official central or local press. Visits to 'model' GACs within Romania were organized. A whole literature promoting collectivization was created, and propaganda movies, produced in Romania or elsewhere in the communist camp, were presented in village halls and rural schools.

If these 'soft' methods were not effective, the communist regime resorted to direct violence, with harassment undertaken through exemplary arrests, deportations, house arrests and, ultimately, conviction and detention. Repressive criminal legislation was adapted in order to serve as an instrument of agricultural collectivization.

The employment of the full arsenal of methods described above created tremendous pressure on the rural world. In 1949, peasant revolts broke out in Banat–Crișana and northern Moldavia and in 1958, a second wave of revolts took place in Oltenia and southern Moldavia. All were brutally repressed (Dobrincu and Iordachi 2009).

Establishing the number of victims (arrested, deported, convicted, mistreated) produced by successive collectivization campaigns is a difficult task. In the period 1949–52 alone, over 89,000 peasants were arrested; of these, almost 35,000 were judged in public trials.

In conclusion, much like the Soviet Union and Albania, Romania organized one of the most state-centred agriculture sectors. Yugoslavia and Poland abandoned collectivization in 1953 and 1956 respectively. Hungary and Czechoslovakia ended collectivization as early as 1960–1, and in Hungary, agricultural farms were orientated towards the market after 1968. Albania achieved the final step of collectivizing mountainous regions in 1966 (Iordachi and Bauerkämper 2014).

Foreign policy: from satellization to 'heresy'

Communist Romania's foreign policy during the rule of Gheorghiu-Dej was determined by the dynamic of relations between the USSR and the US (together with its West European allies) by the political situation in the Kremlin and the power struggle within the PMR.

Foreign policy was the attribute of the single party; the Ministry of Foreign Affairs only played the role of a technical structure, destined to put political decisions into practice. After the purge of Ana Pauker (1952), the office of Minister of Foreign Affairs was assigned to secondary Communist leaders. Much like the whole administration, the Ministry of Foreign Affairs was cleansed of people who were considered unfit according to Marxist-Leninist criteria. These were often replaced with simple workers. The result was a quick de-professionalization of the Romanian diplomatic services.

The presence of Soviet troops in Romania and the imposition of communist leadership had as a consequence satellization in relation to the Soviet Union. The satellization of the region between the Baltic Sea and the Black Sea was achieved through a system of bilateral treaties with the USSR. On 4 February 1948, the 'Treaty of friendship, collaboration and mutual assistance between the Union of Soviet Socialist Republics and the Romanian Popular Republic' was signed, as well as 'The protocol concerning the accurate path of the state border between the Romanian Popular Republic and the Union of Soviet Socialist Republics'. Snake Island in the Black Sea and other small territories were seized by the USSR.

Satellization meant, on the one hand, giving up sovereignty in favour of the USSR and, on the other hand, destroying traditional diplomatic relations. Relations with other countries the 'imperialist bloc' became minimal. Romania denounced even its *Concordat* with the Vatican, which had regulated the situation of Catholics (1948).

The communist leaders meekly accepted satellization towards the Kremlin, as their preservation in power depended on submissive faithfulness to Stalin. In the context of disputes between Stalin and Josip Broz Tito's Yugoslavia, as a result of the latter's refusal to accept Soviet domination, Romania obediently followed the USSR's position. Romanian propaganda against Yugoslavia could not be matched at the level of symbolic violence in the rest of the satellized countries (Anton 2007: 22–1). Romania welcomed anti-Tito émigrés from Yugoslavia and, on 1 October 1949, denounced its bilateral treaty with the country, as the Soviet Union had done two days before.

In 1949, Romania enthusiastically joined the Council for Mutual Economic Assistance (COMECON), in which Gheorghiu-Dej said during a session of the Political Bureau of the PMR Central Committee of 10 January 1949 that he had a founding role together with Vasile Luca. The initiative was meant to be a reaction addressed to the 'imperialist camp', which had proposed the Marshall Plan (Țăranu 2007).

Gheorghiu-Dej continued to conceive Romania's relationship with the Soviet Union as that of a satellite during the post-Stalin era. Confronted with serious economic problems, he demanded a loan of 300–400 million roubles during his visit in Moscow in January 1954, but was only promised 200 million. As compensation from Moscow, in 1954 no less than twelve of the sixteen joint Romanian–Soviet companies (Sovrom), which had exploited Romania's economy since 1945, were abolished.

The signing of the Warsaw Pact by Romania, represented by Gheorghiu-Dej, on 14 May 1955 legally finalized the satellization of the Romanian state towards the Soviet Union. The secret Additional Protocol to the treaty established the military obligations of each state for the creation of the United Armed Forces (Opriş 2008: 62–79). The USSR was in the position of an occupying state, but from a legal point of view, it was contributing to the defence of Romania's borders against a potential attack from 'western imperialism'.

The abandonment of the conflict with Tito by Khrushchev and the visit of the Soviet leader to Belgrade from 27 May to 2 June 1955 led to a resumption of diplomatic relations between Romania and Yugoslavia. Tito visited Bucharest in June 1956, and was enthusiastically received by Gheorghiu-Dej, who only few years before had called him a 'bandit and spy'. The warming of relations between Bucharest and Belgrade, together with the launch of the strategic project of a hydropower plant at the Iron Gates on the Danube, did not, however, mean a geostrategic shift on Romania's part, but was the consequence of an initiative from Moscow.

The strikes in Poznan (Poland) on 28–29 June 1956, followed by the Hungarian Revolution in October–November 1956 raised alarm bells among Romania's communist leaders, who considered that they had to continue showing fealty towards the Soviets. Gheorghiu-Dej offered Romanian troops to defeat the 1956 protests in Hungary. Khrushchev declined the offer but Romania still played a part in the repression of the Revolution, by 'hosting' the Imre Nagy group in Snagov from 1956 to 1958.

Following the events of 1956, the Soviets consolidated their trust in Gheorghiu-Dej. Symbolic gestures on the part of the Soviet Union followed: a minor part of Romania's treasury was returned and the last joint Romanian–Soviet enterprise, Sovromcuarțit was dismantled. Stronger proof of Khrushchev's trust in Gheorghiu-Dej came in April 1958, when earlier demands for the withdrawal of Soviet troops from Romania were met (Scurtu 1996: 233–5). Of course, the Soviet decision was mainly based on considerations deriving from its relations with the West; the withdrawal of

Soviet troops was meant to be a message, together with other decisions (the unilateral reduction of Red Army forces by 300,000, including 41,000 stationed in East Germany and 17,000 in Hungary; the declaration concerning the unilateral cancellation of nuclear experiments) regarding a return to the 'Geneva spirit' (Verona 1992: 137–9).

The withdrawal of Soviet troops from Romania was the fundamental premise for a gradual detachment from the Soviet direction and the imposition of a more autonomous policy. After the deficit of international trust in the USSR, following the repression of the Hungarian Revolution, Gheorghiu-Dej sensed the fact that a new Soviet military intervention could take place only if Romania intended to abandon the communist system or leave the Warsaw Pact and COMECON. The communist leader obviously did not have such intentions.

In parallel with the preservation of good relations with Moscow, Gheorghiu-Dej also sent communist Romania's first diplomatic missions to the West in order to open economic contacts. Achieving economic autonomy and, in this way, political autonomy, became Gheorghiu-Dej's main objective.

It was in the context of the Soviet Union's intention of achieving a specialization of countries within the COMECON, with some countries developing their industry and others their agriculture – a policy supported by East Germany and Czechoslovakia – that the first Romanian–Soviet divergences emerged. The Moscow COMECON meeting of 6–7 June 1962 adopted the document 'Fundamental principles of the international socialist division of labour', elaborated by Soviet economist E.B. Valev, in which the thesis of country specialization in certain industries was specified. Romania was to become a provider of cheap agricultural produce. During the Moscow meeting, Gheorghiu-Dej expressed his veto concerning changing the COMECON decision-taking mechanism, arguing in favour of voluntary coordination (not integration) of economic plans, as they represented an attribute of national sovereignty. This was Romania's first significant rebellious act against the Soviet Union, a tense situation which Khrushchev sought to defuse by making a visit to Bucharest on 18–25 June 1962. However, during the COMECON Executive Committee session of 15–21 February 1963 in Moscow, Romania's representative, Alexandru Bârlădeanu, opposed the creation of the single planning body, arguing that it would affect national sovereignty (Retegan 2002: 50–189). Romanian–Soviet tensions were amplified because Khrushchev had suffered a defeat in the Cuban Missile Crisis in 1962, and China and Albania were contesting Moscow's supremacy within the socialist camp. Romania allied more closely to China during 1963, in order to counterbalance Soviet hegemony. On 24–25 June 1963, Khrushchev visited Romania again in order to calm the situation. The withdrawal of the last Soviet advisors from the Ministry of Home Affairs was demanded (Cătănuş 2011). Gheorghiu-Dej approved symbolic measures: the Maxim Gorki Institute was turned into the Faculty of Slavic Languages within the Institute of Foreign Languages; the Romanian–Soviet Studies Institute was dismantled; the *Cartea Rusă* (Russian Book) publishing house became the Universal Literature Publishing House; the obligatory teaching of Russian in Romanian schools was eliminated; Stalin city returned to its old name, Braşov.

In 1964, the 'Declaration concerning the position of the Romanian Workers Party on the issues of the international communist and workers' movement, also known as the 'April Declaration', was published (PMR 1964). The document synthesized the new vision of Gheorghiu-Dej concerning collaboration within the COMECON and the principles which should ground this collaboration: full equality of rights, respect for sovereignty and national interests, mutual advantages and comradely assistance. On the same line of affirming Romania's autonomy within the Soviet camp, the 'April Declaration' denounced involvement in the internal problems of other parties.

Gheorghiu-Dej continued the strategy of eliminating the instruments of sovietization, immediately after Khrushchev's removal from the head of the CPSU (14 October 1964), demanding the withdrawal of KGB advisors from Romania. They were withdrawn by December 1964 (Moraru 2008: 57). The issue of borders between Romania and the Soviet Union was publicly raised by invoking the 'classics': in December 1964, Karl Marx's volume *Writings about the Romanians*, in which Romania's rights over Bessarabia were confirmed, was published in Bucharest. In China, Mao Zedong, in order to attack the Soviet Union, recognized that Bessarabia had been unjustly taken from Romania.

Simultaneously with distancing itself from the USSR, Romania attempted to normalize relations with Western states. The first successes were recorded in relations with France and the UK, with the upgrading of Romania's representations to the level of embassies in 1963. In October 1963, Romania's representative at the UN (Romania had been accepted in 1955), Corneliu Mănescu, expressed his disagreement with the deployment of Soviet missiles in Cuba, announcing Bucharest's 'neutrality' in the event of a new Soviet–American crisis (Anton 2007: 152). In 1964, Prime Minister Ion Gheorghe Maurer became the first head of government from the communist bloc to visit France, giving a strong political signal of Romania's autonomy within the bloc (Cătănuș 2011: 365).

Until the end of his life in March 1965, Gheorghiu-Dej continued his actions for the empowerment of Romania within the socialist bloc, both by openings towards the West, mainly through economic cooperation (for example, the visit of the US Trade Secretary, Orville Freeman, to Bucharest in August 1963), and by maintaining an attitude close to political confrontation with the Soviet Union. In 1965 Gheorghiu-Dej had reached the position of a national-communist whose 'heresy' consisted in the fact that he wanted to rewrite the satellization relationship with a superpower using the terms of Marxism-Leninism: setting the relation between Romania and the Soviet Union upon an equal, principled footing.

CHAPTER 4
THE NICOLAE CEAUŞESCU REGIME (1965–89)

Having come to power in the context of the communist elites' attempts at a reconciliation with Romanian society after almost two decades of terror, Ceauşescu confiscated political power entirely, and went on to personalize it through an ostentatious personality cult. The capital of hope created by Ceauşescu during the first years of his regime gradually vanished with a resumption of repression and unrealistic economic policies. Much like Gheorghiu-Dej, Ceauşescu also shared a Stalinist vision of society, whose foundations he could not escape in spite of world changes. Intoxicated with the exercise of power, Ceauşescu considered himself a messianic leader: the cost was the collective drama of Romanian society.

The Ceauşescu regime did not develop in a simple linear manner. At first, it continued the liberalization trend from the end of the Gheorghiu-Dej era. However, in the mid-1970s, once he achieved absolute power within the PCR, the regime degenerated into a form of clan domination manifested through repression, dogmatism and megalomaniac economic projects, in the context of a blatant personality cult. The Ceauşescu regime could not be removed except by violent action, as the PCR leader blocked the formation of alternative or dissident groups within the party, which could have facilitated a negotiated transition, as happened in other Eastern European countries.

Ceauşescu gains total power

Gheorghiu-Dej's lung cancer was hidden from the public, in the proverbial secrecy characteristic of dictatorial regimes. Although he was seriously ill, and there were rumours that he had been poisoned by the Soviets, the communist leader tried to save face by being present at public events. However, he died on 19 March 1965. During four days of national mourning, and amidst public expressions of regret, many of them hypocritical on the part of political leaders, a fierce succession struggle ensued. Gheorghiu-Dej had not appointed an official successor and, just as after Stalin's death, a struggle for power was waged. The precise backstage details are not known, as the testimonials of the main actors involved are contradictory, but the result was temporary power sharing under the formula of collective leadership. After two decades of power struggles, marked by bloody revenge, the communist leaders were dominated by mistrust and uncertainty. Most of them wanted peace and stability in office. One aspirant for the PMR leadership was Gheorghe Apostol (born 1913), a party member since the illegality period, who was First Vice-President of the Council of Ministers in 1965.

A second contender was Nicolae Ceaușescu, who was younger (born 1918) and had also been a party member in the illegality period. He had the advantage of knowing the party bureaucracy, as in 1954 he had been the PMR official responsible for organizational issues. The one who was not wanted by all the other leaders was Alexandru Drăghici (born 1913), Minister of the Interior. Like Lavrenti Beria, Drăghici was regarded as a 'master of secrets', dangerous for all, which is why he had to be eliminated from the leadership race. Ion Gheorghe Maurer and Chivu Stoica, supported by the influential Emil Bodnăraș had decided to support the youngest of the three, Nicolae Ceaușescu, for the PMR leadership, hoping that they would be able to control him. On 22 March 1965, Ceaușescu was elected First Secretary of the PMR. Maurer kept the presidency of the Council of Ministers and Chivu Stoica was elected on 24 March 1965 by the MAN as President of the State Council. The collective leadership formula was thus maintained, but not for long (du Bois 2008: 78–112).

Endowed like his predecessor with native intelligence and with guile improved during political struggles, but lacking an intellectual perspective, Ceaușescu was not happy with the status of *primus inter pares*. As a result, he embarked on a complex strategy of separation with the Gheorghiu-Dej regime and of consolidating power, which not only meant the simple elimination of opponents, but also included elements of political symbolism and a change of regime policies.

The Fourth PMR Congress of 19–24 July 1965 changed its name to the Ninth PCR Congress (counting began from the founding congress of 1921), simultaneously with the party's renaming from 'Workers'' to 'Communist' (PCR 1965). The congress was an opportunity for Ceaușescu to consolidate power. The office of 'First Secretary of the Central Committee' was renamed 'Secretary General', to mark the difference between Ceaușescu and the other leaders. During the last day of the Congress, Ceaușescu surprised everyone by dismantling the traditional Political Bureau and replacing it with an Executive Committee, from among which a smaller Permanent Presidium was established. All the 'barons' of the Gheorghiu-Dej era were still present in the Permanent Presidium, but Ceaușescu was preparing the ground for appointing his faithful people to the helm of the PCR, including Virgil Trofin, Paul Niculescu-Mizil and Ilie Verdeț. Following a clever strategy, Ceaușescu managed to remove his main rival, Alexandru Drăghici, from the office of Minister of the Interior and implicitly head of the *Securitate*, invoking the separation between party and state offices. Drăghici was content with his advancement as Secretary of the Central Committee. The PCR Secretary General imposed his faithful people within all important institutions, to ensure their control (Burakowski 2011: 83–5). Ceaușescu was legitimized internationally through the presence in Bucharest of Leonid Brezhnev, First Secretary of the CPSU Central Committee, and of Deng Xiaoping, Secretary General of the Communist Party of China.

Immediately after his consecration as PCR leader, Ceaușescu launched a campaign to win popularity among the common people. In August a new constitution was adopted. The name of the republic was changed from 'popular' to 'socialist' and the spelling of the country's name was Latinized from 'Romînia' back to 'România'. The constitution cemented the PCR's role of 'leading force of the entire society'. Thus the domination of the single party over both the state and society was consolidated, but more attention was paid to rights and freedoms, in order to limit the abuses of repressive institutions. Ideological pressure over intellectuals was relaxed and the economic and cultural opening towards the West continued; the standard of living rose. Simultaneously, the first signs of the intention of imposing a new social engineering project emerged; the most important being the banning of abortion on 1 October 1966 by Decree no. 770. Obviously, Ceauşescu did not intend to abandon the dictatorial state model: this was only a temporary liberalization meant to confer legitimacy on him.

As in the Soviet Union during the post-Stalinist period, the recent past of 'comrades' could be used in the political battle. In October 1965, Ceauşescu ordered his own 'secret report', in the form of an investigation to rehabilitate Lucreţiu Pătrăşcanu. By the time of the public presentation of a small part of the crimes committed under the Gheorghiu-Dej regime, during the PCR Plenary of April 1968, a number of Ceauşescu's opponents had been removed. In January 1967, Apostol was replaced by Ilie Verdeţ in the office of deputy Prime Minister, and in 1969 he also lost his office in the PCR leadership. In December 1967, Chivu Stoica was removed from the presidency of the State Council, so that Ceauşescu now held both the party and the state leadership (Cioroianu 2005: 396). To rehabilitate Pătrăşcanu and Ştefan Foriş, in April 1968, Ceauşescu denounced Gheorghiu-Dej's role in the crimes of the *Securitate*, in a veritable political parricide. Drăghici was rightly considered responsible for the abuses, and was excluded from the PCR. In the context of Ceauşescu's increasing popularity, as a result of condemning the military repression of the Prague Spring of August 1968, several leaders from Gheorghiu-Dej's period (Alexandru Bârlădeanu, Alexandru Moghioroş, Leonte Răutu, and others) were marginalized and replaced with the new leader's faithful people. In August 1969, during the Tenth Congress of the party (PCR 1969), a massive change within the ranks of the Central Committee was achieved by the rise of Ceauşescu's protégés. In order to gain even greater legitimacy, Ceauşescu declared that the PCR Secretary General should now be elected directly by Congress, not by the Central Committee.

After 1970, although he already held as much power as Gheorghiu-Dej had done at the end of his regime, Ceauşescu concentrated ever more influence, which he also distributed to members of his family, especially his wife, Elena. She became a member of the PCR's Central Committee in 1972, and the following year, she entered the Executive Committee, in order to be accepted within the Academy of the Socialist Republic of Romania in 1974, although she had only elementary scientific knowledge. Nicolae Ceauşescu also imposed the modification of the Constitution and the creation of the office of President of the Republic, which he held starting from 28 March 1974. Simultaneously, Ceauşescu accumulated the office of party Secretary General, leader of the National Defence Council, president of the National Council of the Socialist Unity Front and Supreme Commander of the Armed Forces. Political decisions were recentralized and personalized, collective leadership becoming a propaganda fiction (Kunze 2002: 288).

Ceauşescu's transformation in just a decade from a secondary nomenklatura member into an absolute political leader, without resorting to the physical elimination of his competitors, is proof of his Machiavellian political cunning (Andrei et al. 2011). Ceauşescu exploited in his favour the complicities and rivalries between the 'barons' of the Gheorghiu-Dej period, as well as fear of repression. The cowardice of the nomenklatura prevented any opposition to aberrant manifestations of the personality cult. From 1973, Ceauşescu applied 'staff rotation' on a large scale, on the pretext of 'rationalization of the administrative technical apparatus', with the result that the nomenklatura were prevented from building fiefdoms. Within the PCR, which remained the same dictatorial party from the beginning, acceptance of all decisions taken by the 'Comrade', regardless of their content, was encouraged. Submission to Ceauşescu's decisions became an essential condition of political promotion wthin the PCR.

New morphologies of the political regime

After two decades of ruling Romania, the communist leaders headed by Ceauşescu considered that they had acquired enough legitimacy to be accepted by society. Romania's social and economic transformation was visible, and the results of massive industrialization and urbanization efforts strengthened their belief they had achieved a modernizing revolution. To emphasize his role in leading Romania, Ceauşescu adopted the concept of the 'multilaterally developed socialist society'. Derived from scientific socialism, the notion synthesized the idea of moving beyond the stage of power conquest and consolidation, and eliminating the institutions of bourgeois society. A new 'leap forward' was to follow, a new 'revolutionary conquest': the building of the perfect communist society. From the perspective of Marxist-Leninist theory, the 'multilaterally developed socialist society' was superior to capitalism, as it combined equalitarianism and a universal welfare state with civilizational progress, without social polarization and exclusion or criminality and unemployment. In communism, all people had to work, and the result of their work turned, according to propaganda, into fair incomes, cheap housing, and free education and health. For Romania, this meant a transition from a predominantly agrarian economy to a mixed agrarian-industrial one; the objective was to create an industrial economy with a much-diminished agrarian sector. The new society which the communist leaders promised to establish was to be populated by the New Man, in his turn 'multilaterally developed and trained', as Lenin defined him.

The theory of scientific socialism claimed that the transition to a communist society would bring about the disappearance of 'exploitation of man by man' and the dictatorship of the proletariat would then have finished its revolutionary goal. The PCR's role, as a vanguard party, was to end with the 'complete homogenization of communist society and the ever more organic participation of party members in social life in close relation with the popular masses'.

Launched in 1967, the concept of the 'multilaterally developed socialist society' became, during the Tenth PCR Congress in 1969, the fundamental political and ideological objective of the Ceauşescu regime, and remained so until its end. All political, social and economic changes were subsumed to this objective, which was meant to prepare the way for the transition to communism.

The first transformation was undergone by the PCR itself, as it had the 'leading role' in society. From a party of the 'working class vanguard', made up of a small revolutionary elite, the PCR turned into a mass party, which enrolled an ever-increasing share of the population. If in 1965 the PCR had 1.45 million members and candidates, their number had increased to 2.48 million by 1974 and by 1989 to 3.83 million members (Buga 2012: 422–3). Simultaneously with the numerical and organizational expansion of the PCR, the development of other mass structures and organizations took place. The most important was *Uniunea Tineretului Comunist* (UTC – the Union of Communist Youth), the PCR's youth structure, which had existed since 1922. In 1947, it changed its name to *Uniunea Tineretului Muncitoresc* (UTM – the Union of Working Youth), returning to its former name in 1965. The minimum age for enrolling in the UTC was fourteen and the maximum age fluctuated between twenty-five and thirty. If, in the beginning, affiliation to UTC was selective (in 1950 the structure had 650,000 members), it turned into a youth mobilization tool, in order to get young people motivated. In 1960, the UTM had 1.9 million members; this had which increased to 3 million UTC members in 1975 and 4.1 million in 1988 (Tismăneanu et al. 2007: 195).

The inclusion of the whole of society in mass organization also extended to lower ages. In 1949, following the Soviet model, the *Organizaţia de Pionieri* (Pioneer Organization) was founded for children between nine and fourteen (the limit was later lowered to seven). The role of the Pioneer Organization was to educate children 'in the communist spirit'. Ceauşescu went even further, and in 1976, established the *Şoimii Patriei* (Falcons of the Fatherland) organization for children between four and seven. Like the *pionierii*, *şoimii patriei* wore uniforms and were subjected to an early political socialization programme. Romania was the only country in the Soviet camp where a mass organization for such small children existed.

In Ceauşescu's conception, the creation of the communist society, 'the most evolved form of social organization' could be achieved only by the ideologization of the entire social body. Ceauşescu's visit to China and North Korea in 1971 was a political inflection point, as it confirmed in the PCR leader his longstanding belief that a society could only be ruled by an authoritarian regime and using ideological tools. The short period of liberalization was almost over. On 9 July 1971, during a meeting with party activists, Ceauşescu conveyed the so-called 'July Theses' (Ceauşescu 1971). The aim was now to achieve a 'smaller cultural revolution' by which the control of 'party mandarins' over cultural and artistic life would be resumed. Intellectuals and artists were 'called to order' and increasingly rigid limits of freedom of expression and creation were established.

Ceauşescu wanted to impose upon party members a combination between Leninist principles and his rural-conservative vision of social morality, which was to be 'healthy' and not 'decadent' as in the West. In 1974, during the Eleventh Congress of the PCR, the 'Code of communists' work and life, of socialist ethics and equity' was adopted, by which, in thirty-three points, the profile of the 'reliable communist', the prototype of the New Man, was defined. Party members had to: 'serve faithfully the cause of the party and the people'; 'acquire understanding of dialectical and historical materialism'; 'defend more than anything the party's monolithic unity'; 'defend party and state secrets, demonstrate high vigilance and revolutionary combativeness'; and 'manifest the highest intransigence against bourgeois life concepts and the influence of the mentalities of the capitalist world' (PCR 1975a).

The Eleventh Congress of the PCR consecrated the second major political and ideological tendency, national-communism. The traditional internationalist line of communism was not abandoned, but was pragmatically used in international policies, especially in relations with countries of the Third World. In domestic policy, Marxism-Leninism was combined with a nationalist reinterpretation of the whole history of Romania, starting with Antiquity. The political roots of (anti-Soviet) independence and the wish to build a centralized state were identified by official historiography as constants of national history, from the ancient Dacian kings Burebista and Decebal. The creation of a national mythology with the PCR and Ceauşescu at its centre became state policy, with broad reverberations in education, culture and the arts.

Simultaneously with the new directions of ideological justification for power centralization, changes took place in the relations between institutions. Ceauşescu not only personified the idea of Leader, but personalized it to the point of confusion with himself. The source of power was no longer ideology (translated into PCR programmes) or state laws, but the discretionary will of the communist leader, which overcame all political, legal or moral impediments. Just as in Nazism, after the mid-1970s, a veritable *Führerprinzip* (leader principle) was established in Romania. The principle of collective leadership and accountability of the Secretary General to the party were, more than ever, political fictions.

The most important victim of the dictatorial confiscation of power was the governmental institution. Veteran Prime Minister Maurer retired 'on demand' in February 1974, and was replaced with an economist without intellectual scope, Manea Mănescu. The latter had been a PCR member since illegality, and had been promoted by Ceauşescu during the Ninth Congress. Ceauşescu increasingly used the tool of 'presidential decrees', and the role of the government was reduced to that of simple executant of the PCR leader's decisions. Ministers were anonymous figures without political importance. Mănescu's replacement by Ilie Verdeţ in 1979 brought the principle of staff rotation to the highest level. Verdeţ had governmental experience going back to the Maurer government period, but was accepted by Ceauşescu because he seemed to be a faithful executant of orders. As head of the Council of Ministers, Verdeţ had to face an increasingly acute economic crisis, but failed to find solutions for recovery. As a consequence, Ceauşescu, also encouraged by his wife, decided to replace Verdeţ in 1982. He was not completely eliminated from the circle of power, but was rewarded for having accepted marginalization with the presidency of the Central Revision Committee of the PCR. The last of communist Romania's prime ministers was Constantin Dăscălescu. He was also part of Ceauşescu's team. Like his predecessors, Dăscălescu was one of the totally obedient figures towards the Ceauşescu family. He agreed to put into practice decisions in the economic and social field, the most contestable being the early repayment of Romania's foreign debt.

The degradation of the communist regime is emphasized by the imposition of members of the extended Ceaușescu family in various political and state structures. Elena Ceaușescu was promoted in January 1977 to the most important decision-making structure, the Permanent Bureau of the PCR's Political Committee. Between 1980 and 1989 she was First Deputy Prime Minister and in 1985 she took on the leadership of scientific and educational activity in Romania, with disastrous consequences. The youngest son of the Ceaușescu family, Nicu, was propelled in 1982 within the PCR's Central Committee. The following year he became Minister of Youth, and in 1987, he was granted political and administrative leadership of Sibiu County. In 1983, one of the Secretary General's brothers, General Ilie Ceaușescu, became deputy Minister of Defence and another brother, Ion Ceaușescu, was appointed vice-president of the State Planning Committee. In 1986, Vasile Bărbulescu, brother-in-law Ceaușescu, became Secretary of the PCR's Central Committee. Other blood relations and in-laws were appointed to various less important functions. Communist Romania became a unique case among European countries of such a broad extension of a clan within political and administrative institutions, a situation paralleled in North Korea. The promotion of relatives to most important offices could be explained by the Ceaușescu couple's fear of betrayal.

Against the background of clan dictatorship, the theoretical holder of power, the single party, became a decorative institution, ultra-bureaucratized and de-ideologized. The Twelfth, Thirteenth and Fourteenth Congresses of the PCR (1979, 1984 and 1989) were simply ritual moments for instating the personality cult. Communist ideology no longer offered political convictions and motivations, even to political activists. The Central Committee became an increasingly massive structure (245 members in 1979, 281 members in 1989). Apparently more representative, in reality it was an inert political body, dominated by fear of the 'Comrade'. The attack of communist veteran Constantin Pârvulescu against Ceaușescu during the Twelfth Congress, critical of the personality cult, was the last gasp of a minimal opposition to the degradation of the PCR. Pârvulescu was denounced as a 'traitor' and placed under house arrest. A veritable 'dark decade' for society followed and the PCR was purged of all potential dissidence.

In the landscape of political and institutional bankruptcy, the only structure that prospered was the *Securitate*. It received orders not only to learn the population's state of mind and to pre-empt possible revolts, but also to watch important members of the nomenklatura. Elena Ceaușescu placed her children under *Securitate* surveillance, not only for their protection, but also to learn about their activities and friends.

Personality cult

All modern dictatorships saw various forms of personality cult. This essentially consists of the use of some vectors of intellectual and artistic life to promote, by means of official propaganda, an exclusively positive and heroically mythologized image of political leaders, for the purpose of dominating society (Cioroianu 2004: 43–4).

The initial matrix of the personality cult was delivered from Moscow, together with the organizational model of the propaganda apparatus. Romania already had the experience of personality cult in the cases of Carol II and General Ion Antonescu. During the initial stage of the communist regime, Stalin and Lenin were the main subjects of the personality cult, in which local communists ostentatiously participated. The operation of creating a mythologized public image for Gheorghiu-Dej was sinuous, especially after 1952, following the elimination of the Pauker–Luca–Georgescu group and during the second part of the 1950s. Khrushchev's criticism of Stalin's personality cult in the 1956 'Secret Report' made Gheorghiu-Dej cautious about stating too ostentatiously his role in Romanian communism. Criticized during the Plenary of 23–25 March 1956 by Iosif Chişinevschi and Miron Constantinescu for creating a personality cult, Gheorghiu-Dej eliminated his contestants, but did not encourage a blatant personality cult. The propaganda apparatus created an important political moment, however, when Gheorghiu-Dej turned sixty in 1961, the emphasis being placed on his role during the Griviţa Railway Workshop strike of February 1933, which had been repressed by the authorities of the time, and in the establishment of the 'democratic-popular' regime (Pleşa 2016).

After the marginalization of leaders from the Gheorghiu-Dej era, Ceauşescu had no reservations about accepting the personality cult promoted by the party apparatus, which assumed colossal dimensions and ridiculously ostentatious displays after 1980. The personality cult was promoted even in contradiction with Marxist-Leninist doctrine, which stated that the dominant role in history belonged to the masses.

The personality cult was like an infectious disease, which gradually extended throughout Romanian society and ended only with the 1989 Revolution. The propaganda operation of projecting a mythologized image of Ceauşescu in national and international public opinion began with the public display of Romania's disagreement with the repression of the Prague Spring. In August 1968, Ceauşescu condemned the intervention of Warsaw Pact troops in front of a nation which sincerely believed and admired its political leader for his courage. The manifestation of honest popular sympathy, which determined a wave of new enrolments into the PCR, including intellectuals, acted like a drug on Ceauşescu. In December 1989, when he was challenged by the population in the streets, Ceauşescu still honestly believed that he was loved by the 'working class' and that any excess on his part was still allowed.

The personality cult functioned following the snowball principle. Initially it was small, but it gradually became gigantic, suffocating the whole public space. The main functioning scheme of the personality cult was based on the Stalinist model, to which elements from the national tradition (Carol II and the Legionary Movement) were added, as well as Asian features, borrowed from Maoist China and North Korea. This apparently contradictory combination formed an eclectic mixture which was systematically promoted in the public space, after thorough planning. The key phrase was 'Golden Age', assigned to the period after 1965, with the aim of emphasizing the exceptionally positive character of Ceauşescu's leadership. He was called *Conducător* (Leader), just like General Ion Antonescu.

The imagery created around Ceauşescu attributed to him some features of his exceptionalism and uniqueness: 'perfect statesman', 'father of the nation', 'thinker of genius', 'universal ideologist' and 'hero of world peace'. The personality cult was not only limited to Romania, but was also promoted abroad. The *Securitate* spent significant resources on publishing books ostensibly written by Nicolae Ceauşescu, and his wife Elena acquired an increasing number of academic titles, in order to confirm her title of 'world famous scientist'. Chemistry books written by others in the name of Elena Ceauşescu were also published by prestigious publishing houses abroad (Cioroianu 2004; Gabanyi 2003).

The forms of manifestation of the personality cult were diverse, in spite of the thematic monotony. The birthdays of the Ceauşescu couple were turned into national events. Elena Ceauşescu was presented as 'ideal woman and mother', becoming '*Tovarăşa*' (the female comrade). The mobilization of society to become a human background for the personality cult was achieved by the cultural festival *Cântarea României, Cenaclul Flacăra* and the sports event *Daciada*. Romania's national day, 23 August (the moment when Romania stopped fighting against the United Nations in 1944), turned from the 'day of liberation by the Red Army' (as it had been during the Gheorghiu-Dej regime) into the moment of 'liberation from the fascist yoke' and then into the 'anti-fascist and anti-imperialist national liberation revolution, led by the working class guided by the Communist Party'. In order to create the idea of Ceauşescu's popularity among citizens, starting in 1973 massive volumes of letters, wishes and even poems, called 'Tributes', were published. Quotations from Ceauşescu became compulsory in most scientific fields, especially in the socio-political area. Works of historiography could not be published without extended quotations from 'Comrade Nicolae Ceauşescu's thoughts of genius'.

Ceauşescu's transition from the category of mere mortal to that of demigod was achieved through his so-called 'working visits' in the country. From 1965 until 1989 Ceauşescu undertook over 900 visits all over the country (Andrei et al. 2011: 147), which were organized with pomp and ceremony, although popular enthusiasm was increasingly hard to stimulate. Ceauşescu's presence in a locality or enterprise was presented as a veritable epiphany of the 'most beloved son of the People'.

Ceauşescu family's visits abroad were presented in the propaganda as 'historical accomplishments'. Similarly, visits of foreign officials to Romania were considered as proofs of esteem, not for the Romanian state, but for Ceauşescu himself.

The personality cult proved to be profitable for artists and intellectuals favoured by the regime, but for society as a whole it did not have the envisaged results. On the contrary, it provoked an increasing aversion. Romanian society's reaction against generalized lies, especially during the 1980s, was to boycott or participate purely formally in official actions. Political jokes proliferated and were often told in public with much courage, being an indication of accumulated hatred towards the Ceauşescu clan. The Romanian media, dominated by the personality cult, was a credible information source only for sports and the weather. For the rest, in the context of information control, citizens got their information from Radio Free Europe (RFE), Voice of America or other foreign radio stations (Marin 2014). The personality cult initially contributed to consolidating Ceaușescu's power, but the intoxication of public space with the image and messages of the leading family gave rise to a general wave of hatred. The execution of the Ceaușescu couple was regarded by Romanians at the moment of the 1989 Revolution as a fair revenge for the long line of humiliations which they had endured. Instead of bringing together the nation in a massive collective effort to accomplish gigantic projects, the personality cult merely widened the fault line between Ceaușescu and the population.

The main projects of the Ceauşescu regime

If, from the point of view of political symbolism, elements of relatively quick change emerged after Ceaușescu's power takeover, as far as the main projects are concerned, the lines of continuity with the Gheorghiu-Dej era are numerous. Ceaușescu and his predecessor at the party's helm both shared the Leninist belief according to which communism is 'the power of the Soviets plus electrification'. In a broader sense, this meant the single party's hold on political control combined with intensive industrial development.

The socio-economic and political projects undertaken by the Ceaușescu regime are the consequence of a combination of ideological, (geo)political, economic and psycho-political factors. Ceaușescu's wish, but also that of Gheorghiu-Dej, for massive investment in industry must be explained not only by the influence of Marxism-Leninism and the desire of ending development gaps compared to the capitalist West, but also by the leaders' biographies. Gheorghiu-Dej and Ceaușescu had both had a childhood and youth marked by shortage and poverty, in a predominantly rural and unevenly developed Romania. When they became state leaders, their conviction was that the country could set aside poverty, and they would personally have the historical merit of achieving this, only if the country was industrialized and if collectivized agriculture produced according to industrial norms.

Ceaușescu wanted to become the leader of a strong nation, and strength meant first of all being numerous. The pro-birth policy inaugurated in 1966 with the banning of abortion continued until the end of the regime. In 1974 Ceaușescu fixed Romania's demographic targets: 25 million people by 1990 and 30 million by 2000 (PCR 1975b: 92). These were not reached, but they illustrate Ceaușescu's social engineering objectives.

The Romanian communist leader was the partisan of an integral homogenization of Romanian society. The economic component was imposed right from the period of establishment of the communist regime through property nationalizations and confiscations. In order to prevent private capital accumulation, including the formation of a 'red bourgeoisie', a law of illicit wealth was adopted (Law no. 18 of 1968), which allowed for the confiscation of unjustified revenues. The second component, concerning gender, was a major ideological objective. Women continued to suffer discrimination as regards access to office and their role in society. The increase in the number of women in the PCR Central Committee and MAN starting with 1970 was a measure to legitimize the political rise of Elena Ceauşescu. Women were discriminated against in communism as their quasi-exclusive association with fertility and home activity was combined with the expectation that they would participate fully in economic activities. The PCR did not officially recognize gender inequality.

Another dimension of the homogenization of society concerned inter-ethnic relations. During the Ninth Congress of the PCR, the thesis of 'homogenizing the socialist nation' was stated, in which 'co-inhabiting nationalities', as ethnic minorities were called, were 'twinned' with the Romanian people. Unlike in the previous period, collective rights of minorities were no longer recognized. Ceauşescu abolished the Hungarian Autonomous Region in 1968, but was flexible in drawing the borders of counties inhabited by a majority of ethnic Hungarians (he accepted the formation of the 'Szeckler counties' of Covasna and Harghita). Then, in correlation with the policy of internal population mobility in the context of accelerated urbanization, he promoted the settlement of ethnic Romanians in areas inhabited by Hungarian majorities. The selling of Germans and Jews (see Chapter 6) implicitly contributed to a more homogeneous socialist nation.

Territorial homogenization was another favourite preoccupation, with the focus being on two axes: urban–rural and developed–poor. Plans to systemize territory were essentially aimed at gradually cancelling the differences between villages and cities. In order to eliminate poverty from underdeveloped areas budgetary allocations and industrial investment were directed accordingly. Thus, numerous industrial plants were built in traditionally rural areas.

Ceauşescu's third major project was political and military detachment from the USSR. The PCR leader wanted to achieve autonomy within the Soviet camp, but not to leave it altogether. Ceauşescu was conscious of Romania's economic dependence on the Soviets, for which reason he wanted to diversify sources of raw material for resources currently imported from the USSR, and he tried to get technology from the West as a result of his political distancing from the Kremlin. Romania's de-sovietization and return to a part of its national traditions was one of Ceauşescu's main goals. The 1968 administrative-territorial reorganization, which saw a return to counties, also had an anti-Soviet component, as the division into districts was abolished. After manifesting opposition to the invasion of Czechoslovakia in 1968, Ceauşescu lived in fear of subversion from pro-Soviet agents; he began to marginalize them and to keep close watch on them through the *Securitate*. The PCR leader disliked the 'Brezhnev Doctrine', for which reason he obstinately supported the principle of 'non-interference in internal affairs'. De-Russification of culture, initiated during the regime of Gheorghiu-Dej, was energetically continued and national historical traditions were promoted. The consequent rapprochement with the West – in fact a continuation of the foreign policy of the last years of Gheorghiu-Dej– was motivated not by Ceauşescu's sympathy for capitalism, but by the need to obtain technology and commercial benefits for the purpose of internal economic development.

The fourth project was to build a predominantly industrial economy. The Stalinist idea of massive investment in industry, especially heavy industry, prevailed. Additionally, large investments were made in light industry and petrochemicals. Another field which was allocated important resources was maritime transport and, consequently, shipbuilding.

Finally, another strategic direction of the Ceaușescu regime can be identified: the launch of gigantic construction projects. In 1970, a new international airport was built near Bucharest, the first subway lines were laid in 1979; in 1984, the Danube–Black Sea Canal was inaugurated (total length 95.6 kilometres). In 1983 the construction of the iconic building of the Ceaușescu regime began: the gigantic House of the People, comprising 330,000 square metres, which was finalized only after the Revolution. Major projects were launched despite growing discontent on the part of the population towards the regime. If until 1977 Ceaușescu encountered only timid domestic disapproval, thereafter this gradually increased.

Foreign policy: from autonomy to ostracism

The foreign policy orientation legacy of Gheorghiu-Dej fully matched the deeply held belief of Ceaușescu: Romania had to industrialize massively in order to be independent. Only by industrialization could a communist society be built.

As early as the 'confirmation' visit made to Moscow by Ceaușescu in September 1965 as head of the PCR, the Romanian delegation conveyed to the Soviets that it would not abandon the industrialization project in favour of a specialized integration within the COMECON. In order to strengthen its negotiating position, the Romanian delegation demanded the restitution of the treasury, much to the irritation of Brezhnev (Anton and Chiper 2002: 20). Like his predecessor, Ceaușescu did not want to leave the communist bloc, still less to adopt a pluralist regime. The communist leader tried to create an extended framework for political autonomy within the communist bloc, objectively legitimized by the principle of 'non-involvement in the home affairs of other countries'.

Ceaușescu encouraged an active foreign policy which was not only confined to relations within the Soviet bloc, but also concerned relations with Western capitalist countries. A major direction was the establishment of political and economic relations with countries in the Middle East, Asia and Africa.

Aware that Romania's industrialization would not be supported by the Soviets, Ceaușescu turned to the West, helped by Prime Minister Maurer and Foreign Affairs Minister Corneliu Mănescu (1961–72). Contact with Western countries became increasingly intense, as Romania wanted to demonstrate that it had an independent policy. In 1967, in contrast with the bloc policy, Romania signed a trade treaty with Franco's Spain. The most surprising move was the recognition of West Germany by Romania and the establishment of diplomatic relations at the level of embassies (the other satellite states of the USSR only recognized East Germany). In exchange for this political decision, Romania received from West Germany banking credits and access to technology. In any case, secret relations between Romania and West Germany had been important since 1962, when the emigration of ethnic Germans was negotiated in exchange for financial compensation.

On the occasion of the Six-Day War between Israel and a coalition made up of Egypt, Jordan and Syria in June 1967, Romania refused to break diplomatic relations with the Jewish state, as Brezhnev imperatively requested. However, Ceauşescu was careful not to antagonize the Arab world through an openly pro-Israeli position. Romania's neutral attitude was convergent with the interests of the US, which wanted to undermine the USSR by a policy of differentiation among the communist states. Romania also became a model for the rest of the satellite states, and a useful instrument for East–West competition. For political reasons, in September 1967, the US supported Corneliu Mănescu's election as the first president of the UN General Assembly to come from a communist country. This was considered a symbolic prize offered by the US to Romania.

In May 1968, the first visit of a Western political leader to Bucharest since the establishment of communism took place: French President Charles de Gaulle accepted the invitation. The French leader was enthusiastically received; Ceauşescu wished to send the message that Romania belonged to Western civilization (Mâţă 2011).

Ceauşescu became famous at the international level at the moment when the USSR (together with Bulgaria, East Germany, Poland and Hungary) repressed the 'Prague Spring'. Ceauşescu shared the reformist ideas of Aleksander Dubček, who was contributing, in the opinion of the Romanian leader, to the strengthening of communism. In February and August 1968, Ceauşescu visited Czechoslovakia, expressing his solidarity with Dubček's ideas. During the night of 20–21 August 1968, the USSR and its allies invaded Czechoslovakia. Faced with this situation, a huge rally of support for Czechoslovakia was organized in Bucharest, on which occasion Ceauşescu declared that it was unacceptable to a socialist state 'that socialist states should breach the freedom and independence of another state' (Retegan 1998). Romania's distinctive attitude brought him important political dividends and Ceauşescu was regarded as a courageous leader who had to be supported.

On 2 August 1969, US President Richard Nixon arrived in Bucharest and was received on the streets by about a million people. The enthusiasm and trust of Romanians in the communist regime was at its zenith. The main secret purpose of Nixon's visit was to use the Romanian path to facilitate an understanding with China (Komine 2008: 99). As a result of this rapprochement with the US, and much to Soviet discontent, Romania changed its foreign trade legislation, starting to import US technology, including that in the military field (Andrei et al. 2011: 208). Romania helped towards the signing of the peace treaty between North Vietnam and the US and, as a reward, Ceauşescu was received by Nixon at the White House in 1973. Two years later, it received the 'most favoured nation clause' (annually renewed until 1988). In 1975, US President Gerald Ford visited Romania, following the signing of the Helsinki Accords. American diplomacy obviously knew that, in spite of its political opening to the West, Romania was still led by a dictatorial regime. Legitimizing Ceauşescu was one of the practices included in the American strategy of producing cracks within the Soviet bloc, in the hope of weakening it.

In its relations with the West, Romania tried to capitalize on the political gestures of 1967–8, in order to attract investment and technology transfer; Ceauşescu had the illusion of being an internationally recognized leader. In 1970, Ceauşescu led an impressive delegation to Paris, where he was received by President Georges Pompidou. In 1973, Ceauşescu visited Italy, also being received by Pope Paul VI, but the communist leader refused any compromise in the matter of Romanian Greek Catholics. In 1978 Ceauşescu was again received at the White House, this time by President Jimmy Carter. The height of Ceauşescu's international prestige was his visit to London in June 1978, on which occasion the Romanian leader accompanied Queen Elizabeth II in the royal carriage. The reason for inviting Ceauşescu to London was the signing of two contracts with the Romanian state (British Aerospace and Rolls Royce were to produce the BAC-1-11 aircraft in Romania). In 1979, French President Valéry Giscard d'Estaing visited Bucharest and an agreement for building a new car factory in Romania was signed together with Citroën. The next year, Ceauşescu was received by Giscard d'Estaing in Paris and new contracts were signed for technology imports. In 1980, Romania became the first country from the communist bloc to conclude a trade agreement with the European Economic Communities; a joint committee for the industrial field was established. Despite its bad reputation in respect of human rights, Romania's communist leadership was received by the most important leaders of the democratic world. The wish of governments in the capitalist world to conclude profitable contracts and to support dissidence in the Soviet camp explains the success of Romanian diplomacy in the West.

Simultaneously with the action of seducing the West, Romanian diplomacy also used important resources to get to countries outside Europe. Romania's rational interest was to have markets and raw materials sources for its expanding industry. The prevailing political interest was creating an image of Ceauşescu as a world leader, diplomacy being turned into a tool of the personality cult.

Ceauşescu was accepted in the so-called 'Third World' because he fervently promoted the thesis of ending underdevelopment and establishing a new world order, stopping the arms race, nuclear disarmament and the peaceful resolution of conflicts. Romania criticized neo-colonialism and 'capitalist imperialism', supporting the need for peer relations between the great powers and the new states emerging after decolonization (Ceauşescu 1978). In 1971, Ceauşescu visited China, North Korea, Mongolia and North Vietnam. In 1972, the Ceauşescus visited eight African counties, and the next year Ceauşescu was received in six countries in Latin America. In 1974, Ceauşescu was received in four countries in the Middle East (Calafeteanu 2003: 415–51). Thereafter, almost every year the Ceauşescus either visited countries in this region or received leaders from these countries. At the end of the 1980s, when he became an international pariah, Ceauşescu undertook diplomatic journeys only to South Asia, Africa and the Middle East. In all, Ceauşescu undertook over 200 official visits when he was the leader of Romania.

Good relations between Romania and Western states and Romanian diplomatic hyper-activism in the Third World had an impact on Romania's position in the communist bloc. The invasion of Czechoslovakia and the affirmation of the 'Brezhnev Doctrine' concerning limited sovereignty gave rise to increasing tension in Romanian–Soviet relations. The signing of a new friendship and collaboration treaty between Romania and the USSR (July 1970) formed the basis for normalizing relations with the Kremlin (Buga 2013: 165). In Romania's empowerment strategy, Ceauşescu manifested prudence, did not start public conflicts and, what was more important, did not question the country's membership of the Warsaw Pact and the COMECON. Ceauşescu relied on relations with the US and China in order to avoid any frontal attacks from Brezhnev. Within the Warsaw Pact there were frequent disputes between Romanians and Soviets. Bucharest opposed the deployment of Soviet and US missiles in Europe starting from 1976 (Olteanu and Duţu 2014: 29). In 1984, from the position of 'rebel ally', Ceauşescu proposed the simultaneous dismantling of NATO and the Warsaw Pact, an idea proposed from time to time, until 1989. Regarding the 1979 invasion of Afghanistan by the USSR, Ceauşescu no longer adopted a position similar to that in August 1968, but conveyed to the Soviets his disagreement with 'hegemonic policies' (Watts 2013: 257). In 1985, Romania signed the renewal of the validity of the Warsaw Pact for another ten years, although it had tried to reduce this term to only five years. Ceauşescu could not allow a break-up between Romania and the USSR, as the economy was still dependent on Soviet resources and technology.

The Soviet reaction to the positions of Romanian diplomacy was to undermine Bucharest's international position, trying to convince various Western decision-makers, by disinformation, that Ceauşescu's empowerment policy was not sincere but was dissimulated in connivance with Moscow (Watts 2010; Watts 2013: 382). The escape of *Securitate* general Ion Mihai Pacepa to the US in July 1978 and the publication of his book *Red Horizons* in 1987 increased the West's distrust.

Romania contributed diplomatically to the signing of the Helsinki Final Act of the Conference on Security and Co-operation in Europe. The West's perception of Romania started to change after 1980 precisely because it did not respect human rights, as provided for in the 'third basket' of the Final Act. The situation of minorities (especially ethnic Hungarians) became increasingly important on the US diplomacy agenda.

With an economy in crisis, in the context of increasing international prices of oil and raw materials, Romania reached default in 1981. After overcoming the humiliation of being helped by the IMF, Ceauşescu chose the path of autarky and decided in 1982 to repay in advance the foreign debt of $10.54 billion. In order not to pay interest, Ceauşescu sold an important part of Romania's gold reserve in 1986.

The policy of restraining human rights gradually isolated Ceauşescu from the Western world. The rise of Mikhail Gorbachev and the imposition of a 'new course' made Ceauşescu useless to the West in confrontation with the Soviets. The US abandoned the policy of differentiating among states within the communist bloc in favour of direct dialogue with Gorbachev; the Soviets were to decide the limits of political liberalization in communist states. In comparison with Gorbachev, Ceauşescu was perceived as a Stalinist conservative who had to be removed at the first opportunity. In 1988, the US withdrew the 'most favoured nation clause' from Romania, a gesture equivalent to ostracizing Ceauşescu. The Romanian leader was still received, but only by Third World countries. It was not by chance that Ceauşescu's last foreign visit was to Iran, an opponent of the US. Lacking strong foreign allies and isolated from society, the Ceauşescu regime was doomed to dissolution. The tragedy was that this turned out to be violent.

CHAPTER 5
INSTITUTIONS OF 'LEGITIMATE VIOLENCE'

The justice system

One of the essential transformations in society was the subordination of justice to political control, leaving the citizen without tools of legal defence against state abuse. The power monopoly established by the party-state also meant control over justice. By creating 'proletarian justice' a fundamental change in legal theory took place: its role was no longer to defend the rights and liberties of all citizens, but to provide legal justification for political discrimination among citizens according to class criteria. 'Enemies of the people' could be repressed with legal instruments; this concept, which violated the principle of equality before the law, was called 'communist legality'. Magistrates were politically enrolled, although political partisanship had traditionally been forbidden to them. Military courts had an essential role in the political repression, as they had competencies concerning crimes against the state (Pintilescu 2012).

A first measure, taken as early as December 1944, was to suspend the irrevocability of judges, which was no longer established during the communist regime. Judges were independent, but did not have the strong guarantee of irrevocability. The most important judicial court, the Supreme Tribunal, was elected by the MAN, to which it was accountable. The General Prosecutor was also appointed by the MAN, following a proposal from the government. According to Law no. 6 of 1952, the institution of the prosecutor was established according to the Soviet model. In 1968 Ceaușescu tried to achieve a break with Soviet justice by adopting a new Criminal Code and a new Criminal Procedure Code, reorganizing the Prosecutor's Office, which was to function by offering several guarantees for respecting personal rights.

The class character of justice was confirmed by the institution of the *asesor popular* (popular assessor), introduced in December 1947, who accompanied judges during trials. Assessors were at least twenty-three years old, without any obligation to have studied law, appointed by the Communist Party or by satellite organizations, in order to consecrate the 'popular' character of justice. After 1968 the role of assessors was limited to cases concerning labour litigation and those regarding crimes of murder.

From 1945, political control over justice materialized through the gradual elimination of judges who were considered to be compromised. They were replaced by people of limited education. In 1948, the bar associations were dismantled and replaced with colleges; the right to practise as a lawyer was given only to people approved by the PMR. Out of 18,000 lawyers, only 4,500 were initially accepted; their numbers then increased, as those who had not been accepted became legal advisors to enterprises. The consequence of altering the status of lawyers was a drastic diminution of the right to a defence. In all political trials the right to a defence was systematically violated and the benefit of the doubt was replaced by the presumption of guilt. Arrest was followed by a custodial sentence, regardless of the evidence. During the Gheorghiu-Dej regime, mounting a defence was all the more difficult as a good part of the repressive legislation had a secret character, being inaccessible even to lawyers (Crăcană 2015).

In the case of criminal justice, the main issues could be found in the investigation phase; torture, starvation and psychological pressure were frequently used until the mid-1960s. Because the *Securitate* and the *Miliția* had their own criminal investigation structures, they often escaped real surveillance by prosecutors. Judges were intimidated when faced with political files, so that, most often out of conformism, they approved the punishments demanded by the prosecutors.

Although civil justice was not submitted to the same degree of pressure as in the criminal field, it was also guided by Marxist-Leninist values and 'proletarian morality'. During civil cases between the state and citizens, state institutions were systematically favoured.

Political control over justice during the communist period was systemic; it began from the concept of the role of justice in society, continued with the political subordination of magistrates by their affiliation to the PMR/PCR, and reached direct influence of judges' decisions (usually by the *Securitate*) during political trials. There was no institutional, political and professional framework for creating an ethos of magistrates' independence. Like the majority in society, magistrates manifested enthusiastic and sincere attitudes of servitude towards the communist regime, to the point of miming support for PCR policies. Open opposition to communism among magistrates after 1948 was extremely rare. The consequence was a profound lack of trust in the justice system and in the ideas of fairness and equality among citizens. The feeling of belonging to an Orwellian world characterized the communist period, until 1964 and particularly after 1980.

The *Securitate*

At the centre of the mechanisms by which the communist regime dominated society and captured the state, to the point of identification with it, was the institution of the *Securitate*. Established by Decree no. 221 of 30 August 1948 and abolished by Decree-Law no. 33 of 30 December 1989, the *Securitate* had various institutional avatars, but was essentially the tool by which the Communist leaders preserved their dictatorship. According to its founding document, the purpose of the *Securitate* was 'defending democratic conquests and ensuring the security of the Romanian People's Republic against interior and exterior enemies' (Oprea 2008: 69).

Before the creation of the *Securitate* with the help of Soviet advisors, Romania's communization was achieved by using the police, the *Siguranța* (a predecessor of the *Securitate*), the gendarmerie and the corps of detectives. These structures of legitimate violence were not considered to be 'trustworthy', as they represented the 'bourgeois-landlord' regime; their functions were taken over by 'democratic' institutions, starting from 1948.

The *Securitate* was initially organized in directorates (ten in number) at a central level, which had their equivalents in its territorial structures. Initially a tiny percentage of highly trained people (2 per cent) were enrolled, most of the *Securitate* personnel being party activists and proletarians. In order to respond to the demands of the PMR, which wanted the *Securitate* not only to be a violent repression structure, but also to learn the real situation in society, staff trained in the surveillance and control of society and in spying were gradually integrated. The Special Intelligence Service was disbanded in 1951, simultaneously with the creation of a Foreign Intelligence Directorate (DIE) within the *Securitate*. In 1967–8 further important changes occurred in the institution's organization, with the removal of Alexandru Drăghici and the return to the administrative organization of the country into counties. After the defection of General Ion Mihai Pacepa in July 1978, while on a mission in West Germany, the Foreign Intelligence Directorate was reorganized and turned into the Foreign Intelligence Centre (CIE).

At its foundation the *Securitate* organization chart included 4,641 posts. This had expanded to 12,865 by 1955 (including 10,693 officers), and by 22 December 1989, a total of 15,312 people were working there (including 10,114 officers). From the point of view of professional training, *Securitate* personnel at first benefited from the assistance of Soviet advisors; later, people with a superior intellectual status were enrolled to create and manage complex informer and surveillance networks and also to carry out successful spying operations. The main attractions for recruiting staff were high salaries (until the Salaries Law of 1968 a high-ranking officer received three or four times the salary of a university professor) and other material benefits.

The *Securitate* was organized and functioned as the political police of the communist regime. The main repressive actions against 'class enemies' were undertaken by the *Securitate*: arrests, actions to destroy partisan groups and surveillance. It was deeply involved in various state businesses, including selling Jews and Germans (Oprea 2002).

The military leaders of the *Securitate* had a tendency to become autonomous in relation to the party-state, to exercise power in their own personal interest or in the interest of the structure they led. Gheorghiu-Dej and Ceauşescu subordinated the *Securitate* for the purpose of increasing their personal power, tolerating most of the crimes committed by the political police. Surveillance of political leaders by the *Securitate* was a permanent fear. In 1973 Ceauşescu dismissed the leadership of the *Securitate* because he received evidence showing that he and other party leaders were being watched. At a broader level, Ceauşescu decided that the recruitment of collaborators among party members could not be done without PCR approval. From 1973 until 1982 almost 200,000 collaborator files concerning party members were destroyed.

The precise number of *Securitate* collaborators, or of the persons they were watching, at the end of 1989 is not known. In the specialized literature, the figure of 144,289 active collaborators of the *Securitate* in 1989 has been circulated. However this figure has so far not been confirmed by data from the archives. In any case, within Romanian society there was a psychosis of a generalized surveillance: people communicated allusively, often in a codified manner, and were fearful of publicly stating their personal opinions.

The *Miliția*

Another legitimate violence institution was the *Miliția*, created following a Soviet model. It was established by Decree no. 25 of January 1949, as a result of dismantling the Police and the Gendarmerie. Its main role was to preserve public order, but the spectrum of its actions was broader. The new institution only took over a small proportion of former policemen and gendarmes, the rest being subjected to repression (Șinca 2014). The greater part of the staff of the *Miliția* consisted of people with proletarian origins, most of them with a limited education or even illiterate. As in the case of the *Securitate*, those enrolled into the *Miliția* were guaranteed schooling and afterwards were recruited only from the institution's own schools.

Apart from the daily exercise of preserving public order and fighting crime, the *Miliția* had an essential role in communist repression and in police control over society. In rural areas, the *Miliția* played the role of the *Securitate*, establishing collaborator networks for watching citizens.

The activity of the *Securitate* and the *Miliția* was supported by security troops, created as a distinct military structure within the Ministry of the Interior as early as 1949. Within these troops, an anti-terrorist fighting unit was created in 1977. Security troops had an essential role in attacks against anti-communist resistance. Usually, these military units were used for guarding important locations. Security troops were made up of a core of career servicemen together with soldiers fulfilling their compulsory military service.

The army

The first institution which submitted to Soviet control was the army. As early as 1945 the Soviets imposed restraints on staff and disbanded command structures. The principal officers were convicted for 'war crimes', over fifty generals died in detention. Military structures were submitted to the 'democratization' process: the Superior Directorate for Education and Propaganda was created, its goal being the ideologization of the military. Priests were eliminated from its ranks. From 1946, the involvement of the military in political life was allowed and, from 1948, the PMR established political structures within the army, called 'political directorates'. At the core of these political activities were the 996 officers and NCOs of the Tudor Vladimirescu Division (made up of Romanian prisoners from the Eastern Front), who were employed in the army from 1945. Their role was 'building the popular army'. The political and ideological education of officers and recruits was a dominant preoccupation of the PCR; the purpose was to stimulate devotion towards the regime.

The Paris Peace Treaty of February 1947 established a total manpower of 138,000, but Stalin determined an increase of the army to 250,000 men for peace time and 600,000 for war (Şperlea 2003: 102). The army was sovietized, from uniforms to organization and weapons. The creation of the Warsaw Pact offered a legal basis for the Soviets' coordination of the Romanian army. After the withdrawal of Soviet troops from Romania (1958) the army was gradually de-sovietized. Ceauşescu gave a new impetus to army ideologization, using patriotic feelings and national history. In 1969, the PCR adopted the concept of the 'war of the entire people for the defence of the motherland', a year after the creation of paramilitary formations including men and women alike, called *Gărzi patriotice* (Patriotic Guards), in case of a Soviet military intervention in Romania. In fact, from 1968 onwards Ceauşescu neither accepted Warsaw Pact exercises in Romania, for fear of hosting potential occupying troops, nor were Romanian troops sent into other countries for Warsaw Pact exercises.

The army was not used as a direct repression tool against 'class enemies', but it was a huge institutional mechanism by which the Communist Party wanted to ideologize society. For young people fulfilling their compulsory military service the army was a structure within which they were really forced to learn the main elements of the official ideology. Although the army had the main role of ensuring defence, it was increasingly involved in economic activities. Units of army engineers were used to build dams, roads and railways, and during the last decade of communism the army in its entirety was used as a cheap labour force. It not only participated in great construction projects (the Danube–Black Sea Canal, the House of the People in Bucharest, irrigation systems), but also in agricultural works (Scurtu 2010a: 108–13). The situation generated discontent among officers, who no longer had money and time for training, but instead had to harvest maize, grapes or potatoes. During this time, the *Securitate* had a privileged status, much to the dissatisfaction of the army officer corps.

CHAPTER 6
SOCIETY CRUSHED BY TYRANNY

The communist regime continued from previous dictatorships the project of state domination over society, to which it offered an ideological (Marxist-Leninist) justification. According to Arendt's classical totalitarianism thesis, communist societies were 'atomized' and 'massified', under the total control of the party-state, but this is not validated by recent research. Even for the Stalinist period, it can hardly be stated that the 'atomization' process was absolute, as, with the exception of people in the detention system, only a few individuals were in absolute isolation. The communist regime was not exclusively based on coercion and propaganda and, especially during the 1960s and 1970s, it reached a mutual understanding with society, as well as winning real popularity, through seduction, manipulation, integration or mobilization. The brief explanation is that the totalitarian society became 'normal', by its reproduction from generation to generation ('trivialization of Evil'). As the communist regime became increasingly bureaucratized, the party-state de facto abandoned the project of total and transforming control over society, content that apathy did not turn into open disapproval.

The Orwellian description of society is not false, but it cannot be maintained for the entire existence of Romanian communism. The social space was not simply divided between opponents and supporters of the regime; there were intermediate categories. The number of 'certain opponents' of the communist regime, people who directly suffered the effects of repressive policies (prisoners, those administratively hospitalized, displaced, subject to forced domicile, etc.) perhaps extended to 1 million–1.2 million people out of a population of 19 million in 1964. Such a numeric landmark points to a 7 per cent share of Romania's total population. Among the 'unconditional supporters' were the nomenklatura and the repressive apparatus (*Securitate*, justice system), accounting for a little under 200,000 people. In the second circle we include the body of ordinary party members (passive supporters), which had increased from around 600,000 in 1955 to 3.8 million in 1989. At the end of the communist regime, the party membership amounted to 16.5 per cent of the total population, but not all of those who had a party card were also supporters of the regime. What is certain is that, adding together the number of proven victims and the unconditional supporters of the regime, we can conclude that, between them, they did not exceed a quarter of Romania's total population. This leaves three-quarters of the population, whose attitude towards the regime cannot be understood in terms of the resistance versus repression binomial. In quantitative terms, we are speaking about 14 million in 1948 and 18 million in 1989. There were some differences, however: the increasing number of regime opponents in the 1945–58 and 1980–9 intervals, and increasing trust in the regime between 1960 and 1980 (Abraham 2013: 69–74).

The dynamic of social life under communism was complex and contradictory. The communist regime wanted to reduce the individual's areas of uncontrolled freedom, but circles of family and friends were protective shields against the party-state and its policies of repression, mobilization and enrolment. The party-state, by means of its repressive instruments, wanted to reconfigure the foundations of social life, according to Marxist-Leninist values, but it failed. The main reason for the failure of the New Man project can be found at the very heart of the PCR; its utopia was shared only by a reduced number of power fanatics, who could not convince society to follow them.

From armed resistance to dissidence

Armed resistance (1944–62)

The longest action of military challenge against the communist regime in sovietized CEE took place in Romania (Radosav 2006: 88). Its beginning can be recorded during the spring of 1944, with the occupation of northern Bukovina by the Soviets. In collaboration with the Romanian army, partisan groups of 15 to 120 people were formed to fight against the Red Army. After Romania's exit from the war alongside Germany, various insurgents, most of them Legionaries, were parachuted into the country to fight against the Soviets. From the end of 1945, groups of partisans were established in the mountains, prepared for action aimed at overthrowing communism.

The main motivation of the anti-communist resistance was rejection of the regime, but it also feared repression. The widespread belief among those withdrawing into the severe conditions in the mountains was that 'the Americans won't leave us in the hands of communists': a new military conflict was expected, or even the use of the atomic bomb against Stalin. The hopes of the Romanian partisans were fuelled by US involvement in several actions. They sent paratroopers in 1951–3, most of them Romanians (officers, National-Peasantists, Legionaries), but they were caught and most of them were executed.

The main feature of the partisan movement was its fragmented character. Secluded in the mountains and permanently hunted by the *Securitate*, the fighters benefited from the tacit support of the population, but they were not organized in a structure capable of overthrowing the regime. The real dimension of the military resistance movement is hard to establish with precision, even after the opening of the archives and the emergence of abundant memoirs. In any case, in 1969, the *Securitate* identified, for the 1945–59 period, 1,196 'terrorist groups and gangs' organized in 19 centres (Dobre 2003: 9). The evaluation of the *Securitate* must be taken with caution, as it was meant to legitimize the efficiency of the repressive apparatus. Even so, the partisan phenomenon was real, reduced as it was during the post-Stalin period. Groups of partisans did not exceed 200 people, and most of them had, at best, a few tens of fighters. Usually, they avoided direct confrontation with *Securitate* troops. However, during violent confrontations in the mountains, where they were 'hunted' by the *Securitate* and the *Miliția*, the partisans used all the weapons at their disposal, resulting in casualties on both sides.

Permanently pursued by the authorities, betrayed by *Securitate* informers, isolated, but most of all demoralized by the fact that 'the Americans are no longer coming!' while society was beginning to accommodate itself to the communist regime, the number of those who resisted in the mountains after 1956 became progressively smaller. The last significant groups were liquidated by the *Securitate* in 1958, and armed resistance in the mountains was fully eliminated by 1962.

Workers' strikes

The first and most important protest movement involving workers took place between 1 and 3 August 1977 in the Jiu Valley, having at its core miners from Lupeni. Despite the fact that they were considered by the regime's propaganda to be 'the vanguard of society', miners lived in a precarious material situation and their working conditions were poor. The intention of the government to increase their retirement age from fifty to fifty-five and the extension of their shifts from six to eight hours, together with a reduction in other social benefits, generated dissatisfaction. The initial protest of 5,000–6,000 miners was not stopped by Deputy Prime Minister Ilie Verdeț, who was sent to solve the problems. The miners demanded the presence of Ceaușescu, who went to Lupeni on 3 August, where he was expected by 25,000–27,000 miners. Ceaușescu was presented with a total of twenty-six trade union demands, which he only partially accepted. The protest of the miners did not hold political connotations, but the *Securitate* took gradual measures of surveillance and repression. Miners considered undesirable were transferred to other mining centres (Burakowski 2011: 224–6; Rus 2007: 567).

A decade later, the twilight of communism was anticipated by the protest of workers in the Brașov truck factory on 14–15 November 1987. Challenging communism was a desperate action against restrictions in food procurement, heating, electricity and fuel. The factory leadership refused any dialogue with the workers and a few hundred people protested in front of the PCR County Committee, and directly challenged Nicolae Ceaușescu. He ordered the repression of the protest; 300 people were arrested and sixty-one were tried in a political trial. As in 1977, those convicted were transferred to other industrial centres, to eliminate new challenges against the regime (Arsene 1997). The Brașov protest was reported to the population by RFE and Voice of America, and hostility towards the Ceaușescu family increased even more.

The workers' protests of 1977 and 1987 were not isolated; there were also small-scale actions at the Motru mine (in 1981), the Maramureș mines (in 1983) and the Nicolina factory in Iași (February 1987).

Dissidence

In the context of the human rights issue turning into a major issue of Soviet–American relations after signing of the Helsinki Final Act (1975), new forms of challenge to the regime emerged in Romania, starting from its international commitments and constitutional rights and liberties. The main feature of these forms of challenge to the regime, which demanded its improvement and not its disappearance, was their elitist character. The first significant action concerned writer Paul Goma (1977), who publicly expressed solidarity with the Charter 77 movement in Czechoslovakia. Goma was joined within a few months by another 200 people, before being arrested, convicted and then forced to emigrate to France (Cătănuş 2014: 94–5; Petrescu 2013: 115–70).

Other intellectuals manifested, in various forms, their critical position towards the lack of respect for human rights in Romania (for example, Vlad Georgescu, Mihai Botez, Dorin Tudoran, Radu Filipescu, Gabriel Andreescu and Doina Cornea). Dissidence was supported by RFE, which aroused Ceauşescu's anger. The main retaliation was a bomb attack on the RFE headquarters in Munich on 21 February 1981, organized by international terrorist Carlos the Jackal, but this failed to destroy the Romanian section.

Repression was also directed against those who wanted to inform public opinion about the situation in Romania. Engineer Gheorghe Ursu was denounced to the *Securitate* by a colleague who reported that he kept a journal from which it emerged that he had sent materials to RFE. He was arrested in 1985 and died following torture in *Miliţia* custody. The regime presented the case as concerning a common law criminal (he illegally held foreign currency), but the truth was made public in the Western media.

A special initiative was that of doctor Ionel Cană, priest Gheorghe Calciu-Dumitreasa and economist Gheorghe Braşoveanu who founded the Free Trade Union of the Working People of Romania (SLOMR); the declaration was presented on RFE (March 1979). The trade union's initiators were arrested and imprisoned. Calciu-Dumitreasa was only released in 1984, as a result of international protests. The idea of establishing a real trade union was also supported by Vasile Paraschiv, who publicly read the document presented on RFE at his workplace. He was arrested and subjected to torture (Cătănuş 2014: 112–18).

During the end of the Ceauşescu regime, exasperated by the situation in Romania, six former communist leaders (among them Gheorghe Apostol, Alexandru Bârlădeanu, Silviu Brucan and Corneliu Mănescu) sent a message to the Western media in which they criticized the violation of human rights and the deplorable economic situation. Ceauşescu placed them under house arrest (Petrescu 2013: 217–71).

The Romanian Gulag

Just as in the Soviet Union, where the Bolsheviks dominated society through a system of generalized terror, in Romania, too, communization was achieved using the instruments of the totalitarian state: social stigmatization of real, potential and imaginary opponents using state propaganda; physical elimination of the main 'class enemies' (bourgeoisie; political elites from democratic parties; politicians and sympathizers of 'fascists'- Legionaries; intellectuals with democratic orientations; *chiaburi*); social marginalization of the 'people's enemies' through administrative admissions to labour colonies and camps, fixing mandatory residence, removal from jobs or forced emigration; the apparent 'generosity' of the regime, which allowed the societal integration of 'class enemies', on the condition that they converted to the values of the regime, by re-education through labour or ideological re-education.

The repression of society went through several stages. Initially, on the basis of the Armistice Convention, repressive measures were used against 'war criminals and people guilty of the country's disaster' (1944–6). It was not just those guilty of war crimes or for the Holocaust who were punished, but also those considered to be the main opponents of the Soviets. Then, until the death of Stalin, the repression continued at an increasing and increasingly brutal rate, including the arrest and trial of democratic party members, Legionaries, former police officers, clergymen, peasants opposing collectivization, and intellectuals. After 1953, there was a short period of détente, but the Hungarian Revolution caused a new wave of repression, which started with students and was then extended to former Legionaries, intellectuals and members of the historical parties. Simultaneously, repressive action against peasants took place, in order to finalize collectivization. These repressive actions reached their peak in 1958–9, after which their intensity decreased. The pardoning of political prisoners in 1964 ended the Romanian Gulag system, but the control and repression of 'enemies of the proletariat' existed until the end of the communist regime.

The Romanian Gulag was created on the basis of public legislation, whose main document was the Criminal Code of 1948 (an adapted version of that adopted by Carol II in 1937), along with other decrees offering legal support to repression. There was also an extensive secret repressive legislation, which concerned several administrative measures that could be taken against various undesirable categories. The frequent legal justification was 'machination against the social order' (Art. 209 of the Criminal Code). The main political trials took place in military, not civil, courts. In 1950 *unităţi de muncă* (labour units) were established for the 're-education of hostile elements'. These changed their name in 1952 to *colonii de muncă* (labour colonies), and were disbanded in 1954. In 1958 mandatory working places were reintroduced, for a period of two to six years (Tismăneanu et al. 2007: 521–628).

Despite intense efforts on the part of historians after 1990, the map of the Romanian Gulag has not yet been finalized due to difficulties in accessing the archives of the communist penitentiaries. In spite of this, a general profile of the penitentiary system can be created. In 1945, there were 72 prisons with a capacity of 15,000 people. In 1954, there were 64 penitentiaries, 22 camps and 11 colonies for minors. For the 1949–64 period seventy labour colonies, units or mandatory working places were identified. A considerable proportion of the labour colonies were situated in Dobrogea or in the lead mines of Maramureş.

Within the Romanian Gulag, a few prisons were outstanding for the extermination regime applied to political prisoners. The Aiud penitentiary was a place of detention for officers, policemen, politicians, intellectuals and priests (Muraru 2008). In Aiud, political prisoners (defined as 'Legionaries') were submitted to ideological re-education. In the Piteşti penitentiary, from 1949 to 1952, a terrifying experiment of violent re-education took place, ordered by Communist political leaders. This targeted former students who were tortured by other student-prisoners of former Legionary allegiance (Stănescu 2010). Initially tried out within the Suceava penitentiary, re-education by torture was also applied in the Gherla penitentiary, led by the *Securitate* but applied by young former ML members. On a smaller scale, re-education carried out by prisoners also took place in other penitentiaries (Baia Sprie, Târgu Ocna, Ocnele Mari, Târguşor). In order to erase the traces of these crimes, in 1954–5 two trials of prisoners who had used abominable violence against others took place, following which most of those who had carried out the re-education were sentenced to death and executed. The Sighetul Marmaţiei prison is associated with the extermination of the political elites of the interwar period (Iuliu Maniu, Gheorghe I. Brătianu, etc.). Other penitentiaries in which terror was applied included Jilava, Râmnicu Sărat and Oradea.

The most massive repression of Romanian society is associated with the Danube–Black Sea Canal. This is an inland waterway which links the river to the sea across Dobrogea. The project was required of the Romanian communist leaders by Stalin in 1948. Together with civilian and military workers, the Canal (1949–53) was the mandatory working place of 'class enemies'. The total number of political prisoners who worked on the Canal is not known – the communist regime hid information and destroyed documents – but in the eighteen working sites there were approximately 35,000 political prisoners, several thousand of whom died as a result of exhaustion, lack of medical care and malnutrition (Cojoc 2014).

Deportations

'Class enemies' of the regime were subjected not only to the brutality of imprisonment, but also to internal population deportation and the imposition of mandatory residence. The first wave of dislocations were achieved at the beginning of collectivization, the target being former 'landowners' and their families. The procedure consisted of transferring people to other villages in the country and establishing a ban on their leaving their new residence. Peasants who mutinied during revolts against collectivization in 1949 were also deported.

The most important internal deportation action took place in June 1951, as a result of Stalin's conflict with Tito's Yugoslavia. From western Romania (the Banat), 25 kilometres from the country's border with Yugoslavia, 10,099 families, accounting for a total of 43,891 people, were deported to the Bărăgan, a region of drought-prone plains in the south-east. Mandatory residence was imposed on them in eighteen newly established communes (Vultur 1997). In 1956, after the Soviet–Yugoslav reconciliation, population deportation from western Romania ended. In a secret statistic of the *Securitate* from 1967, the deportation and imposition of mandatory residence for approximately 60,000 people from 1949 to 1961, including those deported in June 1951 from the Banat, is acknowledged.

Release of political prisoners

The opening towards the West at the end of the 1950s also involved an attempt by the communist regime to recover its honour by respecting human rights. The first important signal was given in January 1962, when Gheorghiu-Dej pardoned 4,760 peasants who had opposed collectivization. Other pardons followed in 1963 and 1964. A total of 15,035 political prisoners (out of which 6,255 were considered to be ML members) were released by pardon or had reached the end of their sentences. Release from penitentiary was followed by *Securitate* surveillance and sometimes recruitment for collaboration. Having the stigma of 'class enemy', former political prisoners were truly liberated only after their death or following the fall of communism.

By summing up official figures and those resulting from historical research, the number of arrested people assigned to labour colonies or with a fixed mandatory residence can be estimated at 550,000–650,000 people for the 1945–64 period. However, the macabre accountancy of the Romanian Gulag lacks ethical significance, as, even if the number of innocent victims had been smaller, Romanian communism would still have had a criminal dimension (Banu 2009). In any case, individual and collective dramas cannot be understood through the statistical trivialization of victims.

Urbanization and transformation of the rural world

The ideological project of a Soviet-type society had at its core the idea of social homogenization, in its four essential dimensions: abolishing the exploitation of man by man through wealth levelling; erasing ethnic divisions through a policy of integration of minorities into the 'socialist nation'; eliminating differences between cities and villages; and gender equality through the emancipation of women in their double role of labourer and 'hero mother'.

Industrialization and collectivization brought about deep societal changes. The magnitude of the demographic changes is emphasized by a few figures: in 1948 the rural population accounted for 76.6 per cent of the total, but by 1989 it had decreased to 46.7 per cent; and the share of the population employed in agriculture decreased from 74.1 per cent in 1950 to 27.5 per cent in 1989.

The synchronization of the collectivization and industrialization processes meant a decrease in the rural population share by 15 percentage points over almost two decades. Between 1948 and 1977, the village gave over 4 million people to the city, which increased the number of people employed in industry, construction and services. The dominant flux of internal migration was from rural to urban and the main basins fuelling the cities and new industrial areas were Moldavia and Muntenia. During the mid-1980s, city inhabitants became more numerous than those in rural areas. In 1976 Ceauşescu interrupted the development of big cities (Decree no. 68); fourteen of them were declared 'closed' and settling in them was strictly controlled by the administration. The PCR stimulated commuting from semi-urban or rural areas towards big cities, developing regional transport. Internal migration was directed towards medium and small towns or even towards rural areas through the system of mandatory placement for university graduates.

The objective of the communist leaders was to use the peasants to get cheaper food, needed by the expanding cities, and to be able to sell agricultural produce in exchange for the hard currency so necessary for industrialization. In exchange, the PCR 'rewarded' the peasants with a social insurance system; this was, however, far inferior to that for employees.

The quasi-disappearance of private property in rural areas also meant a loss of rural traditions. Traditional customs were prohibited and replaced by the culture of socialist realism; a part of the old way of life was changed by introducing elements of modernity. We can identify an objective component, which can be found in all rural societies subjected to the phenomena of modernization and a repressive social engineering dimension. The disappearance of some crafts, such as wheelwright, cooper, blacksmith or tinker, which were associated with a rural micro-economy based on self-consumption, was a natural transformation, determined by industrial modernization and by widening access to consumer goods. The prohibition of evening gatherings or traditional dances and their replacement by party or trade union meetings undoubtedly represented a punitive mechanism for the cultural transformation of the traditional Romanian village.

In its turn, the urban environment was the crucible of a new social reality. Cities changed radically, both as a result of the building of new enterprises and factories and following ambitious programmes of building residential districts. At the beginning of the 1950s as many as 14,000 apartments were built annually, from the 1970s the figure was as high as 100,000 (Mihalache and Croitoru 2011: 24). Until the mid-1970s residential neighbourhoods developed in the outskirts of cities, but Ceaușescu wanted to completely change the face of urban areas. Starting from 1967, a national urban planning scheme was launched, aimed at rebuilding the centres of the main cities, filling them with new administrative, commercial and residential buildings. Up to the end of communism, the central areas of twenty-nine large and medium-sized cities in Romania were demolished and re-built according to PCR requirements. The Soviet-inspired architectural model of the 1950s and 1960s gave way to the French and Neo-Romanian buildings of the 1970s, only to be replaced by an eclectic style, imported from North Korea, during the 1980s.

A major earthquake on 4 March 1977, which affected the south and east of Romania, claimed the lives of 1,570 people. After this a broad process of architectural transformation was launched. The main objective was to build a new political and administrative centre for Bucharest, with the House of the People (currently the location of the Parliament) as its symbol, a gigantic building with which Ceaușescu wanted to emphasize the force of his regime. Several neighbourhoods of Bucharest were demolished, including centuries-old churches. During the years of the 'great demolition' in Bucharest (1984–7) the main victims were the Cotroceni Monastery (1679) and the Văcărești Monastery (1716), together with over 8,000 houses. The owners of demolished houses received compensation amounting to about 30 per cent of the value of what they had lost.

Starting from the mid-1980s, Ceaușescu was particularly interested in rural planning, which involved demolishing whole villages in order to gain additional land for agriculture. In 1986, out of 13,000 villages, 4,000 were destroyed. In 1988 it was proposed that by the year 2000 no less than 7,000–8,000 villages would be destroyed. The pharaonic plans of a leader increasingly remote from reality led to international protests; in 1988 the 'Operation Villages Roumains' campaign was launched, which reverberated all over the

West. The essence of rural planning consisted in turning villages into quasi-towns: most houses were to be demolished and the population were to be transferred to apartment buildings. Villages were to be endowed with new schools, clinics, libraries and public baths (as villagers' houses were to have only toilets), in order to 'reduce differences between villages and towns'. The project was not received with enthusiasm, even by the nomenklatura, which was conscious of the danger of protests among village inhabitants whose houses were to be demolished. The fall of communism meant the abandonment of this totalitarian social engineering project.

Urbanization and structural change in the rural world also had deep effects on the family, which went through successive crises. The model of multi-generational families living in the same household gradually unravelled, with the emergence of jobs in industry and, subsequently, of apartments offered for rent by the state. The emancipation of women was real, as girls managed to enrol more easily in universities and jobs in industry reduced their dependence on men's revenues. The family witnessed an obvious modernization process, but the fact that this was achieved under an oppressive regime made its effect on society incomplete and traumatic (Dumănescu 2012).

A dictatorial welfare state

The essence of the social contract proposed by the communist regime was giving up freedom in exchange for an extended welfare state in an equalitarian society. According to the Marxist-Leninist project, the state and society were to be revolutionized in an authoritarian modernization process following which everything reminiscent of capitalism would be removed, often violently (by the 'dictatorship of the proletariat'), and in its place a new world would be built. The 'communist welfare state' (Inglot 2008: 25–9) was to be achieved by various targeted policies, which will now be briefly analysed.

The New Man utopia involved a transformation of the educational system. The main issue was illiteracy, as according to the population census of 1930, the share of the illiterate in the population was 42.7 per cent, albeit with a decreasing tendency. In rural areas, illiteracy was much higher and the most affected were women. In the autumn of 1944, the communist media advanced the figure of 49 per cent for illiteracy in rural areas. The communists said that the fight against the bourgeoisie and landowners could not be successful unless peasants and the working class were 'enlightened' by schooling. Therefore, as early as 1946, a campaign to eliminate illiteracy was initiated, which lasted until 1953. Not all people learned to read and write, but the threshold of 90 per cent was exceeded during the mid-1950s.

In August 1948, a broad and controversial education 'reform' took place, using a full replication of the Soviet system. The Russian language became compulsory. A system of single national textbooks was established and their content was deeply ideologized. Free compulsory primary education was reduced from seven to four years, with the possibility of optionally following grades five to seven. This was a downgrade from the solution that had been inconstantly applied since 1925, but pressure from parents led to a significant increase in the number of children who attended school (Rădulescu 2006: 309). Confessional education was abolished and 1,553 schools with 1,856 buildings and their inventory were confiscated. University autonomy was also abolished and the whole educational system was centralized and placed under political control. Also in 1948, the labour contracts of teachers in secondary and tertiary education were cancelled and those considered undesirable were removed. In 1949–50 a new wave of purges followed, which mainly affected universities. The effect of the class struggle in schools and universities saw the removal of some of the most valuable professors, and their replacement by profiteers of the new regime. In 1957 new measures were taken to eliminate 'class enemies' from universities. Class struggle also emerged during student selection procedures. Proletarian origin was an important advantage and few young people from 'reactionary' and 'exploitative' families were accepted until the beginning of the 1960s.

The Soviet model of organizing school cycles proved to be obsolete. In 1956 the duration of elementary school increased to seven years and that of secondary education to four years; this was modified again in 1961 to eight years of elementary school followed by four years of high school.

In 1968 a new education reform was carried out, whose purpose was to break with the Soviet model and recover national traditions. Compulsory education included ten grades, after which two years of high school or professional and technical education could be added. Starting in the mid-1970s, priority was given to industrial and agricultural high schools in order to provide a labour force for the economy. Higher education was orientated towards engineering and other technical disciplines (with over 60 per cent of available places) and places in faculties dealing with the humanities or socio-political disciplines were drastically reduced. In 1977, specializations such as sociology, psychology and pedagogy were abolished. The capital role of education after 1977–8 was to train a qualified labour force for a functioning economy, albeit one following the rigid rules of centralized planning and not the authentic dynamics of internal and international market demand.

The preoccupation of the communist regime with education brought a certain progress to school infrastructure compared to the interwar period. The number of education units increased from 15,879 in 1938 to 27,327 in 1989 and the number of universities from 16 in 1938 to 44 in 1989. There was a significant increase in the number of those advantaged by access to education. In 1938, there were 1,067 pupils and 17 students per 10,000 people; the share increased to 1,504 pupils and 39 students in 1960 and in 1989 it reached 1,963 pupils and 71 students. These figures have to be correlated with the funding provided to the education system by the state budget: 37.8 per cent in 1950, 27.1 per cent in 1970, decreasing to only 15.4 per cent in 1989 (Rădulescu 2006: 315–16). The total number of teaching posts increased from 68,301 in 1945 to 236,190 in 1989. The general picture shows a massive investment in education at the beginning of communism, however, during the 1980s, the education system was submitted to drastic cutbacks, signalling its marginalization. The phenomenon was also emphasized by the

1975 policy of compulsory governmental placements, which meant that higher education graduates were forced to accept jobs offered by the regime, at least during a probation period. Ceaușescu's aim was to transfer a highly qualified labour force to rural areas and mono-industrial centres in order to build 'socialist, multilaterally developed society'. If a graduate refused to accept the job they were assigned, they had to repay the cost of their educational process, which amounted to a large sum.

The school population had doubled its share of the total population by 1988 (24.4 per cent) compared with 1945 (11.8 per cent), but compared with other European countries and even with those in the Soviet bloc, this share was among the lowest.

The communist regime constitutionally assumed the objective of ensuring public healthcare. Following the same policy of centralization and elimination of private property, private health institutions were nationalized in November 1948, after which, in April 1949, pharmacies, laboratories and drug deposits were also nationalized (Bărbulescu 2009: 342–51).

The population's access to medical services was extended and, following investment, the number of hospitals gradually decreased (606 in 1960, 587 in 1970 and, after reorganization, 425 in 1989) while the number of clinics increased (407 in 1960, 385 in 1970, 541 in 1989). In rural areas, medical dispensaries were established and through a centralized vaccination policy, the incidence of serious diseases (tuberculosis, polio, etc.) was diminished. Medical services became more extended, but the phenomenon of 'gifts' for medical staff, who were relatively underpaid, became a usual and generalized practice. Hospitals, despite often precarious conditions, turned into veritable refuges for the elderly and impoverished population.

Communist paternalism had dramatic effects at the moment when it joined with demographic policies. In 1948 abortion was forbidden, but in 1957 it was legalized on demand as a measure to emancipate women (Kligman 1998: 47–9). There was a marked increase in the number of legal abortions: over a million a year between 1963 and 1965. Ceaușescu considered that decreasing birth rates were endangering the objectives of industrialization and national development; abortion was again forbidden (Decree no. 770 of 1966), in the context of several other pro-birth policies (discouraging divorce, increasing allocations for families with several children, etc.). Repressive institutions were charged with watching medical staff in order to prevent illegal abortions. Abortion could only be carried out for medical reasons, with the agreement of prosecutors, on the basis of a coroner's opinion. The consequence was a proliferation of clandestine abortions. According to official figures, 9,452 women died as a result of abortions from 1966 to 1989, though the real number was almost certainly higher. Criminal law restrictions concerning abortion were effective only temporarily; after 1970 the birth rate was again in decline.

In the same spirit of total control over society, a so-called 'rational nutrition' programme was launched in 1982. The proposal came from Doctor Iulian Mincu and was supported by Ceaușescu. The main purpose of 'scientific feeding' was not population health, but a reduction of food consumption, so that the quantities which were produced and not used could be exported to repay the foreign debt as quickly as possible.

The communist welfare state was also manifested in the field of social insurance. Law no. 10 of 1949 abolished the Central House of Social Insurance, the General Pensions House, and other pension houses and funds; the whole social insurance budget was taken over by the state budget. Unemployment was no longer recognized as a labour market reality. According to seniority and difficulty of working conditions, the retirement pension varied between 50–80 per cent of pay. In 1954 some advantages were introduced for early retirement and increasing indemnities for those in hazardous jobs. An important change was the opportunity for housewives and farmers to contribute to and benefit from the pensions system.

In 1977, as a result of increasing costs, a series of changes took place. The minimum seniority period required was increased to twenty-five years for women and thirty years for men. The amount of invalidity pensions decreased. Members of CAPs (*Cooperative Agricole de Producție*, Agricultural Production Cooperatives) and individual non-collectivized peasants benefited from pensions, but these were a lot smaller than those of permanent employees. Separate pension systems were created for the military and employees of the Ministry of Interior, lawyers, clergymen and artists, among others (Zamfir 1999). Although insufficiently developed compared to the Western European 'welfare state', the communist welfare state brought certain benefits to the urban and rural proletariat, through the safety net it offered for old age and for sickness.

Culture, press, art and sport

The Romanian cultural phenomenon did not manage to regain its vitality after the end of the Second World War and was submitted to dramatic new constraints. The communization of society was also brutally manifested in the cultural field. The fundamental objective of the communist government was a radical transformation of cultural life in order to bring about a break with 'bourgeois culture', national traditions and relations with the West. The whole institutional system of cultural and artistic life was replaced and a centralized model was imposed in order to exercise a political and ideological monopoly. In 1948, the Romanian Academy's autonomy was drastically reduced and thirty-two of its forty-seven members were purged. Between 1945 and 1948, no fewer than 8,779 titles were forbidden; these were withdrawn from libraries and bookshops. Consecrated Romanian writers became outcasts. Cultural life was 'Russified' and works of Russian writers, together with those of Marx, Lenin and Stalin, were widely published. The whole cultural phenomenon acquired a 'class dimension' and socialist realism became the main stylistic matrix in art and literature. In science, materialism was imposed against 'idealist-speculative' theories. The synthesis of the PMR's vision was the work of Leonte Răutu who outlined the main directions of *proletkult* (Răutu 1949).

During the communist period, cultural and artistic life were closely linked with important political events in Romania and the rest of the Soviet bloc. The first stage (1948–53) is that of the communization and Russification of culture, characterized by major institutional changes and acts of repression against 'reactionary' intellectuals. Stalin's death led to a decrease in ideological and repressive pressure. After the Hungarian Revolution of 1956, a new wave of repression against intellectuals was unleashed in 1958–9 (Negrici 2010). The main case was the 'Noica–Pillat putsch' in which allegedly 'mystic-Legionary' intellectuals were convicted. Opening to the West and empowerment in relation to the USSR were reflected by a liberalization of cultural and artistic life. After 1971 Ceauşescu imposed a gradual re-ideologization of culture and arts, which were subordinated to his personality cult. The national current in culture was replaced by a sort of national-communism, with its extreme manifestation in the form of *protochronism* (by which Romanian chronological priority with regard to certain international inventions was stated). In 1971 the Council of Socialist Culture and Education was created, which was subordinated both to the PCR and to the Council of Ministers. Its purpose was 'directing and orientating all cultural and educational activity' taking place in Romania. The objective of creating a mass culture and the New Man was resumed with vigour and re-conceptualized in 1974, in order to build the 'multilaterally developed socialist society'. The *'Cântarea României'* ('Singing Romania') festival was created in 1976, which generated mass involvement in cultural and artistic activities ordered by the regime. At the same time, repressive actions against intellectuals were resumed (Diaconescu 2012).

The Communists' political interest in controlling cultural, artistic and sports life was not manifested only in oppressive forms but also through investments in infrastructure. Budgets allocated to cultural and scientific activities (Vasile 2011a), or to sport, were permanently in crisis, as industry and agriculture were the priorities in terms of investment. However, the network of cultural institutions (museums, theatres, cinemas and concert halls) and sports facilities became denser than in the interwar period.

Literature also went through the contradictions of cultural life. Some of the main writers marking Romanian culture during this period were Tudor Arghezi, Lucian Blaga, George Călinescu, Mihail Sadoveanu, Nichita Stănescu, Marin Sorescu, Camil Petrescu and Marin Preda.

Historiography was deeply ideologized and mystified; traditional historians were removed from universities and research centres. The epitome of perverting historiography by party-state control is represented by Mihail Roller (Müller 2003). The main institutional effort was to publish between 1960 and 1964 four volumes of *Treatise on the History of Romania*, a synthesis of the historical materialist perspective. Starting with the 1970s, this was subjected to pressure to adopting the autochthonist-nationalist theory, which invented a past of uninterrupted statehood going back as far as pre-Roman Antiquity. However these phantasmagorias were not accepted by the leading historians of the period: Dan Berindei, Constantin C. Giurescu, Andrei Oţetea and David Prodan.

Mass media

For the party-state, control of information and implicitly of the mass media was essential, as this was its main communication channel. The media was turned into the central component of the propaganda system and its role was to create a class consciousness among individuals, and to generate enthusiasm, trust and optimism in relation to the communist regime.

As early as 1944 the media was 'purged' of 'fascist' elements and the press organs of the democratic parties (*Dreptatea* of the PNȚ, *Viitorul* of the PNL, etc.) were disbanded simultaneously with the disappearance of the parties themselves. The communist media (*Scânteia, Scânteia tineretului, România liberă*) led virulent campaigns against 'enemies of the people' in the press.

From 1948, the PMR exercised an absolute control over the mass media. Following nationalization, the state became the single owner and the communists restricted access to information. Journalists were 'ideologically guided' in order to avoid any temptation of free expression of opinions; from 1949 to 1977, censorship was officially acknowledged by the regime, being within the competency of the Press and Printing Committee. Press distribution was also under state control. Within the PMR/PCR Central Committee there was a press section (under various titles) which ensured full political control over the press. Media Law no. 3 of 1974 introduced the obligation that all journalists be PCR members, thus strengthening political and ideological control over the mass media. The official dismissal of censorship in 1977 did not mean it really disappeared, only that it was transferred to the level of editorial teams; self censorship of journalists was also frequent (Șercan 2015).

The media was centralized and standardized step by step by issuing template messages approved by political activists. The main caretakers concerning ideological control over media were Leonte Răutu under Gheorghiu-Dej, and Dumitru Popescu (nicknamed 'God') in the Nicolae Ceaușescu era.

The media developed quantitatively, simultaneously with increasing circulation, in the context of a growth in the number of literate people. Cultural publications, minority, sports, technical or children's magazines increased in number and in circulation. The number of printing houses and the capacity of paper factories also increased. The price of the publications was reduced, being centrally controlled, precisely to facilitate access to the press.

Scânteia was the central press organ of the PMR/PCR; one or two publications were also created at the level of each county/region, usually with a weekly issue and during the 1970s even daily. In 1950 the press had a total circulation of 4.6 million copies, compared to 2.5 million in 1946 (Giurescu 2013: 975). Later, during the 1970s, the daily press alone reached a total circulation of approximately 4 million copies; this level was diminished starting with 1979, following the PCR's decision to save paper.

Radio was also under political control. The number of broadcasting hours and the territorial coverage increased; regional stations emerged and radio receivers became ever more accessible. In 1952 a new radio headquarters was inaugurated in Bucharest.

On 31 December 1956, public television began broadcasting, initially with a small number of subscribers, although the number quickly increased (there were 500,000 subscribers in 1965 and 1.5 million in 1970). In 1970 the television service received a new headquarters building and its coverage increased to over 80 per cent of the territory. From 1983 colour television was introduced, but in 1985, much to the discontent of the population, the daily programme was reduced to only two hours and broadcasts by the second national channel (TVR 2), which had also hosted regional stations were stopped.

Ceaușescu attracted tremendous hatred from the Romanian people because he deprived them of the right to watch television, to listen to uncensored information on the radio and to read quality newspapers. In 1989, the national television station was broadcasting only two hours a day and the newspapers contained articles obsessively serving the cult of personality, sports news or classified ads. Unlike the communist media, Western radio stations (Voice of America and RFE), which militated against Ceaușescu's dictatorship, had very high audience shares and credibility, although listening to them was officially forbidden and their transmission was jammed. At the end of the communist regime, possessing a satellite dish and a video-player became elements of social prestige. Watching television stations from Bulgaria, Yugoslavia, Hungary or the USSR with the help of dishes became daily practice.

Far from representing the 'fourth power', the media was used as a favourite tool of political propaganda. The critical message was carefully controlled and political leaders were the object of a personality cult.

Performing and visual arts

Turning art into a propaganda tool did not exclude the theatre. At the beginning of the communist era, the theatre was dominated by the influence of Russian plays, which regularly opened the season. According to the Soviet model, new theatres were opened, including in small towns, for the purpose of 'enlightening the people'. A great number of amateur theatre companies were established. Old theatre buildings were extended and culture houses were built in rural areas and small towns, which were used for theatre, music shows, or for political meetings. By the end of the 1960s resources were being invested in new monumental buildings: the I.L. Caragiale Theatre of Bucharest and the National Theatre of Craiova being examples.

From the mid-1950s the number of Soviet plays in the socialist realism style decreased and a comeback to the rules of dramatic art took place. The opening to the West from the mid-1960s facilitated tours abroad by Romanian theatre companies. During the 1980s, the theatre suffered a decline as a result of political control and a reduction in the budgets of cultural institutions.

The conservatories of Bucharest, Cluj and Iași continued and developed their activity. The most important event in the field of classical music was the George Enescu Festival, which was held eleven times from 1958 to 1988. The event was supported by the regime as it offered a positive image abroad. As far as pop music was concerned, starting from 1963 the *Mamaia* festival took place, with a pause between 1977 and 1982. Traditional music was supported by the regime starting in the 1960s, as it strengthened the idea of rediscovering national identity. Western rock was considered 'decadent music' and hardly crossed the barriers of censorship. The alternative to rock music favoured by the PCR was folk music, whose main representation was the *Flacăra* (Flame) Cenacle (1973–85), established by the poet Adrian Păunescu. The *Flacăra* Cenacle became very popular, but was stopped after 1,615 shows as a result of a stampede in which five people were killed.

The movie industry was also nationalized. With Soviet assistance, a large amount of projection equipment was bought to be used for propaganda campaigns (literacy, collectivization). Film studios were built near Bucharest in order to make original productions. Starting in the 1960s, movies with higher budgets were produced, the predominant theme being national history (*Dacii, Mihai Viteazul, Horea*, etc.). The movies with the greatest audience were those directed by Sergiu Nicolaescu, who also had the leading role in a number of them (Căliman 2000; Vasile 2011).

The elimination of a 'bourgeois' influence was also carried out in the field of the visual arts. Public sculpture and painting (especially murals) were privileged by the regime, as they were integrated into official propaganda. The abandonment of socialist realism at the beginning of the 1960s left some place for aesthetic autonomy in painting, sculpture and other decorative arts. Despite its limited freedom of expression, the communist regime offered significant and regular resources for artists, who managed to maintain a decent standard of living, so challenges against the regime from artists were rare (Cârneci 2013).

Sport

The communist New Man not only had to be the bearer of Marxist-Leninist progressive ideals, he also had to be a strong person, with a harmoniously developed body maintained by the practice of sport. Youth had to be educated through sports, not just in the spirit of Marxism-Leninism. The sports phenomenon was turned into a means of mobilization in favour of the party-state. Affiliation to the Olympic movement (Romania came back in 1948 at the Winter Olympic Games held in St Moritz) turned into useful propaganda at international level, and the successes of communist states' sportspeople were promoted as victories against the 'capitalist imperialist' system. Sportspeople were considered 'the best ambassadors' of communism.

In 1953, Bucharest hosted the World Youth and Students' Festival, during which several sports competitions unfolded. In preparation for the event, a huge stadium with a capacity of 80,000 was built (called *23 August*). Ceaușescu would go on to use the Olympic Games in international politics. Romania participated in both the 1980 Summer Olympic Games held in Moscow, which were boycotted by the US, and also in the 1984 Summer Olympics held in Los Angeles, which were boycotted by the USSR and fourteen other countries from the Soviet sphere of influence.

Apart from the propaganda use of sports events by the PCR, after the Second World War sport turned into a mass phenomenon. In 1949, the position of the new regime concerning the issue of sport was synthesized (PMR 1949): it had to include all socio-professional categories (including peasants and the military); the sports movement could not be limited to football, but had to include the development of several other sports. The

Physical Culture and Sport Committee was established (replaced in 1967 with the National Council for Physical Education and Sport) and physical education became mandatory within the education system, including universities. Nicolae Ceaușescu continued his support for sport and sports events were included in his personality cult. Following Romanian success at the Summer Olympics of 1976, a new sports competition was launched at national level, called the *Daciada*. Although it was dedicated to amateur sportspeople, being a mass competition, professionals were also encouraged to compete, to improve their performances. Held every two years, the *Daciada* was also integrated into the Ceaușescu family personality cult.

From the very start of taking over power, the PCR was preoccupied with creating an extended network of amateur sports associations and clubs within enterprises, trade unions and cities. Within the army a sports club was created in 1947, which took the name *Steaua* (The Star) in 1961. Following rivalry with the army, the personnel of the Ministry of the Interior created their own sports club in 1948, called, in the Soviet tradition, *Dinamo*. During the 1980s, the *Miliția* and *Securitate* from Bucharest had a football team which they supported, *Victoria*. Investment in sports infrastructure increased. This was not just limited to stadiums (at least one seating several thousand in each important city), but also included building gyms, swimming pools and sports centres.

Football results at international level were not significant, with the exception of Steaua's winning of the European Cup after a dramatic final against FC Barcelona in 1986. The men's handball team managed to win four world cups between 1961 and 1974. The most important Olympic results were gymnastics, rowing and canoeing. The result with the greatest sports and media impact was the score of 10 obtained by gymnast Nadia Comăneci at the Summer Olympics in Montreal in 1976. Another world-class sportsman was Ilie Năstase in tennis, who was world number one in 1972–3.

At ten Summer Olympic Games (Helsinki 1952 to Seoul 1988) Romania garnered fifty-five gold, sixty-three silver and eighty-one bronze medals. The best results were recorded in the 1984 Summer Olympics in Los Angeles, where Romania took second place (in the absence of the USSR, but ahead of West Germany and China), with fifty-three medals, twenty of them gold. It was the peak of Romania's international sporting achievements obtained despite the increasingly persistent economic crisis within the country.

Ecclesiastical institutions

Starting with Karl Marx, communist ideology had stated that religion was the 'opium of the people', which had to be counteracted with the arguments of historical and scientific materialism. Atheism was to be the axiological attribute of the New Man. However, the ideological objectives of Marxism-Leninism were one thing, the reality of leading society was another. Stalin was forced to move from religious persecution to accommodating the Russian Orthodox Church during the Second World War, using it to mobilize society.

Within the communist constitutions of 1948, 1952 and 1965, freedom of conscience was guaranteed by the state. Religious denominations could administer themselves freely, but their organization and functioning had to be approved by the government. Consecrating the principle of the secular state, the constitutions established that 'school is separated from church' and confessional schools of all denominations were abolished. Building new places of worship was difficult, needing approval from the state.

The exercise of the right to religious freedom turned into a social practice that was tolerated but not encouraged, as individuals were afraid of being socially stigmatized or watched by the *Securitate* for participating in religious ceremonies (weddings, baptisms and funerals). Religious holidays were not officially recognized, being considered working days. An attempt was made to replace Christian with pre-Christian mythology. From 1949 onwards, *Moş Crăciun* (Father Christmas) was replaced with *Moş Gerilă* (Jack Frost), of Russian inspiration, who brought presents on New Year's Eve.

Breaching constitutional provisions and international regulations in the field of fundamental rights, the communist regime tried, by various means, to control all ecclesiastical institutions. The communist leaders knew they could have serious opponents among the ecclesiastical hierarchy, so they tried to subordinate or even destroy it. Under the 1948 Law of Religions, the state recognized fourteen religious denominations, whose organization was controlled by the Ministry of Religions, which became the Department of Religions in 1957. Under the political control of the communists, this governmental institution closely collaborated with the *Securitate* and the *Miliţia* (especially in rural areas), to attract collaborators or promote controllable hierarchies, from the bottom levels up to the high clergy (Petcu 2005).

The communists' attitude towards religious denominations was differentiated. Their intention of controlling *Biserica Ortodoxă Română* (BOR – the Romanian Orthodox Church) was manifested as early as 1944, when the so-called 'democratic priests' emerged. Their leader, Constantin Burducea (a former ML member) became Minister of Religions in the Groza government. On the pretext of the fight against 'fascists', some diocese were dismantled (such as that of the Metropolitan of Oltenia) and parts of the hostile hierarchy were retired. In 1948, Justinian Marina was elected as Patriarch; he openly collaborated with the communist regime, but he saved monasticism, which the communists had intended to abolish. The following patriarchs, Iustin Moisescu (1977–86) and Teoctist Arăpaşu (1986–2007) continued the strategy of accommodation with the communist regime, in order to avoid open conflict (Gillet 2001). Collaboration with the communist state was justified by the concept of 'symphony' between the political authority and the church, according to which believers had to recognize the authority of *Caesar* (the state) (Leuştean 2008: 23). After the regime turned towards national-communism at the end of 1960s, the BOR was a de facto partner in the political use of the patriotic feelings of the population. Starting with 1968, the role of the BOR in building national identity was recognized by Ceauşescu. This did not, however, mean the creation of a relationship based on trust between party and church; the *Securitate* continued to watch the BOR, for which purpose it enrolled numerous collaborators from among the Orthodox clergy, at all levels.

Orthodox monasticism was not abolished, but it was numerically reduced. In 1959–60 alone, no less than ninety-two Orthodox monasteries were disbanded, but over 100 remained functional. Religious classes were forbidden in schools and theological education at university level was subject to constraints. Dozens of churches were victims of the destructive plan of 'territorial systematization', by relocation or demolition. The Văcărești Monastery of Bucharest, built in the eighteenth century, was the most important church to be demolished, in spite of international protests.

Over 2,000 Orthodox priests and monks were arrested during the Gheorghiu-Dej regime, under various accusations, from 'Legionarism' to opposition to collectivization (Rădulescu 2011: 194–204).

Total repression was unleashed against *Biserica Greco-Catolică* (BGC – the Greek-Catholic Church), as a result of Soviet orders, in the context of the USSR offensive against the Vatican, which was considered an instrument of capitalist imperialism. The Groza government failed to convince the Greek-Catholic clergy to accept union with the BOR. On 1 December 1948, the BGC was dissolved and all its possessions were nationalized. Part of them were transferred to the BOR, which supported the 'unification' action, considering it 'a historical act for the Romanian people' (Patriarch Justinian). The six bishops of the BGC were arrested and their conversion to Orthodoxy was attempted. Six bishops clandestinely appointed were also arrested. Following failure to enrol them into the BOR, they were sent to prison, where some of them died. The whole ecclesiastical elite, but also ordinary BGC priests, were subjected to repression by imprisonment or mandatory residence. There were some Greek-Catholic priests, however, who accepted the 'union' in order to save their lives. The BGC continued to function clandestinely, but all efforts on the part of the Vatican to re-establish the Church failed. Greek-Catholic believers were systematically watched by the *Securitate* (Vasile 2003).

The communist regime also hit hard at the Roman Catholic Church (BRC), after denouncing the *Concordat* between Romania and the Holy See on 17 June 1948. Confessional schools and religious congregations were disbanded. Most properties were nationalized and some of the dioceses were abolished. Bishops and a part of the Roman Catholic clergy, monks and nuns were arrested. The repression continued until 1964, and was followed by *Securitate* surveillance and enrolment of collaborators from among the clergy and laity.

Other historical churches (Lutheran, Reformed and Unitarian) fared no better during the communist regime. A considerable part of the ecclesiastical hierarchy was either arrested or subjected to forms of repression. Even if it did not undertake massive actions of repression against the leadership of the Jewish faith, the communist regime tried to attract it towards collaboration. The Muslim faith was subjected to repression: dozens of mullahs were arrested. Turks and Tatars were watched in case they proved to have subversive connections with Turkey, a NATO member state.

On the basis of the Law of Religions of 1948 the state recognized the existence of four non-traditional Protestant denominations: Baptist, Pentecostal, Seventh-day Adventist and Evangelical. Initially regarded with sympathy (they rejected the ecclesiastic hierarchy of the historical denominations, and as it was hoped that they could be attracted towards collaboration) these denominations came to be treated with hostility, due both to their religious proselytism and to their relationships with similar denominations in the West (Chivu-Duța 2007: 143–90). During the 1980s, non-traditional Protestant denominations saw a fast numerical rise, as the BOR was considered compromised. The wish of members of these denominations to emigrate to the West brought them onto a collision course with the Ceaușescu regime; they were politically persecuted and socially marginalized. Despite repeated international protests during the 1980s, the situation regarding freedom of belief did not improve.

Policies regarding ethnic minorities

The policy regarding ethnic minorities underwent significant fluctuations during the 1945–89 period. Until the full establishment of communism, the problems created by the war were predominant: dealing with the German and Jewish minorities, and preventing Romanian–Hungarian conflicts in Transylvania until the clarification of the border issue following the Peace Treaty. The PCR cooperated with minorities in order to consolidate its power. In 1948, the communist regime considered the issue of minorities solved, in alignment with proletarian internationalism. The integrated concept was the Soviet-inspired 'socialist nation', in which ethnic groups coexisted in harmony, as a result of respecting each other's cultural identity. By using the concept of 'co-inhabiting nationalities' the vision of a multi-ethnic society was promoted, in which harmony predominated, without hierarchy according to ethnic criteria, nationalities being presumed to be equal. The only acceptable cleavage in society was the social one, generated by the theory of class struggle, and not the national one, originating from the period of 'bourgeois order'. According to the communist constitutions, ethnic groups had the right to use their mother tongue in education at all levels. In administration and justice the mother tongue could be used orally and in writing; public servants were appointed who knew the languages of the local population. The vernacular language could be used in books, newspapers and theatres.

A gradual change in the attitude towards minorities started to emerge at the end of the 1950s, with the affirmation of national identity and sovereignty. Ethnic minorities benefited from the liberalization of social life during the first years of the Ceaușescu regime. Following the transition to national-communism after 1971, however, the situation of minorities started to deteriorate, to reach a paroxysm in the mid-1980s, when Ceaușescu tried to increase solidarity among the majority population through nationalism (Copilaș 2015).

Hungarians

At the end of the Second World War, Hungarians in Romania hoped that their fate would be different from that which had followed the dissolution of Austro-Hungary, either through a part of Transylvania being given to Hungary or by their being granted a broad territorial autonomy. The first signs seemed favourable, as in May 1945 the existence of two distinct universities in Cluj was confirmed: Babeş (Romanian) and Bolyai (Hungarian). *Uniunea Populară Maghiară* (UPM – the Hungarian Popular Union) became the political instrument of the Hungarian elites, who allied themselves with the communists. After the signing of the Paris Peace Treaty in 1947, the Hungarian elites were demoralized, especially as restrictions on travel to Hungary were imposed.

In 1952, Stalin decided to create the Hungarian Autonomous Region, which included 13 per cent of Transylvania's territory, much to the surprise of the Romanian Communist leaders (Bottoni 2010: 103). The new administrative-territorial structure was mentioned in the 1952 Constitution. However, Hungarians were also subjected to repression and their resistance against collectivization was punished just as in the case of ethnic Romanians. Following the 1956 Hungarian Revolution, repressive actions of a political, not an ethnic character, were directed upon Romanian society as a whole (Bottoni 2010: 370), but they were particularly directed against ethnic Hungarians. The unification of Babeş and Bolyai universities in Cluj in 1959 was motivated by the fear that an anti-communist intellectual opposition might take shape, following the model of Budapest. Leadership posts in the unified university were equally divided between ethnic Romanians and Hungarians.

Wishing to break with Gheorghiu-Dej's heritage, in 1968 Ceauşescu disbanded the Hungarian Autonomous Region, as part of a national administrative reform. The Hungarian community was affected by the dissolution of confessional schools, but education in Hungarian was maintained in state schools. Books and newspapers in Hungarian, as well as theatres and other cultural structures were supported by the state, as they were for other minorities (Olti and Gidó 2009). The Hungarian language was also used in administration. From 1958, Radio Târgu Mureş broadcast shows in Hungarian. In 1969 shows in Hungarian and German were launched on Romanian Television, although they were discontinued in 1985, in the context of reducing the programme to two hours per day.

During the 1980s a number of Hungarian high schools were disbanded and the general policy of ethnic homogenization through the system of compulsory placement also affected Hungarian elites, who were sent to jobs outside Transylvania. Political tensions between Bucharest and Budapest after 1980 also marked the Hungarian local community, which manifested its wish for legal emigration or escape towards the 'goulash socialism' of Hungary. Simultaneously, the *Securitate* intensified the process of recruiting collaborators among ethnic Hungarians, in order to keep watch on 'nationalist-chauvinistic manifestations'.

Germans

After Romania's withdrawal from the alliance with Hitler, the fate of the German community in Romania dramatically changed, as they bore a Nazi stigma. The German Ethnic Group (GEG), established following Germany's request in November 1940, included most of the ethnic Germans (Saxons and Swabians) in Romania. On 7 October 1944, the GEG was dissolved through a royal decree and its goods were nationalized.

This was only the beginning of the repression, as GEG members were now deprived of their civil rights. Following an imperative request from Moscow and in spite of protests from Bucharest, in January 1945 the deportation of Germans to the USSR began (69,332 were deported from the territory of Romania and 5,324 from western Transylvania under the Hungarian administration). Of those deported, only two-thirds returned to Romania in 1948–9 (Tismăneanu et al. 2007: 359; Betea et al. 2012).

Ethnic Germans received a heavy blow with the agrarian law of 1945, following which a good part of their properties were confiscated. Then, in 1954, in order to put right some of these errors, over 64,000 peasant families received land from state reserves, which was used to bring them into GACs.

The Communist leaders wanted to expel all ethnic Germans from Romania, but the Soviets did not agree with a similar solution to that applied in Czechoslovakia, Poland and Hungary. Romania remained the country with the largest German community in Eastern Europe. There was an issue of reuniting German families from Romania and divided Germany. At the beginning of the 1950s, the Groza government allowed the emigration of only small numbers of Germans, in spite of increasing demands. In this context, following the model of Jewish emigration, in 1962 secret agreements were established between Romania and West Germany in order to allow for the emigration of ethnic Germans. The *Securitate* was the main institution in charge of this secret operation. In exchange for granting emigration permission, variable sums were paid, according to the educational level of each person (e. g. 1,800 German Marks for an ordinary person, 11,000 Marks for a university graduate). The immoral sale of ethnic Germans fuelled the wish of the Communist leaders not just for cash, but also credit and technology delivery or other advantages (Dobre et al. 2011). Up until 1989, approximately 230,000 ethnic Germans were involved in this kind of 'ransom'. Over 150,000 more left Romania in 1990–3, and the German community was reduced to a minor presence.

The elimination of collective civil bans on Germans in 1948 led to the gradual normalization of this minority's situation. Cultural rights, as they were established by the regime, were restored. For example, in 1953, the German section of the State Theatre in Timișoara was founded and a similar section in Sibiu was opened in 1956. *Neuer Weg* was the main German-language newspaper in Romania. In spite of the respect shown for their cultural identity, Germans were attracted by the mirage of life in capitalist Germany and the main collective objective was emigration at any cost.

Jews

The main phenomenon marking the Jewish community was emigration to Palestine/Israel. On 7 May 1946, the ship *Max Nordau* left for Palestine from the port of Constanța, carrying 1,754 passengers. Up until 1989, there were several waves of Jewish emigration to Israel or the West. Emigration was conditional on payment of 'compensation', which differed according to the educational level of the people in question (from a few US dollars in some cases to US$10,000 for a doctor). The essential role in the operation of selling Jews (in exchange for money, agricultural products or technology) was again played by the *Securitate*, which intermediated several agreements with Israel (Ioanid 2015). As in the case of German emigration, the dynamic of selling Jews was approved at the highest political level. By 1989 there were only 25,000–30,000 Jewish people left in Romania.

The life of the Jewish community followed the general line of the rest of society. Chief Rabbi Alexandru Şafran, who did not adhere to PCR politics, was forced to leave Romania in 1948, and was replaced by the more pragmatic Moses Rosen. Jewish cultural organizations aligned themselves with the regime and *Partidul Evreiesc* (the Jewish Party) dissolved itself (Tismăneanu et al. 2007: 368–70). *Comitetul Democratic Evreiesc* (the Jewish Democratic Committee), a mass organization created in 1945 to support the Communists, was dissolved in 1953, in the context of Stalinist anti-Semitism. Repression did not spare the leaders of the Jewish community; from 1949 to 1953, no fewer than twenty trials of Romanian Zionists were organized (Rotman 2004). The Jewish faith was officially recognized by the state which supported the Yiddish media and Jewish theatre. Like the Germans, Jews also lived during communism with the objective of emigrating, in their case to Israel, despite the uncertainty created by war in the Middle East.

Roma and other minorities

As they were a minority without elites, the main problem for the communist regime in the case of the Roma was integration through settlement. The Roma were recognized as an ethnic minority only in 1990; during the communist period they were denied the status of 'co-inhabiting nationality', as they were considered a social, not an ethnic minority (Achim 2010). The PCR saw the distinctiveness of the Roma as a social issue, so efforts were made to encourage their schooling and assimilation by offering jobs and housing. In 1962, measures were taken for settling nomadic Roma. 'Social parasitism' was countered by the regime by repressive tools for social integration. From 1977 to 1983, over 65,000 Roma were settled, but due to their precarious education and the preservation of their clans, they did not adapt to the new way of life (Achim 2004b: 196).

The other ethnic minorities (Armenians, Bulgarians, Poles, Russians, Serbs, Slovaks, Tatars, Turks and Ukrainians) were not submitted to systematic repression, and led their lives under the same conditions as the Romanian majority.

CHAPTER 7
THE ECONOMY

Any account of the history of economic life in Romania during the communist period has to overcome the barrier of the unreliability of official statistical information concerning macroeconomic data. As the success of the communist regime was related by its own official propaganda on economic results, which had of necessity to be glorious in order to offer legitimacy to the PCR, official statistics were structurally flawed. Reconstructing the statistical data is impossible, as there were no pre-defined criteria for the falsification of information, which was manipulated according to the political context. In a regime of generalized lies, the manipulation of statistical information became a fact of everyday life.

The delimitation of a rigid chronology concerning economic history is a risky enterprise, as it is impossible to establish single moments which determined profound changes in the economy. Economic cycles follow other rhythms than political life and the economy has multiple determinants, which cannot be easily controlled by the political authorities (for example, the contagion of international economic crises). Nevertheless, we can outline a number of stages in the post-war economic history of Romania. The first of these (1945–8) was post-war reconstruction, characterized by the payment of war debts to the USSR, simultaneously with transition to the command economy. During the second stage (1949/50–60/62), the command economy was fully established, following nationalizations and the collectivization of agriculture. The main features were rapid industrialization, total collectivization and economic integration in the Soviet bloc through the COMECON. The third stage (1962–80/82) was dominated by the continuation, acceleration and diversification of industrialization, in the context of economic opening to the West and to extra-European areas (the Middle East, Africa and South-East Asia). The fourth stage (1982–9) was marked by the increasing influence of the raw materials crisis (which began, at international level, with the first 'oil shock' of 1973) on industry, which became non-competitive. The level of foreign debt increased due to the fact that industrialization was achieved by means of international credits. Ceauşescu tried to stop economic stagnation using austerity and autarchy to repay foreign debt at an accelerated pace. This was the period when the economy was influenced to the highest extent by personal (irrational) decisions. Megalomaniac building projects consumed a part of the resources which could have been orientated towards industrial recovery and increasing the standard of living of the population.

In spite of the previously mentioned methodological issues concerning the use of statistical data from the communist period, a complex attempt at evaluating the dynamic

Table 7.1 Total and per capita average GDP dynamic (1945–89)

Years	GDP in million dollars 2000 (ppc*)	GDP per capita in dollars 2000 (ppc*)
1945–7**	10,621	672
1950–4	28,375	1,700
1955–9	39,869	2,241
1960–4	55,653	2,977
1965–9	84,700	4,350
1970–4	129,653	6,270
1975–9	179,123	8,264
1985–9	211,037	9,401

Note: * PPC – Peercoin. ** For the years 1948–9 there is no data available.
Source: Axenciuc 2012: 37.

of Romania's Gross Domestic Product (GDP) (Axenciuc 2012) emphasizes a few major elements (see Table 7.1). The average GDP during the first three years after the end of the war was the equivalent of US$10.6 billion at 2000 currency values, and the GDP first exceeded US$100 billion in 1970, and US$200 billion in 1979. The investigation of the national wealth dynamic reveals the fact that, compared to 1950, the total GDP multiplied 10.2 times until 1989, while the value reported per capita during the same period increased 7.2 times. The situation can be explained by the fact that the demographic dynamic was quicker than the economic dynamic (Axenciuc 2012: 40).

The legacy of war

Romania's territory was not subjected to systematic destruction during the Second World War, and US bombings between 1942 and 1944, although on a relatively massive scale, did not dramatically affect the economic infrastructure. The destruction was also limited as a result of Romania's withdrawal from the war alongside Germany on 23 August 1944. In spite of this, in the context of losing Bessarabia and northern Bukovina to the USSR and southern Dobrogea to Bulgaria, the national revenue in 1945 was half that of 1938 (Constantinescu 2000: 93). Romania was confronted, like most countries after the war, with the issue of industrial conversion and finding jobs for demobilized servicemen. The state was involved through governmental orders for metallurgy and the car industry. The whole of Europe was in ruins and the economic crisis was profound.

Romania was confronted in 1945–6 with a prolonged drought which severely reduced agricultural production. In Moldavia and Oltenia, the drought went on until 1947. Food shortages fuelled both speculation and inflation, which reached high levels. The government created controlled-price stores (called *economate*), by which a third of the country's population was supplied. But administrative measures could not compensate for the deficit of products and raw materials necessary to re-launch production.

In the wake of actions to eliminate the consequences of war and prepare for the command economy, the agrarian reform was carried out in 1945, and the National Bank was nationalized in 1946, monetary stabilization was accomplished in 1947, the main means of production were nationalized in 1948 and a state monopoly over foreign trade was established in 1949.

Economic hardships were increased by payment of the war debt to the Soviet Union, as established by the Armistice Convention. Its value was US$300 million (at an exchange rate of US$35 for a gold ounce), to be paid in six years, which amounted to over 55 per cent of Romania's national income in 1945. The war debt was not paid in money, but in goods. Even before the war was over, the Soviets transferred several factories to the USSR, together with raw materials, the maritime and river merchant fleets, 490 railway locomotives and 7,200 wagons. Some of this was returned by the Soviets to Romania, as proof of 'friendship with the democratic-popular regime', but the massive 'booty' burdened the development of the national economy (Murgescu 2010: 333–4).

Soviet domination over Romania's economy acquired new legal forms as a result of the bilateral economic cooperation treaty signed in Moscow on 8 May 1945. On the basis of this agreement sixteen joint Soviet-Romanian enterprises (Sovrom) were created on an equal basis in key economic fields. The Soviet contribution mainly consisted of German properties (or 'other enemy capital') on Romania's territory. Until 1948, Romania accepted any economic demands of the Soviets through mixed companies; thereafter, until their dissolution in 1956, there was an attempt to respect the principle of parity collaboration (Banu 2004: 145). Following the dissolution of Sovrom, Romania repurchased the Soviet share of these companies.

The command economy

The nationalization of the economy in 1948–50 was undertaken to introduce centralized command economy mechanisms, following the Soviet model. The Marxist-Leninist argument was that centralized planning was necessary because only thus could a quick and balanced development of the economy be achieved. A command economy was the instrument by which the objectives of the Communist Party could be realized. The first step was the creation, in 1948, of the *Comisia de Stat a Planificării* (CSP – State Planning Commission), which changed its name in 1952 to the State Planning Committee. This was an administrative institution subordinated to the government, and had a key role in economic planning. Another important institution for the command economy was the State Committee for Prices (1950), which approved and monitored prices in the economy (Costache 2012: 76).

Conscious of the difficulties of transition from an economy based on supply and demand to one based on centralized planning, the PMR leaders showed prudence, in spite of support from Soviet advisors. In 1949 and 1950 the economy was led on the basis of annual plans. From 1951, simultaneously with other COMECON countries, Romania took over the Soviet model of five-year plans, which had been introduced in the USSR as early as 1928 (Oprişan 1951). Economic planning was synchronized with the fifth five-year plan of the USSR (1951–5), thus increasing economic integration within the Soviet bloc.

Five-year plans were elaborated starting from the general objectives established by the PMR/PCR, and ministries, enterprises and the administration had to comply with them. Reaching bureaucratically established economic results by neglecting the real economy was a fundamental objective of the PMR/PCR (Mureşan 2012: 253–8).

The command economy also brought about changes in the employee income policy, by making it more rigid. In 1950 a Labour Code favourable to employees (Law no. 3 of 1950) was introduced, establishing a regular working day of eight hours. In 1972 a new Labour Code was adopted (Law no. 10), according to which 'Remuneration is made according to the quantity, quality and social importance of labour, ensuring equal remuneration for equal labour' (art. 81, para. 2). The main problem of labour relations during the communist period was the weak motivation of people to work more and more efficiently. The PCR tried to motivate employees to be more efficient by using ideological and ethical arguments, but the labour force was used extensively. During those times, it was said, in order to emphasize the domination of bureaucracy over the working class, that 'ten dig and one keeps the files!'.

In the context of the economic crisis at the beginning of the 1980s, Ceauşescu tried to remedy the situation by using labour accountability and salary differentiation according to performance. The model was not new, having already been adopted in Tito's Yugoslavia as early as 1950. Law no. 2 of 1983 provided that: 'Working people, as owners, producers and beneficiaries, are fully accountable for the good housekeeping of socialist property belonging to the entire people, their revenues being closely related to production achievement, increasing labour productivity and the economic efficiency of the whole activity'. Employees formally became owners of the enterprises in which they worked and were accountable for self-management. To the discontent of workers, their income was no longer guaranteed, as the principle of 'global agreement' was introduced and incomes became related to the achievement of the plan. The new policy of motivating employees did not have the envisaged effects, as the central planning achieved by the CSP lacked realism. The perverse effect was that false reporting of production increased and the quality of products decreased even further. The party bureaucracy entered into a game of general complicity with the technocrats in order to camouflage reality and create the appearance of high productivity. However, where plans could not be achieved, those who were financially penalized belonged to the auxiliary or leadership staff and not to the working class. The main consequence of the apparent economic decentralization and labour accountability was a deeper economic crisis and a dramatic decrease in product quality; few Romanian products were accepted abroad, even within contracts politically negotiated with countries in the Third World (Burakowski 2011: 276).

Simultaneously with centralized planning at national level, the party assumed the role of 'mobilizing the working class'. The propaganda model was the Soviet one: *Stakhanovism*.

Starting with 1951, the PMR officially assumed the 'Stakhanovite competition' of workers, for intensive labour, for the purpose of accumulating as soon as possible the necessary resources for industrialization. Although references to Stakhanovism disappeared from official propaganda at the end of the 1950s, up until the fall of communism there was a constant preoccupation with the early achievement of five-year plans. At the beginning of the 1970s, Ceaușescu promoted the propaganda formula of achieving 'the five-year plan in four-and-a-half years'.

Agriculture

The main branch of the economy, agriculture, underwent a structural transformation during the post-war period. Connecting to modernization meant that the number of people working in agriculture dropped from 6.2 million in 1950 to 3 million in 1989. This was the cumulative consequence of collectivization, of introducing modern technology and of industrialization. Due to the reduced and uncertain incomes of peasants and industrialization, the labour force remaining in agriculture underwent a rapid aging process after 1970.

The structure of agricultural property went through dramatic changes. After the fragmentation of property following the agrarian reform of 1945, the nationalization and collectivization processes begun in 1949 gradually brought about the concentration of property and the expansion of its exploitation. The total agricultural area in 1960 was 14.54 million hectares, which was extended through deforestation and draining to 15 million hectares by 1985. After the completion of collectivization, the structure of property remained relatively stable. A first form was that of State Agricultural Households (renamed Întreprinderi Agricole de Stat, IAS – State Agricultural Enterprises in 1967), created after the agrarian reform of 1945, after the nationalizations of March 1949 or after various 'voluntary donations' during the collectivization period. The property of the state increased from 11.8 per cent of the total agricultural land in 1962 to 13.9 per cent in 1989. IASs were elite farms, which incorporated animal and plant production; there were 560 in 1960 and 411 in 1989 (Lup 2014: 149).

The second form of property was cooperative ownership. In 1965, TOZs and GACs were turned into CAP. The main phenomenon was that of concentrating surfaces and administrative structures: in 1962 there were 5,398 CAPs, covering 62.5 per cent of the agricultural surface, but by 1989 the number had been reduced to 3,776, covering 60.7 per cent of the total agricultural area. The form of private households was preserved in mountain areas, under the form of lots received by peasants for exploitation to their own benefit, but their share amounted to under 10 per cent of agricultural land.

In agriculture, important efforts were made for modernization. In 1945, there were fewer than 2,000 agronomists in Romania. Agricultural education was allocated important resources, most of them for vocational schools (agricultural mechanics and technicians). From 1949 to 1989, around 75,000 specialists with higher education were trained

Table 7.2 Evolution of the employed population per activity fields (1950–89)

Field (thousand people / per cent)	1950	1965	1980	1989
Industry	1,000.7	1,862.9	3,678.8	4,169
	(12%)	(19.2%)	(35.6%)	(38.1%)
Construction	186.3	609.3	857.4	766.7
	(2.4%)	(6.4%)	(8.5%)	(7%)
Agriculture	6,207.7	5,476.5	3,048.1	3,012.3
	(74.1%)	(56.5%)	(29.5%)	(27.5%)
Transport and communications	168.6	348.9	707.7	757.1
	(2.2%)	(3.7%)	(6.9%)	(6.9%)
Other fields	775.3	1,367.6	2,016.5	2,240.6
	(9.3%)	(16.2%)	(19.5%)	(20.5%)

Source: Constantinescu 2000: 493.

(agronomists, zoo-technicians, veterinarians, mechanical engineers), 150,000 agricultural technicians and 40,000 graduates of agricultural high schools (Lup 2014: 418).

The technical endowment of agriculture saw obvious progress. From fewer than 9,000 tractors in Romania in 1945, their number gradually increased to 13,700 in 1950, 107,300 in 1970 and 151,700 in 1989. Simultaneously, the number of other items of agricultural equipment (combines, seeders, ploughs, etc.) also increased. From the 1970s chemical fertilizers were widely used. The potentially irrigated surface grew significantly, from less than 0.1 million hectares in 1950 to 3.1 million hectares in 1989.

Agriculture followed the path of production diversification. Cereals remained the basis of agriculture, but the areas cultivated with industrial plants (flax and cotton) increased, as did those for supporting animal production (forage plants), vegetables and oil plants (sunflower). Large livestock farms were created, both for cattle and for pigs and poultry. The number and dimensions of orchards and vineyards also increased.

The surface of forests remained stable (6.4 million hectares), in spite of industrial timber exploitation. This was due to systematic programmes of forestation and forest management.

This real progress was undermined by the system of organizing the economy. Production planning was centralized and prices were fixed, without reflecting real costs. CAPs and IASs had a reduced capitalization and their development was difficult. The incomes of agricultural workers fluctuated and were smaller than those of industrial workers. For these reasons, socialist agriculture remained extensive rather than intensive, with a lower productivity than in the countries of Western Europe. For example, milk and cereal production was systematically lower in Romania than in France (Lup 2014: 562, 602). However, agriculture fulfilled its main mission from the PCR perspective: supporting industrialization and urbanization by providing cheap food for a growing population and as a resource for export (Murgescu 2010: 368). Hard currency obtained from trade in agricultural products was mainly used for acquiring industrial technologies.

The cycle of underdevelopment was not broken, however, as agricultural products were exported at a small profit and technology imports had a high added value.

The industrialization of the economy

The fundamental political and economic objective of the communist regime was industrialization. Investment in industrialization exceeded 40 per cent of the total, and in 1980 it accounted for more than half of the total capital. The absolute priorities were industries in 'group A' (the steel industry, car-making and mining), while those in 'group B' (production of consumer goods, textiles and food) were considered of secondary importance. Industrial development was extensive, being manifested in an increase in the number of enterprises (while their productivity was secondary); an accumulation of fixed assets through several investment programmes (though in the 1980s, wear and tear of equipment began to affect productivity and the use of obsolete technology further reduced competitiveness); and an accelerated increase in the population employed in industry up until 1980, after which the rhythm decreased in the context of territorial homogenization policies on the urban–rural axis (Mureşan 2012: 260–2).

Dividing the national income into a consumption fund and an accumulation fund during the eight five-year plans indicates the following dynamic: in 1951–5, the consumption fund was 75.7 per cent (the rest being the accumulation fund); in 1955–60, the consumption fund increased to 82.9 per cent, as a result of de-Stalinization; in 1961–5, the consumption fund decreased to 74.5 per cent following the resumption of industrialization, and the trend continued during the next five-year plans (1966–70, 70.5 per cent; 1971–5, 66.3 per cent; 1976–80, 64 per cent); the consumption fund increased again during the last two five-year plans (1981–5, 69.3 per cent; 1985–9, 74.3 per cent), as a result of the repayment of foreign debt and reduced investment (Murgescu 2010: 337).

The first plan that had a major impact on both the economy and on society was electrification (Petrescu 2010: 129). Launched in 1950, the ten-year plan (1951–60) aimed to connect villages to the electricity network (from 445 to 13,000). New units for producing electrical energy were created: hydropower plants (Porţile de Fier, Bicaz), thermoelectric plants (Paroşeni, Işalniţa), and, starting from 1980, the grandiose project of a five-reactor thermonuclear plant (Cernavodă) with the support of a Canadian consortium (though, in fact, only two reactors were finalized, in 1996 and 2007). Closely linked with energy production was development of coal mining. As a consequence, energy production increased from 130 kWh per inhabitant in 1950 to 3,276 kWh per inhabitant in 1989.

Metallurgy was considered to be pivotal to the economy, and together with the extension of older plants in Reşiţa and Hunedoara, new ironworks were built in Galaţi and Târgovişte, as well as plants for nonferrous metals (Slatina). In close relation with metallurgy, the car industry developed. Romania produced cars under Renault (Dacia) and Citroën (Oltcit) licences, diesel and electric locomotives, heavy ocean vessels, oil extraction equipment and aircraft. The petrochemicals industry developed rapidly during the 1970s, on the basis of the chemical industry created during previous

Table 7.3 Percentage structure (%) according to investment destination (1950–89)

		1950	1960	1970	1980	1985	1989
Industry	Total	43.6	42.7	47.5	50.9	48.4	43.7
	Group A*	37.6	36.3	40.2	42.7	43.5	37.7
	Group B**	6	6.4	7.3	8.2	4.9	6
Construction		5.9	1.9	4.5	4.6	4.6	4.7
Agriculture and forestry		11.8	19.7	16.4	13.3	18.2	17.5
Transport		14.9	7.4	9.8	11.2	10.3	10.3
Communications		0.6	0.7	0.8	0.8	0.4	0.4
Merchandise circulation		2.3	2.7	3.5	2.2	2.1	2.4
Municipal housing and other non-productive provision of goods		12.2	19	12.7	13.5	13	14.9
Education, art, culture		3.1	2.6	2	1.3	0.4	1.1
Science		1.7	1.2	0.5	0.6	0.6	1.0
Healthcare and social assistance		2.4	1.4	1.4	0.5	0.4	0.3
Administration		1.2	0.6	0.6	0.6	0.6	4.1
Other branches		0.3	0.2	0.2	0.5	1.1	0.4

Note: * Group A: heavy industry, mining, steel industry, etc. ** Group B: Industries producing consumer goods.

Source: Murgescu 2010: 338.

decades. Light industry had a secondary role as regards investment and salaries. The textile, footwear and leather industries also developed, being mainly orientated towards exports.

The general strategy for developing heavy industry during the 1960s was to acquire technology from the West, often on credit, and to use cheaper raw materials from the USSR. Exports were mainly orientated towards the COMECON and Third World countries. During the 1980s a serious economic crisis occurred, caused both by increasing prices of raw materials and by the decision to make early repayment of Romania's foreign debt. Investment in industry could not be continued and its equipment and technology became uncompetitive; it was obsolete and worn out as a result of overuse.

The civil and industrial construction sector was also supported by industrialization and urbanization. From 1951 to 1989, over 5.5 million homes were built, almost 3 million of them with the funds of the state, enterprises and cooperative organizations and the other 2.5 million with the population's own funds. The state ensured cheap financing for home building and purchasing. Up until 1970, the state and the enterprises built only 750,000 apartments, the remainder of the 3 million being entirely created during the Ceauşescu regime (Constantinescu 2000: 184). There were, however, significant differences in comfort and area between private and state homes, the latter usually being smaller. In correlation, the domestic production of furniture and consumer goods (refrigerators, washing machines, television sets and cookers) developed; imports from COMECON countries were increasingly smaller in number and those from the West prohibited.

Industrial buildings, public architecture and hydraulic works consumed most of the public resources. The Danube–Black Sea Canal, the Porţile de Fier and Bicaz hydropower plants, the House of the People, the Vidraru dam and the Transfăgărăşan road through the southern Carpathians are only a few of the representative construction projects achieved during the period of the communist regime.

Transport, post and communications

The recovery and development of transport infrastructure destroyed by war was an important preoccupation as early as 1945. The basis of passenger and freight transport was the railway system. Efforts to develop the railway structure since the nineteenth century meant that there was little need to extend it. In 1950 Romania had 10,853 kilometres of railways, which had been increased only to 11,343 kilometres by 1989 (Mureşan 1995: 128). Investment was directed towards modernizing the existing network. In 1989, a third of the network was electrified and the share of double tracks increased from 4.3 per cent in 1950 to 26 per cent in 1989.

The recovery and extension of the road network was a political and economic necessity after 1945. The total length of roads (national, county, local) was 66,460 kilometres, including 11,960 kilometres of national roads. The development of the road infrastructure required its extension and by 1975 it had reached 77,949 kilometres. Subsequently, some local roads were closed in order to turn them into agricultural land, and by 1989 the total length of public roads had decreased to 72,816 kilometres. However, the length of national roads increased to 13,117 kilometres by 1975 and 14,483 kilometres by 1989. The most important problem was motorway building; only a 96-kilometre segment linking Bucharest with Piteşti was completed. Road transport witnessed the highest development, its flexibility being a competitive advantage compared to railways. Urban passenger transport developed as a consequence of rapid urbanization; by 1979 there were transport networks in 223 of the 236 towns. After 1980, urban transport diminished in order to save fuel. In 1979, subway transport was introduced in Bucharest, and it expanded continuously until 1989.

The share of railway transport decreased from 90.7 per cent of passenger transport in 1950 to 35.2 per cent in 1989, and from 81.6 per cent to 29.9 per cent for freight. Road passenger transport increased from 8.8 per cent in 1950 to 64.4 per cent in 1989 and the road transport of goods from 2.8 per cent to 11.1 per cent, during the same interval. The most important increase was in the maritime and river shipping of goods, from 13.8 per cent in 1950 to 56.6 per cent in 1989 (Mureşan 1995: 131–3). The spectacular increase of maritime shipping can be explained by massive investment in the shipbuilding yards of Galați, Constanța and Mangalia amongst others. The main maritime port was Constanța, and the most important river ports were Galați, Orșova and Tulcea.

Air transport developed with difficulty. The main development occurred during the 1970s, following the opening of new airports and the endowment of the state company, Tarom, with several aircraft which were also used on international routes.

Technical progress in the field of radio and communications gradually entered into communist Romania. The network of post offices was extended (1,579 in 1950, 4,596 in 1989), and they became available not only in towns, but in almost all communes. Private telephones increased in number from 0.043 million in 1950 to 2.2 million in 1989 (Constantinescu 2000: 251). The number of telephone subscribers and of newspaper shops increased, but not enough to satisfy private demand.

Trade, services and tourism

The negative consequences of nationalizing property and introducing centralized planning emerged almost instantly in trade and services. While in 1948 over 90 per cent of trade was private, its share drastically diminished until its disappearance during the 1960s. The change of the trading system initially meant a reduction in the number of shops (65,800 in 1950, 50,800 a decade later) and the building of state and cooperative retail chains (the latter being associational structures subordinated to centralized economic planning). From the 1970s the number of shops increased, reaching over 82,000 in 1989 (state and cooperative in equal shares). From the 1960s, so-called 'universal stores' began to be built, positioned at the centre of towns and cities.

The communist regime began and ended under the sign of crisis in domestic trade, mainly concerning strictly necessary products. The legacy of war and the drought of 1945–7 led to a crisis in agricultural production, resulting in speculation and hyperinflation. During the 1980s, queues at food stores reappeared and became systematic, despite the introduction of a system of an individual minimum food basket (through the so-called 'cards'). Speculation with produce and black-market trade became a daily practice that could not be controlled by the repressive apparatus.

Romania's foreign trade reflects the transformation of the economy from one which is predominantly agrarian to one with a significant industrial sector. The structure of imports and exports emphasizes this dynamic. While in 1950, the share of car, machinery and transport equipment was only 4.2 per cent and that of industrial consumer goods was 1.3 per cent, by 1989 these indicators had significantly changed their values: to 29.3 per cent in the first case and 18.1 per cent in the second. The share of food and non-food raw materials systematically decreased with industrialization. The import structure also indicates Romania's economic vulnerabilities: in 1989 more than half was accounted for by fuel, raw materials and metals. Imports of cars, machinery and transport equipment were never less than a quarter of total imports during the whole post-war period, a situation indicating technological dependence on both the West and the USSR.

Romania's foreign trade during the communist period was at first mainly orientated towards socialist countries, but their share later decreased, dropping from 80 per cent in 1950 to less than half at the end of the Ceaușescu regime. Trade with capitalist countries began to develop after 1960, and was accelerated during the 1970s by Romania's joining GATT (General Agreement on Tariffs and Trade) in 1971 and receiving Most Favoured Nation status from the United States in 1975.

During the second half of the 1970s a third orientation in Romania's trade emerged, different from the COMECON and the West: that is, towards developing countries in Africa, the Middle East, South-East Asia and Latin America. Western markets were hard to conquer for Romanian industrial products, which were poor in quality. Trading relations with COMECON countries often functioned on the basis of barter, which was a disadvantage beyond a certain point for an economy in need of currency liquidity. Trade with developing countries was politically supported by Ceaușescu through several visits to those countries; the level of these trading relations comprised one quarter of Romania's total trading exchanges during the 1980s (Constantinescu 2000: 298; Murgescu 2010: 358).

Romania's balance of trade was predominantly negative from the 1950s to the 1980s, with only some years (1956, 1959–60, 1965, 1976) being positive. From 1980 until the fall of communism the balance was positive. However this was not as a result of changing the economic structure, but due to the drastic and irrational limitation of imports, in the context of the policy of accelerated repayment of foreign debt (Constantinescu 2000: 386). In spite of the predominantly negative parameters regarding the balance of trade, foreign trade represented, on the whole, an important resource for Romania's economic development.

The public services sector witnessed slow development, as a result of the political objective of increasing the capacity to invest in industry. Education and health, essential public services in a modern society, functioned with difficulty in spite of important infrastructure investments, because of reduced budget allocations for materials and salaries.

Cultural and entertainment services (libraries, theatres, cinemas, museums, etc.) developed from the point of view of infrastructure, in the context of urbanization. However, gaps between the urban and the rural environment with regard to access to socio-cultural services could not be overcome, despite all the PCR's efforts.

Tourism was a marginal political preoccupation at the beginning of the communist period, but developed with urbanization. In 1970, a Minister of Tourism was created and activity increased, but after 1980 investment was drastically reduced even in this field. The building of new tourist resorts began as early as the mid-1950s, but the rhythm increased after 1965. By 1970, there were 497 hotels and motels and by 1989 their number had increased to 828. The most spectacular increase was that of camps for children and high-school pupils, from 76 in 1970 to 218 in 1989 (Rădulescu and Stănculescu 2012: 307). The General Trade Union Confederation built tourist spas in Herculane, Felix, Sovata and Călimănești. Youth organizations were assigned tourist resorts in mountain areas (Predeal, Poiana Brașov) or at the seaside (Costinești). New seaside resorts were built (Olimp, Neptun) and existing ones were extended. The number of chalets in mountain areas multiplied. By 1980, at least one hotel had been built in each county or other large town. The accommodation capacity (including private providers) increased from 2.48 million beds in 1970 to 4.18 million beds in 1989. In 1970, no fewer than 5.44 million tourists came to Romania, and in 1989 their number reached 11.6 million (Constantinescu 2000: 318–2).

Until the mid-1960s, Romania was visited for tourism only by citizens of socialist countries; tourism offices were then opened by Romania in the West, in order to demonstrate political opening and to inject hard currency. Romanian citizens' visits abroad, even to socialist countries, were controlled by the regime, as internal tourism was encouraged. Through their trade unions, employees received holiday tickets at reduced prices, and the system of governmental subsidy for tourism was extended to farmers, retired people, students and schoolchildren.

Table 7.4 Percentage structure (%) of exports and imports (1950–89)

Groups of products	1950		1960		1970		1980		1989	
	Exp.	Imp.	Exp.	Imp.	Exp.	Imp.	Exp.	Imp.	Exp.	Imp.
Cars, machinery and transport equipment	4.2	38.3	16.7	33.7	22.4	40.3	24.9	24.6	29.3	25.5
Fuel, mineral raw materials, metals	33.8	23.5	37.0	34.3	22.6	31.1	29.5	50.3	32.1	56
Chemical products, fertilizers, rubber	1.7	4.5	2.1	7.4	7.2	6.0	9.7	6.4	9.5	5.6
Construction materials and accessories	4.4	1.1	2.5	1.0	2.8	1.5	2.2	1.0	2.0	0.9
Non-food raw materials and processed products	28.9	21.4	14.7	13.4	10.2	10.1	4.8	5.7	4.1	5.4
Raw materials for production of food goods (including livestock)	11.6	0.7	9.1	2.5	4.5	2.5	4.2	5.7	0.6	1.7
Food products	14.1	0.3	12.1	2.5	12.1	3.0	8.5	3.2	4.3	1.5
Industrial consumer goods	1.3	10.2	5.8	5.2	18.2	5.5	16.2	3.0	18.1	3.4

Source: adapted from Constantinescu 2000: 288, 294.

Banking sector

The nationalization of the National Bank was followed by the other banks in 1948 and the reorganization of the system according to Soviet criteria. From 1949, a system was imposed in which the National Bank became the depository of all available money from enterprises and public institutions. The *Casa de Economii și Consemnațiuni* (CEC – the Home Savings Bank) provided deposit and credit services to the population and the Investments Bank was meant to support industrialization and urbanization. The Romanian Bank of Foreign Trade (1968) and *Banca Agricolă* (1970) were later established as specialist branches of the state's banking institutions. The state had a monopoly over credit and currency exchange operations.

The 1947 monetary reform was not sufficient, as inflation could not be eliminated. In 1952 a new monetary reform was undertaken by the massive reduction of the quantity of money in circulation. The exchange was not limited in terms of value, but people with less money to change benefited from a more favourable conversion rate. The conversion rate varied from 20:1 to 400:1.

Crediting resources were directed as a priority towards supporting industrialization and urbanization. During the first two decades of the communist regime, the crediting of economic activities was made by default, simply because it was mentioned in the five-year plans. After 1967, an element of economic rationality was introduced, distinguishing between profitable and non-profitable enterprises. At the same time, Ceaușescu intensified industrialization by using foreign credit, both from the USSR and from the capitalist West. In 1972 Romania became the first country in the Soviet bloc to join the International Monetary Fund (IMF) and the World Bank. Three loans were taken from the IMF: in 1975, 1977 and 1981. The IMF tried to introduce an element of economic flexibility in exchange for financing, but its policies were not accepted by Ceaușescu.

It was the obsession of the Communist leaders with quick industrialization using foreign loans that brought Romania into crisis. In 1977–80, Romania undertook massive imports of Western machinery and equipment. However, in 1979, the second oil shock occurred, manifested by an increase in the prices of raw materials. The Iranian Revolution and the beginning of the war between Iran and Saddam Hussein's Iraq limited Iranian oil exports to Romania. To his annoyance, Ceaușescu was again forced to turn to the USSR for oil imports. In 1979, the US increased the interest rate on loans and credit became more expensive. In 1981, Romania had arrears of US$1.14 billion and a total foreign debt of US$10.54 billion. The real issue was not so much the value of the debts as their structure, a fifth of them being short-term loans. Ceaușescu turned for help to the IMF, which initially agreed to finance Romania. However, for fear of contagion from Poland (which was in default), the inter-banking credit lines were cancelled. Demands for a rescheduling of foreign debt were turned down at first by foreign creditors and Romania defaulted. Two agreements to reschedule the debt were subsequently signed. Considering himself humiliated by the situation in which he found himself, Ceaușescu committed Romania to a revision of the five-year plan and an early repayment of its foreign debt, which should normally have taken place over twenty-five years.

Industrial investments were not stopped, and new megalomaniac building projects were launched, but the effort to repay the debt was supported by drastic austerity measures. Imports were seriously limited, including those necessary for industry, and everything that could be sold was exported, often at prices which did not cover production costs, in an effort to get hard currency (Ban 2012: 758–61).

Ceauşescu's irrational stubbornness extended to the point of selling 80 tonnes of gold from the National Bank reserves in 1986 for US$1.04 billion. After the repayment of the foreign debt had been finalized in April 1989, the redemption of only 21 tonnes of gold was approved (Constantinescu 2000: 379). Romania had apparently won its economic independence, but the price paid by the population was not only huge but also unfair.

A predominantly positive balance?

A superficial evaluation of the economic statistical data presented in this chapter might create the impression of 'factual confirmation' with regard to the theses of authoritarian modernization theory, which were fashionable in the 1970s. Economic analyses regarding Romania's history from the mid-nineteenth century to the present day (Axenciuc 2012; Murgescu 2010; Vlăsceanu and Hâncean 2014) emphasize the quantitative accumulation of economic progress during the communist period, at a quicker rate than during any previous period. This is a statistical certitude and the main explanation lies in the dictatorial political system, which favoured the mobilization of the population and the concentration of resources for politically determined objectives, while limiting consumption.

However, if we evaluate Romania's economic progress compared with other Soviet bloc countries and with most European countries (Murgescu 2010: 331), we may observe that Romania did not manage to overcome its historical gaps in relation to the West, where the first industrial revolution was launched as early as the nineteenth century, and did not stand out in its progress among the other Central European states. The essential conclusion is that, in spite of immense efforts to break with the economic underdevelopment matrix, Romania did not manage to overcome its existing historical gaps. Indeed they grew even greater during the 1980s, a period in which the international economy entered the era of globalization. An economy based on knowledge, services and a strong financial sector replaced models centred on industry in the West.

CHAPTER 8
THE FALL OF COMMUNISM

Ceauşescu and the 'domino effect'

The peaceful end of the Cold War and the fall of communist regimes in Eastern Europe, followed by the dismantling of the Soviet Union, were hard to predict by even the most optimistic and subtle sovietologists. The mystery around the *annus mirabilis*, 1989, still looms, and fascinates Europeans. The Romanian revolution is not without historical controversy, since it was an exception from the general model of peaceful transitions from communism to pluralist regimes, and the only system change with a large number of victims.

Historians are accustomed to finding *a posteriori* various causes of revolutions. Scholars researching the fall of communism often use the concept of 'root causes', also called structural, such as the lack of legitimacy of the communist ideology and power; societal opposition following economic failure; loss of confidence by the communist elite in its capacity to rule and the refusal to use force to remain in power; and the resurgence of nationalist feelings in the USSR. Furthermore, according to the theoretical grid being used, historians base their explanations on 'conjectural' or 'specific' causes, such as: the 'Gorbachev factor'; the spread of revolution from one country to another; external influences and actions; and internal conspiracies and protests (Abraham 2013: 110–41; Brown 2009: 503–617). Despite the complexity of the conceptual framework employed to explain revolutionary events, respectively the abundance of documentary sources, the historian of the 1989 revolutions has a hard time coping with the teleological temptation to think of communism as inherently doomed to failure. However, labelling the fall of communist regimes as a 'genetically-programmed event' could be a serious epistemological error. For instance, the Soviet Union did not have to accept the peaceful undoing of her European spheres of influence by the abandonment of the Brezhnev doctrine, and communism would have lasted, since the US and her Western allies would have refrained from decommunizing Europe by military intervention. It is very likely that the Polish 'Round Table Agreement' would not have been possible had Poland been ruled by Nicolae Ceauşescu instead of Wojciech Jaruzelski. These heuristic examples show us the importance of understanding the full dynamics of revolutionary changes, against the backdrop of the national particularities of states.

It is vital for the historian to understand and explain why Romanian communism was overthrown by a bloody revolution instead of the negotiated change in the rest of Eastern Europe. An assessment of the main actions challenging Ceauşescu's policies – the workers' strikes of the Jiu Valley (1977) and Braşov (1987) – quickly put down by the communist repression system, shows that the regime had not been under a real threat from such protests, given the geopolitical stalemate of the Cold War. Likewise, the 'Letter of the Six' and the protests by Doina Cornea's and other dissidents were individual actions, lacking the unity of a group providing an alternative or being an influential focus point for a negotiated transition.

At least as important as the lack of a united civic opposition against the Nicolae Ceauşescu regime is the quasi non-existence of alternative currents within the PCR, which could have extended to the *Securitate* and the army. The fear of marginalization or repression, the general mood of suspicion, respectively the competition and mistrust between the communist elites (between the army and the *Securitate*, or the Party and the *Securitate*) prevented the aggregation of any opposition, much less of an authentic political alternative. Even the dynastic transfer of power from Nicolae to Nicu Ceauşescu, expected to occur at the fourteenth Congress of the PCR in November 1989, proved all but an illusion. At the age of 71, Nicolae Ceauşescu trusted only his wife Elena and a very narrow group of sycophantic collaborators, and was not willing to organize his own withdrawal from the top of the PCR and the Romanian state.

Ceauşescu regarded the Eastern European changes of 1989 as 'deviations from Socialism'. At the meeting of the Political Consultative Committee of the Warsaw Pact states in Bucharest on the 7 to 8 July 1989, in the presence of Mikhail Gorbachev, the Romanian leader expressed concern at 'the tendencies to question socialist values' (Scurtu 2006: 100). In turn, Gorbachev insisted on strengthening the political dimension of the Warsaw Pact, supporting 'compliance with the will of brotherly parties'. Things were becoming clearer than ever: to Ceauşescu, the new Soviet leader was a heretic to Marxism-Leninism; for Gorbachev, the Romanian communist was becoming increasingly obsolete against the new backdrop of *Glasnost* and *Perestroika*. The historical idiosyncrasy of Ceauşescu was also stressed by the visits of George Bush, the US president, to Poland and Hungary in July 1989, with the US leader conveying moderate messages in favour of democracy. From being the favourite Eastern European partner of the West in the 1970s, Ceauşescu had become the outcast of East–West relations after 1985, diplomatically isolated and vilified by the international press.

The *coup de grâce* of Polish communism was to be given on 19 August 1989, when Tadeusz Mazowiecki became the first non-communist prime minister in Eastern Europe. Ceauşescu's first reaction was to summon the Soviet ambassador in Bucharest to pass on his misgivings for events in Poland. On that day, the PCR Secretary General also submitted a letter to the Central Committees of European socialist parties, requesting a review of the Polish situation, since 'Socialism is in danger'. On 21 August 1989, Ceauşescu called a meeting of the Executive Political Committee of the Central Committee of the PCR, dedicated to evaluating the situation in Poland. The answers of Mikhail Gorbachev and the Polish and Hungarian communists were highly critical towards Ceauşescu's conservatism (Scurtu 2006: 105–6). This revealed the isolation of the Ceauşescu regime not only from the West, but also from some of the communist countries. However, the *Perestroika* 'dissident' Ceauşescu was not entirely isolated, considering the gerontocracies of Bulgaria and the German Democratic Republic. They were about to fall one after another, though, following the 'domino principle' (Preda 2000).

Erich Honecker was the first of Ceauşescu's chance allies to fall. Several street rallies for democracy took place in the German Democratic Republic from September to October 1989. The East German communist regime had received a major blow from Hungary, which had opened its borders to allow East Germans to immigrate/travel to Austria, then to West Germany. On 18 October 1989, Erich Honecker was forced to resign, and was replaced by Egon Krenz, a close collaborator of the former leader. The latter soon found himself under fire, and on 7 November, the East German communist government resigned. On 9 November, the border crossings were opened, including the Berlin Wall. One of the most important symbols of the Eastern bloc had thus fallen.

As calamities only come in pairs for dictators, Ceauşescu's counterpart in Sofia, Todor Zhivkov, was forced to resign from the Political Bureau, and was then dismissed from all party and state positions on 10 November 1989. The decisive role in ensuring change in Bulgaria was played by pro-Soviet army generals, who encircled Sofia with their loyal troops. Thus, in just two days, two of Ceauşescu's potential allies against *Perestroika* were ousted from power.

In Czechoslovakia, the communist regime struggled with the pressure of the street rallies which began on 17 November 1989. At the end of the PCR's fourteenth Congress on 24 November 1989, which reconfirmed his leadership, Ceauşescu was informed of the *en masse* resignation of all Czechoslovak Communist Party leaders, with Karel Urbanek replacing Miloš Jakeš. On 10 December, Gustáv Husák was forced to resign as President of Czechoslovakia. A new government with a non-communist majority was formed, led by Marián Čalfa (Pop 2002: 268–78). A new communist stronghold was falling, and Ceauşescu remained the second to last European communist, next to the Albanian Ramiz Alia.

The changes in Central Europe, and particularly the prospect of German reunification, demanded a direct clarification between the US and the Soviet Union. This took place at the Malta conference between George Bush and Mikhail Gorbachev on the 2–3 December 1989. The meeting gave rise to various comments and interpretations. The documents made available so far (notes of the US State Department, press releases, memoirs, etc.) indicate that the 'Nicolae Ceauşescu' topic was not on the official agenda, but it may have been marginally approached during the discussion on the right of communist states freely to choose their course. Gorbachev undertook to brief the party and state leaders of the Warsaw Pact countries on the results of the Malta talks at the Moscow meeting of 4–5 December 1989. This was the venue for the last Ceauşescu–Gorbachev meeting. The Soviet leader rejected Ceauşescu's calls for an international debate on the 'communist movement' (Olteanu 1999: 216). Gorbachev's message was quite clear: the modernization of communism was to continue. Honecker was presented as a negative example, and a serious warning was given to the Romanian leader: retire from the frontline of politics or share the fate of his German counterpart.

Oddly, the Romanian communist leadership, although informed of the political transformations in CEE, seemed hardly aware of their dynamics and actual direction.

The 'under siege' syndrome took over the upper ranks of the PCR, the *Securitate* and the army. On 2 December 1989, commanders from the leading structures of the Ministry of Defence met under the authority of General Ilie Ceauşescu, in an atmosphere of confidence that the 'democratic' virus would not affect the Romanians (Kunze 2002: 456). On 1 December 1989, Nicolae Ceauşescu received a 'top secret', hand-written report from the head of the *Securitate*, Iulian Vlad, stating that: 'Our data shows that the Bush–Gorbachev meeting will also discuss the exertion of pressures on the Socialist countries which have not implemented [real reforms] up to now, particularly the Popular Republic of China, Cuba and Romania.' In spite of all this information, Ceauşescu became truly worried only in the aftermath of his final meeting with Gorbachev. After the meeting, he returned straight from Moscow, giving up on the next day's hunt, his favourite pastime. The Romanian communist propaganda depicted the Malta conference as an agreement of the superpowers, going over Romania's head. While anticipating external actions against him, Ceauşescu thought that he had the nation on his side, with the army, the *Securitate*, and especially the 'working class' bound to defend him. Since the full reimbursement of foreign debt in the spring of 1989 had given Ceauşescu the illusion of absolute independence, he believed the nation could not go against the 'hero among national heroes' that the communist propaganda presented him to be. This would not be the first case of a dictator at odds with his nation, who thinks of himself as loved and respected, while the truth is entirely the opposite: Ceauşescu was deeply hated and despised for the suffering and humiliation he had inflicted on his people. The Romanian dictator became the indirect victim of his own cult of personality.

The unfolding of the Romanian revolution

Changes in Eastern Europe were undoubtedly known by Romanian citizens thanks to Western radio stations (RFE, Voice of America), and later Radio Budapest, whose broadcasts could be understood in Transylvania and Banat. The Ceauşescu regime sought to restrict access to information to the greatest possible extent, and foreign radio stations were jammed. Although Romanians might not have fully discerned the dynamics of events, they created significant expectations. Information on the fall of communist regimes generated both hope that something was going to happen after all and frustration that the Ceauşescu regime continued to stay in power. The psychological prerequisites (apprehension, social anxiety, individual and collective frustration) of a revolutionary movement were being created. For most Romanians, the only problem was related to the timing and main actors of change.

The first potentially dangerous internal action against the Ceauşescu regime was the attempted revolt of 14 December 1989 in Iaşi. Leaflets on behalf of the Romanian Popular Front were circulated in Iaşi, urging the population to take part in a protest rally in Unirii Square against the 'terror unleashed by the Ceauşescu dictatorship'. The action did not take place, as the movement leaders were quickly suppressed by the *Securitate*: Cassian Maria Spiridon – writer; Ştefan Prutianu – professor; Vasile Vicol – engineer; Aurel

Ştefanachi – writer; Ionel Săcăleanu – engineer; Valentin Odobescu – lawyer (Florescu and Spiridon 2000). It was a doomed attempt, since Iaşi was under the tight control of the *Securitate*, which inhibited any significant protests.

The chain of events leading to the fall of the communist regime started in Timişoara, on 15 December 1989, when a protest erupted against the attempt by PCR and *Securitate* decision makers to evict reformed pastor László Tökés. The pastor had recently criticized the regime in the international press, and the PCR leaders accused him of incitement to ethnic hatred. (The *Securitate* thought that its former informant under a 1982 commitment had in the meantime also become an agent of the ÁVH – the Hungarian secret police.) Pastor Tökés was visited on 15 December 1989 by Dennis Carry of the American Embassy in Bucharest, a first step towards the international dissemination of his case.

On the second day, 16 November, crowds supporting László Tökés gathered in Timişoara, with the participation of even larger numbers, Romanians and Hungarians alike. From 5.00 pm on 16 December, a group of young people blocked traffic in the centre of Timişoara, breaking shop windows. Slogans against Nicolae Ceauşescu were shouted, and 'Deşteaptă-te române!' ('Awake, Romanian!') and 'Hora Unirii' ('The round dance of the Unification') were sung. The forces of the Ministry of the Interior (*Miliţia*, *Securitate* troops, firemen) repressed the demonstrators, by arresting around 180 people. A fully-fledged manhunt was organized in Timişoara on the night of 16 to 17 December, with people arrested on the streets, some of whom were tortured (Oşca 2009: 126–63; Milin 2009).

In the morning of 17 December, the situation in Timişoara seemed under control; the army was on the streets, and Pastor Tökés had been evicted to the village of Mineu in Sălaj County, in the north-west of the country. But the demonstrations continued, and Nicolae Ceauşescu gave a verbal order for a forcible intervention (a state of necessity was declared in Timişoara, but without issuing a legal presidential decree), to be executed by General Vasile Milea, the minister of defence. Barricades were raised throughout the city. After 5.00 pm, units of the army and Ministry of the Interior (*Miliţia* and *Securitate*) began firing live rounds randomly at the demonstrators. The first deaths and serious injuries occurred. Other reprisals followed during the night of 17 to 18 December. On 18 December, an official state of necessity was established in Timişoara. The first count of the communist authorities found 58 dead, 200 wounded and 700 arrests. Some of the bodies were housed in the Timiş County Hospital, and on Elena Ceauşescu's orders, forty-three were transported to Bucharest and cremated to erase all traces of the murders. Of the forty-three people cremated at the *Cenuşa* crematorium, thirty-eight were later identified.

A meeting of the Executive Political Committee of the PCR was organized on 17 December. Nicolae Ceauşescu blamed the Timişoara protests on foreign subversion, 'both from the East and the West'. He offered his resignation as a test of loyalty of the PCR leadership, but they did not accept. As a precaution against foreign subversion, Ceauşescu ordered the interruption of all tourist activities, with only North Korean, Chinese and Cuban citizens being allowed entry into Romania (Scurtu 2006: 187).

On 18 December, Ceauşescu left for a short visit to Iran, as a sign of his belief that he was in control of the situation. In the meantime, the international media (using Yugoslav and Hungarian sources) began reporting on the Timişoara crackdown (with accounts of thousands of deaths, a figure considerably distorted). Several governments, including Washington and Moscow, protested against the loss of human lives and demanded compliance with human rights. The international pressure against the Ceauşescu regime intensified on 19 December, despite the attitude of denial put forward by Romanian officials in the country and abroad, as they tried to keep up the appearance of having the situation under control.

On 19 December, Timişoara was on strike as a protest against the use of abusive violence. On 20 December, the workers of the major industrial platforms rallied on the streets, despite efforts by the authorities to block them in the factories. The occupation of the Opera Square by Timişoara residents generated a first defensive action by the army, which retreated into barracks on the order of General Ştefan Guşă (endorsed by General Milea). Thus, Timişoara became the first 'free Romanian city'. Almost at the same time, Ceauşescu returned from Iran only to find that the protests had spread instead of stopping, despite the army's shooting of the Timişoara demonstrators. A political delegation led by Prime Minister Constantin Dăscălescu arrived in Timişoara on 20 December. Dăscălescu tried to address the demonstrators, but he was booed and the negotiation attempt ended in failure. They demanded Ceauşescu's resignation, free elections, and the punishment of those responsible for the crackdown.

Informed of the failure to pacify Timişoara, Ceauşescu first organized a teleconference with party activists at county level, and then addressed the nation directly on the evening of 20 December, hoping to convince people that the events of Timişoara were the results of actions by 'reactionary, imperialist, irredentist and chauvinist circles' connected to various foreign intelligence services. It was in the spirit of national-communism to blame internal crisis on foreign orchestrations. However, the appeal 'Country in peril' was not credible for a nation informed by foreign radio stations that Ceauşescu's crackdown had left thousands dead or wounded in Timişoara. Such information seemed credible because Ceauşescu was desperately holding on to power. Fortunately, the number of victims proved much lower than announced by the international media, but it left the Romanian people with the strong conviction that, unless they had the courage to protest, they might be the next victims. This could be one explanation for the extraordinary courage shown by them during the days and nights of the revolution.

On the night of 20–21 December, a 'Proclamation of the Romanian Democratic Front of Timişoara' was drawn up; it was read the following morning from the balcony of the Opera. It was the first political programme of the Revolution: the Front defined itself as a 'political organization' seeking negotiations with the government for the democratization of the country. They requested free elections, freedom of speech and of the press, and the opening of state borders (Oşca 2009: 372–3).

The anti-communist protests did not begin in Timişoara by chance. Lying close to Romania's western border, Timişoara is located in one of the relatively rich regions of the country. The small cross-border traffic with Yugoslavia and Hungary provided Timişoara's residents with subsistence resources not available elsewhere in Romania. Banat's inhabitants received information about the changes in Central Europe from both the Yugoslavs and the Hungarians. Moreover, they often took pride in their pro-Western orientation (Siani-Davies 2006: 86). Thus, the revolution broke out in a relatively rich city, with a civic culture orientated towards modernity, in which frustration at being confined in a 'camp' was the main source of the protest.

On the morning of 21 December, the protests spread from Timişoara all across the country. Rallies were organized in Arad, Cluj-Napoca, Craiova, Sibiu, Târgu Mureş and Lugoj, amongst others. In Bucharest, Ceauşescu called an assembly to support the regime and condemn the protests of Timişoara, certain that the industrial workers would be on his side. But instead of pre-recorded ovations, Ceauşescu's speech was interrupted by gunshots and yelling broadcast through the audio station from the Palace Square. Stunned, Ceauşescu said to the people in the square, 'Silence! . . . Silence! . . . Calm down! . . . Silence! . . . Calm down!' But very few people were listening. The city centre was filled with more than 70,000 people, workers, pupils and students, who organized and raised barricades at the Intercontinental Hotel and University Square. In Bucharest, the crackdown began in the afternoon of 21 December. During the night, the repression forces acted with brutality. Fifty people were killed, 462 were injured, and 1,245 were arrested and incarcerated at the Jilava prison.

After the crackdown of 21–22 December in Bucharest and the removal of the University Square barricade by the army, the population of Bucharest was fraught with fear, but also revolt. Confusion and uncertainty dominated. On the morning of 22 December, columns of protesters formed at the large industrial plants (Republica, IMGB, 23 August) and started marching towards the PCR Headquarters. At 10.59 am, the national radio station announced that the Minister of Defence, General Vasile Milea, had 'committed suicide'. A state of necessity was immediately declared for the entire country. General Victor Stănculescu was verbally designated by Ceauşescu to replace Milea. But the new minister of defence ordered the two regiments, one armoured and one motorized, heading for the Central Committee of PCR to return to quarters. This prevented a new bloodbath, and the angry crowds could continue to exercise pressure on the dictator couple. Fear of the Bucharest residents' reaction ultimately pushed Ceauşescu to seek refuge, after one last attempt to appease the nation by addressing them through a megaphone from the balcony of the Central Committee, at around 11.30 am, had been met only with booing from the protesters.

General Stănculescu warned Ceauşescu about the imminence of an attack on the Central Committee. He also provided the solution: leave by helicopter to another command centre, less exposed to crowd pressure (Andreescu and Bucur 2009: 51–150). At 12.06 am, Nicolae Ceauşescu and his wife Elena left Bucharest by helicopter, together with two loyal henchmen, Emil Bobu and Manea Mănescu. The flight of the Ceauşescu couple happened as crowds were already entering the building of the Central Committee in search of them. Had they stayed five minutes more, they would have been caught by the angry mob and probably lynched.

The fugitives flew to Ceauşescu's residence in Snagov, then further to Târgovişte. They abandoned the helicopter near the town of Titu, after the pilot was ordered from the ground to land. The army had closed Romania's air space. While travelling by car, the Ceauşescu couple were taken into custody and sheltered in a military garrison in Târgovişte.

In less than an hour from the flight of the couple, Romanian television broadcast the first instalment in the series of live revolutions with the announcement that the dictator had fled, presented by the actor Ion Caramitru and the poet Mircea Dinescu. In the new power and authority vacuum, the fight for succession was on.

A first power centre was apparently taking shape in the building recently left by Ceauşescu, the headquarters of the PCR. Here, former prime ministers Ilie Verdeţ and Constantin Dăscălescu each sought to form a new government, made up of former nomenklatura members and demonstrators. But the initiative did not last more than twenty minutes, as the crowds from the Palace Square booed the initiators (Portocală 1991: 97). At almost the same time, a core of political power was seemingly forming at the television building, united by the mere fact of their presence in the building. An essential factor in the evolution of events was the army, which 'fraternized with the revolutionaries' after Ceauşescu's flight.

The literature on the revolution still holds many unknowns on the role of the army in the power transfer, but it was undoubtedly essential. Responsible for a large proportion of the revolution victims, the army abandoned its supreme leader, Ceauşescu, feeling humiliated by him and resenting being unwillingly turned into a tool of repression. Instead of defending the country against foreign aggression, it had been called to defend an unpopular political regime. When forced to fire on civilians, the army often fraternized with the demonstrators. The soldiers thought of themselves as part of the nation, and their involvement in repressive actions, although not openly disapproved of, was half-hearted or even sabotaged by cooperation with civilians.

A significant role was that of General Victor Stănculescu, who decided to betray Ceauşescu, also benefiting from the passive attitude of the head of the *Securitate*, General Iulian Vlad, who was not willing to follow Ceauşescu to the end. At 1.30 am on 22 December, General Stănculescu invited Ion Iliescu to the Ministry of Defence to offer him protection, recognising him as Ceauşescu's successor. Stănculescu thought that Ion Iliescu, also supported by Iulian Vlad, seemed a more viable option than Verdeţ–Dăscălescu (Stoenescu 2005: 487–91). On the afternoon of 22 December, a second, wider meeting took place at the Ministry of Defence, with the participation of generals Victor Stănculescu, Ştefan Guşă and Nicolae Militaru, and civilians Ion Iliescu, Petre Roman, Gelu Voican-Voiculescu, among others. In the aftermath of this meeting, Ion Iliescu was recognized as the new leader of the post-Ceauşescu team.

Even if the army leaders recognized the authority of a power group headed by Iliescu, the full take-over of power was not an easy task, since any new leadership had to secure popular support. Neither the military nor the new political team grasped the direction of the changes. Everyone's common denominator was the removal of the Ceauşescu family from power, but the extent of the social and political changes was unclear. At first, Iliescu defended 'socialism with a human face', while other revolution leaders (Petre Roman, Dumitru Mazilu) were the partisans of radical political change. The military-backed leaders were under strong pressure from the masses to bring deep political change (including freedom and free elections).

The flight of Ceauşescu and the chaos following the demise of the dictatorship brought the first 'televised revolution' in history. The events were eagerly followed in the country as well as abroad. The symbolic core of the revolution was transferred into the studios of Romanian television, which became an ad-hoc command centre (Tatulici 1990).

The escape of Ceauşescu from the headquarters of the PCR brought a general feeling of euphoria, manifested by repeated chanting of the slogan 'Ole, Ole, Ole, Ole, Ceauşescu nu mai e!' ('Ole, ole, ole, ole, Ceauşescu is gone') in all the large squares in the country. But with Ceauşescu still alive, the fear of his return was still present, as the news of his arrest was not broadcast until the evening of 23 December (Duţu 2010: 216).

The mystery of the Ceauşescu family's fate and the hope that the dictatorship was over led to the appearance of several revolution programmes on the afternoon of 22 December. The most important document was the Communication of the National Salvation Front to the Country. The proclamation, read by Iliescu, was broadcast by Romanian television on the evening of 22 December. The text was based on a draft prepared before the flight of Ceauşescu, and subsequently amended by Silviu Brucan. It is divided into three parts. The preamble announces the establishment of *Frontul Salvării Naţionale* (FSN – the National Salvation Front), which is 'supported by the Romanian army and comprised of all the healthy forces of the country, regardless of their nationality, all the organizations and groups which valiantly rose to defend freedom and dignity during the years of totalitarian tyranny'. It announces the dissolution of all 'power structures of the Ceauşescu clan. The Government is dismissed, the State Council and its institutions cease their activities, the entire executive power is assumed by the Council of the National Salvation Front.' (Andreescu and Bucur 2009: 240–3).

The second part of the proclamation contains ten main objectives, including: '1. Abolition of the single-party system and establishment of a democratic and pluralist form of government. 2. Organization of free elections in the month of April. 3. Separation of the legislative, executive and judicial branches of the State and election of all political leaders for one or no more than two terms. No one may claim power for life anymore.' Thus, the communist regime was abolished, while setting the foundation for a new pluralist regime.

Other provisions refer to the restructuring of the economy and of agriculture, stopping the destruction of villages, reorganization of education, and protection for the rights and liberties of national minorities. The leaders of the revolutionary government wanted to convey the message of a continued unity of the state: 'We will abide by the international commitments of Romania, firstly regarding the Warsaw Pact'. Furthermore, to assure the Soviet Union that the FSN leaders did not intend to change Romania's international status, General Militaru, who had been marginalized by Nicolae Ceauşescu specifically for being exposed as an agent of the Soviet army intelligence service GRU (Main Intelligence Directorate), was appointed as the Minister of Defence the next day.

The third part contains a provisional list of thirty-eight members of *Consiliul Frontului Salvării Naționale* (CFSN – the Council of the National Salvation Front). The initial composition of the CFSN was designed to confer representativeness and thus legitimacy on the new power structure: anti-communist intellectuals (Doina Cornea, Ana Blandiana, Mircea Dinescu), members of the military (generals Ștefan Gușă and Victor Stănculescu), members of the PCR nomenklatura marginalized by Ceaușescu (Alexandru Bârladeanu, Silviu Brucan, Ion Iliescu), revolutionaries (Marian Baciu, Bogdan Teodoriu, Eugenia Iorga, Paul Negrițiu, Manole Gheorghe), artists and symbolic personalities (Ion Caramitru, Sergiu Nicolaescu, László Tökés). It was a heterogeneous conglomerate in which the real power was held by the political founders of the CFSN (Iliescu, Brucan, Mazilu and Roman) and the representatives of the army. Iliescu was elected head of the CFSN on 27 December.

The fall of the Ceaușescu regime also became spectacular due to the so-called 'terrorists' episode'. It is known that between 22 December and the announcement of the trial, conviction and execution of the Ceaușescu couple on 25 December, an intense psychological war was waged in Romania, also fought with electronic means. Much unverified information was spread, such as information on helicopter infiltrations, poisoning of water sources, mining of dams, or a supposed aerial assault by 70,000 Libyans on Bucharest. Phoney targets appeared on the screens of military radar and were fired upon. And since all these mysterious characters had to bear a name, they were called 'terrorists'.

As the fight against 'terrorists' raged on, the issue of possible Soviet military aid in favour of the revolutionaries was raised. There is no evidence of a specific call for Soviet military help from Romanian revolutionary leaders. The Soviet political and military leadership rejected a military intervention in Romania since the 'Brezhnev doctrine' had been repudiated in Moscow, and the interventions in Czechoslovakia and Afghanistan had already been branded as mistakes. The Soviet refusal seems even more surprising as the US ambassador in Moscow, J. Matlock, enquiring in a phone conversation with I.P. Aboimov, the deputy foreign minister of the USSR, wanted to know whether 'the possibility of Soviet military assistance for the National Salvation Front was entirely out of the question' (Sava and Monac 2000: 178–1). The Soviet answer was that 'we are not yet prepared to start considering such a virtual possibility'. The US suggestion, initially made through diplomatic channels, was also voiced publically by the US Secretary of State, James Baker, who said on 24 December on NBC TV that the US were not going to object 'if the Warsaw Pact judges it necessary to intervene' in Romania. In fact, the Americans wished to receive an indirect justification of their intervention in Panama on the 20 December 1989 to oust the Noriega regime.

The explanations for the 'terrorists' of the Romanian revolution are manifold and contradictory. Some claim that the terrorists did exist, while others think it was a ruse designed to justify the execution of Ceaușescu. At least ten explanations of the terrorist issue are given in the literature: members of the *Securitate*, Arab terrorists, officers of the army and the Ministry of the Interior, foreign agents (Soviet and Hungarian); but no irrefutable proof has been advanced so far in support of any of these variants (Cesereanu

2004). The competing explanations do not provide full answers for the entire string of revolutionary events in Bucharest and the rest of the country. Manipulations did exist, but they were the result of chaos and uncertainty. The most likely explanation for the many dead after 22 December was that the victims were caused by the existence of several command centres of the army (up to 23 December) and the *Securitate*, which lacked coordination. The rivalry between them could also explain some of the victims of the period from 22 to 31 December 1989. The handing of weapons to civilians in cooperation with the army, together with the actions of the Patriotic Guards explain, at least in part, the large number of victims: many shots were fired 'blindly', not knowing whether the targets were indeed 'terrorists' or other revolutionaries.

Uncertainty was still dominant, as it was known that the former communist leader was under arrest, but his fate was unclear. An Extraordinary Military Tribunal was convened on the evening of 24 December to convict Ceaușescu. A faction of the CFSN members (Silviu Brucan, General Stănculescu and Gelu Voican-Voiculescu) wished for a quick execution. Iliescu did not initially agree to an execution, but his hesitant behaviour was used by the other members of the FSN Executive Bureau to impose the death penalty. On Christmas Day, 25 December, Nicolae and Elena Ceaușescu were sentenced to death by a drumhead military court in a mock trial, for a series of accusations, such as genocide (an alleged figure of 60,000 deaths was invoked), and were executed by an army firing squad in the courtyard of the Târgoviște garrison. The footage of the trial and the final part of the execution was partly broadcast on national television on 27 December (Durandin 2011: 145–70). National and international public opinion looked at the dead bodies of the Ceaușescu couple with both satisfaction and horror. After the video confirmation of the couple's execution, the intensity of military confrontation decreased; it completely stopped over the following days.

Ceaușescu's trial and execution marked a symbolic, violent end to the communist regime, which had been both established and manifested through violence. Romanians set forth with hope and enthusiasm on the long and winding road of 'transition' to freedom and prosperity.

The victims of the 1989 Revolution

According to official data, the number of deaths and mutilations by shooting before 22 December 1989 was approximately seven times lower than that of the victims after this date. The Institute of the Romanian Revolution of December 1989 (IRRD) identified 1,290 dead in the revolution, 1,283 of them Romanians and seven foreigners. No less than 748 children were registered as the offspring of martyr-hero parents (dead or wounded).

As per the IRRD estimates, 306 of the victims (245 civilians, 61 servicemen) were killed between 17 and 22 December 1989, (allegedly) by the forces of the Ministry of Defence, Ministry of the Interior and Patriotic Guards. There were a further 743 victims between 23 and 25 December (489 civilians, 254 servicemen), and 85 victims between

26 and 31 December 1989 (57 civilians, 28 servicemen). The main historical controversies are related to the responsibility for the victims of the Romanian revolution between 23 and 31 December 1989. The investigations by institutions of the Romanian state and the historical research are not sufficiently accurate to identify the perpetrator of each killing or wounding (Bucur 2012: 165–74).

The prosecution of the perpetrators of repression during the revolution is not yet complete. In 1990, extraordinary tribunals to judge the guilty were established due to popular pressure, with the most important trial being that of the members of the Executive Political Committee of the PCR, charged with complicity in genocide, and sentenced to periods of incarceration of between ten and twenty years. Most of those convicted were released by 1994 or 1995. Also significant are the 'Trial of the Twenty-five' of Timișoara, or the Chițac-Stănculescu trial. Other trials were organized for the killings in Cluj-Napoca and Sibiu. In 2008, General Victor Stănculescu and General Mihai Chițac were sentenced to fifteen years in prison for the repression of the Timișoara protests. Victor Stănculescu was released on parole in May 2014 for both 'good behaviour' and medical reasons.

The dominant feeling in Romanian society, outspokenly manifested by the victims of the revolution and the descendants of the deceased, is that the perpetrators of the crimes of December 1989 have not been exemplarily punished. The victims of the revolution, particularly those after Ceaușescu's flight from the Central Committee, are considered a regrettable consequence of 'terrorist' actions, with the responsibility thus dissipated. The topic of the revolution and its victims has been a hot topic for debate since the beginning of 1990, impacting on political life in the transition period.

In 2011, Romania was convicted by the European Court of Human Rights (ECtHR) because it had not efficiently and duly finalized criminal files concerning victims of the 1989 Revolution. Despite controversies about the 'Revolution File', Romania's judiciary system has not revealed the expected truth.

PART II
RETURN TO DEMOCRACY: LOST
IN TRANSITIONS

After the fall of communism, countries of the former Soviet bloc had the objective of simultaneously accomplishing a double transition: on the one hand, creating institutions and practices specific to representative (liberal) democracy and, on the other hand, establishing institutions and practices specific to a market economy (Linz and Stepan 1996; Gill 2002; Haynes 2012).

This double transformation, generically defined as 'transition', took place following certain general parameters: domination of neo-liberal ideology, according to which there is a codetermination between market economy ('capitalism') and representative democracy; existence of a societal quasi-consensus both concerning democratization and regarding transition to a market economy. The double transformation was legitimized by the need for Euro-Atlantic integration (belonging to NATO and the European Union – EU): external assistance of the transformation process and imposition of a conditionality regime for fulfilling assumed objectives. The main actors that influenced the transition process of Central and Eastern Europe were: the EU, the US, Germany, the IMF and the Council of Europe (CoE).

The duration of the socio-political and economic transformation of the Central European region remains a controversial subject among experts (Tucker 2015). The restrictive perspective considers that (electoral) democracy was reached during the second series of free elections (in the mid-1990s), after which democratic maturity was emphasized. The second broad interpretational current considers that the end of transition has an important geopolitical component, the guiding element being NATO accession (1999 for the Czech Republic, Poland and Hungary; 2004 for Romania, Bulgaria, Slovakia, Slovenia and the Baltic States). The general conclusion that can be drawn is that transition is a lengthy process marked by several difficulties and political traps (Rose 2009; Møller 2009).

For Romanians, jumping into the unknown post-communist world equally raised hopes and anguishes. The dominant perception was that Ceaușescu's death was a moment of historical fracture, a liberation from the past. There was no detailed textbook for 'piloting' a nation towards an unclear or moving destination. Three visions emerged concerning the future of the country. The first was promoted by the historical parties, which wanted restoration, by returning to the political situation before communism, the latter being defined as a bracket or accident of history. This uchronia was abandoned under the pressure of reality. The second concept, of a libertarian inspiration, stated that society would transform without the project of elites, following the 'invisible hand' of individual will. Finally, a third perspective stated that a social engineering project was needed, and must be assumed and applied by elites through institutions. The main promoter of this approach was Ion Iliescu, who initiated as early as 2 January 1990 the organization of the National Institute for Economic Research, led by Tudorel Postolache, for the purpose of designing a strategic vision on transition. In April 1990 the government received the 'Outline Concerning a Strategy for Establishing Market Economy in Romania' (Murgescu and Murgescu 2010: 436). The initial social engineering project was adapted to reality and continued by Iliescu through the 'Snagov Strategy' (1995) and then by the 'Sustainable Development Strategy – Horizon 2025' (2004).

The historical reality proved, however, to be much more complex than could have been anticipated and programmed; the transformation of society followed not only rational, national or international, projects, but also informal rules impossible to predict a priori. The 'prophecy' of Silviu Brucan, communist ideologist and a leading figure in the FSN, that Romanians would need a decade to balance social life and 'twenty years' to 'learn democracy' became famous (Brucan 2004: 9–18). Brucan's saying became paradigmatic through its profound meaning: historical changes take place in the long term and values and social practices change the slowest.

The feeling of a 'permanent transition' or a repeating one became established within Romanian society. There were political declarations concerning the end of transition and the beginning of a 'new era', starting with President Emil Constantinescu (1997), in the context of the first democratic alternation in power, and continuing with Prime Minister Adrian Năstase in 2002, in the ideological document 'Towards Normality'. The governor of the National Bank, Mugur Isărescu, considered in 2013 that the transition economy cycle, with macroeconomic imbalances, was over. Beyond the erudite definitions of political and socio-economic transition, the feeling that a great number of citizens were captive to a fluid reality, lacking stability landmarks, in a chaotic race to nowhere remains the dominant issue of Romanian society after 1989. Affiliation to Euro-Atlantic institutions failed, in the context of economic and military crises after 2008, to eliminate the sense of being doomed to a race through the labyrinth of history.

CHAPTER 9
POLITICAL PARTIES

The history of political pluralism begins with the euphoria of participating in the first free elections resulted in a massive turnout (86.2 per cent on 20 May 1990). Political activism was considered a path to national rebirth, as proven by the seventy-one political groups which participated in the first elections. Party inflation was natural, being favoured by the fact that a political party could be established by the association of only 251 people. Until 1996 almost 200 parties were registered, but only a few dozen were active (Radu 2000: 16). Party fragmentation, specific to early democracy, was overcome by introducing electoral thresholds for parliamentary elections and by changing the registration rules for political parties.

After an initial stage of trust in political parties, starting in the late 1990s, a chronic mistrust emerged. Disappointment towards politics was determined by the transformation of political actors into *cartel-parties* (Katz and Mair 1995, 2009). Following a logic of their own survival, parties organized themselves as bureaucratic structures, mostly orientated towards annuities from exploiting public offices. The financing of parties from public sources allowed party bureaucracy to become self-sufficient, with interest in the electorate's issues being maximized before elections (Gherghina and Chiru 2013). The increasing costs of electoral campaigns led all the parliamentary parties to create informal systems of getting 'dirty money' from public resources. According to the custom, several public procurement contracts (given by city halls, county councils or even ministries) were conditioned by a 10 per cent 'commission' used both for political activities (including media financing) and for enriching politicians.

Parties had different internal structures. The Social Democrats were the only ones with the ambition of having an extended network of members in each locality, much like a mass party, of over half a million people. The other political actors structured themselves as ad hoc cadres parties, with at best 150,000 members each. The total estimated number of parliamentary party members did not exceed one million people after the 2000s, correlating with the fall of trust in political parties. Approximately 10 per cent of election participants were formally enrolled in parties. The number of members increases when a party is in government and decreases, often dramatically, when it is in opposition (Gherghina 2015: 113).

Political parties were structured not only according to exhibited doctrinal identity, but also according to temporary societal tensions. Far from having the historical stability of the cleavages identified in the West by the theory of Stein Rokkan (Rokkan 2010), until the mid-2000s political life in Romania was dominated by two main tensions. The first opposed 'anti-communists' to 'post-communists' (Barbu 1999: 16–17). This tension (de Waele 2003) was only conjectural, as the 'anti-communists' had not all shown this orientation by dissidence during communism and not all those that were labelled as 'post-/neo-communists' had been part of the nomenklatura. Society was not truly divided among supporters of the old regime and those of the new democratic order, as nostalgia for communism meant regretting the loss of its social stability rather than an active wish to restore the communist regime.

Privatization and the rhythm of reform were issues around which a second great tension accumulated, between 'maximalists' or 'reformists' and 'minimalists' or 'conservatives'. The first advocated a quick transformation of the economy, while 'minimalists' proposed a reduction of the social costs implied by the transition to capitalism or even denied the latter's utility. The manner in which the transition in the Romanian economy took place created an additional urban/rural tension, in the sense that minimalist orientations were usually supported by the rural areas and maximalist ones by urban areas.

The doctrinal structuring of parties was not a uniform and continuous phenomenon. 'Ideological conformity' of national parties was more important for the progressive left (Party of European Socialists – PES, Socialist International – SI) and European liberal (Alliance of Liberals and Democrats for Europe – ALDE), while conservatives (European People's Party – EPP) privileged pragmatic advantages of affiliation to the European political family instead of doctrinal coherence. Party de-ideologization at European level, in the context of an increased domination of political marketing in political communication, also affected the Romanian political space, which was in any case poor with regard to the parties' doctrinal consolidation.

After NATO and EU accession, parties had the tendency to get closer to an imaginary centre, each wanting to represent the nation as a whole and not just particular segments (owners, workers, minorities, etc.). Subsequently, parliamentary parties made their de-ideologization chronic, with parliamentarians in general being supporters of liberal democracy, market economy, rule of law and the country's Euro-Atlantic orientation. There were fewer real differences between party policies; what made them different was their leaders and their capacity for electoral mobilization. Against such a background, the emergence of left–right coalitions was only natural, the main obstacles being conflicts between leaders, not between radically different visions regarding society.

The plural left

The political manifestation of the left was, from the very beginning, plural and competitive-conflicting. On 17 January 1990, *Partidul Social Democrat Român* (PSDR – the Romanian Social Democratic Party), the declared continuer of traditional interwar social democracy, re-emerged. Marked by the prison experiences of their leaders, traditional social democrats promoted a radical vision over the communist inheritance. They became allies of the National Peasant Party and of the Liberals, opposing the FSN and Ion Iliescu. With a tiny electoral share, the PSDR was accepted into the SI in 1993.

Much as in other Central and Eastern European countries, there was also a successor to the Communist Party in Romania. If *de jure* this was no longer possible, as the PCR had been disbanded during the 1989 Revolution and its properties nationalized, some smaller groups emerged *de facto*, which organized into party formulas, claiming to be the continuers of the old regime's 'positive legacy'. The political vehicle was *Partidul Socialist al Muncii* (PSM – the Socialist Party of Labour), under the leadership of former Communist Prime Minister Ilie Verdeț. The 1992 parliamentary elections were the apex of the PSM. The PSM's past-ridden orientation, with nostalgia towards national-communism, is highlighted by the establishment, together with the far left, of the parliamentary group called the 'National Party', led by Senator Adrian Păunescu and Deputy Tudor Mohora. The latter split from the PSM, as he wanted an 'enlightened socialism', and established *Partidul Socialist* (PS – the Socialist Party). The PSM and PS were left outside of the Parliament in 1996 (Abraham 2006a: 344–5; 357–8).

The predominant influence of the left is related to the transformation of the FSN into a political party on 6 February 1990, winning elections with a massive score (66 per cent), and to the state leadership by Ion Iliescu from the very early days of the 1989 Revolution.

After the 20 May 1990 elections, the FSN polarized between a current militating for quick economic reforms by privatization and an orientation promoting a gradual change of the economy, which was wanted by a majority of the population. The first idea was represented by the prime minister and FSN leader Petre Roman. The second, with a vision inspired by the orthodox left, close to the centralist state, was coagulated around Ion Iliescu. After the removal of the Roman government, the FSN divided into two groups, at the National Convention of 27–29 March 1992. The partisans of Roman won, inheriting the FSN infrastructure, and the supporters of Iliescu established a new party, *Frontul Democrat al Salvării Naționale* (FDSN – the Democratic National Salvation Front).

The winner of the 27 September 1992 elections was the group profiting from the credibility and public image of Iliescu, who won his first constitutional presidential mandate. The formation of an FDSN government, under the leadership of technocrat Nicolae Văcăroiu, offered the opportunity for the party's institutional consolidation and in-depth social democratization. In 1993, the FDSN changed its name to *Partidul Democrației Sociale din România* (PDSR – the Party of Social Democracy in Romania), to signal its propinquity to the European social democratic family.

Roman's FSN consolidated itself from an organizational and doctrinal point of view by social democratizing (it even changed its name to *Partidul Democrat*, PD – the Democratic Party). The 1996 elections were lost by Iliescu and PDSR; PD became a governmental party, in a coalition supporting President Emil Constantinescu.

The PDSR failure in 1996 brought about an increase in internal tensions, the battle for Iliescu's support being waged between two former ministers Meleșcanu and Năstase. Iliescu supported Năstase, and Meleșcanu established a new party, together with other MPs, *Alianța pentru România* (ApR – Alliance for Romania), which wanted to become a social-liberal force, following the Blair–Schroeder–Clinton model. The ApR was initially seen as an attractive choice, but accusations of corruption against its leaders led to its failure in the 2000 parliamentary elections. A faction of the ApR returned to social democracy while Meleşcanu and the rest of his party were integrated into the PNL in 2001.

While in government, the PD wanted to block the initiatives of right-wing parties regarding property restitution, and the warlike attitude of its ministers within the coalition was perceived as duplicitous (Gallagher 2004: 221). During the 2000 elections, the PD suffered a major failure and the party leadership was taken over by Băsescu, who had won Bucharest City Hall.

Iliescu returned victorious in the 2000 elections and the PDSR formed the government, under the leadership of Năstase. From the position of party chairman Năstase made it his business to achieve the unification of the left. First of all, in June 2001, the PDSR and PSDR merged, forming the PSD; thus, historical legitimacy overlapped with the legitimacy of the anti-communist revolution. In 2003, the PSD engulfed other left wing parties, trying to impose a monopoly over social democracy. Fusion with the PD was blocked by Băsescu, and the battle between the two successor parties of FSN continued to grow ever-fiercer. In spite of PD opposition, the PSD became an SI member in 2003, thus also acquiring international ideological legitimacy (Abraham 2007).

The 2004 elections determined new changes. Băsescu pulled the PD out of the SI, orientating it towards the European right (EPP). The PSD, being in opposition, entered the stage of internal conflicts. In 2005, Iliescu lost the party leadership to Mircea Geoană, former minister of foreign affairs in the PSD government. Năstase, after losing the presidential elections, was politically marginalized. Under the leadership of Geoană, the PSD witnessed the emergence of local leaders, pejoratively called 'barons' by the mass media. Geoană lost the 2009 presidential elections to Băsescu, and maintaining the party in opposition brought Victor Ponta to party leadership in 2010; under his lead the party won the 2012 elections, together with the PNL. Ponta entered the 2014 presidential competition as prime minister, but lost the election to Klaus Iohannis. In July 2015, Ponta resigned from the leadership of the PSD, remaining as prime minister until November 2015.

Initially within the plural left sphere was the *Partidul Umanist Român* (PUR – the Romanian Humanist Party), established in 1991 and led by Dan Voiculescu, a media tycoon. The PUR played an important role starting with 2000, as it was used as exchange currency for the support of Voiculescu's media trust. As in 2000, in 2004 PUR entered Parliament with the support of the social democrats. After Băsescu's victory in the presidential election, Voiculescu reorientated himself, and the PUR became, in 2005, the *Partidul Conservator* (PC – the Conservative Party), with the ambition of playing a prominent political role. In 2015, following its merger with a liberal party, it ended up becoming an ALDE member.

Popular conservatives

Together with Enlightenment-inspired liberalism, conservatism was a major ideological doctrine in Romania before the First World War (Brătescu 2014). After the fall of communism, several parties emerged in Romania which assumed, at least partially, the values of Anglo-American neo-conservatism in combination with Christian-democracy, subsumed to the formula of the 'popular' doctrine.

Popular conservatism was represented in the beginning by the PNȚ, founded in 1927, and re-established on 11 January 1990. In order to indicate relations with Western Christian-democracy, the party assumed the Christian-democratic identity (PNȚCD). Led by leaders who had been convicted on political grounds during the communist regime, the PNȚCD demanded a return to monarchy and the 1923 Constitution, and quick retrocession of land properties and buildings nationalized during the communist period. The PNȚCD took up the anti-communist message, demanding the application of lustration. Corneliu Coposu became the leader of the PNȚCD; he had been close to Iuliu Maniu and had served seventeen years' political imprisonment. The failure of the PNȚCD during the elections of 20 May 1990, when it achieved only 2.5 per cent of the vote meant that it participated in subsequent elections as part of political alliances, as it had the support of some civic associations (Ionescu 2002).

The PNȚCD headed the 1996 winning coalition, with two prime ministers subsequently being appointed from its ranks: Victor Ciorbea and Radu Vasile. The position of the main governing party from 1996 to 2000 proved fatal to the PNȚCD. Lacking sufficiently numerous and experienced human resources for administering the country, the PNȚCD leaders were permanently on the defence against the PD and the Liberals. Confronted with economic and political difficulties, with growing social distress, caught in underground political struggles and discredited by the perception of corruption and inertia, PNȚCD leaders were incapable of ensuring efficient political communication. From being a pivotal party of government in 1996, the PNȚCD failed to enter Parliament in the 2000 elections, although it tried to conceal its identity through a new political alliance. From 2001, despite EPP political support, the PNȚCD failed to awaken the sympathy of voters, and remained outside Parliament.

The EPP's political interest in Romania was major, as, in its competition with the PES in the European Parliament, it needed every vote. The solution was offered by President Băsescu, who removed the PD from the SI and PES and transferred it into the EPP in 2005. The PD became the main partner of the European right in Romania, and even if in terms of its doctrine the party was weakly consolidated, the ambiguous 'popular' doctrine was considered sufficient.

The PD, from 2007 *Partidul Democrat Liberal* (PDL – Democratic Liberal Party), was the political arm of President Băsescu during his two mandates, behaving as a pragmatic party. Emil Boc took over its leadership, but acted only as a temporary replacement for Băsescu. In the position of presidential party, the PDL had its major electoral win in 2008, but the failure of an efficient administration during the economic crisis brought the party back to the status of secondary actor following the 2012 elections.

The establishment of a large right-wing party in Romania, after the fusion between PDL and PNL in 2015, ended the period of the intense multi-party system, as two main political blocs can now be envisaged: social democratic and conservative popular, although in between there are still some secondary political groups.

Liberals

Romanian liberals, inspired by the democratic revolution of 1848–9, had a major role in modernizing Romania. Having the advantage of this prestigious historical legacy, the PNL was re-established as early as January 1990, under the leadership of Radu Câmpeanu.

The first decade after the fall of communism was dominated by conflicts and tensions between various liberal factions. Fighting for supremacy with the PNŢCD and divided with regard to relations with Ion Iliescu, liberals created several rival political structures. The first dissidents opposed Radu Câmpeanu in 1990, aiming for a minimal state, under the name of *PNL-Aripa Tânără* (PNL-AT – PNL-Young Wing). Radu Câmpeanu removed the party from *Convenţia Democratică* (CD – the Democratic Convention) after the 1992 local elections, hoping for a higher score than the PNŢCD. The Liberal leader proposed that King Michael I should stand in the presidential elections of 1992, to the dismay of liberals. The PNL did not manage to enter Parliament in 1992, and a new crisis was generated. In 1993 Radu Câmpeanu was replaced at the top of the PNL by Mircea Ionescu-Quintus, but other factions resulted.

At the moment of the PNL's exit from the CD, a faction led by Niculae Cerveni decided to remain with the PNŢCD and the civic associations, establishing the PNL-CD (PNL-Democratic Convention), which acquired parliamentary representation in 1992.

Separated from historical liberalism, another party of anti-communist intelligentsia, *Partidul Alianţei Civice* (PAC – the Civic Alliance Party), was initially integrated into the *Convenţia Democratică din România* (CDR – Romanian Democratic Convention). The neo-liberal orientation was promoted by *Partidul Alternativa României* (PAR – the Alternative for Romania Party), which turned in 1997 into *Uniunea Forţelor de Dreapta* (UFD – the Union of the Forces of the Right). It entered Parliament in 1996 on the list of the coalition led by Emil Constantinescu, and in 2003 it was absorbed by the PNL.

The years 1993–6 saw a Brownian movement of liberal parties, the most important event being the return of the PNL (Quintus wing) to the CDR (1994) and, afterwards, to participation in government. With the advantage of a governmental party, from 1997 onwards the PNL gathered in the small liberal parties. Leaving the CDR in 2000 proved to be a saving move for the PNL, as it managed to get into parliament in its own right. The main architect of this strategy was lawyer Valeriu Stoica, who became PNL chairman in 2001. Lacking charisma, but a good negotiator, Stoica ceded the PNL leadership to Theodor Stolojan in 2002, counting on the latter's image as a technocrat. Stolojan continued the strategy of unifying liberal parties and in 2003 established an alliance with the PD. Stolojan withdrew from the 2004 presidential contest and from the PNL's leadership, being replaced at the helm by Călin Popescu-Tăriceanu. From the position of first PNL prime minister after 1989, Tăriceanu tried to expand the party's electoral pool over the threshold of 20 per cent. Internal tensions continued and the pro-Băsescu faction within the PNL, led by Stolojan and Stoica, left the party in 2007 to form *Partidul Liberal-Democrat* (PLD – the Liberal Democratic Party), which was eventually assimilated by the PD.

In preparation for the presidential elections of 2009, Tăriceanu was replaced as PNL leader by Crin Antonescu. The latter, self-willingly leading the PNL, refused any collaboration proposed by President Băsescu and kept the party in opposition. He formed an alliance with the Social Democrats against Băsescu in February 2011. The PNL got an unprecedented 28 per cent of seats in the Senate in the parliamentary elections of 2012. Following the logic of 'all or nothing', Antonescu, for reasons which were not fully clarified, later forced the PNL's withdrawal from the Ponta government, followed by an alliance with the PDL for the presidential elections. The PNL abruptly withdrew from the ALDE in 2014, becoming a member of the EPP, reasoning that they could thus have a greater role in European politics. Iohannis became PNL leader and the Liberals united with Băsescu's former party, keeping the same name. Iohannis became the first PNL leader to win Romania's presidency, thus including the Liberals in the category of major parties, together with the PSD.

The exit from the family of European liberals was not accepted by all Romanian liberals. A faction led by Tăriceanu merged with the PC in 2015, establishing *Alianța Liberalilor și Democraților* (ALD – Alliance of Liberals and Democrats), which was immediately accepted as member of the homonymous European party.

Populist nationalism

Nationalism was not 'frozen' by Marxism-Leninism and, after 1989, it became manifest both as a force of national reawakening from under Soviet influence and as an ideological exclusion force based on ethnocentrism (Andreescu 2003). Populism found several forms of political expression among which the most frequent was a combination with nationalism (Gherghina and Mișcoiu 2010).

The activism of the Hungarian community's elites at the beginning of 1990 determined a counter-reaction, informally supported by personnel of the Army and the former *Securitate*, in the form of a regional political party, *Partidul de Uniune Națională a Românilor din Transilvania* (PUNRT – the National Union Party of the Romanians of Transylvania). The structure was meant to be the protector of Transylvanian Romanians against the 'Hungarian irredentist danger', and it claimed to be a continuation of the Austro-Hungarian tradition of *Partidul Național Român* (PNR – the Romanian National Party), which had participated decisively in the achievement of Greater Romania. The PUNRT was the political arm of the *Vatra Românească* (Romanian Hearth) cultural organization, whose main leader was Radu Ciontea. The party acquired national scope by a few mergers, renouncing the specification of 'Transylvania' in its name and becoming simply PUNR. During the 1992 local elections, Gheorghe Funar won the city hall of Cluj-Napoca, the main city of Transylvania, and during the parliamentary elections of the same year he gained around 8 per cent of the vote. Funar took over the PUNR leadership in October 1992, giving it an ultranationalist direction. The party supported Romania's union with the Republic of Moldova. In 1994, the PUNR became a part of the Văcăroiu government, being assigned the ministry of agriculture (Valeriu Tabără). Funar was a virulent critic of the Romanian–Hungarian reconciliation initiated by Iliescu. In the 1996 elections, the PUNR received 4.3 per cent of the vote, a failure which led the party to split. Funar moved towards *Partidul România Mare* (PRM – the Greater Romania Party), opening the gate towards the electorate of Transylvania, while Tabără eventually ended up in the PD. The PUNR failed to enter Parliament in 2000 and eventually faded away, despite several resuscitation attempts (Abraham 2006a: 387–90).

In the same first generation of ethnocentrism promoters was the PRM, a political group led by the former communist journalist Corneliu Vadim Tudor. The party was born as a social movement generated by nationalist, anti-Semitic and knee-jerk law-and-order messages ('Down with the Mafia! Up with the Motherland!'), conveyed by *România Mare* (Greater Romania) magazine, which in 1990 had a circulation of half a million. Built by a group of writers, army generals and personnel of the former *Securitate*, as a bastion for defending the communist past, the PRM was the main defender of Ceaușescu's nationalist communism.

The party had the role of being a collecting basin of social frustrations, which progressively increased. In 1992 the PRM received 3.9 per cent of the vote in the parliamentary elections, rising to 4.5 per cent in 1996 and almost 20 per cent in 2000, before dropping again to 13.3 per cent in 2004 and 3.57 per cent in 2008, thus falling below the threshold to enter Parliament.

Despite its warlike rhetoric, the PRM was an instrument used by the main political operators against their opponents. In 1991, it was Petre Roman's weapon against *Alianța Civică* (the Civic Alliance). From 1994 to 1995, it supported the Văcăroiu government. During the period of PSD rule, the PRM aligned with the PNL and PD against the Năstase government.

Tudor's populism was violent. He proclaimed his identification with the interests of the Romanian people, while all others were real or potential enemies of the nation. The theory of international conspiracy against Romania was part of the ideological structure of the messages issued by PRM. Tudor's discourse was a mixture of populist themes of the left and of the extreme right: xenophobia, racism and violence (Abraham 2006a: 390–401).

The climax of the PRM's rise was in 2000, in the context of a collapsing Emil Constantinescu regime. Tudor reached the second round of the presidential election, promising the exemplary punishment of corruption. He lost against Iliescu, but he went on to make allegations of electoral fraud and a 'Judaeo-Masonic' conspiracy. The PRM then saw a gradual erosion of support, as Tudor's messages were no longer considered new and attractive but sterile and useless. Incapable of reforming from within, with a leader who was politically marginalized due to his extremism, which was considered incompatible with European values, the PRM left the political scene, to the regret of its militants supporters.

The political exhaustion of the PUNR and PRM left space for new forms of expression for ethnocentric social values. A second wave of nationalism emerged in the context of Romania's affiliation to the Euro-Atlantic world, being less visceral and aiming to be 'enlightened'. The first such group was *Partidul Noua Generație* (PNG – the New Generation Party), which was established in 1998, but acquired notoriety for being bought by the owner of Steaua football club, George Becali, in 2004. Originating from a family of Macedo-Romanian shepherds, Becali had become rich following real estate speculation and his national fame was acquired through super exposure in the media and by ostentatious charitable donations. In 2006, the PNG assumed a 'Christian-democratic' identity (PNG-CD), Becali being a believer who shocked with his mysticism, but also with his generous donations to church building.

The PNG-CD did not bring any significant innovations compared to the traditional national-populist line with law-and-order accents practised by PRM. Unlike the past-ridden discourse of the PRM, Becali often used an anti-communist discourse. Becali's party participated in the parliamentary elections in 2004 and 2008, but, lacking territorial structures, received less than 3 per cent of the vote. Sympathy towards Steaua and Becali's celebrity failed to transform the PNG into a parliamentary party. Becali's most important success was his election as member of the European Parliament in 2009, on the PRM's list.

Another political experiment was that undertaken by media owner and television journalist Dan Diaconescu. Through his OTV television station, Diaconescu became noticed for his populist law-and-order, anti-capitalist and anti-parliamentary rhetoric. In 2010 he founded *Partidul Poporului – Dan Diaconescu* (PP-DD – the Dan Diaconescu People's Party). In the context of economic crisis and the discrediting of the traditional parties, the PP-DD attracted almost 12 per cent of votes in the parliamentary elections of 2012 by using the strategy of aggressive law-and-order populism. Although it was large, the PP-DD parliamentary group quickly unravelled, as the party lacked any ideological and functional elements.

Following Diaconescu's sentencing to five-and-a-half years in prison for blackmail in March 2015, the PP-DD merged, a few months later with *Uniunea Națională pentru Progresul României* (UNPR – the National Union for the Progress of Romania). This party was born in 2010, as a parliamentary group built by political migration. Its leader was a former quartermaster general, Gabriel Oprea, who was previously a member of the PSD. Displaying a sort of moderate nationalism, the UNPR played the role of a 'hinge party' for the PDL and PSD, serving as a collecting basin for political migration. UNPR leaders sought to offer an honourable justification of this political role by an ambiguous appeal to 'national interest' directed towards preserving the stability of governmental coalitions. In the 2012 elections, the UNPR entered Parliament in alliance with the PSD, as the 'national interest' party failed to attract voters' support in its own right.

The ban against fascist groups forced ML admirers to organize as *Noua Dreaptă* (ND – New Right), but this remained at the stage of a non-governmental organization (Gherghina 2011: 177). Romania was thus spared the rise of anti-system nationalist-populist parties in the context of the European economic crises after 2008. The 12 per cent share obtained by the PP-DD in 2012 is that of the Romanian electorate with ethnocentric values. The traditional parties were not threatened with a massive rejection vote because, from the 2000s onwards, voters willing to search for alternative political formulas migrated in search of better paid jobs in the West and their interest in Romanian politics dramatically decreased. In spite of a chronic mistrust of parties, the Romanian electorate still hoped that the traditional parties could offer a better life.

Ethno-parties

The main ethnic minority of Romania, the Hungarians, took the initiative of creating a political vehicle dating back to the days of the 1989 Revolution. *Uniunea Democratică a Maghiarilor din România* (UDMR – Democratic Alliance of Hungarians in Romania) was legally established in April 1990 (Bucur 2014: 37), but not as a classical political party, so much as a structure gathering various ideological platforms (Christian-democratic, liberal, socialist) and apolitical organizations. Even if within the UDMR several ideological orientations coexist at international level it is affiliated to the EPP. The founding leader was Domokos Géza (1990–3), followed by Markó Béla, who handed the leadership to Kelemen Hunor in 2011.

The UDMR's doctrinal core is nationalism, with the main objective of achieving personal, local and regional autonomy, according to the political programme adopted in 1995 (Andriescu and Gherghina 2012). The issue of territorial autonomy was the strategic objective of the UDMR's political action. As far as political tactics were concerned, the Hungarian elite were divided into two factions. The first, with a gradualist orientation, sought participation in government and the progressive accomplishment of objectives through negotiation with the other political actors in Bucharest. The second, initially called *Blocul Reformist* (the Reformist Bloc), having a conservative-nationalist doctrine, wanted radical action (including the proclamation of secession in areas inhabited by a Hungarian majority, in central Romania), which would force the Romanian parties to accept territorial autonomy according to ethnic criteria. Hungary's support and internationalization of the ethnic issue in Transylvania were considered essential tactical elements. This faction finally separated from the UDMR and founded *Uniunea Civică Maghiară* (the Hungarian Civic Union), which went on to become *Partidul Civic Maghiar* (the Hungarian Civic Party) in 2008, politically and logistically supported from Hungary by the Hungarian Civic Alliance (FIDESZ). The political leader of the conservative-nationalist orientation was László Tökés, who often criticized the UDMR's gradualist tactics.

The gradualist grouping around Markó Béla and Kelemen Hunor favoured participation in government, as a form of attracting resources necessary to the Hungarian community. The UDMR entered government in 1996, and in December 2000 engaged in the parliamentary support for the Năstase government, returning to government in 2004–8, 2009–12 and 2014. The UDMR became an almost indispensable ingredient of governmental coalitions.

The strategic objective of the UDMR leadership was to preserve a monopoly over ethnic Hungarian votes. Its internal organization was conceived to bring into its deliberative structures as many community elites as possible. The designation of candidates for parliamentary elections is made following an internal ballot within the community, in order to generate consensus. Ecclesiastical structures are also involved in the administration of political power, the Catholic and Reformed churches being important electoral mobilization channels.

The UDMR managed to conserve its dominant influence among ethnic Hungarians, in spite of attacks from the nationalist-conservative camp, which intensified after 2000, also following foreign suggestions. The UDMR's internal oligarchization, manifested by the very low degree of renewal regarding its parliamentary elites, mainly masculine, did not remain without an effect among voters. During the 1990 parliamentary elections the UDMR obtained 1 million votes for the Senate, but in 2004 received only 0.63 million and by 2012 only 0.38 million (Stănescu 2014: 152). The decrease in the number of UDMR voters must also be explained by a decreasing trust in and loyalty to political elites, against the general background of diminishing voter turnout.

The German community, less numerous, did not manage to produce a competitive party at national level, just a regional structure, *Forumul Democrat al Germanilor din România* (FDGR – the Democratic Forum of Germans in Romania). The Roma community, although more numerous, lacked the necessary elites to promote its interests at national level, and remained fragmented into several small parties.

Agrarians

Quite strong during the interwar period, agrarian orientations were revived after 1989. *Partidul Democrat Agrar din România* (PDAR – the Democratic Agrarian Party of Romania) assumed the objective of reviving agriculture and the rural world. It had a minor parliamentary share following the 1990 and 1992 elections. It failed to enter Parliament in 1996 and was thus removed from political life.

Greens

The post-modern current of environmentalism was institutionalized in Romania in 1990 by the establishment of *Mișcarea Ecologistă* (MER – the Romanian Ecology Movement) and *Partidul Ecologist* (PER – the Romanian Ecology Party). During the 1990 elections, the MER managed to send to Parliament twelve deputies and one senator, while the PER won eight seats in the Chamber of Deputies and one in the Senate. Even before the May 1990 elections a section of the MER split and formed *Federația Ecologistă din România* (FER – Romanian Ecology Federation), though it did not, however, take part in the ballot.

The PER and FER became part of the CDR, achieving parliamentary representation in 1996, but failing in the 2000 elections. The MER orientated itself towards an alliance with parties close to the PDSR, but did not enter Parliament in 1996. Close to Romania's accession to the EU, *Partidul Verde* (PV – the Green Party) was established, in a laboratory initiative aimed at covering the whole European ideological spectrum.

The Greens did not manage to perform well as within society there was no structured preoccupation with environmental issues. Dominated by the logic of confrontation, environmentalist parties lacked a sufficiently visible political personality to be able to consolidate post-modern values in society.

Political and electoral alliances

The categorical domination of FSN and the political impact of the University Square protests led to the creation of political structures for consolidating the Opposition. On 15 December 1990, leaders of the PNȚCD, PNL, PSDR, PER and UDMR signed the protocol for establishing *Convenția Națională pentru Instaurarea Democrației* (CNID – National Convention for Establishing Democracy), whose objective was the creation of a democratic decommunized society. While preparing for the 1992 elections, CNID member parties and other political and civic organizations decided, on 26 November 1991, to form an electoral alliance, CD, which participated in local elections. Following this moment, the PNL left the CD, wanting to have candidates under its own name. In June 1992, a new political and electoral alliance was established, the CDR, which supported Emil Constantinescu in the presidential elections. As an opposition group, the CDR was left in 1995 by the PSDR and UDMR, but the PNL returned. In 1996, the CDR was reorganized, being composed of eighteen parties and civic groups. From its position as the main structure supporting the government after the 1996 elections, the CDR gradually unravelled, the most important moment being the PNL's exit (2000). The PNȚCD remained the main party within the CDR, but it chose to establish another alliance, with other small parties and civic associations, CDR 2000, which did not manage to enter Parliament in the 2000 elections (Pavel and Huiu 2003).

Another political alliance entering parliament after the 1996 elections was the *Uniunea Social Democrată* (USD – the Social Democratic Union), established in 1995 by the PD and PSDR. The USD unravelled in 1999, as the PSDR was preparing for another project, fusion with the PDSR.

The political imbalance created after the 2000 parliamentary elections, following which the PSD dominated political life, was meant to be ended by the cooperation between PD and PNL, within *Alianța 'Dreptate și Adevăr'* (ADA – the Justice and Truth Alliance), created in September 2003. Its presidential candidate, Traian Băsescu, won the 2004 elections. In the context of the PD's becoming a presidential party and of Băsescu's conflicts with the PNL, the ADA de facto ceased to exist in 2007 (Radu 2009).

Băsescu's domination over political life led to the creation of *Uniunea Social Liberală* (USL – the Social Liberal Union), made up in 2011 between the PSD, PNL and PC. For the general elections of 2012, an enlarged USL was formed out of two associations, *Alianța de Centru-Stânga* (the Centre-Left Alliance: PSD and UNPR) and *Alianța de Centru-Dreapta* (the Centre-Right Alliance: PNL and PC). The USL won the 2012 parliamentary elections but unravelled in 2014, in the context of political tension caused by the PNL's disbelief that Victor Ponta would respect the political agreement to support liberal leader Crin Antonescu in the presidential elections. After the Liberals left the government, the PSD announced its own candidate, Ponta, and the PNL joined with the PDL in *Alianţa Creştin Liberală* (ACL – the Christian Liberal Alliance) to support Klaus Iohannis, who won the 2014 presidential elections.

Another specific feature of political life was participation of the Social Democrats in alliance with other parties after their 1996 defeat. In 2000, *Polul Social Democrat Român* (the Romanian Social Democratic Pole) was created by the PDSR, PUR and PSDR. The Social Democrats continued their collaboration with PUR in 2004, under the name *Uniunea Naţională* PSD+PUR (the PSD+PUR National Union). In the 2008 parliamentary elections, the collaboration between the Social Democrats and Dan Voiculescu's party took the name *Alianţa Politică* PSD+PC (the PSD+PC Political Alliance). During the 2014 presidential elections, the PSD, PC and UNPR established another version of *Uniunea Social Democrată* (USD).

The dynamic of political life showed that parties made alliances in order to achieve electoral gains, but these political constructions did not resist the test of government. The CDR and the USL unravelled after winning elections. Also, associations among parties were trans-ideological, the wish to gain power or to survive being stronger than doctrinal identity.

The electoral system

The dynamic of the party system was also influenced by electoral mechanisms. After the fall of communism a classical list-based proportional representation system without an electoral threshold was established, which favoured a broad representation. In the 20 May 1990 elections, eighteen parties and political groupings were represented in the Chamber of Deputies with seven in the Senate. The 1992 parliamentary elections took place on the basis of a new electoral law, providing for a blocked-list proportional system with a 3 per cent threshold. The number of parliamentary political actors were reduced to seven. In 2000, the electoral threshold was raised to 5 per cent for parties and 8 per cent for alliances made up of two parties (Morar 2000).

In 2008 a new electoral system was introduced. Candidates competed in uninominal colleges, but the distribution of parliamentary seats was made according to proportional criteria and did not follow majority system rules. The national 5 per cent threshold was preserved. Law no. 35 of 2008 was replaced in 2015 by a return to a blocked-list proportional system, with a 5 per cent threshold. Thus ended the Romanian electoral experiment with uninominal college elections.

Party access to Parliament was also influenced by two other features of the ballots. From 1990 until 2004 parliamentary elections took place simultaneously with presidential elections, thus favouring parties with strong presidential candidates. Parliamentary elections have been preceded since 1992 by local elections for mayors, city halls and county councils. The local ballot, taking place six months before the parliamentary one, is a major test for parties, and winning local power is an important asset for the national competition.

Elections for the European Parliament, taking place for the first time in Romania in 2007, preceded presidential elections in 2009 and 2014, thus serving as a predictor of party popularity. Elections for the European Parliament also take place according to a blocked-list proportional system, with a 5 per cent threshold.

Even if the proportional system is the most democratic, it does not ensure the full representation of voters' options within Parliament. During the 1996 and 2000 elections, around 20 per cent of valid votes did not translate into parliamentary representation, being redistributed to parties which reached the electoral threshold (Radu 2012: 257–76). For Romanian society, however, the proportional system was adequate, as it allowed significant minority options in society to find a parliamentary political expression, thus limiting the potential for political conflict.

Parties and parliamentary mandates

Viewed from the perspective of the seven parliamentary elections from 1990 to 2012, the party system shows us that the left had the higher parliamentary representation, followed by liberal parties. The nationalist-populist current did not manage to be represented by the same party, but by political structures from two generations. The only political actor participating under the same name during the seven parliamentary elections was UDMR. There was only one independent MP, Antonie Iorgovan in 1990, after which election was no longer possible without party support, despite attempts by other well-known public personalities.

Electoral participation

The voting turnout of 86.2 per cent on 20 May 1990 was the peak of political mobilization, and participation in the political process gradually reduced thereafter: 76.29 per cent in 1992; 76 per cent in 1996; 65.3 per cent in 2000; 58.5 per cent in 2005; and 39.2 per cent in 2008. In 2012, there was a slight increase to 41.8 per cent. Participation in parliamentary elections was usually lower compared to presidential and local elections. European elections aroused the lowest interest (Tufiş 2014: 295; *Declinul participării* 2009). The level of voting turnout also witnessed regional differences, being higher in Oltenia, Moldavia and Muntenia, and lower in Transylvania and Bucharest. The predominant tendency was that turnout in rural areas and small towns was higher than in medium-sized towns and big cities (Iaţu 2014).

The relatively low level of electoral participation, compared to Western European countries, can also be explained by a lack of trust in the political institutions of representative democracy (parliament, parties), which were often perceived to be inefficient and corrupt (Tufiş 2012: 202–19).

Table 9.1 Parliamentary seats won by parties in elections (1990–2012)

Parties/ Elections	1990 CoD	1990 Sen	1992 CoD	1992 Sen	1996 CoD	1996 Sen	2000 CoD	2000 Sen	2004 CoD	2004 Sen	2008 CoD	2008 Sen	2012 CoD	2012 Sen
FSN/PD/ PDL	264 (66%)	91 (76%)	43 (12.6%)	18 (12.5%)	43 (12.5%)	22 (15.4%)	31 (8.9%)	13 (9.2%)	47 (14.2%)	21 (15.3%)	115 (34.4%)	51 (37.2%)	56 (9.6%)	24 (16.9%)
FDSN/ PDSR/PSD	–	–	117 (34.3%)	49 (34.2%)	91 (26.5%)	41 (28.6%)	149 (40%)	59 (42.1%)	112 (33.7%)	46 (34%)	110 (32.9%)	48 (35.1%)	152 (38.3%)	58 (31.7%)
PSDR	2 (0.5%)	0	10 (2.9%)	1 (0.6%)	10 (2.9%)	1 (0.7%)	10 (3.1%)	2 (1.4%)	–	–	–	–	–	–
PUR/PC	–	–	–	–	0	0	6 (1.7%)	4 (2.8%)	20 (6%)	11 (8%)	4 (1.3%)	1 (0.7%)	13 (3.3%)	8 (4.4%)
PNȚCD	12 (3%)	1 (0.8)	41 (12%)	21 (14.6%)	82 (23.9%)	27 (18.8%)	0	0	0	0	0	0	0	0
PNL	29 (7.3%)	10 (8.4)	0	0	25 (7.2%)	17 (11.8%)	30 (8.7%)	13 (9.2%)	65 (19.6%)	28 (20.4%)	65 (19.5%)	28 (20.4%)	100 (25.4%)	51 (27.9%)
PNLCD	–	–	3 (0.8%)	4 (2.8%)	6 1.7%	4 (2.8%)	–	–	–	–	–	–	–	–
PNL-AT	–	–	11 (3.2%)	1 (0.6%)	0	0	–	–	–	–	–	–	–	–
PAC	–	–	13 (3.8%)	7 (4.9%)	0	0	–	–	–	–	–	–	–	–
PAR/UFD	–	–	–	–	3 (0.8%)	3 (2.1%)	0	0	–	–	–	–	–	–

(Continued)

Table 9.1 Continued

Parties/Elections	1990 CoD	1990 Sen	1992 CoD	1992 Sen	1996 CoD	1996 Sen	2000 CoD	2000 Sen	2004 CoD	2004 Sen	2008 CoD	2008 Sen	2012 CoD	2012 Sen
UDMR	29 (7.3%)	12 (10%)	27 (7.9%)	12 (8.4%)	25 (7.2%)	11 (7.7%)	27 (7.8%)	12 (8.5%)	22 (6.6%)	10 (7.3%)	22 (6.6%)	9 (6.6%)	18 (4.6%)	9 (4.9%)
PRM	–	–	16 (4.7%)	6 (4.2%)	19 (5.5%)	8 (5.6%)	84 (24.3%)	37 (26.4%)	48 (14.4%)	21 (15.3%)	0	0	0	0
PUNR	9 (2.2%)	2 (1.6%)	30 (8.8%)	14 (9.8%)	18 (5.2%)	7 (4.9%)	0	0	–	–	–	–	–	–
PDAR	9 (2.2%)	0	0	5 (3.5%)	0	0	–	–	–	–	–	–	–	–
PSM	–	–	13 (3.8%)	5 (3.5%)	–	–	–	–	–	–	–	–	–	–
PER	8 (2%)	1 (0.8%)	4 (1.1%)	0	5 (1.4%)	1 (0.7%)	0	0	0	0	–	–	–	–
FER	–	–	0	0	1 (0.3%)	1 (0.7%)	0	0	0	0	–	–	–	–
MER	12 (3%)	1 (0.8%)	0	0	0	0	–	–	–	–	–	–	–	–
UNPR	–	–	–	–	–	–	–	–	–	–	–	–	9 (2.3%)	5 (2.7%)
PP-DD	–	–	–	–	–	–	–	–	–	–	–	–	47 (11.9%)	21 (11.5%)
Minorities (other than UDMR)	12 (2.7%)	–	13 (3.8%)	–	15 (4.3%)	–	18 (5.2%)	–	18 (5.4%)	–	18 (5.3%)	–	18 (4.6%)	–

Other parties	12 (3%)	0	0	0	0	0	0	0	0	0	0	0	0	0
Ind.	0	1 (0.8%)	0	0	0	0	0	0	0	0	0	0	0	0
Total	397	119	341	143	343	143	345	140	332	137	334	137	412	183

Symbols: CoD – Chamber of Deputies; Sen – Senate; Ind – Independents; (–) – party had not been created or no longer existed; (0) – party won no parliamentary representation.

Source: Compilation based on Abraham 2006a and Stănescu 2014.

CHAPTER 10
POLITICAL INSTITUTIONS

The Parliament

The transition from the communist pseudo-parliamentarianism of the Great National Assembly to liberal democracy followed several stages. The first phase was that in which the revolutionary power organ, the CFSN, also had the prerogatives of a Parliament: appointing and revoking the government, issuing legislative decrees, appointing and revoking the president of the Higher Court of Justice, regulating the electoral system, approving the state budget, ratifying and denouncing international treaties (Decree-law no. 2 of 1989).

As a result of street confrontations between supporters of traditional parties (PNL, PNŢCD) and the FSN, on 1 February 1990 an agreement was reached concerning the establishment of *Consiliul Provizoriu de Uniune Naţională* (CPUN – the Provisional National Unity Council). The institution was the first form of a parliamentary regime. From 9 February 1990, the date of the first CPUN meeting until the establishment of the elected Parliament on 20 May 1990, on the basis of Decree-law no. 92 of 1990, the attributes and manner of functioning of the CPUN remained those provided for by the CFSN (*Documente privind Revoluţia* 2009).

Decree-law no. 92 of 18 March 1990 on the election of the Parliament and the President of Romania represented a 'small constitution'. Instead of the CPUN, a unicameral organ, a Parliament made up of two assemblies was established: the Chamber of Deputies and the Senate. Instead of the CPUN President the office of President of the Republic was created. The CPUN Executive Bureau disappeared. A state administration emerged: the government led by the prime minister. According to the same decree, the President of the Republic was requested to exercise a series of attributes specific to the institution of head of state in parliamentary regimes.

The end of the constitutional transition stage took place at the end of 1991, with the validation of the new Constitution by referendum. Implicitly sanctioning the principle of separation of state powers, the fundamental law designates the Parliament as the single legislative authority of the country, having a bicameral structure: the Chamber of Deputies and the Senate. The duration of a legislature is four years and can be prolonged by organic law only in case of war or catastrophe.

The initial idea of the Constitutive Assembly was to establish a unicameral parliament, but the 1991 Constitution created the so-called symmetric or 'perfect bicameralism', as a result of FSN internal conflicts and of proposals to preserve democratic tradition. The two chambers were made up of the same type of voting (universal, direct and secret, with simultaneous elections for both chambers). What differed was the necessary number of votes for electing a member or a senator, the same governmental majority resulting in the two chambers. Romania is the only case of symmetrical bicameralism in the EU.

The chambers had identical competencies and, until 2003, there was a procedure of mediation between the Senate and the Chamber of Deputies in case of divergence upon a certain draft law. By an amendment to the Constitution in 2003 competencies related to the order of chamber reference were divided. The lower chamber is the first referred to in the case of legislative projects for ratifying treaties or other international agreements and of legislative measures resulting from these treaties or agreements, as well as for draft organic laws concerning administrative litigation, the organization and functioning of the Superior Council of Magistracy, of judicial courts, of the Public Ministry and the Court of Auditors, and the general organization of education (art. 75).

The most virulent attack against bicameralism took place in 2009. Traian Băsescu, from his position of presidential candidate, convened simultaneously with the first round of elections (22 November) a referendum during which citizens were asked if they wanted a unicameral parliament and a reduction of the number of MPs to 300. Obviously, in the context of a bad reputation for Parliament, the majority of those voting answered positively both regarding the turn to unicameralism (77.78 per cent, out of a turnout of 50.95 per cent of the electorate) and the reduction in the number of MPs (88.84 per cent). But abandoning bicameralism, which is linked with Romania's democratic tradition, in favour of unicameralism, which is reminiscent of communist pseudo-parliamentarianism, was not accepted by Parliament itself. With the exception of Traian Băsescu, the other important political actors did not yield to the populist temptation. The trend within the EU is that countries with a larger population (over 15 million inhabitants) have larger and bicameral parliaments and smaller states proportionally have less numerous legislative assemblies.

Is the Romanian Parliament 'overweight'? From 1990 to 2012, the Parliament was made up of a number of MPs varying between 486 (in 1990) and 469 (in 2004). The representation ratio, established in 1992 and kept thereafter, was 70,000 inhabitants for a Deputy and 160,000 citizens for a Senator. The uninominal system with compensation, established in 2008, showed its effects during the 2012 elections, when 588 MPs were elected, 117 more than in 2008. The cause was political domination by the USL; it won a larger number of mandates with more than 50 per cent plus one vote, but after applying the principle of proportional compensation, there were 117 additional mandates compared to 2008, most of them for smaller parties (PDL, UDMR, PP-DD). Even if we do not take into account the 2012 Parliament, the other legislatures show that, in relation to Romania's population, the Romanian legislative assembly is oversized, being more appropriate for a country with Poland's population (38 million people). If we take into account the principle that the size of a Parliament should be the cube root of the total population, then the 'ideal Parliament' in its bicameral organization and with automatic representation of minorities should have had between 270 and 300 MPs. The interests of all the political parties have determined the establishment and preservation of an 'overweight' legislative, with about 100 MPs more than necessary.

The application of the democratic principle of mutual checks between powers places the Parliament in a strong constitutional position, offering multiple instruments for exercising parliamentary control. The Constitution introduces the mechanism of the *no-confidence vote* which, once adopted, determines the fall of the government. A no-confidence vote can be initiated by at least a quarter of the total number of MPs and is adopted if it gets the vote of an absolute majority. In order to avoid excess use of such motions, the Constitution provides that if an action against the government is rejected, the same MPs cannot introduce another no-confidence motion during the same session.

From 1992 to 2015, a total of thirty-two no-confidence motions were introduced, but only two were successful. The first of them was initiated just before the 2009 presidential election campaign, and was supported by the PNL and UDMR, but voted also by the PSD. The Boc government was brought down on 13 October 2009 and immediately a PSD–PNL–UDMR coalition proposed Klaus Iohannis, mayor of Sibiu at the time, as its candidate for the post of prime minister. The candidate-president Traian Băsescu refused to consider the existence of a new majority and adopted a stalling strategy by proposing two ghost-candidates (Cătălin Croitoru, advisor to the BNR governor and Liviu Negoiță, a mayor from the PDL), so that the Boc government, though *ad interim*, offered him an advantage in organizing the presidential elections. After the controversial victory of Băsescu, Boc was re-appointed as prime minister, with the support of a majority gathered by political migration and the inclusion of the UDMR in the governmental coalition.

The second successful no-confidence motion, on 27 April 2012, demolished the Ungureanu government, led by a former Director of the *Serviciul de Informații Externe* (SIE – the Foreign Intelligence Service). The PSD and PNL managed to defeat the government promoted by Băsescu, with the support of some UDMR and minority group MPs. The unusual element from the point of view of parliamentary practice was the fact that MPs from the majority coalition (PDL–UDMR–UNPR) were instructed not to vote, with the result that only nine votes were expressed in favour of the government. In the context of the economic crisis and massive street protests, Băsescu was forced to entrust the formation of a new government to Victor Ponta, PSD chairman and leader of the Opposition.

The greatest number of no-confidence motions (eleven) were introduced between 2009 and 2012, as the governments proposed by Băsescu (Boc and Ungureanu) had a fragile majority and the economic and social crisis increased the political pressure on MPs from the majority coalition. The lowest number of no-confidence motions (two) was introduced against the Năstase Cabinet (2001–4), which was supported by a solid parliamentary majority.

Another instrument of parliamentary control is the *simple motion*. This is a parliamentary exercise by which the Opposition expresses its position concerning a domestic or foreign policy issue, but without being able to dismiss a Cabinet member. From 1992 to 2015, no fewer than 161 simple motions were introduced (108 in the

Chamber of Deputies and 53 in the Senate), out of which only eleven were adopted (three in the Chamber of Deputies and eight in the Senate). If for the Opposition a simple motion is an instrument for criticizing and eroding the government, the parliamentary majority wishes to show its solidarity and support for the cabinet, automatically rejecting criticism from the Opposition.

Other forms of parliamentary control are *questions* and *interpellations* addressed by MPs to the government. However, the prime minister or other ministers rarely show up in person to engage in dialogue with MPs.

The domination of the executive over the Parliament is emphasized by the dynamic of the legislative process. The supremacy of the executive power over the legislative was achieved by *emergency ordinances*, designed to be an exceptional instrument for governmental use in crisis situations. The use of emergency ordinances must be understood in relation to the general trend of the legislative process. Until 2000 no more than 300 laws were promulgated each year, after which, in the context of the EU accession negotiations, the number of laws increased. Only in 2010 was there a return to the situation of promulgating less than 300 laws each year (see Figure 10.1).

Emergency ordinances come into force immediately, but not all are accepted by the Parliament, thus generating an unstable legislative situation. A situation has been reached in which ordinances are voted by different legislatures than those during which they were initiated by the government. During the Văcăroiu government (1992–6), the share of laws that originated as emergency ordinances was 3.06 per cent. During the CDR–PD–UDMR government (1996–2000), the share of emergency ordinances adopted by the Parliament out of the total number of promulgated laws significantly increased, to 67.14 per cent. In 1999–2000, the government issued more emergency ordinances than the number of laws promulgated by the president (1999: 218 ordinances, 210 promulgated laws; 2000: 297 ordinances, 223 promulgated laws). Some 14.4 per cent of emergency ordinances introduced by the government between 1997 and 2000 were rejected by the Parliament. The great number of emergency ordinances can be explained by the fragility of the parliamentary majority and the conflicts within the governing coalition.

During the Năstase government (2001–4) the share of emergency ordinances from the total of adopted laws decreased to 25.38 per cent, though at the same time there was an overall increase in the number of laws adopted. In the context of a stable

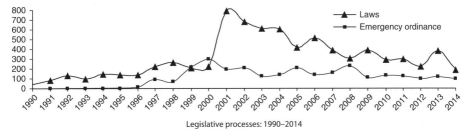

Legislative processes: 1990–2014

Figure 10.1 Dynamics of the legislative process in Romania (1990–2014)

Source: Chamber of Deputies (www.cdep.ro), own data compilation.

parliamentary majority, the share of emergency ordinances rejected by parliament diminished to 1.96 per cent.

During the 2005–8 legislature, the share of ordinances increased to 44.71 per cent, the greatest number of emergency ordinances (229) being introduced in 2008. The share of rejected emergency ordinances decreased to 0.4 per cent (*Parlamentarismul în România* 2011: 21–2). In the 2009–12 legislature, the share of emergency ordinances decreased appreciably to 38.27 per cent, and that of rejected ordinances remained under 1 per cent.

The analysis of the legislative process indicates the fact that coalition governments are more likely to use emergency ordinances, regardless of the declared ideology of the governing parties. Excessive use of governmental ordinances is the foundation of the phenomenon of legislative inflation, with the effects of legislative over-regulation and unpredictability.

The domination of the executive over the Parliament was also visible in the constitutional provision of the *governmental responsibility procedure*. If a no-confidence motion, introduced three days after the presentation of the government's initiative, is successful, the government is dismissed. If the motion is rejected, the legislative text is considered adopted. Only the president can demand the re-examination of that law by the plenary assembly of both chambers. The governmental responsibility procedure is at the same time a political and legislative tool; governments want to prove their strength and MPs cannot intervene over the legislative proposals. Until the end of 2015 there were sixteen such procedures: Ciorbea – 1; Vasile – 1; Năstase – 3; Tăriceanu – 2; Boc – 7; Ponta – 2. The inflation of governmental responsibility procedures under Prime Minister Emil Boc was determined not so much by the weakness of parliamentary support as by the authoritarian impulses of President Traian Băsescu, who in this way, on the pretext of 'economic crisis' and 'reform', wanted to diminish the legitimacy of the Parliament (*Parlamentarismul în România* 2011: 24–6).

The Tăriceanu government introduced the harmful innovation of simultaneously introducing the governmental responsibility procedure over several fields/issues, formally gathered in a single law, and thus to be voted on as a single parliamentary event ('Draft law on property and justice reform', 14 June 2005). The precedent created by Prime Minister Tăriceanu was fully used by Boc, who included several austerity measures, which changed or abrogated several laws, in a single draft law, in order to offer the abuse of executive power an appearance of lawfulness.

The Parliament, together with parliamentary parties, was among the institutions with a low level of public trust. Anti-parliamentary populism could be witnessed both among politicians and the media. The ideas of diffuse evil and collective responsibility ('they are all the same') were widely spread in collective thought, being systematically maintained by the mass media (especially electronic media). Ridiculing parliamentary life, only partially justified by the MPs' behaviour, became an obsessive media emphasis as early as 1990. The media industriously cultivated the spectacular, shocking elements of parliamentary and political party life. There was even a fashion of trapping politicians with trick questions, to which they did not know the answer. Newspapers commented widely on some parliamentary situations and declarations. Some defining elements about politicians were outlined: 'incompetence', 'inactivity', 'uselessness'. The costs related to parliamentary activity and the Parliament's endowments (cars and luxury offices), contrasting with poverty among voters, led to a general decrease of confidence in politicians (Abraham 2006a: 214).

The domination of the executive over the legislative was possible not only as a result of discrediting the parliamentary institution but also as a consequence of changes in the structure of the parliamentary body. The Parliament witnessed a high rate of newcomers after each election: 71.8 per cent (1992); 64.1 per cent (1996); 60.9 per cent (2000); 58.4 per cent (2004); 62.3 per cent (2008); 53 per cent (2012) (Ștefan 2012: 164). The predominant share of newcomer MPs can be explained by the dynamics within political parties, by infighting between factions and by the results of parliamentary elections (electoral volatility), after which some parties (for example, PNȚCD, PRM) remained outside the Parliament. Only five MPs (four of them from the UDMR) were elected in all legislatures from the CPUN to the 2012 elections. Parliament renewal is a positive fact because it favoured the circulation of the parliamentary elite, but it also contributed to a decrease in the quality of the legislative act; experienced parliamentary politicians were structurally in the minority. 'Experts', mainly high-value professional lawyers, grew fewer within the Parliament. The main tendency was a decrease in the numbers of teachers, researchers, engineers, doctors and economists, simultaneously with an increase in numbers of businessmen, public servants, officeholders and political advisors (Ștefan 2012: 112; Matichescu and Protsyk 2011). The 2008 and 2012 elections accelerated the de-professionalization of parliamentary elites, by an increase in the share of entrepreneurs and local elites, often with a precarious level of education. In fact, the shrinking of the proportion of MP with a higher academic profile (which could contribute to a qualitatively better legislation) in favour of 'sponsors' (people capable in the first place of attracting money and votes), is the consequence of the Romanian political parties' cartelization, which caused their gradual break-up with society, benefiting from the public financing of their activity and following their own logic of survival.

Politics was and remained a predominantly masculine preoccupation in Romania; this conclusion was also supported by the gender distribution of MPs. The lowest level of female representation in the Parliament can be found between 1992 and 1996: 3.7 per cent, representing eighteen women MPs. A 10.8 per cent share can be found between 2000 and 2004, representing forty women deputies and twelve women senators. In 2012, sixty-seven women were elected to the Parliament (fifty-five deputies and twelve senators), meaning a share of 11.5 per cent (Autoritatea Electorală Permanentă 2013: 1).

The Parliament was not the favourite shelter of the former Communist nomenklatura. During the 1990–2004 legislature, the share of old elite members from the former regime did not rise above 15 per cent (Grosescu 2006: 244), and with the new electoral system of 2008, the former nomenklatura dropped to an insignificant share. Two decades after the fall of communism, the parliamentary political elite was completely detached, in professional terms, from the Communist nomenklatura. New parliamentary elites emerged, made up of people professionally educated after 1989, although the latter were not *ab initio* more competent or more honest.

A profoundly negative phenomenon for the Parliament's legitimacy is political migration. The main element which makes possible the migration of MPs between parties is the constitutional insistence on the representative mandate and the interdiction on the imperative mandate. The Constitution states that: 'Any imperative mandate shall be null' (art. 69, align. 2). Constitutional provisions are based on the theory of the representative mandate, according to which MPs are representatives of the nation as a whole, not only of the community that elected them, so that they cannot be conditioned in any way during the exercise of their mandate. Parliamentary migration in the case of the Chamber of Deputies had the following dynamics: 1992–6: 79 deputies; 1996–2000: 91 deputies; 2000–4: 46 deputies; 2004–8: 81 deputies; 2008–12: 99 deputies. The practice of multiple migration was established, with cases of deputies who, during the same legislature, migrated to two or three parties. In the Senate, migration had a lower magnitude than in the Chamber of Deputies, but followed much the same trends.

At a general glance over parliamentary political migration we may notice two dominant tendencies. A first category essentially concerns migration as an individual strategy, determined by the MP's wish to get a new mandate, on the list of a party better situated in the opinion polls. There were also cases of dissident groups originating from a bigger party, but which remained in opposition (for example the case of the ApR between 1997 and 2000). The second situation regards parliamentary migration encouraged by the executive power, in order to get parliamentary support in exchange for advantages, often personal, for the migratory MPs. This process began after 2004, when thirty-one MPs left the PRM and PSD in order to create a solid parliamentary majority for the presidential party. In 2009, after the break-up of the grand coalition between the PDL and the PSD, Traian Băsescu again encouraged parliamentary migration, and in 2010 the UNPR was created especially in order to stabilize a parliamentary majority for the Boc government. The UNPR was also used by Prime Minister Ponta to collect parliamentary migration after the 2012 elections, thus becoming an essential pillar of the parliamentary majority (2014–15) around the PSD, after dissolution of the USL.

It may be observed that the parliamentary migration phenomenon is favoured by coalition governments, being significantly lower in the case of one-party governments, such as that of the PSD during the 2000–4 legislature. After 2004, the practice of coalition governments was established: Justice and Truth PNL–PD (2004), PDL–PSD (2008), USL (2012). After the unravelling of these coalitions, the party having the office of prime minister had a certain advantage, and tried to ensure its fragile majority by stimulating parliamentary migration. Although this phenomenon is criticized by parties when they are in opposition, it is used by the same political actors as an instrument for preserving governmental stability when it is favourable to them. Though it is immoral, parliamentary migration has become trivialized, becoming a usual practice which arouses neither enthusiasm nor repulsion. The deeper cause of migration can be found in the precarious human and professional quality of parliamentary elites and in party de-ideologization, as the parties were more interested in attracting 'sponsors', often people with no direct link to the history and ideological values of the party in whose name they had become MPs.

The President of the Republic

The functional and symbolic profile of the institution of President of the Republic was marked by the political inheritance of Ceaușescu. The image of the dictator-president remained alive in the collective memory and democratically elected presidents wanted to avoid association with the communist leader (Verheijen 2004: 197).

The republican option was the only desirable one for an electorate which had just exited from communism, as monarchy was associated with the interwar 'bourgeois-landowner' regime. Leaders of historical parties either supported a return to the 1923 Constitution or the organization of a referendum concerning the form of government, considering that the abolition of the monarchy had been illegal and, as a consequence, Romania ought to return to constitutional monarchy. After four decades of communism, however, support for the monarchy did not reignite and, by the beginning of the 1990s, sympathy for King Michael I (born in 1921) had reduced. Therefore, two days after the execution of the Ceaușescus, when the CFSN established the republican form of government by Decree-law no. 2 of 1989, a restoration of the monarchy was no longer possible.

Original semi-presidentialism?

Defining the presidential office was a process influenced by the political conflicts centred around Ion Iliescu. The street protests of January–February 1990, the FSN's metamorphosis into a political party and the launching of the 'neo-communist' restoration theme, used by the historical parties against Iliescu, determined the countenance of Romania's pre-constitutional regime. By Decree-law no. 92 of 1990, the President of Romania had attributes specific to heads of states in parliamentary regimes: appointing the prime minister from the ranks of the party or political movement which obtained most seats in the Parliament; promulgation of laws; mediating competition among parties; while enjoying an impartial position and not being directly engaged in the act of governing. The president had limited powers concerning the dissolution of Parliament. However, the most important fact was ultimately the election of the president by direct, universal and secret vote, which conferred on him a strong popular legitimacy.

After 20 May 1990 and the transformation of the Parliament into a constituent assembly, a question was raised concerning the constitutional definition of the political regime. A presidential model was not acceptable, as it was reminiscent of Ceaușescu. The classical parliamentary model was not desirable for Iliescu, as he knew his political legitimacy would be much reduced if he were elected by Parliament. The French semi-presidential regime seemed the ideal model, evoking the traditional French influence in

Romania. In fact, far from being simply an option in the interest of Iliescu, the preservation of a strong legitimacy for the President of the Republic, by his direct election, fitted within the international trend of the presidentialization of politics (Poguntke and Webb 2007). A soft semi-presidential model, with presidents elected by direct vote, proliferated among former communist countries, such as Poland, Bulgaria and Ukraine.

The 1991 Constitution does not depart significantly from the fundamental guidelines established as early as March 1990. The president has great legitimacy, but he is part of a two-headed executive, together with the government. The President of the Republic is not politically accountable to the Parliament, but he can be suspended for 'grave acts infringing upon constitutional provisions'. The decision of suspension must be validated by a national referendum; if not, the president remains in office.

The pressure of society for creating constitutional mechanisms that would avoid possible authoritarian sideslips determined the fragmentation of power between president and government. The president cannot dismiss the prime minister, a limitation explicitly included in the 2003 Constitution. The president can participate in government meetings, if he is invited by the prime minister. The Head of State does not have the prerogative of legislative initiative. His principal competencies are in the fields of foreign policy and defence, but his attributes in these fields are also limited, as the government 'ensure[s] the implementation of the domestic and foreign policy of the country' (art. 102). The president concludes international treaties on behalf of Romania, which are negotiated by the government. In the field of defence and security the Supreme Council of National Defence (CSAȚ) was created, which is chaired by the president and brings together the heads of the special services and cabinet members with national security attributes (defence, foreign affairs, justice, interior, and economy).

On the basis of a comprehensive interpretation of the Constitution, Romania has a parliamentary regime with a directly elected president or a parliamentarized semi-presidential regime. The ambiguous definition of presidential competencies gave rise to several political conflicts (Stan and Vancea 2015: 203–13). The attempt to turn the presidential institution into a 'republican monarchy', by extending the president's mandate from four to five years in the 2003 constitutional revision, proved to be a failure. Traian Băsescu, the first beneficiary of the five-year mandate, did not break with the custom established by Iliescu of dominating his party of origin in the shadows, but instead consolidated this pathology by creating a real presidential party (the PD), ostentatiously led by the President of the Republic. Partisan political involvement of presidents took place despite constitutional provisions which forbid them to be members of a political party. The original meaning of the constitutional norms was supposed to be a protection against the president's political partisanship.

Ion Iliescu (1989–96, 2000–4)

Ion Iliescu (born 3 March 1930) became a national political leader during the exceptional circumstances of the Revolution, and his career was favoured by the legitimacy acquired by overthrowing Ceaușescu. Iliescu was part of the enlightened elites of the communist regime, in which he served as Minister of Youth (1967–71) but was gradually marginalized by Ceaușescu in 1971, after a divergence of views.

Iliescu was elected President in three polls; the first being on 20 May 1990, when he received 85.07 per cent of the vote. Haloed by his role during the Revolution, a good orator, empathic with the crowds, Iliescu easily defeated his competitors: Radu Câmpeanu (10.64 per cent) and Ion Rațiu (4.29 per cent). The main accusation against Iliescu was that he had previously been a communist, but for most Romanians in 1990, this was an asset, a proof of competence. Iliescu won the elections with such a high score, not because there were frauds, but because the model of society promoted by the FSN was based on consensus, stability and silence, even if this meant immobility and a slow rhythm of democratic transformation.

After the adoption of the Constitution, the stage of institutional transition ended, and in 1992, new parliamentary and presidential elections were organized. Iliescu's image began to be eroded by the 1990–1 mineriads, the FSN break-up in March 1992 and, most of all, by the emergence of the first social costs of the transition to a market economy, in the context of liberalizing prices. Iliescu's electoral programme of 1992, proposed, in essence, continuing democratization and economic reform, to be achieved, however, with 'moderation and balance', overcoming 'the crisis of ruptures, incidents and fervent approaches'. The consensual message of Iliescu, who was associated with the slogan 'A president for your tranquillity!' satisfied the expectations of most categories within society. His most important opponent was Emil Constantinescu of the CDR, who proposed 'the country's total separation from communism'. Iliescu got 47.34 per cent in the first round (27 September 1992), and 61.43 per cent in the second round (11 October 1992).

Iliescu lost the presidential elections of 1996, but came back in a spectacular manner in 2000. Constantinescu's refusal to stand for a second mandate created confusion among the forces that had supported him in 1996. In the context of an economic and social crisis, accompanied by a fragmentation of the right-wing forces, Iliescu entered the second round of elections against extremist leader C.V. Tudor. The mobilization of society against the extremist danger, which was unacceptable even to many who would otherwise have opposed Iliescu, decided the outcome of the presidential final. Iliescu, becoming the 'saviour of democracy', achieved 66.83 per cent (10 December 2000).

Iliescu started from a broad political base, which transcended emerging social categories and existing cultural cleavages, as a result of his prominent role in the system change. His power base quickly eroded, however, becoming reduced to FSN voters and later to only a part of them. After the FSN's break-up in March 1992, his power base during his 1992–6 mandate was made up of the PDSR and, during his third mandate, of the PSD. The axis of his political base was in the administrative apparatus: industrial technocracy, the army and the secret services, which felt threatened by the anti-communist radicalism of the Opposition. To all these factors of institutional power Iliescu guaranteed stability during the 1990s, in exchange for their supporting his gradualist policies, for a 'quiet transition'. Having the experience of manoeuvring institutional relations since his youth, Iliescu did not enter into conflict with the power structures, as happened to Emil Constantinescu, nor was he their loud supporter, like Traian Băsescu. He was the 'quiet force' who offered resources and legitimacy, without giving the impression that he would be dominated by them. Iliescu considered that the administration, technocracy, army and intelligence services were subordinated to the political power and that the president had a central role in managing power fluxes.

Iliescu's vision of society underwent some changes. At the moment of the Revolution, Iliescu's ideological horizon was at the level of a communist favouring *Perestroika*, who gradually became a social democrat. Iliescu was a leftist president who wanted to imprint his own vision on Romanian society (Iliescu 2004: 269). From his office of president he wanted to impose on the Roman, Stolojan and Văcăroiu governments a 'gradualist-reformist' economic vision, with minimal social costs. Prime Ministers Stolojan and Văcăroiu, originating from the communist regime's technocracy, avoided entering into conflict with Iliescu, and adapted to his vision. Petre Roman, however, who assumed the identity of a quick-reform leader, entered into conflict with the president, a stage ending up with his removal from government following the September 1991 mineriad.

In his relations with the Năstase government, President Iliescu wanted to preserve his political authority within the PSD, for which reason he opposed several governmental initiatives. He was against the intention of renouncing the progressive taxation of individual income in favour of a flat-rate tax in 2002, claiming it was not a social democratic measure. He also blocked Prime Minister Năstase's intention of forcing early elections immediately after Romania was invited to join NATO the same year, which would have offered a clear advantage to the Social Democrats, but would have left Iliescu out of the power equation in the PSD after the end of his mandate. In the context of the simmering conflict with Iliescu, Prime Minister Năstase, following unconvincing results in the local elections and divergences which followed within PSD, briefly resigned as head of government in July 2004, but he came back in order not to deepen the political crisis.

In exercising his role of mediator, Iliescu used the instrument of periodic informal consultations, usually attended by the prime minister and the speakers of the two chambers of the Parliament. Thus, institutional bottlenecks were avoided and political conflicts rarely became public.

Immediately after the fall of communism, Iliescu hoped to establish an 'original democracy' and a social system that would combine the prosperity of capitalism with the social security of communism. Iliescu did not wish to amplify conflicts within society, but instead to generate consensus. For example, after the 1992 parliamentary elections he wanted a Romanian 'Moncloa Pact', by a political agreement between the FDSN and the CDR. Corneliu Coposu, leader of the Opposition, refused the offer to participate in government, thinking that a minority government around the FDSN would not survive, and that, following early elections, the CDR would win. The CDR leaders were wrong, as the Văcăroiu government survived until the 1996 elections. The defining moment for Iliescu's belief in building national political consensus was the 'Snagov Declaration' on 21 June 1995, by which the main parties and institutions of Romania committed themselves to supporting Romania's EU accession.

Iliescu's prudence, synonymous with inaction for his critics, was useful to Romania during the tense atmosphere of the 1990s, as the danger of escalating interethnic conflicts was avoided after the Târgu Mureş episode in March 1990. On the other hand, his hesitant character (Boda 1999: 243; Dobrescu 1997: 109) and desire to be the 'providential man' by his calm and tolerance, not only for society, but also for the party he tutored, consequently lead to a proliferation of corruption. Iliescu wanted to be 'poor and honest', but his action was limited to criticizing, albeit often heavily, the 'flunkeyism' and 'crony capitalism' even within his own party. The institutional tolerance for corruption manifested by Iliescu can be also explained by his belief that the primitive accumulation of capital could not be made only with legal means: a 'law of history' could not be avoided by Romanian society; only its effects could be limited.

The approach of the monarchic issue by Iliescu proves his capacity of reinventing himself. In January 1990, Michael I asked the CPUN to re-establish the democratic Constitution of 1923. The CPUN refused, and the former monarch's entry to the country on the occasion of Easter 1990 on 13 April was forbidden. Later, on 24 December 1990, after initially allowing Michael I to enter Romania, the government changed its mind and the former monarch was expelled. On 23 April 1992, Michael I came back to Romania for Easter. He was welcomed enthusiastically by tens of thousands of Romanians. Following this triumphal reception, Iliescu blocked any further visits by the former monarch, for fear of the rising popularity of the Opposition and the monarchy.

During his final mandate, with the prospect of Romania's Euro-Atlantic integration, Iliescu became reconciled with the former monarch on 19–20 May 2001, in a meeting that was meant to symbolize the closing of past wounds. The Romanian state recognized the property rights of the Royal House over some properties nationalized by the communist regime and Michael I gave his support to Romania's candidature for NATO accession.

In the same spirit of closing past wounds, Iliescu acknowledged the responsibility of the Romanian state for the Holocaust, following the activity of the Elie Wiesel Commission in 2004. As far as communism was concerned, Iliescu had an ambivalent attitude: he criticized crimes from the time of Gheorghiu-Dej and Ceauşescu's dictatorship, but he always considered that there were numerous positive factors. Regarding the victims of the Revolution, Iliescu had a constant attitude of respect and he favoured material rewards for revolutionaries. Using his influence over the army and the justice system, he tried to offer protection to some of the army generals who had supported the FSN. During Iliescu's mandates, the criminal trials arising from the Revolution involved only second-rank communist politicians and officers.

On the issue of restoring property, Iliescu retained a statist vision, accepting the resolution of this issue only under the influence of foreign factors (ECtHR decisions convicting the Romanian state and clarification of the property issue in preparation for EU accession). Iliescu seemed convinced that 'one injustice cannot be undone by another' and that *restitutio in integrum* would cause serious social problems, leaving millions of people homeless. Iliescu wanted a moderate compromise solution, refusing the *restitutio in integrum* principle with regard to property, both in order to keep a body of voters which had something to lose and because the accumulation of large land or industrial properties would have led to growing inequalities within society. Or because, as a convinced socialist, Iliescu wanted a cohesive and equalitarian society.

The only initiative aimed at suspending Iliescu from the office of president was blocked in Parliament because the CDR did not have enough votes; it started from his Satu Mare declaration of 20 May 1994, according to which the courts should not admit claims concerning nationalized houses from the former owners, as no legislation to this end had yet been adopted.

Romania's international policy can also be looked upon from the perspective of Iliescu's political vision dynamic and manner of action. The collapse of the USSR was not anticipated in Bucharest until the middle of 1991; Iliescu wanted to maintain cordial relations with Moscow (Iliescu 2011: 181). Romania under Iliescu was the last of the CEE countries to accept the dissolution of the Warsaw Pact and the COMECON. Although it had connections with NATO within the North-Atlantic Coordination Council, the Bucharest regime remained distant towards the Alliance, initially refusing direct military cooperation. In August 1991 and October 1993, after Muscovite putsches, the reactions of the Romanian president were equivocal. Ion Iliescu waited to see who the winners were, before assuming a public position. The conclusion of the Romanian–Soviet Treaty on 5 April 1991, while the Soviet security system in Central Europe was in full disarray, was a major diplomatic error. It can be explained, on one hand, by Iliescu's excessive prudence, as he wanted to maintain close relations with Gorbachev's USSR, and, on the other hand, by his reticence towards the capitalist system. Gorbachev's USSR, with its limited pluralism, a market economy but with the state massively involved in the economy, seemed adequate to Iliescu's political vision during the 1990s.

Understanding that the dissolution of the USSR completely changed the rules of the international game, Iliescu wanted to completely eliminate doubts about Romania's pro-Western orientation. Thus, he contributed to an exit from international isolation by cultivating relations with Western countries. The main achievement of Iliescu's first two presidential mandates was the Treaty with Hungary in 1996, which made possible the full normalization of bilateral relations, opening the path towards Euro-Atlantic integration.

Iliescu became a staunch supporter of Romania's connection to NATO and the EU, but promoted a flexible multi-dimensional foreign policy, with openings to China, Russia and the Middle East, especially in the field of economic relations.

During his third presidential mandate, Iliescu dedicated himself to Romania's Euro-Atlantic integration. He and Prime Minister Năstase distributed their foreign policy tasks, wanting to send a message of unity and solidarity. As chairman of the CSAT, Iliescu approved the close relations of Romanian security structures with their Western counterparts, going so far as to agree to the opening in Romania in 2002 of a centre of the US Central Intelligence Agency, around which speculations later emerged that it was a detention centre in which terrorism suspects were tortured. Under Iliescu, Romania joined NATO and finalized EU accession negotiations, thus crowning ten years of exercising the presidential office.

Emil Constantinescu (1996–2000)

Professor of geology, rector of the University of Bucharest, and a supporter of the protests in University Square, Emil Constantinescu (born 19 November 1939) was the beneficiary of favourable political conjunctures. Although he was not the leader of a political party, in 1992 he became the CDR presidential candidate, as the Opposition's main political leader, Corneliu Coposu (1914–95), was too old to enter into a presidential competition. In 1996 he was reconfirmed as CDR candidate, as he was the Democratic Convention's personality with the highest public exposure (Pavel and Huiu 2003).

In a political context dominated by expectations of political change, Iliescu received the highest number of votes in the first round of the 1996 elections, but Constantinescu won the second round (54.41 per cent, 17 November 1996) with the support of a broad coalition which no longer wanted the PDSR in power, made up of the CDR, USD and UDMR.

Emil Constantinescu essentially defined himself as a civil society man, originating in and being legitimized by it. His supporters considered him a 'Romanian Havel'. He had not had a relevant political career during the communist regime; nor had he been a political dissident. Constantinescu did not build a party, as Iliescu or Băsescu did, but he was the chairman of the CDR in 1992–6, an eclectic structure which could not ensure the political support needed to lead the country in the long term. Constantinescu considered the authority of the presidential office to be sufficient to generate the necessary basis for exercising power. He wanted to follow the model of a moderator-president, being prudent in showing political partisanship. He surrounded himself with advisors who did not hold political influence within the CDR, considering that they were recommended by their professional and human qualities and not by a potential role of intermediaries for presidential interests with political parties.

Constantinescu did not have the ambition of being a political doctrinaire or visionary. His perspective over society was moralizing, impregnated by the national 'fear of failure' as a result of communist history and transition (Constantinescu 2002). The politician Constantinescu was a convinced democrat; his democratic ethos was authentic, aiming for a 'political revolution' by which Romanian society would Westernize and detach itself from its totalitarian past.

The Constantinescu administration proved precarious in the pragmatic use of political tools for reaching its objectives. Constantinescu's relations with political forces which supported him during the presidential elections had undergone a transformation. Constantinescu managed to impose on the coalition parties, in the first place the PNȚCD, the appointment of Victor Ciorbea (mayor of Bucharest, elected in 1996) to the office of prime minister, despite significant support within the same party for Radu Vasile, a senior leader of the party (Diaconescu 2003: 199–200). Prime Minister Ciorbea was a docile collaborator with Constantinescu, even if there were moments when the head of government wanted to preserve his decisional autonomy (Vălenaș 2003: 37).

The first political conflict with the support base was with the Civic Alliance, when Constantinescu refused to accept the ideological patronage of its leaders and the expected jobs of presidential advisors were not received by public intellectuals. In March 1997, Constantinescu declared that the lustration project (supported by the Civic Alliance) was no longer necessary, the priority being to reconcile society. In addition, Constantinescu abandoned the idea of returning to monarchy, to which he had acquiesced before winning the elections. These changes meant a transition from ideology to the reality of exercising power. The cost was the alienation of Constantinescu's most ideological supporters, who had hoped that the president would be a docile instrument in their hands.

Following the political crisis generated by the PD when they left government in February 1998, Constantinescu was politically weakened, and was forced to accept the sacrifice of Prime Minister Ciorbea in March 1998. Radu Vasile won the support of the PNŢCD for the office of prime minister, against the presidential favourite, Sorin Dimitriu. Presidential influence over the government decreased very much in favour of the PD and the Vasile faction within the PNŢCD. Constantinescu took his revenge in December 1999, forcing the replacement of Prime Minister Vasile by extra-constitutional means. The price imposed by the PD for preserving the governing coalition was the acceptance of a technocrat as the head of government. Constantinescu chose Mugur Isărescu, governor of the National Bank. This decreased even more the president's influence over the government and the coalition and Constantinescu became ever more politically isolated. His dramatic decline in the opinion polls turned Constantinescu into a subject of the media's daily ironies. Constantinescu did not have the ability and authority to keep the CDR united, and the PNL's game of political survival by leaving the CDR in 2000 left all the failures of government in the charge of the PNŢCD and the president.

Constantinescu's presidential mandate was marked by political tensions and social protests, which culminated with the mineriads of the winter of 1999. Accepting the IMF's premise that Romania's economy could recover only after 'shock therapy', in the context of a diminishing of the country's financial resources, numerous state enterprises were closed, the mining sector was radically restructured by closing mines and the banking sector was to be cleared of bankrupt banks. Inflation reached almost 155 per cent in 1997 and the national currency suffered massive depreciation. Poverty quickly extended and the enthusiasm for political change turned into disappointment and contempt towards the governing coalition and Emil Constantinescu. The economic crisis was exacerbated by the proliferation of corruption. The CDR was notable for its lack of competent technocrats, although it had undertaken to bring '15,000 specialists' into the government. The numerous protest movements strongly undermined Constantinescu's political legitimacy.

The perception of failure concerning Constantinescu's presidency, bitterly acknowledged even by his supporters, was also determined by limited success in the issue of property restitution. The main achievement remains Law no. 1 of 2000, extending the land surface which could be restored from 10 to 50 hectares. At the end of the Constantinescu administration a law was drawn up concerning the legal status of some buildings that had been abusively nationalized between 1945 and 1989. This was eventually adopted, after amendments, in January 2001 by the PSD government. The adoption of a law concerning the disclosure of the *Securitate* (Law no. 187 of 1999) was not followed by a transfer of files towards a civilian institution in order for the action of recognizing and assuming the past to become effective.

The undisputable achievements of President Constantinescu can be found in the field of international politics. After Romania's failure to join NATO during the Madrid Summit (July 1997) and the visit of US President Clinton to Bucharest, Constantinescu continued efforts to connect to the Euro-Atlantic world. In relations with the major international actors, the most important elements were the Strategic Partnership with the US and the Special Partnership with France in 1997, the opening to China (the project of rebuilding the Silk Road) but also the maintaining of cold relations with the Russian Federation. Another event with a special symbolism was the visit of Pope John Paul II to Bucharest in May 1999, the first visit of a Roman Catholic pontiff to a country with an Orthodox majority; the main credit for this was due, however, to Prime Minister Radu Vasile (a Catholic convert).

The moment of maximum tension for Constantinescu was his support for the Anglo-American position during the Kosovo conflict, including the bombing of Belgrade, in the face of opposition from public opinion. As a consequence of the support given in the Yugoslav issue, on 4 May 1999, British Prime Minister Tony Blair committed himself in Bucharest to supporting the Romanian cause of joining the EU. During the European Council of Helsinki (December 1999), Romania was invited to begin EU accession negotiations. However, the moment of the 1999 Yugoslav War accelerated the population's loss of faith in President Constantinescu; socio-economic failures contributed to his quick and irreversible political decline (Gallagher 2004: 167–270).

During the second part of Constantinescu's presidential mandate, when signs of failure were becoming visible, he left the impression of a person profoundly disappointed by society. For example, in March 1999 he publicly declared that 'the political world is dirty and miserable'. Ultimately, politically isolated, Constantinescu acknowledged his failure, announcing his abandonment of the political battle for a new presidential mandate on 17 July 2000. Constantinescu seemed at the end of his mandate to be a politician sacrificing himself, quitting politics in the hope that posterity would recognize his merits. Constantinescu offered a conspiracy-theory explanation for his political failure, responsibility being attributed to the 'forces of the dark' (*Securitate*, Communist nomenklatura). It is true though that neither the intelligence structures nor media owners linked with the communist regime had any interest in supporting him, but his political failure was essentially determined by an inefficient, unprofessional and often corrupt government, whose failings he had allowed himself to be identified with, albeit also by his own inaction.

In 2000 Constantinescu did not take the risk of a humiliating electoral failure, hoping that a future comeback would still be possible. In 2003 he created the *Acțiunea Populară* (the Popular Action), a vehicle for his return to politics. However, his historical moment had passed and he found few allies ready to link their future to a leader associated with a major failure, the CDR-dominated government.

Traian Băsescu (2004–9, 2009–14)

A former merchant navy captain approved by the *Securitate* to become head of a Romanian maritime transport agency (NAVROM) in Antwerp, Belgium in 1987–9, Traian Băsescu (born 4 November 1951) had a political career within the FSN (Minister of Transport), then became mayor of Bucharest in 2000, then chairman of the PD in 2001. Băsescu became President of Romania in October 2004, after replacing at the last moment the candidate of the PNL–PD Alliance, Theodor Stolojan. The change of candidate was announced by Băsescu, seen shedding tears in front of an astonished audience, in order to justify the unexpected replacement of a candidate with no chance. The pretext of replacement was an imaginary 'illness' and 'blackmail'. Năstase, the prime minister in office, started out as front-runner in the election, as a result of economic success, of NATO accession and of ending the EU accession negotiations. In the first round on 28 November 2004, Năstase got 40.94 per cent and Băsescu 33.92 per cent. Immediately after the first round of the election, Băsescu accused Năstase of election fraud. The serious accusation was only a trick in a dirty electoral campaign, but it helped mobilize undecided voters. Băsescu legitimized himself by promising to punish corruption and to introduce a flat-rate tax on personal income. In the context in which in the neighbouring Ukraine the 'orange revolution' was under way with significant street protests, Băsescu won the presidential election on 12 December 2004 in the second round, with 51.23 per cent of the vote.

Băsescu became the first president with two consecutive mandates under the 1991 constitution, managing to win the 2009 presidential election (with 50.33 per cent in the second round, 6 December 2009) against Social Democrat Mircea Geoană. Băsescu got a second mandate following an electoral campaign during which his main message was an anti-parliamentarian populist law-and-order one. Simultaneously with the first round of the presidential election, he convened two referenda by which he proposed a unicameral parliament and a reduction of the number of MPs to a maximum of 300. However, his victory was brought about by a major mistake on the part of Geoană, who met a few days before the second round with oligarch S.O. Vântu; Băsescu speculated that his opponent was controlled by tycoons. Geoană confirmed the visit, but said he had gone to the oligarch 'to discuss financial and banking issues', a statement which bewildered even his electorate. In spite of this, Băsescu lost the election in Romania, but won as a result of the diaspora vote. Băsescu's victory was the more spectacular in that most parties and most of the mass media were allied against him, with the exception of the presidential party (PDL), but the small and controversial difference (Geoană alleged election fraud) deepened the division of society.

Unlike previous presidents, Băsescu began his mandate with a limited political basis which he managed to extend. He became increasingly popular by displaying uninhibited behaviour, using direct colloquial language, which created the image of a 'man of the people'. For example, in 2006 he partied all night with George Becali, owner of the football club Steaua, after they had qualified for the UEFA Cup semi-finals, and in the morning he drove home. Băsescu became increasingly popular by using systematic messages against corruption, criticizing political parties, the Parliament and 'tycoons'. In order to de-legitimize critical media, he repeatedly stated that it acted following the political commands of its owners, which was not so far from the truth. In fact, even the media supporting him was responding to the commands of oligarchs just as much as the critical media; Băsescu, however, considered the former to be 'unbiased' and 'professional'.

Băsescu's mandates unfolded under the sign of systematic attempts to match an authoritarian vision of human relations with the attributes of a president mediating between state and society, according to the constitutional provisions. Băsescu declared himself a 'player-president' aiming to get involved in all issues of society, ignoring the separation and mutual checks of state powers. Presidential voluntarism was justified by Băsescu as the defence of 'popular' interests against corruption. Băsescu's 'neo-caesarist' regime was characterized by the leader's action of restraining the legitimacy of democratic institutions (Parliament, parties), by permanently discrediting them.

Significant for Băsescu's 'neo-caesarism' are his relations with governments. As early as December 2004 he refused the idea of coalition, threatening the PUR and UDMR, initially allied with the PSD, which had won the parliamentary elections of 2004, that, if they did not participate in a government led by Călin Popescu-Tăriceanu of the PNL, he would call for early elections. The PUR, named by Băsescu in January 2005 the 'immoral solution', and the UDMR yielded to the blackmail and joined the governmental coalition forced by the president.

Attempting to have all the power, Băsescu and Tăriceanu initially wanted to organize early elections for July 2015, but the prime minister changed his mind after the president implied that he wanted a totally obedient head of government (Săftoiu 2015: 225). Tăriceanu thwarted Băsescu's ruse, refusing to resign and in 2006 personal conflicts between the two began. The institutional consequence of the wish for absolute power was a generalized political conflict following which the PNL–PD Alliance unravelled, the presidential party (PD) was removed from government on 1 April 2007, and eventually there was an attempt to dismiss Băsescu.

After the parliamentary elections of 2008, Băsescu 'saw his dream coming true', as he confessed, as it was now possible to impose a prime minister willing to follow presidential directives verbatim: Emil Boc. The real headquarters of the executive power transferred from the government to the presidency and ministers became, most of the time, mere executors of the presidential will. The symbolic moment of Băsescu's domination over the government was the announcement of austerity measures on 6 May 2010. This was not made by Prime Minister Boc, who had the constitutional right, but by the president himself.

Loss of control over government, following the dismissal of the Ungureanu cabinet after a no-confidence vote and the establishment of the Ponta government in May 2012 saw a resumption of public conflict between Băsescu and the prime minister.

Băsescu's 'neo-caesarism' is highlighted by the use of the consultative referendum, provided by the constitution as an extraordinary manner of solving divergences within society. Instead of negotiating with political parties and other relevant actors in society, Băsescu wanted to impose his own vision, at all costs, by setting the will of the 'people' against the will of the parties and the Parliament. Presidents Iliescu and Constantinescu never used the consultative referendum, but Băsescu organized no fewer than three. The first referendum took place on 25 November 2007, simultaneously with elections for the European Parliament. The issue at stake was the election of MPs in uninominal constituencies, 'on the basis of a majority vote in two rounds'. The referendum was invalidated due to lack of quorum. A further two referenda were organized simultaneously with the first round of 2009 presidential elections, the subjects of consultation being the abolition of the Senate and reducing the number of MPs to a maximum of 300. We may notice that the referenda were organized around issues concerning political institutions and not themes of major interest to society as a whole.

Băsescu's authoritarian vision on political and human relations can be seen in his relations with the PD. First of all, on his election as president and resignation from the PD, Băsescu directly 'appointed' Emil Boc to succeed him as party chairman. Afterwards, in June 2005, suddenly and without any debate, the PD abandoned the PES in favour of the EPP. Băsescu's aim was to create a great right-wing party in Romania through a merger of the PD and the PNL, a project refused by the Liberals. In response, Băsescu activated a liberal dissidence led by Theodor Stolojan, who created the PLD in December 2006, only for it then to be taken over by the PD in January 2008, thus establishing the PDL, after a short-lived attempt at destabilizing the Tăriceanu government.

Băsescu's loss of political vitality in the later part of his second mandate led the PDL to emancipate itself from presidential control. Băsescu tried to impose Elena Udrea, a charming blonde about whom there were rumours that relations were more than just professional, at the helm of the PDL, but his attempt failed. In spite of Băsescu's wishes, Vasile Blaga became chairman of the PDL on 23 March 2013, and openly expressed an independent attitude. Băsescu's furious reaction was to allege fraud in the PDL elections, thus announcing a definitive break-up with the former presidential party.

Political tensions between Băsescu and most political parties, his refusal to mediate conflicts and his frequent attacks against opponents, in the name of the fight against corruption and the 'reform' of justice also led to two actions to remove him from office.

The first suspension was initiated by the PSD, as a method not only of defending democracy, but also of consolidating the political position of Mircea Geoană, leader of the Opposition at that time. The PNL associated itself with this initiative of suspending Băsescu, as it hoped that it could thus consolidate the government, which was under constant attack from the president. The UDMR joined the suspension action, as Băsescu was openly encouraging a rival structure, the Hungarian Civic Union, which was nationalistic and conservative. As a consequence, a broad coalition made up of 322 MPs emerged within the Parliament, which voted to suspend Băsescu from office on 19 April 2007. Băsescu's dismissal referendum (19 May 2007) was however clearly won by him (74.48 per cent of votes against dismissal). The initiators of the suspension lost to Băsescu because they did not know to convince people about the danger the president's actions presented for democracy. The parties initiating the suspension were perceived as being corrupt and illegitimate. In his defence, Băsescu stated that he had been suspended because he had fought for the interests of the 'people' and for the independence of justice. Băsescu claimed that his dismissal was wanted by the oligarchs and by Russia (*Referendumul* 2007).

The second suspension action was initiated in the summer of 2012, shortly after the USL took over the government led by Victor Ponta. Băsescu was blamed for multiple breaches of the Constitution, in essence that he was behaving according to the autocratic principle '*L'Etat c'est moi!*' In fact, the USL wanted to eliminate an unpopular president, following austerity policies. Băsescu was increasingly irritating a population growing tired of permanent political conflicts. At the same time, an accusation of plagiarism concerning Ponta's doctoral thesis emerged, which was interpreted by Ponta as a manoeuvre of a group close to Băsescu. On 6 July 2012, Băsescu was suspended from office by the Parliament, with 256 votes in favour, and the second USL leader, Crin Antonescu, became *ad interim* president by virtue of his position as Speaker of the Senate. The dismissal referendum of 29 July 2012 was clearly lost by Băsescu, whose strategy was to allege a 'coup d'état', asking citizens to boycott the popular vote, in order not to fulfil the necessary quorum for the referendum to be validated. The electorate voted massively in favour of dismissal (7.4 million votes), wishing to punish Băsescu both for austerity policies and for behavioural excesses which citizens no longer so as picturesque, as in the beginning, but rather grotesque and improper for a head of state (Radu and Buti 2013). However this was not enough to reach the threshold of 50 per cent of the total electorate plus one, which was required in order for the referendum result to be validated by the Constitutional Court. After this second dismissal attempt, Băsescu returned to his office, in spite of some political and constitutional controversies, but with his legitimacy strongly shaken. From this point until the end of his mandate his political role ceased to be significant.

The two attempts to dismiss Băsescu and the constant tension between the president and the prime minister must be explained not only by the voluntarist presidential style, but also as symptomatic of the failure of institutional cohabitation specific to republics with presidents elected by universal suffrage (Ghergina and Mişcoiu 2013).

Băsescu's mandates were marked by a series of actions to change Romanian society. Although initially he was not convinced of the necessity of condemning communism, which was demanded by a part of the *intelligentsia*, being rather reticent in this regard (Săftoiu 2015: 129–34), in December 2006 he condemned the communist regime in the Parliament, considering it 'illegitimate and criminal', on the basis of a report elaborated by a presidential committee led by Vladimir Tismăneanu. A positive fact was the pressure on the intelligence services to transfer to a civilian institution most of the former *Securitate*'s files between 2005 and 2006. Even if Băsescu was blamed for his personal interactions with the *Securitate* (insufficiently clarified by the archives) the transfer of the files created the possibility of clarifying a sensitive issue for society.

Băsescu sensed the opportunity of using presidential committees around various fields, which would offer expertise for future public policies. Constitutional reform was not achieved due to the fact that conflicting approaches over the issue did not offer chances of success. The intention of reforming health, by reorganizing the system according to market economy criteria, generated public protests in 2012 and was abandoned. The demographic crisis was also analysed by a presidential committee, but its recommendations were not turned into a framework for public policies. Băsescu made numerous efforts at the reform of education. However, forcing the adoption of an education law (Law no. 1 of 2011), not by parliamentary debate, but by governmental responsibility of the Boc government, raised the hostility of both trade unions and political parties, with the result that the legislation was subsequently changed by the Ponta government.

In the field of international politics, Băsescu distinguished his approach by stating his Atlanticism under the form of the 'Washington–London–Bucharest Axis'. He closely followed American policy in the region and in Afghanistan and Iraq, though he was unsuccessful in his attempts to bring about a greater US involvement in solving frozen conflicts in the Black Sea region and the Caucasus. He wanted to go down in history through the unification of the Republic of Moldova with Romania, but international conditions were not prepared for such an undertaking. His anti-Russian rhetoric maintained bilateral relations at a very low level. In European politics, Băsescu followed a strategy of mimetic connection to the strategy of the Great Powers, first of all to Germany's. He imposed the austerity policies promoted by Germany within the EU after 2008. Romanian influence in the EU was undermined by permanent internal conflicts, thus consolidating the perception that Romania was a 'problem child'.

Băsescu's greatest passion was the secret services; he often stated that he was 'the best informed person in Romania', a situation which led to several debates concerning the services' partisan involvement in politics. The intelligence services and the prosecution service were the institutions that acquired the highest influence during Băsescu's mandates, a situation justified by the fight against corruption (Poenaru and Rogozanu 2014).

After a decade of conflicts, Romanian society came out of the 'Băsescu era' divided, conflictual and confused to the point of anomy. Băsescu left the presidential office deserted by his former allies and with the stigma of his own brother Mircea Băsescu's arrest under the accusation of receiving €250,000 from a Roma criminal clan in exchange for the promise of getting some favourable decisions for them in court.

The government

The cabinet of ministers in the aggregate executive power

Abandoning the party-state system left an open area for redefining the executive power in a democratic context. Overcoming the stage of system change ambiguity, the government is defined by Law no. 37 of 1990 as 'the central body of executive power, which exercises, according to law, public administration over the whole territory of the country'. Then, the constitution extensively establishes the role of government: it 'shall (...) ensure the implementation of the domestic and foreign policy of the country, and exercise the general management of public administration' (art.102, align.1).

The relations between government and Parliament are specific to a parliamentary regime. The government is empowered by Parliament to use emergency ordinances, with the exception of fields in which a qualified majority is needed for adopting laws.

The main ambiguity and source of political tension was the relationship between president and prime minister, both parts of a two-headed executive. The president cannot dismiss the prime minister, a provision included in the 2003 constitutional revision as a result of the forced dismissal of Prime Minister Radu Vasile by President Constantinescu in 1999. In order to ensure governmental stability, it is difficult to call early elections: 'the President of Romania may dissolve Parliament, if no vote of confidence has been obtained to form a government within 60 days after the first request was made, and only after rejection of at least two requests for investiture' (art. 89, align. 1). The president can chair Cabinet meetings in exceptional cases and only following an invitation from the prime minister. The head of government has an important disadvantage: the president is the *de facto* coordinator of the intelligence services. This situation offers the president great influence, through access to information, which has often been used in political battles. The very fact that the president chairs the CSAȚ, and a number of ministers take part in its sessions, means that heads of state have tried to tutor some members of the cabinet (especially from foreign affairs and defence), an attitude accepted or rejected by prime ministers, according to the political context.

This two-headed executive, taking over from the semi-presidentialism of the French Fifth Republic, brought about the emergence of cohabitation. This is only formal when the president and the prime minister originate from opposing political camps. In Romania, this situation occurred for the first time in 2007, between President Băsescu and Prime Minister Tăriceanu, then resumed after 2012 between Presidents Băsescu and Iohannis and Prime Minister Ponta. There was an attempt to regulate the cohabitation situation by an 'Institutional Collaboration Agreement' signed on 12 December 2012 by Băsescu and Ponta (Radu and Buti 2013: 257–9). The document, without legal value, was signed after the second failed attempt to dismiss Băsescu and following the USL's victory in the parliamentary elections. The meaning of the agreement was to reassure Western governments regarding the political situation in Romania, and also to assure both signatories that the country would be governed without escalating political conflicts anew.

There was also an informal cohabitation, when conflicts took place between presidents and prime ministers from the same political structure: Iliescu and Roman after the 1990 elections until the 1991 mineriad; Constantinescu and Vasile (1998–9); Băsescu and Tăriceanu, from the middle of 2005, when the Prime Minister refused to resign, until April 2007, when the pro-presidential party (PD) was removed from government (Stan 2009). The cohabitation stage had multiple consequences. It mainly affected public trust in politicians, following frequent conflicts. Society became divided and radicalized between supporters of the President and of the Prime Minister. Much as in the case of French cohabitations (Lazardeux 2015), the efficiency of public institutions decreased. The conflictual division of executive power made administrative institutions under governmental and government parties' influence reticent in cooperating with the President and lead those from the presidential sphere (especially the intelligence services) to collaborate only selectively with the government.

The area of governmental competency was gradually reduced. The decentralization of administration brought about a transfer of attributes and resources towards local authorities, and the role of government turned from administrator to regulator and controller of national policies. Additionally, the limitation of governmental power was achieved by a transfer of competencies from ministries towards new agencies and authorities, created during the European integration process. A part of these new structures remained under the government's coordination; others, especially market regulating and control institutions, left the sphere of direct political control. After 2000, no less than thirty authorities and agencies were created, which either took over some of the ministries' tasks or received new sectors of activity, which had not previously been assigned to ministries. The demarcation of competencies among ministries, authorities and agencies was not sufficiently precise, for which reason institutional overlapping occurred and bureaucracy expanded.

Table 10.1 Cabinets after 1989: political composition, parliamentary support, dimensions

Legislature	Cabinet/Term	Main parties in cabinet	Parliamentary political support	Number of portfolios*	Number of ministers**
1989–1990***	Roman I 22/12/89–28/06/90	FSN	FSN	31	34
1990–1992	Roman II 28/06/90–16/10/91	FSN	FSN	25	32
	Stolojan 16/10/91–19/11/92	FSN, PNL, MER	FSN, PNL, MER, PDAR	21	21
1992–1996	Văcăroiu 19/11/92–11/12/96	FDSN (PDSR)	FDSN (PDSR), PUNR, PRM, PSM, PDAR	22	46
1996–2000	Ciorbea 11/12/96–15/04/98	PNȚCD, PNL, PD, PSDR, UDMR	CDR, USD, UDMR	28	41
	Vasile 15/04/98–22/12/99			24	33
	Isărescu 22/12/99–28/12/00			20	22

2000–2004	Năstase 28/12/00–28/12/04	PSD	PSD, PUR, UDMR	27	46
2004–2008	Popescu-Tăriceanu I 29/12/04–5/04/07	PNL, PD, PC, UDMR	ADA, PUR, UDMR	25	39
	Popescu-Tăriceanu II 5/07/07–22/12/08	PNL, UDMR	PNL, UDMR, PSD+PUR	17	24
2008–2012	Boc I 22/12/08–23/12/09	PDL, PSD+PC	PDL, PSD+PC	21	26
	Boc II 23/12/09–9/02/12	PDL, UDMR, UNPR	PDL, UDMR, UNPR	18	29
	Ungureanu 9/02/12–7/05/12	PDL, UDMR, UNPR	PDL, UDMR, UNPR	18	18
	Ponta I 7/05/12–21/12/12	PSD, PNL, PC, UNPR	USL	21	31
2012–2015	Ponta II 21/12/12–5/03/14	PSD, PNL, PC, UNPR	USL	28	31
	Ponta III 5/03/14–17/12/14	PSD, PC, UDMR, UNPR	PSD, PC, UDMR, UNPR	26	30
	Ponta IV 17/12/14–4/11/15	PSD, ALDE, UNPR	PSD, ALDE, UNPR	22	25

Notes: * Number of portfolios (prime minister; deputy prime minister; state minister; minister; minister delegate); ** Number of cabinet members, without *ad interims*; *** The term legislature for the period December 1989–June 1990 is not appropriate, as there were no parliamentary elections during this time span.

Source: Own compilation using Abraham 2006a, Radu 2012, Ştefan 2012, www.gov.ro

The Petre Roman governments

Launched as political leader during the days of the Revolution, Petre Roman (b. 1946) led the first two cabinets of post-communist Romania. The day after the execution of Nicolae Ceauşescu a provisional government was established, led by the charismatic Polytechnic professor Roman. Relations between the cabinet and the CFSN Council were characterized by subordination and not by mutual checks and balances, a situation which can be explained by the fact that political legitimacy belonged to the Front. Two-thirds of the first Roman Cabinet was made up of deputy ministers or directors from the old regime. The provisional government, whose main role was to manage current affairs until the first parliamentary elections, was a technical and administrative annex of the CFSN, with the latter retaining the political initiative. The cabinet was influenced by competition among various ministers, but Roman prevailed as a leader of government (Stoenescu 2006).

The Roman government was the target of street protests in January–February 1990. Political pressure was doubled by that existing within the army. Appointed Minister of Defence since 26 December 1989, General Nicolae Militaru was challenged by the Action Committee for Army Democratization (CADA), created by officers. Militaru replaced senior officers with officers who had studied in the USSR. For fear of an officers' revolt, the CFSN replaced Militaru with his rival, Victor Stănculescu.

The first Roman cabinet took measures which made it popular: the working week was reduced to five days and salaries were increased. The FSN got over 66 per cent of parliamentary seats in the 20 May elections and Roman received from Iliescu the mandate to form a second government. This cabinet presented its governing programme on 28 June 1990 at the Romanian Athenaeum hall in a 'Programme-declaration' announcing courageous directions of economic and institutional reform (Abraham 2006a: 235). All had to be rebuilt for a new society.

The ambitious objectives had to be fulfilled by a slimmer cabinet, with twenty-five portfolios and nineteen ministries, filled by people from among the old regime's technocracy, but who had not held top ranks in the PCR apparatus. The newly appointed Minister of Foreign Affairs was an academic without experience in the old regime's diplomatic service, Adrian Năstase. Lawyer Adrian Severin had an important role in conceiving economic reform (Severin 1995). Most members of the second Roman Cabinet did not hold prominent offices within the FSN but tried to acquire political power by means of government.

The second Roman Cabinet had two main strategic objectives. The first was to end the international isolation resulting from the June 1990 mineriad and to regain international confidence. The 'hot' discussion issues with the West were ethnic minorities, human rights, media pluralism and the former *Securitate*. Assistance for economic and institutional transformation was reduced. Subsequently, the government closely followed regional evolutions, first of all the unravelling of the COMECON and of the Warsaw Pact. International policy decisions mainly belonged to Iliescu; in this area, the government only had the role of implementing presidential decisions.

The transition to a market economy, the second strategic objective, generated increasing tensions between the cabinet and a part of the FSN parliamentary group. Partial price liberalization on 1 November 1990 resulted in a rapid increase in the rate of inflation, and privatization was rejected by a faction led by Alexandru Bârlădeanu, president of the Senate and a former communist leader (Betea 1997: 242–3). Rising prices caused broad social protests and, starting with the 1991 winter, tensions within the FSN began to increase. The adoption of a new privatization law in July 1991 was accomplished only after new conflicts, as a group of MPs even left the FSN.

The steps taken by the second Roman Cabinet for the reform of society and the economy were bold; an institutional framework was created for functional democratic institutions, the establishment of a market economy (banking system, privatization, foreign investment), property restitution (Law no. 18 of 1991) and the regulation of working relations. However, conflicts within the FSN and with President Iliescu, as well as a deficient management of public expectations, raised mistrust in the second Roman Cabinet. The miners arrived in Bucharest in September 1991, in order to protest against the government, and the political crisis situation gave Iliescu the occasion for removing the government. The gesture of Prime Minister Roman of making his mandate available to President Iliescu turned into a concealed dismissal.

The Theodor Stolojan Cabinet

The solution identified by Iliescu following consultations with the political parties was the establishment of a 'national union' government. The proposal was not accepted by Corneliu Coposu (PNȚCD), but the PNL, PDAR and MER agreed to be part of a limited mandate government, until the organization of new parliamentary elections, after the adoption of a new constitution. As prime minister of this new government, a technocrat was appointed: economist Theodor Stolojan (b. 1943).

The institutional legacy of the Stolojan transition government is significant, including the Constitutional Court, the Court of Auditors, the National Audiovisual Council, the justice system, organization of the Romanian Intelligence Service and electoral laws.

The Nicolae Văcăroiu government

The 27 September 1992 elections brought the first major political fragmentation: the FDSN received 34.3 per cent, the CDR 24.1 per cent, the FSN 12.6 per cent, the PUNR 8.8 per cent, and the UDMR 7.9 per cent of seats in the Chamber of Deputies. Re-elected as President, Iliescu proposed the formula of a grand coalition government between the FDSN and the CDR, but the strategy of the PNȚCD leaders was different. They preferred to stay in opposition, hoping for the quick departure of Iliescu and the FDSN. Iliescu preferred a FDSN minority government led by a technocrat. His choice was Nicolae Văcăroiu (b. 1943), an economist professionally validated within the State Planning Council of the communist period, but not an FDSN member. Văcăroiu got the parliamentary investiture vote, with the FDSN counting on the parliamentary support of the PRM, PSM and PUNR which did not want early elections.

The Văcăroiu cabinet was a return to the power system specific to a provisional government, in which the government does not play any political role, being only an administrative interface: the political role was played by Iliescu and the governing party. Văcăroiu did not adopt the confrontational attitude of Petre Roman, but closely followed the political lines established by Iliescu.

The Opposition tried to bring down the government by no-confidence votes during each parliamentary session, but they failed. In order to save the Văcăroiu cabinet, the PDSR first concluded a government protocol with the PUNR in 1994, in exchange for two portfolios, and in January 1995 a political cooperation protocol was signed between the PDSR, PRM, PSM and PUNR, called the 'red quadrangle' by the Opposition. With the exception of the PUNR, the PDSR's partners did not receive places in the executive (the PRM received only three places of state secretaries and one of prefect; the PSM received the office of Mehedinți county prefect), but otherwise only the usual budget allocations and diplomatic offices, in exchange for parliamentary support. In spite of the collaboration agreement, political relations among the government parties were tense. During the autumn of 1996, the PUNR was removed from government due to the fact that Gheorghe Funar opposed the normalization of Romanian–Hungarian relations.

The first important measures of the Văcăroiu government were the introduction of Value Added Tax (VAT) on 1 July 1993 and a total liberalization of prices on the same date. The Văcăroiu government slowed economic decline by interventionist policies and massive subventions. Privatization took place at reduced rhythms, being dominated by a state-centred orientation. In 1995–6, massive loans were contracted from the foreign market, at high interest rates and low maturity, which affected Romania's repayment capacity. The small business sector developed, as a result of tax breaks. However, economic results were overshadowed by extended corruption and a widespread feeling of stagnation and isolation from the Euro-Atlantic world (Abraham 2006a: 248–64).

The Victor Ciorbea Cabinet

Following the parliamentary elections of 3 November 1996 the first democratic alternation in government took place. The results for the Chamber of Deputies were: CDR, 35.5 per cent of seats; PDSR, 26.5 per cent; USD, 15.4 per cent; and UDMR, 7.3 per cent. As a result of the USD's support for Emil Constantinescu during the second round of the presidential election, on 6 December 1996 a governing coalition was created, which was made up of the CDR, the USD and the UDMR. The prime minister accepted by the coalition was lawyer Victor Ciorbea (b. 1954), who had become mayor of Bucharest earlier in the same year. For the first time, the UDMR became part of the government, thus breaking a political taboo.

The Ciorbea Cabinet was a political government, in which the parties appointed important leaders (vice-chairmen), but without mandating ministers to take decisions on behalf of the parties they represented. Governmental decisions were taken by the chairman of the political parties, under the influence of President Constantinescu. Ciorbea did not have a strong position within the PNȚCD and became captive to negotiations and confrontations among the governing parties' leaders.

The Ciorbea Cabinet was the first to be based on a 'coalition of coalitions' made up of structures with diverging values and orientations, whose main binder was the desire to acquire power. The CDR parties wanted properties confiscated by the communist regime (lands, forests, houses, enterprises that still existed) for their clientele. The PD had an electoral basis made up of those who were, in one way or another, linked with the state, and its elite originated among the leadership of state enterprises. These diverging interests became the main source of political conflicts.

The coalition parties introduced an 'algorithm' not only for dividing central state administration offices but also for politicizing the whole state bureaucratic structure. After the PDSR had politicized the administration with its clientele, the coalition government carried this phenomenon to the point of absurdity (down to the level of school watchmen!). The zero-sum game dominated relations among the parties.

Convinced that Romania had to be saved through shock therapy, the government decided to completely liberalize energy and food prices between February and May

1997. The result was an increase in prices, rampant inflation, a fall in domestic production as a result of decreasing consumption, and quickly increasing interest rates, so that financing the economy became a lot more difficult. The exchange rate depreciated in real terms by approximately one-third, after severe devaluation at the beginning of 1997. Social protests emerged in the summer of 1997, becoming increasingly numerous and outside trade union control.

After Romania's failure to be invited to join NATO at the Madrid Summit (July 1997), coalition conflicts became increasingly frequent, the main adversaries being the PNȚCD and the PD. In December 1997, the Minister of Transport, Traian Băsescu (PD), publicly criticized Ciorbea, and the crisis escalated until the PD ministers left the government in February 1998. Ciorbea was politically isolated, being attacked also from within the PNȚCD by Radu Vasile, and the PNL and even President Constantinescu considered that another political solution had to be identified. Disappointed, Prime Minister Ciorbea announced his resignation on 30 March 1998 (Abraham 2006a: 265–75; Gallagher 2004: 165–92). The governing coalition was resumed, but with another prime minister.

The Radu Vasile government

The rise of economic historian Radu Vasile (1942–2013) from Secretary General of the PNȚCD to prime minister was due to a favourable political context. Vasile's inclination towards compromise was acceptable for the PD, the PNL and the 'pragmatic' group in the PNȚCD, in spite of opposition from President Constantinescu. Prime Minister Vasile brought with him new conflict fault lines: between Cabinet and President, within the PNȚCD, between the executive and Romania's foreign partners (IMF, World Bank, EU) and between the government and a part of society (mineriads).

Romania's internal situation became increasingly tense in the context of a prolonged political crisis and the imposition of austerity policies following IMF rules. In March 1998 the stand-by agreement signed with the IMF in 1997 was suspended. The currency reserves of the National Bank stood at approximately US$500 million at the beginning of 1998, while Romania had to face a payment peak of over US$2.5 billion in 1999, debts contracted above all in 1995–6. There was a clear prospect of default, following Bulgaria in 1996. In order to avoid such a scenario, one of the most important state companies, Romtelecom, was privatized in 1998, selling its shares to another state company, OTE of Greece. The mass media then developed a concerted campaign concerning this privatization, suspecting corruption among high governmental officials. In 1998–9 almost 150 large companies in key sectors were privatized: energy (Petromidia), banks (BancPost, BRD). The government and the National Bank managed to pay Romania's debts in 1999, with the help of money from privatization (mainly Romtelecom and BRD) and from other international and domestic resources, thus avoiding default.

The tacit truce between the parties of the governing coalition, achieved after the change of prime minister, was quickly forgotten, however, and tensions re-emerged. The PD and PNȚCD faced each other over the issue of property restitution. The PNȚCD wanted *restitutio in integrum*, the PD only limited restitution. At the end of 1999 a compromise was achieved, resulting in Law no. 1 of 2000, also called the 'Lupu Law', which established restitution of forests up to ten hectares and of agricultural lands up to fifty hectares for each owner. The UDMR also demanded the satisfaction of its own agenda and threatened to leave the government. The compromise was the creation of a multicultural university, Petöfi-Schiller, in Cluj-Napoca in 1998.

Romania received the invitation to open EU accession negotiations at Helsinki in December 1999. Immediately, President Constantinescu decided to remove Prime Minister Vasile, under the pretext of preparing for EU accession. Large trade union cartels had been on strike since 23 November and the protest only ended on 22 December 1999. Constantinescu removed the prime minister from office on 13 December and Romania found itself with two premiers: Radu Vasile, who refused to resign, and Alexandru Athanasiu, appointed *ad interim*. Vasile gave in on 17 December 1999, after the coalition ministers collectively resigned. Isolated, Vasile left the cabinet with a feeling of general betrayal (Vasile 2002).

The Mugur Isărescu Cabinet

Governor of the National Bank since September 1990, Mugur Isărescu (b. 1949) agreed to become prime minister only on condition that he would be able to return to the banking institution after his term ended. The solution of a technocrat prime minister was intended to preserve the governing coalition, which was preparing for elections. The Mugur Isărescu executive was a political oddity: it was led by a technocrat, but all the other positions were allocated according to the political algorithm and the ministers were also political leaders. Petre Roman became Minister of Foreign Affairs, the first chairman of an important party to enter one of the CDR–PD–UDMR cabinets, in an attempt to increase public confidence in view of the forthcoming presidential campaign.

Besides preparing for the elections, Isărescu's mission was to begin the EU accession negotiations. Isărescu promoted 'The medium term 2000–2006 economic development strategy', which was approved by all the parliamentary political parties. After President Constantinescu's decision not to stand for a new presidential mandate and the PNL's exit from the CDR, Isărescu agreed to become the presidential candidate of the coalition created around the PNȚCD (CDR 2000). Government was reduced only to the administration of current affairs.

The government prepared for the electoral year by reducing VAT on some services and products from 22 per cent to 19 per cent and reducing corporate tax from 38 per cent to 25 per cent. Salaries for public employees were raised. The Isărescu Cabinet can be credited with stopping the decline of the Romanian economy, reducing inflation to 40 per cent and beginning a re-launch of industrial activity.

The Adrian Năstase government

The main beneficiaries of the Constantinescu regime's failure were Ion Iliescu and the PDSR. During the 2000 parliamentary elections, the PDSR received 44.9 per cent; the

PRM, 24.3 per cent; the PD, 9 per cent; the PNL, 8.7 per cent and the UDMR 7.8 per cent of seats in the Chamber of Deputies. Iliescu appointed lawyer Adrian Năstase (b. 1950) as the head of the government. Năstase established a minority cabinet, with the parliamentary support of the UDMR, for the duration of the four years of government and of the PNL until May 2001.

The main governmental objectives were NATO accession and finalizing the EU accession negotiations, both of which were accomplished. As a result of combining the offices of party chairman and prime minister, Năstase strengthened his position as undisputed leader both of the government and of the PSD.

The Năstase government took several measures in consultation with foreign partners, concerning macroeconomic stabilization, reducing the inflation rate, real economy monetization, and increasing currency reserves. The first success of the Cabinet was the conclusion, in October 2001, of an agreement with the IMF. The Năstase government launched broad social projects (for example 'Roll and milk' for pupils, and the minimum wage), and a Labour Code favourable to employees was implemented. These were measures to consolidate the social democratic identity of the government.

Năstase decided to restructure his cabinet twice, in June 2003 and March 2004, aiming both to attract voters' sympathy and to increase electoral performance.

The main failings of the PSD government were the wish to overextend political power, involvement in the mass media by means of state advertising, the weak pace of justice reform, certain authoritarian tendencies in relation to the opposition, and a decrease in Parliament's relevance as a result of excessive use of emergency ordinances and diminishing political debates. At institutional level, the Năstase government elaborated action plans and programmes to fight corruption; the National Anticorruption Prosecuting Office was created, but its results were below citizens' expectations. On the positive side, the Adrian Năstase government succeeded in creating an environment of stability and relative predictability (Abraham 2006a: 290–303).

The Călin Popescu-Tăriceanu Cabinets

During the 2004 parliamentary elections the political scene was re-balanced: PSD+PUR, 39.7 per cent; ADA, 33.8 per cent; PRM, 13 per cent and UDMR 6.6 per cent in the Chamber of Deputies. Băsescu's victory in the presidential election redefined the political equation. PNL leader, Călin Popescu-Tăriceanu (b. 1952), formed an ADA government, after breaking the PUR and UDMR's commitments towards the PSD (Radu 2009: 91). The first important decision was to introduce a flat-rate tax for individual incomes, thus replacing the progressive system. Another important economic measure was the adoption of a legal package providing for full property restitution in 2005. The main foreign affairs preoccupation of the Tăriceanu Cabinet was to sign the EU accession treaty and ensure its ratification.

At the political level, Tăriceanu's time in government was dominated by conflict with President Băsescu. This happened at a gradual pace: after Tăriceanu's refusal to resign in order to organize early elections in July 2005, mutual attacks increased in intensity (Dima

2009), leading to the unravelling of the cabinet following the dismissal of the PD ministers on 1 April 2007. A minority PNL–UDMR government was established, which was tacitly supported by the Social Democrats and which resisted until the 2008 parliamentary elections. The second Tăriceanu Cabinet was weak, as it depended on PSD support and, as a consequence, it was forced to make several concessions. In 2008, a law was adopted to increase teachers' pay by 50 per cent, although such a raise was unrealistic. In order to protect PNL interests, a new electoral law was adopted, with elections held in uninominal colleges but with a proportional distribution of mandates. This proved to be a major failure.

Tăriceanu was the prime minister during whose mandate Romania joined the EU, and economic growth was significant. The main error, though, was lack of control over crediting policy and a real estate speculative bubble emerged. A massive foreign capital influx after 2005 and a fast growth in consumer debt left Romania vulnerable to the 2008 international economic crisis.

The Emil Boc governments

The results of the 2008 parliamentary elections offered several alternatives for governmental majorities: PDL, 34.4 per cent; PSD + PC, 34.1 per cent; PNL, 19.5 per cent and UDMR, 6.6 per cent in the Chamber of Deputies. President Băsescu continued to block a renewal of the alliance between the PSD and the PNL from the Tăriceanu mandate. Initially he named Theodor Stolojan as candidate for prime minister and after the latter's withdrawal he proposed lawyer Emil Boc (b. 1966), the president of the PDL. Faced with the option of entering government or continuing their opposition, the Social Democrats led by Mircea Geoană agreed to form a grand coalition government with the PDL.

Băsescu's skilful manoeuvre was in fact preparing for the presidential election, in the context of the international economic crisis. The first Boc cabinet postponed its reactions to the economic crisis, as the PDL and PSD refused to take unpopular decisions in an electoral year. On the contrary, a loan of €19.95 billion was contracted with the IMF, World Bank and EU, which allowed coverage of a good part of public spending.

On 1 October 2009, the PSD ministers withdrew from the cabinet and Boc formed an *ad interim* government, whose existence was prolonged through political tricks until after the presidential elections. Băsescu's re-election meant a new mandate for Prime Minister Boc, who formed a new government with the UDMR. Gabriel Oprea, Minister of Defence, who had recently resigned from the PSD, led an intense campaign of recruiting MPs, which later established the UNPR. The second Boc Cabinet was thus ensured parliamentary support.

After the presidential elections, the government had to face economic realities. With GDP reduced by 6.6 per cent and a budget deficit of –7.3 per cent of GDP in 2009, public spending was not sustainable. Băsescu took over de facto leadership of the government; during 2010, austerity measures were taken to balance the budget. Reducing public sector pay by 25 per cent, as well as childcare and unemployment benefit, taxing pensions, increasing VAT from 19 to 24 per cent, and blocking hiring in the public sector were some of the measures taken by Traian Băsescu and applied by the second Boc cabinet.

The complementary solution to austerity during the economic crisis was investment in infrastructure, but available resources were limited. Elena Udrea, Minister of Regional Development, wasted around €1 billion on several useless projects (for example, mountain gondolas in areas without tourists). The persistence of the economic crisis led to an increase of social tension, which exploded in the winter of 2011–12, the political stake being the removal of Băsescu and the Boc government. In order to offer Băsescu new political options, Boc resigned on 6 February 2012.

The Mihai-Răzvan Ungureanu Cabinet

Băsescu's hope of preserving control over government was pinned on historian Mihai-Răzvan Ungureanu (b. 1968), who became prime minister of the PDL–UDMR–UNPR government straight from his office of SIE director. His main mission was to prepare for the local and parliamentary elections.

Replacing Emil Boc calmed the political situation, but the presidential party (the PDL) lacked credibility and was demoralized. A small group of PDL MPs migrated to the PNL, seeking political survival. Following the no-confidence vote initiated by the PSD and PNL, components of the USL, the Ungureanu government was dismissed on 27 April 2012. During its eighty-seven days the Ungureanu cabinet failed to achieve anything of note and its dismissal deepened the crisis in the Băsescu regime.

The Victor Ponta governments

Faced with a new political reality, Băsescu appointed as prime minister lawyer Victor Ponta (b. 1972), chairman of the PSD. Ponta established a USL government, which also included some technocrats; the most important of these was Minister of Finance, Florin Georgescu (Radu and Buti 2013: 50–4). The main political objective was winning the local and parliamentary elections. The government corrected part of the consequences of the austerity measures taken by the Boc government. Recomposing public sector pay and increasing pensions were some of the main measures taken.

The USL tempestuously launched a second dismissal attempt against President Băsescu. This was unsuccessful due to a failure to meet the referendum quorum for dismissal, but the 7.4 million votes against Băsescu gave the USL a major advantage for the parliamentary elections. The USL won 66.3 per cent of seats in the Chamber of Deputies, so Ponta was sure of a new mandate as Prime Minister. This was also a political government, in which the USL was joined by the UNPR. The main governmental objective remained the elimination of the consequences of the austerity policies. However, despite having massive parliamentary support, the cabinet failed to attain its main objectives. Constitutional reform was postponed in the Parliament, awaiting the result of the 2014 presidential election. Administrative and territorial reorganization, promised by the government, was blocked by the Constitutional Court.

Initial enthusiasm turned to mistrust between Liberals and Social Democrats. Crin Antonescu was supposed to be the USL's candidate in the presidential election, but Ponta was convinced that he had to stand for the presidency himself (Buti and Radu 2015). As a result, to prepare for the presidential election, the PNL left the government in February 2014; USL de facto unravelled (Stănescu 2014: 158). A third Ponta government was formed, taking up the USL's governing programme, but also including the UDMR. Following Ponta's defeat in the presidential election of 2014, the UDMR left the government. Ponta remained prime minister in a new cabinet, which continued to stand by the USL's governing programme, with a parliamentary majority gathered by political migration; the UNPR became the main collecting basin. Within the fourth Ponta Cabinet some portfolios were attributed to liberals close to Tăriceanu, who had left the PNL and formed the ALDE in 2015, following a fusion with the PC. Ponta resigned on 4 November 2015, after street protests following a fire during a rock concert in Bucharest on 30 October in which sixty-four people died.

Comparative elements

Governmental stability was favoured by collaboration between the president and prime minister. The medium lifespan of the sixteen cabinets led by eleven prime ministers from 1989 to 2015 (from Roman I to Ponta IV) was one-and-a-half years. Until 2015, only three prime ministers completed a four-year mandate: Văcăroiu, Năstase and Tăriceanu. The Văcăroiu and Năstase cabinets, in theory supported by a minority, were based on parliamentary coalitions and not on extended governmental alliances. Two governments (Roman II and Vasile) fell as a result of conflicts with Presidents Iliescu and Constantinescu. The Ciorbea, Tăriceanu I, Boc I and Ponta II cabinets unravelled following conflicts within the governing coalition. The only prime minister who lost office following a no-confidence vote was Ungureanu. These data show that governmental instability is greater within coalition governments and in dual President–Prime Minister cohabitations. Surprisingly, governments supported by a large majority (Boc I and Ponta II) were fragile; the idea of a grand coalition between left and right was undermined by diverging political interests.

The medium size of the sixteen cabinets analysed was twenty-three portfolios, including the prime minister, deputy prime ministers, state ministers, ministers and ministers-delegates. The magnitude of the cabinets was smaller than had been the case in communist governments, respecting the trend among EU governments. Over the period analysed, there were a total of 528 cabinet members, excluding *ad interim* members. The 134 changes in the cabinets' composition took place as a result of reshuffles and resignations for political or personal reasons. Reshuffles were an important instrument by which prime ministers sought to revive activity and regain voters' trust. Reshuffles or collective resignations were also used to solve political crises or to create new political situations (for example, the resignation of the PSD ministers from the Boc I cabinet and that of the PNL ministers from the Ponta II Cabinet, both before presidential elections).

Romanian governments were overwhelmingly male, with women representing only 5 per cent of cabinet members. Left-wing governments had more women in governmental positions, but their percentage is still far from the feminist ideal of gender balance. The dominant tendency was to gather professional politicians, with a corresponding reduction in the number of technocrats (Stănescu 2014: 250–68; Ştefan 2012: 187–95). Parties engaged technocrats only for technical fields (finances, foreign affairs, etc.); political leadership of ministries was rather the rule. Technocrats were put forward among state secretaries.

Governmental stability was also an important factor for economic and social dynamics. Economic crises (1997–9, 2009–11) were also associated with political instability, while the economic momentum of 2000–8 was supported by governments led by strong prime ministers (Năstase and Tăriceanu).

The main tendency was a decrease in the cabinets' influence among state power institutions, with the exception of the Năstase government. Following conflicts between president and prime minister, government leaders lost prestige and influence. Prime ministers often seemed uninformed and vulnerable in front of presidents enjoying absolute immunity. The limitation of the national government's area of action following EU accession and the massive influence of the IMF over macroeconomic policies, as well as the management of security issues under NATO coordination and of justice issues by professional structures led to an emasculation of the cabinet as the main state leadership institution. The paradox is that the governmental institution was designed to have extended powers, having the necessary constitutional competencies, but the gradual erosion of its capacity to exercise power made mutual checks and balances rather become an ideal than a modus operandi. This is why the perception of occult governance and lack of governance became widespread in Romania, thus increasing the sense of democratic deficit.

Local administration

The return to democracy reset relations between the central state leadership and local administration. The constitution establishes the national and unitary character of the state and the limits of local authorities' attributes are provided by this organizational matrix. The forty-one *judeţe* (counties) and the municipality of Bucharest enjoy local autonomy. Cities, towns and *comune* (rural districts consisting of one or more villages) elect their mayors and local councils; at county level, the 1991 constitution introduced county councils. The government preserved an intervention instrument in local affairs, being able to challenge decisions of local authorities in court, by means of a prefect, one for each county. According to the fundamental law, the prefect 'shall direct the decentralized public services of ministries and other bodies of the central public administration in the territorial-administrative units' (art.122, align.2).

Local administration witnessed an unsustainable expansion process. If in 1990 Romania had 260 towns and cities (56 of them classed as *municipii*) and 2,688 *comune*, after 2000 their number rapidly increased; by 2015 there were 320 towns and cities (including 93 *municipii*) and 2,861 *comune*. The increase in the number of local administration structures was carried out in the context of a decreasing national population, being determined by local political interests rather than demographic considerations.

The most important phenomenon was the transfer of attributes and resources from central to local authorities. During 1991–4, local taxes were introduced, providing an important revenue resource for local administrations. The GDP share of local budgets was increased, with several services being assigned to town halls or county councils. Until 2000 the share of local budgets did not go beyond 4.6 per cent of GDP (Stănescu 2014: 271). Afterwards, in the context of the regional development policy promoted by the EU, an increasing number of competencies were transferred to local authorities. Not only were schools and hospitals transferred under their administration, but town halls also received the right to have local police in the fields of public order, road traffic and other local matters. In 2015, the GDP share of local budgets was about 9 per cent, while the consolidated budget accounted for a GDP share of about 33 per cent. Nearly a quarter of all public spending was accounted for by local authorities.

Local autonomy also included an election process, in order to confer legitimacy on institutions. The first local elections took place in 1992; they usually precede parliamentary elections every four years. For political parties, local elections have acquired an increasing importance, as they are an instrument for selecting political elites and establishing electoral fiefdoms.

The importance of local elected officials is emphasized by political migration. The main reason for mayors' and councillors' migration between parties was the financial dependence of local institutions on government and county councils. The practice was inaugurated after the 1996 parliamentary elections, in favour of the PNȚCD, PD and PNL, but also extended to include about a third of all mayors during the PSD government (2001–4). The 2004 change in government determined a new wave of political migration from the opposition (PSD) to the parties in power (PD and PNL), which included almost a quarter of all mayors. In 2006, political migration of local elected officials was forbidden, but it continued informally. In 2014, in preparation for the presidential election, the Ponta government legalized limited political migration (only once and during a limited period of 45 days), in the hope of gaining a political advantage. The PSD and UNPR were indeed the main beneficiaries of this measure and the PDL and PNL were the main losers. However, Victor Ponta's defeat in the 2014 presidential election showed that the mayors' political influence had been overestimated.

The transfer of competencies and resources from central level to the local administration was accompanied by the consolidation of local power poles. During the 2000s, some county council leaders accumulated not only political but also economic power, becoming media shareholders and building clientele networks. The media ironically called them 'local barons'. They became indispensable to the parties by virtue of their capacity for building electoral fiefdoms. Local leaders, many of them with the ambition of acquiring a major political role in national affairs, concentrated political power in the institution of county council chairmen. Initially elected from among county councillors, the holders of this post overcame the status of *primus inter pares*, and from 2004, they could be dismissed only in exceptional cases. The influence of county council chairmen increased even more in 2006, as they acquired the role of local executive power, being the decisive factor in allocating budget resources towards mayors. From 2008, county council chairmen were elected by direct vote in a single round, reaching the climax of their power. Prefects, the government's representatives in the territory, were appointed only after the formal approval of local leaders from the governing party. Gradually, feudal types of power networks emerged, endowed with political legitimacy, which often spent public resources according to their own interests. Leaders ensured the loyalty of mayors by preferential resource allocation. Governments began to allocate an increasing share of resources in a non-transparent manner, favouring mayors from ruling parties. Clientelism became systematic.

The extended political influence of local leaders, doped by the idea that 'we are leading the country', was sensed to be a danger to the state's unitary character, incurring the risk of functionally atomizing administration. After 2012, force structures (the Romanian intelligence service and the prosecutor's office) began a systematic action of eliminating 'local barons'. The project was tacitly supported by both President Băsescu and Prime Minister Ponta. The first hoped to weaken his opponents and the second saw in the elimination of strong local leaders, by means of judicial investigations, an instrument for consolidating his position within the PSD. Force structures and the justice system saw the elimination of 'local barons' (county council chairmen, mayors of municipalities) as a way to strengthen their authority in relation to political power; this was why they acted against local leaders from all parties. The decisive blow to the local leaders' power system was dealt in 2015 by a return to the indirect election of county council chairmen.

CHAPTER 11
MAIN PUBLIC POLICIES

Education

Education reform was not a priority at the beginning of transition, because after the immediate abandonment of social mobilization practices concerning pupils and students (education institutions were de-politicized after the Revolution, with the dissolution of the PCR; high school and university students were no longer used for agricultural work or on construction sites), the predominant perception was that the only issue was the politicization of education under communism. The idea of reforming the education system emerged in the mid-1990s, and was related to the project of modernization through Europeanization, of preparing Romanian society for NATO membership and EU accession. Several successes of Romanian students in international Olympiads (in maths, physics and chemistry) strengthened the belief that the Romanian educational system was advanced. However, the public highlighting of the crisis of traditional education eventually defeated the mythology of Romanian exceptionalism and recovery measures were sought.

Decentralization of pre-university education was one of the first reform directions, on the basis that city halls would know best how to manage schools for the benefit of their communities. After 1999, successive measures were adopted for the decentralization of school management; the Ministry of Education only retained responsibility for controlling educational content. Another important change was to adapt educational content to the reality of a pluralist and contradictory world. Beginning in 1997, alternative textbooks were introduced for each subject, with schools being able to choose the textbooks they preferred. A mantra of educational content reform was 'to educate citizens, not turn children into encyclopaedias!' Polemics were generated by the first 'alternative textbooks' for the history of the Romanians in 1999, as the inclusion of media stars or the caricature of political leaders from national history (Stephen the Great, Michael the Brave, etc.) in the interests of 'demythologizing' the past were, and still are, accepted with difficulty in society.

Written exams for high school and college entry were abandoned, being replaced with national exams ('Capacity' at the end of the eighth grade for high school entry, and Baccalaureate for college entry), whose results acquired a predominant share in the admission requirements. In the face of the danger of building false educational hierarchies, exigency during the Baccalaureate exams increased after 2011, with fraud being gradually eliminated through draconian video surveillance measures.

A real explosion took place in the field of higher education. In 1990 there were forty-eight universities in Romania with around 192,000 students; by 2002 there were

126 higher education institutions, with a maximum of one million students in 2013 (Drăgoescu 2013). Technical education witnessed a massive decrease, from 68 per cent of all students in 1990 to only 25 per cent in 2011. The most important areas of interest were economics, law and fields with a pedagogical outlet (philology, history and socio-political subjects). The numbers studying medicine diminished, from 10 per cent of students in 1990 to 4 per cent in 2004, only to rise again to about 10 per cent after 2010. The evolution in the number of students enrolled for different subjects reflects changes in Romanian society. Industrial decline was reflected by a lack of interest in technical studies. Social sciences and humanities faculties increased the number of students because education offered secure jobs, even if they were poorly paid. Interest in medicine revived with the westward migration of doctors after EU accession.

The quantitative expansion of higher education was achieved by both state and private universities. Following an upward trend, in 2010 almost half of the total number of students were enrolled in private universities, but the majority of these were mere 'degree factories' orientated towards profit and not towards research, as institutional evaluation showed (Vlăsceanu et al. 2010). A new Education Law (Law no. 1 of 2011) imposed more rigorous standards on universities. The demographic decline after 1990 and the youth migration to the West brought about a financial crisis for private universities, which was exacerbated when state universities were allowed to offer fee-paying places in addition to their quota of state-funded places. As a consequence, private universities entered a merciless fight for survival. Among state universities, differences increased between traditional academic centres (Bucharest, Cluj-Napoca, Iași, Timișoara) and universities in medium-sized towns, which have made great efforts to survive.

Education and research witnessed a process of budgetary marginalization. As trade union representation in the education system was fragmented, teachers did not have great negotiating force. Only after a number of crises, following general strikes in 2000 and 2005, was the education budget increased, but salaries remained insufficient to attract valuable people into pre-university education. Salaries in universities and research were very low, especially at entry level, so that a part of the intellectual elite either emigrated or entered better paid fields (banking, insurance, law, etc.). In 2008, during the parliamentary election campaign, Traian Băsescu and the leaders of all the parliamentary political parties signed the 'National Pact for Education' which consensually assumed the objective of providing 6 per cent of GDP for education and 1 per cent for research. The highest budget allocations came in 2008, at about 4.5 per cent of GDP, but the average annual budget allocation has remained under 4 per cent. Political commitments from 2008 were quickly abandoned by all parties.

According to constitutional provisions, state education is free of charge at all levels. In 1990, compulsory education was reduced from ten grades to eight grades, against international trends; the situation was remedied in 2003 by the introduction of compulsory education for ten years; this was increased to eleven in 2011. Social reality shows that compulsory education is not effective, however, as 2 per cent of children abandon school at primary level (Apostu et al. 2015: 32). The rate of school dropout is higher in rural areas than in urban areas and pupils from the countryside suffer from precarious studying conditions (poorly qualified teachers, obsolete educational and sanitary facilities) (Stanef 2013). In secondary education the dropout rate was double that in primary education. On the whole, only about 80 per cent of the school-age population (7–23 years old) is included in the educational system. However, the most dramatic problem occurs in the case of university access for rural young people: only a quarter proceed to higher education and even fewer complete their studies, despite scholarships allocated by the government (Pricopie et al. 2011).

The main feature of education reforms is their deeply personalized character. Almost every minister of education envisaged changing the system 'from the very foundations', the result being a long row of projects which were started but not finished and which demoralized teachers, parents and pupils/students. The convulsive internal dynamics of the education system increased mistrust in the functioning of the social progress based on education and personal merit.

The medical system

The efforts from the middle of the communist era directed at building a broad health infrastructure were stopped by an investment reduction at the end of the Ceauşescu regime. After 1989 the spirals of economic and social system change left deep traces throughout the health system, which was already in crisis. Health was a major political concern for all governments, at least rhetorically, but miraculous solutions for universal and high-quality medical services, in the conditions of budgetary precariousness, were difficult to find and hard to implement. The health system was the testing lab for a variety of transformation strategies, but its inertia was tremendous. Informal payments by patients ('bribes') were an old custom; governments did not allocate significant financial resources for decent salaries, believing that doctors and auxiliary medical staff received an income from patients' 'gifts' (Allin and Mladovsky 2008; Administraţia Prezidenţială 2008).

At the beginning of the 1990s, the health network (hospitals, clinics, dispensaries and other medical units) was centrally coordinated by the Health Ministry. Between 1990 and 1998 a dual financing system was used, including state budget and complementary financing (a special health fund based on the contributions of employees, as well as external financing from the World Bank). Under IMF and World Bank pressure, the Ciorbea government made some system changes (Law no. 145 of 1997): compulsory health insurance was introduced, based on the solidarity principle (the Bismarck system) together with a network for managing contributions (the National Health Insurance Fund – CNAS), which is autonomous from the government (the CNAS has a tripartite leadership made up of trade unions, employers and state authorities). The government, through the Health Ministry, bears the main political responsibility for managing the health of the population, but the most important resources are autonomously managed by the CNAS. The institution has accumulated large financial resources, even a surplus, while the pension fund has recorded increasing deficits. In 2002, government control was established over resources paid by insured employees, part of the sum being transferred towards pension payments. From 2006, the CNAS received more resources and more autonomy (Law no. 95 of 2006), but medical services did not significantly improve. The situation could seem strange, as while in 1990 health expenditure amounted to 3.5 per cent of GDP, in 2000 the percentage increased to 5 per cent, reaching 5.6 per cent in 2009 and then decreasing to below 5 per cent during the economic crisis. In spite of this increase in financial resources, the general perception was that the quality of medical services was decreasing (*Percepţii asupra sistemul medical* 2010). This had two main causes. The first was pricing above the European average for medication and medical equipment, Romania being a sort of El Dorado for the pharmaceutical industry. During negotiations with big pharmaceutical and medical equipment companies, health system managers often proved inefficient, if not indeed corrupt, being willing to accept very high prices. Against the lobby of the great pharmaceutical companies (in 2002 and 2004, former US Secretary of State Madeleine Albright supported the interests of the company Merck in Bucharest in discussions with the Năstase government), Romanian politicians proved to be weak negotiators. Second, hospitals were great consumers of resources (almost half of the budget), as preventative health and outpatients were not considered priorities. In 2010, in the context of the economic crisis, Băsescu forced the Boc government to implement massive decentralization, by transferring 373 of the 435 hospitals in Romania to local and county authorities. Additionally, 67 small town or rural hospitals were closed and some hospitals were turned into medical centres without a programme of round-the-clock assistance (*Analiza funcţională a sectorului sănătate* 2012). Hospital maintenance costs decreased, but hundreds of thousands of people were deprived of medical assistance. The Ponta government reopened twenty-seven of those hospitals situated in areas of medium population density.

One of the causes of the precarious situation characterizing the health system is its financing below the European average. Although the whole population of Romania has the constitutional right to medical assistance, approximately half of the inhabitants of the country do not pay contributions to the health insurance fund, either because they are exempt from payment (pupils/students, some pensioners, etc.) or because they work on the black market and do not contribute. A significant number of economic agents do not pay their dues towards the health fund. Romania is below the EU average for health system financing, but the collection rate is reduced and the number of those who can benefit without paying is significant.

The general underperformance of the public health system was the effect of a congruence among several factors: population ageing, with a disproportionate incidence of heart disease; increasing social stress; an unhealthy diet, especially for poorer social categories; the precarious medical education of marginalized categories; lack of access for the poor to medical services, often conditioned by the requirement for informal payments; high costs of medication and medical products, coupled with a delay in introducing the newest pharmaceutical products; massive fraud within the health system, including the use of fake prescriptions; externalization of simple medical services towards the private sector and the preservation of costly medical services by public hospitals; and emigration of medical staff and transfer of experts from the public to the private sector.

Trying to eliminate health hazards, an increasing number of middle-class Romanians have moved, through private insurance, towards the private health sector, which is in continuous expansion. After 1998, more and more private clinics and hospitals opened in the main cities, but without being able to offer assistance to more than 20 per cent of the population. There have been many attempts, often in good faith, to fight against the reality that the health system is seriously sick, by means of several administrative-bureaucratic experiments, but generally disappointing results have strengthened the feeling that personal solutions are preferable to institutional-collective ones.

The social state

The ideal of Romanians after the fall of the Ceaușescu regime was to have the social stability of communism and the consumerist exuberance of capitalism. It was not by accident that the idea of a 'third way' between communism and capitalism was very popular in the Romania of the 1990s. This proved to be difficult to achieve, even if the constitution defines Romania as a 'social state'. The introduction of market economy mechanisms brought about deep changes within the social structures, in the direction of social polarization and the re-emergence of the phenomenon of extreme poverty.

The pensions system witnessed negative structural changes. Starting with 1990, governments reduced the pressure of massive unemployment by encouraging early retirement, and disability pensions were obtained very easily and often fraudulently. The consequence was an increase in the number of pensioners from 3.58 million in 1990 to 5.3 million in 2015, in the context of a decrease in the number of employees from 8.15 million in 1990 to 4.58 million in 2015. The reversal of the ratio between employees and pensioners, to which may be added the increase in life expectancy and demographic decline, brought about a crisis in the pensions system, which was based on the idea of individual contribution and intergenerational solidarity (Șeitan et al. 2012: 18–76).

Governments tried to prevent the collapse of the pensions system and to reduce the level of transfers from the state budget by several methods: increasing the level of contributions to pension funds, from 14 per cent in 1990 to 35 per cent in 2002, and also extending the number of contributors (imposing contributions for income from intellectual property rights and rents); increasing the retirement age to sixty-five years for men and sixty years for women, and imposing a minimum limit of fifteen years of contributions in order to benefit from a pension; introducing compulsory pensions managed by private pension funds and optional private pensions; and ending the rigorous correlation of pensions with the evolution of salaries, so that the average net pension would be half of the average net salary.

The dissolution of some industries and the increase in unemployment, high inflation until the beginning of the 2000s, an economic structure based on the comparative advantage of a cheap labour force, black market labour in the private sector, de-industrialization of some mono-industrial areas and a return to subsistence agriculture based on self-consumption, and the alternation of crises with periods of economic growth caused millions of people to be thrown into the vicious circle of poverty. Oligarchic capitalism, orientated towards quick profit obtained by any means, in conjunction with the interest of foreign capital in keeping labour costs as low as possible, translated into the establishment of an economically deeply polarized society. The transition in 2005 from the progressive taxation system to the flat-rate tax of 16 per cent of individual income deepened economic inequalities (Voinea and Mihăescu 2008). The low level of income brought about the emergence of a new phenomenon: the impoverishment of people with jobs but whose incomes are not sufficient for a decent standard of living (about 20 per cent of employees), a phenomenon present at the European level (*Labour Market* 2013: 24–6). According to international statistics (Gini Index), Romania is one of the most uneven countries of the EU. The absolute poverty rate was 5.7 per cent in 1990, rising to 35.9 per cent in 2001, after which a downward trend followed (5.7 per cent in 2008), followed by an increase again in the context of austerity measures in 2010–12 to the level of 10 per cent. During the economic crisis unleashed in 2008, about a million people were affected by extreme poverty and relative poverty was felt by almost 4 million people (*După 20 de ani* 2010: 18–29).

Anti-poverty programmes were especially associated with social-democratic governments, but measures for limiting poverty were also taken by liberal-conservative governments, especially during preparations for elections. The state assumed the obligation of offering minimal financial aid (the minimum wage, Law no. 16 of 2001) at the request of people affected by extreme poverty. Minors receive an allocation of symbolic value (less than €20 per month in 2015) and people with disabilities benefit from special allowances and free medical assistance. The most extended form of social protection consists of unemployment benefits, which vary according to work experience, from six months to one year, the sum also being correlated with the income of the person before losing their job.

Labour market regulation can consolidate or weaken the social state. The communist Labour Code (1972) was preserved with some amendments until 2003, precisely because it offered employees the illusion of social stability. In 2003, the labour legislation was unified and compacted by a new code, which preserved a relative balance between the rights and obligations of employees and companies (Law no. 53 of 2003). In 2011, following requests from the IMF and large foreign companies present in Romania, labour legislation was changed to make the labour market more flexible, especially in the private sector. Permanent labour contracts decreased in favour of temporary or part-time (2-, 4- or 6-hour) employment. The consequence was a deepening of social marginalization for people who are without permanent labour contracts.

The establishment of a real social state in Romania was delayed not only by the ideological opposition of neo-conservatives (e.g., former president Băsescu) but, most of all, by the incoherent action of governments, orientated towards extinguishing immediate crises (Administrația Prezidențială 2009b: 5–7). Social policies ranged between the imperative of diminishing poverty and the desire to protect private, national or international capital interests. Poverty levels above the European average have fuelled feelings of dissatisfaction with regard to political life and evoked nostalgia for the communist past. Romania is not a singular case among CEE countries, but it completes the image of a flawed transition towards democracy and a market economy.

CHAPTER 12
FOREIGN POLICY AND EURO-ATLANTIC INTEGRATION

The euphoria following the fall of the communist regime, which dominated Romanian society during the first part of 1990, was quickly replaced by the anxieties of geopolitical incertitude. Romania not only wanted internal stability, but was in a feverish search for new foreign allies. The peaceful end of the Cold War brought about major changes in international politics, which the political and diplomatic decision makers in Romania sought to understand and anticipate, because the 'iron law' of Romanian diplomacy is to adapt to changes in order not to endanger state integrity. The success in establishing the modern Romanian state (1859–60), winning independence (1877–8) and creating Greater Romania (1918–20), but also the losses of territories and population in 1940 have created among diplomats, the military and statesmen an ethos of sacrifice for the defence of state borders. Romanian elites consider that the strength of the country's borders is conferred not only by demographic principle, economic power and national policy, but also by the interests of and competition among the Great Powers. Preserving close relations with at least one Great Power which would guarantee borders has been a strategic objective from the mid-nineteenth century to the present day. This is the main line of continuity in Romania's foreign policy, regardless of the succession of political regimes. After 1990, NATO and EU membership were considered the safest instruments for ensuring national security and border integrity. Important domestic resources were mobilized, attributes of national sovereignty were ceded, and the population stoically accepted significant social sacrifices to achieve Euro-Atlantic integration, considering that these were costs which had to be borne to ensure national security. Romania's international policy was thus placed upon the solid foundation of popular support for major objectives (Abraham 2006b; Georgescu 2011; Ivan 2009).

Stages in Romania's international policy

For over a quarter of a century, Romania's international policy followed three main stages, determined both by the evolution of national policy and, most of all, by changes in relations between the Great Powers and major events in the neighbourhood.

The first stage was that of 'incertitude' (1989–93). In 1991, the dissolution of the COMECON (28 June), of the Warsaw Pact (1 July) and of the Soviet Union (25 December), and also the Yugoslav wars convulsed and fragmented the regional situation (King 2010). Czechoslovaks, Poles and Hungarians revived the notion of *Mitteleuropa*, as a formula of differentiation from other East Europeans, hoping for a privileged relationship, not only with Germany, but also with the United States. Romania was not accepted as a member of the Vişegrád Group because it was considered to be a 'Balkan state'. Romania was internationally isolated because the inter-ethnic tensions in Târgu Mureş and the 1990–1 mineriads had created the image of an ungovernable country. The US had a marginal interest towards Romania and Bulgaria, which is why they encouraged the differentiation of the Vişegrád Group from the other ex-communist states (Puşcaş 2000). Romanian diplomacy exhibited prudence towards the USSR and the Russian Federation, but it was conscious that its future lay in the West. Romania managed to emerge from international isolation only in 1993, with its accession to the CoE. Romania demonstrated its internal stability and the minorities issue was wisely dealt with, so that other inter-ethnic conflicts were avoided.

During the second stage, the major preoccupation of Romanian diplomacy was accession to Euro-Atlantic institutions (1994–2007). The period covered three democratic changes in government (1996, 2000, 2004), during which parties acted consensually for the country to become a member of both NATO and the EU. The main events of this period were the NATO Summit in Madrid (1997), the invitation to start EU accession negotiations (Helsinki, December 1999), the Kosovo war (1999), the invitation to join NATO (Prague, November 2002), military participation in the US-led coalition in Afghanistan and Iraq, NATO accession (29 March 2004), signing the EU accession treaty (April 2005), and, finally, accession to the EU (1 January 2007). Romania's international policy (in its regional, European and global dimension) of this period was focused on the main human and material resources towards NATO and EU accession. Decision-makers in the international policy field acted with the massive support of public opinion (Denca 2013).

After EU accession, the main objective of Romania's international policy was the creation of a credible country profile, with the ambition of supporting an effective economic diplomacy, and also of attracting the Republic of Moldova towards Brussels (Popescu 2010). Without the idea of singularity within the EU being abandoned, the annexation of the Crimea by the Russian Federation in 2014 marks the beginning of a new stage, during which military security has again become a dominant preoccupation. The major risk for Romania, of being in the neighbourhood of a huge conflict, has led to an increasing interest in attracting NATO/US military capabilities, so that territorial protection is not just covered by the force of international documents, but also by troops on the ground.

Political and institutional mechanisms

Romania's international policy is managed by a number of institutions whose functionality depends on relations within the executive. Romania's Constitution assigns to the government responsibility for undertaking 'the domestic and foreign policy of the country'. The President of the Republic has a rather symbolic role (signing international treaties negotiated by the government, appointing and recalling ambassadors), but in practice it is customary that foreign policy is led from the Cotroceni Palace, at least as far as its strategic lines are concerned. During 1990–2004, when presidents and governments had the same political colour, foreign policy was de facto shared between the President of the Republic and the government. Prime ministers between 1990 and 2004 have accepted that the foreign affairs minister collaborates with the presidency in planning and carrying out foreign policy, the more so as the president also chairs the CSAȚ and is implicitly the priority recipient of information sent by the SIE.

International policy was not so consensual in 2006–8 and 2012–15, when the president and the prime minister came from different parties. On 29 June 2006, Prime Minister Tăriceanu demanded the withdrawal of Romanian troops from Iraq, without consulting President Băsescu or the Foreign Affairs Minister, Ungureanu, and also without giving prior notice to the United States. The liberals hoped for an electoral gain following this decision, as the military deaths had reduced public support for continuing the mission in Iraq. The sudden withdrawal from Iraq was blocked in the CSAȚ, but the risk of a major rift between foreign policy decision-makers was highlighted for the first time.

Tensions between the foreign affairs minister and the presidency became systematic from 2012 to 2014, the main stake being Romania's representation on the European Council. Prime Minister Ponta wanted to participate in the European Council, invoking the functionalist argument that the President of the Republic does not possess the constitutional competence to apply decisions taken in Brussels. In June 2012 the foreign affairs minister sent to the European Commission the composition of Romania's delegation for the European Council reunion of 28–29 June. This included Prime Minister Ponta as head of the delegation, the foreign affairs minister, the European affairs minister, but not President Băsescu. He did not participate in the European Council, although he had intended to do so. He referred the issue to the Constitutional Court, which decided by a majority vote that the President of Romania does participate in European Council meetings as Head of State, and that this duty can be delegated by him expressly to the prime minister. By a political and judicial decision an inefficient mechanism of international policy decision-making was established during the periods of president–government cohabitation.

Parliamentary diplomacy also significantly developed in Romania, contributing to the promotion of national interests. Cultural diplomacy has as its main support structure the Romanian Cultural Institute, which has offices in the most important cities of the world (New York, London, Berlin, Rome, etc.), with the objective of promoting Romanian national identity and artistic creation.

NATO accession

For Romania, as for other Central European states, NATO membership meant the accomplishment of a strategic objective. The massive popular support of Romanians for

NATO accession (over 70 per cent) must be understood as a hope of living in peace, with territorial integrity guaranteed.

Romania's race to NATO was not a solitary exercise; it did not depend only upon Romania's internal changes towards democratization or on its military capacities but, above all, on the dynamics of international relations (including the role of CEE within the world balance of power, US–Russian Federation relations, the shift of the centre of conflict from Europe to the Middle East, the emergence of new kinds of threats, and the prevalence of asymmetrical risks after the 11 September 2001 attacks in America).

During the early 1990s NATO's Eastern enlargement was not a priority on the agenda of Western countries, in spite of the ex-communist states' insistence (Năstase 2006–11). The US, Germany and the UK were more preoccupied with avoiding a deterioration in their relations with Russia, which was entering a phase of internal instability, implicitly honouring informal commitments from the end of the Cold War, according to which NATO would not enlarge eastwards nor would it install new bases in the former Soviet empire (the 'Russia First' policy) (Asmus 2002: 18–47).

In the context of incertitude regarding NATO's future, as it was considered that the organization had lost its reason for being with the end of the Cold War, but also in order to answer to the ever-persistent pressures of Central Europeans to be integrated into the organization, the US launched, in January 1994, the Partnership for Peace (PfP). The Americans wanted to prevent a destabilization of Central Europe due to the power vacuum in the region (Paşcu 2014: 67). Romania was the first country which signed the 'Framework Agreement of the Partnership for Peace' on 26 January 1994. This led to the emergence of internal polemics over the opportunity of signing this agreement, as the Partnership was much less than NATO membership, and its member states had not received authentic security guarantees. Poland, the Czech Republic and Hungary again demanded the enlargement of NATO and not just transitory formulas. The gesture of Romanian diplomacy of being the first country to join the PfP should be interpreted as a decision to use any anchors which could bind Romania to the West, avoiding a new international isolation. It also helped to legitimize those in political power (Ion Iliescu and the PDSR) externally, as they proved to be an accepted partner in the West, despite the contrary claims of the Opposition (the CDR).

In April 1995, the US launched a resolution by which NATO's enlargement to the east was proposed. Immediately, Russia threatened to cancel the START 2 treaty and the treaty concerning Conventional Forces in Europe (CFE). Internally, these events gave more impetus to debates about belonging to Europe. The most important decision taken in Bucharest was to re-launch a political dialogue with Hungary, following the model of French–German reconciliation. This was finalized by the signing of the Basic Treaty on 16 September 1996.

The elections at the end of 1996 brought the first democratic government change in Romania. President Constantinescu and the Ciorbea Government started a desperate campaign to join NATO at the Madrid summit in July 1997. In April 1997, the Romanian Parliament unanimously adopted a message addressed to the sixteen NATO members, demanding support for a favourable decision during the Madrid summit. The mass media in the country launched an irrational campaign suggesting the country's destiny was linked with Romania's invitation to join NATO in Madrid (Rusu-Toderean 1997–8: 93–110). NATO membership was mythologized, and was promoted as being a solution to all Romania's fundamental problems, which was obviously far from the truth.

At the diplomatic level, although following the elections Romania had seen a change in leadership to an openly pro-Western government, the US strategy could not be changed. France became the most vocal supporter of inviting Romania into NATO, raising the Americans' suspicion of a new francophone 'Trojan horse'. Germany and the UK did not yet support the consolidation of NATO's south-eastern flank. As a consequence, the political decision agreed by the Americans was to receive into the Alliance only the Czech Republic, Poland and Hungary, to which it was considered the West had a 'moral obligation', due to their resistance against communism. The 'consolation prize' received by Romania was the visit to Bucharest of President Bill Clinton in July 1997. He was received with unusual enthusiasm, considering that he had just refused to offer security guarantees through NATO membership. The US message was to encourage accession preparations, with a new evaluation being due after two years, at the Alliance summit in Washington in April 1999. This had also been promised at the end of the Madrid summit.

The Kosovo crisis of 1998–9 emphasized for NATO strategists the need to consolidate its south-eastern flank, where the most important state was Romania. The George Bush Jr Republican administration brought a more realistic perspective in relations with Russia. At the same time, the US considered that it had to eliminate any security vacuum in Europe by a broad enlargement of the Alliance, hoping at the same time to attract allies from the 'New Europe' against the French–German couple, which was reticent towards US hegemony (Larrabee 2003: 4–5; 159–60). The 11 September 2001 attacks and the beginning of the war in Afghanistan strengthened Romania's application for NATO accession. In September 2001, Parliament decided, by an overwhelming majority, on Romania's participation as NATO's de facto ally in the fight against global terrorism by all means, including military. Romania guaranteed access to its airspace, airports, land and sea facilities in the event of a NATO request to this effect. On 30 April 2002, the Parliament approved Romania's offer to participate in Operation 'Enduring Freedom' in Afghanistan. In June 2003, the Romanian Parliament approved participation with forces in the stabilization and reconstruction of Iraq.

Romania was behaving as a de facto NATO member, so that the invitation addressed to it, alongside another six ex-communist states at the Prague NATO summit (21 November 2002) was an important political moment. The visit of President George W,. Bush to Bucharest, immediately after the Prague moment, was meant to send to Romanians the message that they had eventually solved the fear of foreign aggression. Romania effectively became a NATO member on 29 March 2004, when accession instruments were exchanged in Washington between the new member states and the Alliance.

On a psychosocial level, Romania's NATO membership eliminated the fear of a new foreign invasion, but its position as a border state and the proximity of areas of instability, from the Western Balkans to Afghanistan, preserved public interest in the Alliance. During the presidential mandates of Băsescu, when he spelled out the so-called 'Washington–London–Bucharest Axis', Romania closely followed US interests. Romania was among the last countries to withdraw its troops from the 'Iraqi Freedom' operation in July 2009. It had contributed a total of 8,400 soldiers (with a peak of 730 military in 2007), most of them under US and British command. Romania repaid NATO membership with twenty-seven dead and over 130 wounded by 2015. The Romanian army also has a relatively large contingent in Afghanistan (ISAF – Enduring Freedom).

Romania's most visible moment within NATO was the Alliance's summit in Bucharest in April 2008, which represented the most important foreign policy event ever organized in the country. In the history of NATO, the Bucharest summit did not bring any significant innovations, either from the perspective of military doctrine or concerning essential military decisions. However it had the largest political participation (twenty-three presidents and twenty-two prime ministers) during the entire existence of NATO.

European integration

Romania already had ties to the European Communities (which became the European Union after the Maastricht Treaty) during the communist period, but due to the mineriads of 1990–1 and the period of international isolation that followed, the Romanian state signed the Agreement of Association to the European Union (the Europe Agreement), the legal basis for bilateral relations, as late as 1 February 1993, much later then the other Central European states.

In June 1993, at the European Council in Copenhagen, the political and economic criteria that states would have to fulfil in order to be part of the EU were established. The European Council reunion in Essen in December 1994, which adopted the programmatic document 'A Strategy for Preparing Associated States in Central and Eastern Europe for accession to the EU', as well as the enforcement of Romania's Association Agreement to the EU on 1 February 1995, determined the acceleration of the internal process for building political support for the vision of European integration. On the initiative of President Iliescu, the Commission of Snagov was created. Between March and June 1995, this acted with the clear objective of identifying solutions which would prepare Romania to become a full member of the EU. On 21 June 1995, the political leadership of Romania, the heads of parliamentary parties in power and in the opposition, adopted a declaration which institutionalized what would later be known as the 'Snagov spirit' (Ioan-Franc 2000). Significantly, one day after the signing of this declaration at the Palace of Snagov, Romania forwarded its request for accession to the EU, together with a 'National Strategy for Preparing Romania's Accession to the European Union'.

In 1997, the EU's 'Agenda 2000' was adopted, and it established the pre-accession strategy, incorporating two new elements: a partnership for accession and the extended participation of candidate states in Community programmes and the mechanisms which implemented the Community *acquis* (legislation). The European Council held in Luxembourg in December 1997 took the necessary steps to launch the enlargement process. On 30 March 1998, the process of accession for Cyprus, Hungary, Poland, Estonia, the Czech Republic and Slovenia was launched and for Bulgaria, Latvia, Lithuania, Romania and Slovakia the process of analytical examination of the *acquis* was opened (Papadimitriou and Phinnemore 2008: 40–51).

At the European Council in Helsinki in December 1999, the beginning of accession talks was decided for another six states: Romania, Slovakia, Latvia, Lithuania, Bulgaria and Malta. This decision was politically prepared by letters to the Romanian president signed by the prime ministers of Britain and Finland before the summit in Helsinki. It was underlined that compliance with the political criteria settled in Copenhagen in 1993 was essential in order to begin negotiations for accession, and candidate states were asked to solve problems regarding their borders.

The European Council in Copenhagen in December 2002 decided that the historic enlargement of the Union should take place on 1 May 2004 with reference to ten states. As far as Romania and Bulgaria were concerned, EU leaders established 2007 as the date for accession. This was the first decision of the Union which accepted the date of 2007 which had been proposed by Romania in 2000. The year 2007 constituted itself as an important political and symbolic reference point, with internal political actions being judged according to this date.

Accession negotiations were undertaken according to the Copenhagen criteria: the political and economic criteria, as well as the Community *acquis*. The thirty-one chapters of the Community *acquis* include basic conditions regarding the economic and social transformations a candidate state must undergo. The negotiations were led by Aurel Ciobanu-Dordea between February and December 2000 and chief-negotiator Vasile Puşcaş between December 2000 and December 2004, until the finalization of the negotiations calendar (Puşcaş 2006a; Puşcaş 2003–6).

Undergoing accession negotiations involved an important political component because of the need to get support for the acceptance of certain chapters by the Commission and ministerial councils. The Romanian government managed to persuade the President of the European Commission during 1999–2004, Romano Prodi, and the Commissioner for European enlargement, Günther Verheugen.

During the accession negotiations between Romania and the EU there were tense moments that concerned two sensitive issues. On 30 May 2001, Baroness Emma Nicholson, the European Parliament's Special Rapporteur on Romania's EU accession, recommended that the Parliament's Foreign Affairs Committee propose that the European Commission suspend accession negotiations because of concern about international child adoptions from Romania. Romania imposed a moratorium on international child adoptions, but it was not strictly respected. At the same time, throughout the West (US, France, Italy), there were demands for a complete resumption of adoptions. In 2004, Baroness Nicholson again threatened suspension of the accession negotiations, and was supported by the Commissioner for Enlargement, Günther

Verheugen. The Năstase government completely blocked international adoptions and thus avoided deepening the political crisis (Abraham 2006b: 109–15; Gallagher 2009/2010: 48–53).

A second subject which created a crisis situation between Romania and the EU was the International Criminal Court. Tensions between Bucharest and Brussels were high when Romania became the first country to sign, on 1 August 2002, a bilateral agreement by which it undertook to prevent the rendition of US citizens to international courts for war crimes. This diplomatic gesture aroused a negative reaction from the EU, with some European states not only criticizing the American pressures to which Romania was apparently subject, but also the fact that Bucharest had succumbed to them. Romania's gesture had a major importance for the US, as it created a precedent which could be used by other states in order to sign bilateral agreements. The reasoning of the Năstase government, when it signed the agreement, was that it expected that Romania would receive an accession invitation during the November 2002 NATO summit in Prague (as indeed happened), so the priority remained ensuring US support. By the time the EU accession negotiations were finalized, any negative effects would be in the past (Abraham 2006b: 116–18).

The accession negotiations were eventually finalized on 17 December 2004, after the end of the election process, and the signing of the Treaty took place on 26 April 2005. However the Treaty was signed with certain 'safeguarding clauses'. The European climate had changed, however, after the failure of referendums regarding the Treaty establishing a Constitution for Europe in France and the Netherlands in 2005, becoming less favourable to receiving new member states. In a political climate dominated by disputes between President Băsescu and Prime Minister Tăriceanu, which had the effect of decreasing governmental cohesion and orientating the political parties towards promoting their public image, the European Commission took advantage of the fragility of political power in Bucharest and Sofia to impose a surveillance format not included in the Accession Treaties. The Cooperation and Verification Mechanism (CVM) does not have a time limit, and it was a trade-off accepted by the two governments in order to have the calendar for accession on 1 January 2007 respected. This way Romania, together with Bulgaria, tacitly accepted that they represented 'exceptional cases'. No other member state, including the ten states that had become EU members on 1 May 2004, had accepted, or had even been asked to accept, such a status.

Romania's accession to the EU on 1 January 2007 symbolically ended a historic stage started by the Revolution of December 1989.

Similarly to NATO accession, Romania's European integration was the result of multilateral interests. The national political and diplomatic activity was convergent with the EU's interest in enlarging eastwards, for its political consolidation and economic expansion. The dynamics of the Union's enlargement were essentially determined by Brussels' evaluations concerning its own capacity of absorbing new states and by the social, economic and political situation in each candidate state. Delaying Romania's and Bulgaria's accession until 2007, together with the establishment of a new set of conditions for accepting accession (through the CVM), reflects not so much substantial difference between the countries of

Central and Eastern Europe (Hungary's democratic regression after 2010 confirms the superficiality of Euro-bureaucratic evaluations of the situation in Eastern Europe), as the fears of Western countries that the accession of an additional 30 million Romanians and Bulgarians would be too costly for the minuscule Community budget. Delaying the accession of new members left time for the Union to prepare the 2007–13 multi-annual budget, which also included envisaged funds for Romania and Bulgaria.

Romania's acceptance into the EU was not only part of the major project of Europe's political reunification, but also involved significant economic concessions. An important sponsor of Tony Blair's Labour Party, Lakshmi Mittal, was recommended to the Năstase government and benefited from advantageous conditions in the privatization of the biggest Romanian steel mill, Sidex Galați. Austria was very active in its relations with Romania, considering that the accession negotiations could be a favourable context for the purchase of companies in profitable fields. In 2004, the biggest Romanian oil company, Petrom, was purchased by OMV (a partly state-owned Austrian company), together with a 100-year concession on the energy resources of the Romanian state. The biggest bank in Romania, BCR, was privatized in 2005 in favour of another Austrian company, Erste Bank. Also in 2004, Romania privatized an important part of the electricity distribution network in favour of the Italian company Enel. In 2005, a good part of the gas distribution network was privatized in favour of Gaz de France. We may notice that during the period of negotiation and ratification of the accession treaty, Romania undertook privatizations in strategic fields (energy, banking and the steel industry). Not all these privatizations were the result of 'special conditionings' (support of accession in exchange for selling important companies), but they were the consequence of the European Commission's strategy of pushing ex-communist states to create a functional market economy by privatizing major companies. This meant, in fact, transferring property of the Romanian state into the ownership of other European countries (Austria, France, etc.) via big corporations. The promise of European funds was to compensate the ceding of important national companies in favour of Western companies. Tacitly, the privatization of some strategic companies was considered by the artisans of Romania's European integration a 'reasonable economic price' for the removal of the country from an uncertain geopolitical area and its integration into the EU.

The road from formal accession to real integration into EU institutions was marked by obstacles. The appointment of the first European commissioner from Romania was turned into a subject of political conflict between Băsescu and Tăriceanu. The government's initial proposal, Varujan Vosganian (a PNL minister), was withdrawn after the emergence of speculation concerning his collaboration with the *Securitate* (it was implied that withdrawal of ethnic Armenian Vosganian might have been motivated by the fact that he was perceived as Russia's agent of influence). The second proposal was the technocrat Leonard Orban, the former deputy EU negotiator within the Năstase government, who received the less prominent portfolio of multilingualism. The second European commissioner from Romania, in the second Barroso Commission (2009–14), was the technocrat Dacian Cioloș, who received the important portfolio of agriculture, with the support of France. Corina Crețu, former Member of the European Parliament and a Social Democratic politician, became the third European commissioner from Romania, in the Juncker Commission. Romania's mediocre influence within Community institutions must also be correlated with the teams of MEPs, which, with some exceptions, have lacked prominent national political personalities.

Romania's accession on 1 January 2007 was conditioned by accepting the CVM, in order to reach the consensus of the twenty-five member states, as a result of the reticence of Germany and the Nordic countries (Gallagher 2009/2010: 216–17). The CVM initially referred to the reform of the criminal justice system and the fight against corruption, but these themes were increasingly extended to wider issues related to the judicial system. From a formula of temporary support for the Romanian judicial system (conditions were accepted for a period of three years after the accession date), the CVM turned into a mechanism for maintaining the marginalization of Bulgaria and Romania within the Union. By their exceptional character, a false perception was created that Bulgaria and Romania were the only countries in Europe who had problems with their judicial systems. Romania was not accepted into the Schengen Area because of issues presented within the CVM reports, although the EU treaties and Romania's accession treaty do not include such conditions. The European Commission stated in June 2011 that Romania fulfilled the technical conditions for accession to the Schengen Area, but within the Council of the EU there was always a country which opposed enlargement. After repeated postponements of a favourable decision on the Schengen issue, Băsescu adopted a public attitude of reproof against the Netherlands' blocking of a decision at the end of 2011, and the accreditation of the Dutch Ambassador in Bucharest was delayed for several months. The CVM was also used to justify the opening of the labour market for Romanian citizens, but at the same time blocking access to certain Community funds. Despite intense diplomatic efforts and the European Commission's support, Romania has not been accepted in the Schengen Area. In 2013, the Ponta government radically changed the strategy: as the Romanian state fulfilled all technical conditions, it was no use undertaking new diplomatic action; rather Romania would wait for a decision from the other member states, when the subject of Romanian immigration ceases to be on some parties' agendas in France, the Netherlands and Germany.

From the perspective of Romania's international policy, accession to the Union meant an important success, but EU affiliation is incomplete without adopting the Euro and entering the Schengen Area. The perception that Romania is treated as a second-class country has led to a decrease in Romanians' Euro-enthusiasm, but without establishing, yet, a massive bloc of Eurosceptic options.

Relations with the Great Powers

History has developed in Romanian elites an acute sense of orientation towards gaining the support of the Great Powers, as an essential instrument for defending national interests. Relations with the Great Powers have influenced both Romania's internal policy and its neighbourhood policy strategies. Romania's diplomacy has permanently sought room to manoeuvre to avoid becoming a collateral victim in the conflicts among the Great Powers. Living under the syndrome of borders modified by force (the main reference points being Yalta (1945) and Malta (1989)), political elites after 1989 have ranged between excessive prudence and an irrational attachment, similar to unconditional submission, towards Great Powers.

United States of America

Romanian's relationship with the US has always been in a dual mode: on the one hand diplomacy, with the cold reasoning of state interest, on the other hand an imaginary relationship, mythologized around the American Dream. For a long time, Romania's main stake was not a limitation of the US sphere of influence but attracting it as much as possible. Suffering from the 'syndrome of loneliness' or insularity, Romanians have built an emotional relationship with the US; they have always been 'waiting for the Americans'. If Russia embodies the negative pole in the Romanians' modern political imaginary, the irreducible foe, the US was associated with the highest qualities, a land of 'all possibilities'. Romanians' sympathy towards the US is widespread in society, remaining at high levels even in periods of decline concerning international confidence, such as the failures in Afghanistan and Iraq (*Percepția opiniei publice* 2005: 59–60).

The December 1989 regime change created conditions for a new Romanian–US relationship, after the freeze at the end of the Ceaușescu era. The US interest in Romania in this first phase was limited by Soviet–US relations; the US wanted to avoid Moscow's hostility by being too closely involved near its borders. There were suspicions about those in power in Bucharest (Iliescu and the FSN), who were considered not to be irrevocably separated from communism. From the perspective of Romania's doubly 'original' evolution (violent revolution and a first government that was left-wing, of the FSN), the Bush administration was circumspect towards political developments in Bucharest, as the Cold War mentality was still present within US diplomacy.

The visit of Secretary of State James Baker to Bucharest (February 1990) took place in a context marked by street violence in Romania. After the mineriad of 13–15 June 1990, bilateral relations were frozen, as it was considered that there was not a democratic regime in Bucharest, a perception strengthened by the September 1991 mineriad. In addition, the issues of inter-ethnic relations and of the *Securitate* frequently returned to the diplomatic agenda of the 1990s. Bilateral relations were normalized in 1993, when Romania recovered Most Favoured Nation status; this was perpetuated in 1996 (Pușcaș 2006b).

In order to compensate politically for the refusal to receive Romania into NATO at the Madrid summit, the US–Romania Strategic Partnership was launched on the occasion of President Bill Clinton's visit to Bucharest in July 1997. This was meant to be an extended framework for collaboration aimed at consolidating bilateral relations, supporting the reform process and Romania's steps towards Euro-Atlantic integration, and promoting Romania's role as a factor of stability and security in South-East Europe.

But, while the US sought a concrete mechanism with limited objectives, Romanian politicians at first offered an original interpretation: a grandiose design involving massive economic and financial aid. In fact, the idea of the strategic partnership became a tool for internal political use in Romania. Emil Constantinescu's return visit to Washington took place in July 1998, but it did not change the US strategic decisions concerning Romania. During the Washington summit in 1999, a new NATO enlargement was not envisaged.

In Washington, Romania was considered a secondary state among ex-communist countries, the priority being Poland, the Czech Republic and Hungary. The whole region of CEE was less important than relations with Russia or the Middle East (the Israeli–Palestinian issue). During the 1990s, US economic assistance for post-communist countries remained less than 1 per cent of the US budget, in spite of the large Eastern-European community in America. Israel and Egypt benefited from more funds than the whole of CEE.

For the US, Romania was geographically too close to Russia to be at the centre of the first NATO enlargement, but also too politically and historically remote by tradition from Russia to be completely ignored. The US politically sponsored the creation of a distinct group among ex-communist countries (the Vişegrád Group), the general interest being the democratization of CEE. The 'new international order' announced by George Bush in 1990 meant US support for democratic change and market economy development in former communist states. Mineriads, inter-ethnic conflicts and events in University Square had created the perception of a neo-communist regime in Bucharest. The democratic change of 1996 was not sufficient of itself to bring Romania into the position of privileged US partner in the area. The US intervention in Bosnia in 1995 and the Kosovo crisis in 1999, determined by the inefficiency of European diplomacy, consolidated the perception of Romania's geostrategic importance as a meeting point of the Western Balkans and the Black Sea, two regions prone to conflict.

After the terrorist attacks against the US in September 2001, in the context of changes in US foreign policy philosophy (Schonberg 2009), Romania truly became important within the 'coalitions of the willing' in Afghanistan and Iraq and also for counterbalancing 'Old Europe', reticent about the US interventionist strategy, with a 'New Europe'. After 2001, top-level political contacts intensified: George W. Bush visited Romania on 23 November 2002, and both President Iliescu (October 2003) and Prime Minister Năstase (November 2001, July 2004) were received at the White House (Năstase 2012). As a political recognition for sending Romanian troops to Afghanistan and for Romanian diplomatic support for the US intervention in Iraq, on 10 March 2003, the American authorities granted Romania the status of 'market economy', at a time when the EU was still reluctant, which was important for finalizing the accession negotiations.

Turkey's initial refusal to participate as an ally in US operations in Iraq in 2003 strengthened Romania's role in the US strategy of securing the Black Sea basin and also the Middle East. Romania's accession to NATO was part of a broader strategic process by which the geopolitical vacuum from the Baltic to the Black Sea was eliminated.

Romania became a NATO and EU border state, and its potential value increased as regards political, military and economic processes in the Western Balkans and the Black Sea area (Turkey, Ukraine and the Caucasus).

The main controversy of that period was the signing, in 2003, of a \$2.3 billion contract with US company Bechtel to build the 415-kilometre Transylvania Motorway from Braşov to Oradea. It was said that this contract was a sort of bribe for the acceptance of Romania into NATO. After the 2004 elections, the Bechtel contract was blocked by the Tăriceanu government, following a request from Traian Băsescu, on the grounds of suspected corruption. After several resumptions and blockings of the contract, without the existence of acts of corruption being proved, it was terminated in 2013. Romania had paid €2.2 billion for only one-eighth of the initial project. The Transylvania Motorway is one of Romania's great failed projects.

'The Washington–London–Bucharest Axis will be a priority in the foreign policy of the next five years,' declared president-elect Băsescu on 13 December 2004 (Roncea 2005: 15). Neither the US nor the UK responded enthusiastically to Băsescu's initiative; they never referred to their relation with Romania as one with geostrategic virtues. An 'axis' also involves not only a privileged bilateral relation, but also a connection meant to establish a common conduct of the axis' poles towards third parties, as well as imposing on the latter a certain behaviour favourable to these poles. During Băsescu's visit to Washington in March 2005, President George W. Bush did not mention this so-called axis, declaring only that Romania was a 'special ally'. Romania was indeed important for the US as a military transit point towards Afghanistan and Iraq, as well as a location for its troops. To this end, an agreement concerning the activities of US forces stationed on Romanian territory ('Access Agreement') was signed, which entered into force on 21 July 2006.

The use of the term 'axis' was explained by Băsescu by a colourful formula: instead of having subordinate relations with several powers (called 'fire flies'), he preferred to interact with the 'Great Fire Fly', towards which he would have an attitude of total obedience (Abraham 2006b: 176–7). Thus Băsescu expressed a cynical realism: if you want protection you have to fulfil every demand without objection. It is not clear if the obedient behaviour was really demanded by Washington or if it was just a local initiative. If we analyse the Polish–US relationship by comparison to the Romanian–US one, we may consider that political obedience was Băsescu's initiative, in exchange for toleration of his authoritarian attitudes. US Ambassador to Romania Mark Gitenstein (August 2009 to December 2012), a former professional lobbyist, was an open supporter of all policies designed by Băsescu. After ending his mandate as ambassador, he became a member of the board of the 'Property Fund', a structure created by the government of Romania in 2005 to personal compensation to people dispossessed by the communist regime. The 'Property Fund' holds shares in the most profitable companies in Romania (for example, Petrom and Nuclearelectrica). Several Romanian political commentators interpreted Mark Gitenstein's presence among the leadership of the 'Property Fund' as a 'reward' for support given to Băsescu, including during his second suspension in 2012.

Romania remained in Iraq until the end of the missions there, in contrast to other European states (for example, Spain) which adopted a moderate Atlanticism. In 2011, the idea of privileged relations was revitalized by the adoption in Washington of the 'Common Declaration on the Strategic Partnership for the 21st Century between Romania and the US', during a meeting between Traian Băsescu and Barack Obama. Other collaborations were also established in the areas of science and technology, research, education and culture. Deploying some parts of the US Theatre Missile Defence in Romania (the 13 September 2011 agreement for a US military base) increased the level of Romanian–US bilateral relations.

After 1990, the Romanian–US relationship has significantly changed: from a lack of interest at the start of the 1990s to one of close collaboration in the military field and information exchanges in the 2000s. The ironic aspect of the strategic relationship idea is the fact that Romania was not even included in the Visa Waiver programme, so that it is often difficult for Romanian citizens to travel to the United States. Direct investment by the US in Romania remains at a modest level, as the big US corporations have not been attracted by South-East Europe, although the area is under NATO's security umbrella. No large US bank has ever been present in Romania to undertake massive investment.

USSR/Russian Federation

The feeling of insecurity created by the 'great neighbour in the East', which was the main enemy of Romanian statehood during the modern era, is the main defining element of Romanian–Russian relations. The imposition and securing of the totalitarian communist system by the Soviet Union only exacerbated the Romanians' traditional 'Russophobia'. Opinion polls undertaken after 1990 in Romania have identified Russia among the states most disliked by Romanians (*Percepţia opiniei publice* 2005: 68). Russia traditionally perceived Romania as a 'potential province' and Romanians as a small Orthodox but neo-Latin nation, different and exotic in the 'Slavic sea' surrounding it.

During the first part of the 1990s, the Russian–Romanian relationship was undoubtedly dominated by geopolitics. With the Soviet Union in the process of disintegration, two issues were of maximum importance on the bilateral relations' agenda: first, Romania's search for a security system in which it would quickly integrate and, secondly, the potential unification of Bessarabia with Romania.

Central-European states, recently emancipated from Soviet domination, each in turn demanded the dissolution of the institution which had formalized their belonging to the communist world, the Warsaw Pact. On 15 February 1991, the Vişegrád Trilateral was established in Budapest, joining Czechoslovakia, Poland and Hungary. Romania was not accepted as a member, despite a request by the Roman government. On 25 February 1991, foreign affairs ministers of the Warsaw Pact Member States signed in Budapest an agreement for dissolving the military structures of the alliance. On 1 July 1991, in Prague, the Warsaw Pact officially ended.

The solution identified by the Soviet Foreign Affairs Ministry for the dissolution of COMECON and the Warsaw Pact was to create a network of bilateral treaties with all ex-communist countries. Negotiations initiated by the USSR with Hungary, Poland and Czechoslovakia were blocked when it came to the articles providing for the withdrawal of Soviet troops from those countries. After the dissolution of the USSR, bilateral agreements were quickly signed with the Russian Federation: the Czech and Slovak Federative Republic (1 April 1992), Poland (22 May 1992) and Bulgaria (4 August 1992).

Romania chose a different path. Under the coordination of Iliescu, on 5 April 1991 the 'Treaty of collaboration, good neighbourliness and friendship' between Romania and the USSR was signed in Moscow. The agreement, not ratified by the Romanian Parliament, included in article 4 a clause according to which:

> Romania and the Union of Soviet Socialist Republics will not participate in any alliances directed one against the other. Neither of the Contracting Parties will allow that its territory be used by a third party for committing aggression against the other Contracting Party. Neither of them will, to this end, provide to a third party its ways and means of communication or other infrastructures, nor will it give any support to such a state that would enter into armed conflict with the other Contracting Party.

Soare 2010: 96–8

Iliescu's acceptance of conditioning from Moscow concerning NATO accession was, obviously, a serious political mistake. It can be explained by the fact that Romanian diplomats were taken by surprise; they did not understand that the Soviet Union was in a process of quick dissolution, and, by means of a traditional double game of Romanian diplomacy, the treaty was signed but was never ratified by the Parliament when it realized that it could create important internal and external problems.

The regulation of Romanian–Russian relations became difficult in Romania, for home affairs reasons. In April 1996, a treaty formula considered to be mutually advantageous for both Moscow and Bucharest was reached. It came close to being signed but, for electoral reasons, Iliescu gave it up, although the Russian minister of foreign affairs, Yevgeny Primakov, had come to Bucharest all the way from China precisely for this reason.

From 1997 to 2000 no significant progress was achieved in relations with Russia, a situation which changed with the preparation of NATO accession. The new international context created by the events of 11 September 2001 modified both relations between the US and the Russian Federation (during the Rome Summit of 28 May 2002 the new NATO–Russia Council was established) and the role of NATO. The US perspective on Romania's sub-regional role, in the new international context, was synthetically expressed by President Bush during his visit to Bucharest on 23 November 2002. The US leader said that Romania must become a 'bridge towards the new Russia' and that 'a Russia fully integrated in Europe does not need a buffer zone'. These declarations must not be interpreted in the sense that Romania would have the role of spokesperson or emissary within NATO in relations with Russia, but that Romania could represent a secure space in the vicinity of the Russian Federation.

Romania and Russia finally agreed to conclude a bilateral treaty, which was signed by Ion Iliescu and Vladimir Putin on 4 July 2003. The principle according to which the Romanian–Russian treaty was negotiated was 'the problems we cannot solve are avoided'. The 2003 agreement, entering into force on 27 July 2004 following the exchange of ratification instruments on the occasion of the visit of Prime Minister Năstase to the Russian Federation, left the parties with the possibility of joining any political and military alliance (Article 3). The issues of the restoration of the Romanian treasury and the condemnation of the Ribbentrop–Molotov Pact were not included in the text of the treaty. They were included in a political declaration of the ministers of foreign affairs which was not legally binding. A formula was reached by which both parties condemned the Ribbentrop–Molotov Pact and Romania's participation on the side of Axis powers in the war against the USSR (Buga and Chifu 2003: 13). The treaty does not include clauses that would prevent the deployment of NATO or US bases on Romania's territory, although concerned Russian officials openly manifested their hostility towards the positioning of Western military bases in the immediate vicinity of the Russian border.

The year 1999 was marked by significant political tensions. Emil Constantinescu considered that the mineriads of January–February 1999 were carried out with Russian support:

> [I]n the context of the escalation of the Kosovo conflict and of the preparation of the NATO intervention, it was necessary that Romania either become a transport corridor for oil, weapons and munitions, or become a completely destabilized country which could not be used by NATO as a basis for solving the Kosovo problem. Today, these are not even suppositions; they happened while the Serbian Parliament voted the union with Russia. Belarus had already united!
>
> Abraham 2006b: 199

Afterwards, following the cessation of NATO bombing in Serbia (24 May to 10 June 1999), Russia requested an air lane in order to 'carry out some military transports towards the region of Kosovo' (13 June 1999). The government granted the right to overfly without the Parliament's agreement, but the Russian Federation violated regulations stipulating the manner in which this right could be exercised. The agreement was suspended altogether and on 26 June 1999 Romanian military aircraft were used to enforce that decision. Russian Ilyushin aircraft were escorted out of Romanian air space. The prospect of a military incident was avoided.

After stating the 'Washington–London–Bucharest Axis' doctrine, Băsescu, in his wilful manner, visited Moscow in February 2005, recognizing the legitimate interests of the Russian Federation in the Black Sea area and addressing an invitation to participate in a future multilateral cooperation format around the Black Sea. At the High-Level Meeting of the Sixtieth Session of the UN General Assembly in September 2005, Băsescu declared: 'The Russian Federation treats the Black Sea as a Russian lake, as it does not want to internationalize problems in the area'. Băsescu's anti-Russian rhetoric intensified as the resolution of frozen conflicts was postponed and because Romania could not counterbalance Russia's influence in the Republic of Moldova. Băsescu turned the relationship with Russia into a major electoral campaign issue, accusing his opponents (principally Mircea Geoană, former Romanian Ambassador to the US) of being 'Moscow's men'. The situation affected the normalization of bilateral relations and Vladimir Putin visited Romania only on the occasion of the NATO summit in Bucharest in 2008.

The acceptance of US bases and the deployment of some elements of the Theatre Missile Defence in Romania (Deveselu airbase) provoked warlike rhetoric towards Romania from various Russian officials. Romania wanted Ukraine and Georgia to be offered a calendar for NATO accession, a proposal which was not supported by Germany and France.

The Russian–Georgian war of 2008 and, later, Russia's aggression against Ukraine in 2014 confirmed Romanians' worst geopolitical fears. Romania was one of the European countries which supported the adoption of a firm attitude by NATO and the EU against Russia and a harsh sanctions regime to guarantee the integrity of Ukraine (or of most of it). In the context of EU sanctions being applied to Russia, the Russian vice-premier Dmitri Rogozin threatened Romania with bombardment.

The issue of the reunification of the Romanian state by returning Bessarabia was not on the official agenda of Romanian–Russian relations. Russia has several instruments for influencing Chişinău's policy, so that Moscow's agreement is necessary for any unionist project. There was a competition between Romania and Russia to influence the situation in the Republic of Moldova. If, for Moscow, maintaining the separation of Bessarabia from Romania is part of its imperial policy of controlling its neighbourhood (Oliker et al. 2009), for Romania, uniting with the Republic of Moldova is part of a long-term political process, starting from the idea of a linguistic, historical and religious community.

Another important issue is the Romanian treasury in Moscow, given to Tsarist Russia in return for protection from the Central Powers' armies during the First World War. Important quantities of gold, jewels and art objects were never returned to Romania, as they were confiscated by Bolshevik Russia. Three partial restitutions took place (1935, 1956 and 2008), but they constituted only a small part of the goods sent for storage to Tsarist Russia (Scurtu 2014). Russia's official position is that it does not know what happened to Romania's treasury; in 2003 a mixed commission of Romanian and Russian historians was created, in order to find out about Romania's lost fortune. This has become an instrument for delaying the issue, not for solving it.

Another major theme of Russian–Romanian relations is energy. Gazprom wanted to buy Petrom (the largest national oil company in Romania), but its bid was not accepted. Russia then became a shareholder in OMV, which bought Petrom in 2004. Romania did not want to participate in the Russian South Stream project of transporting gas towards Europe through the Black Sea area, a project eventually abandoned by Gazprom in 2014. Romania diversified its energy production in order to reduce its energy dependence on Russia. A few small trade wars also took place (for example, Romanian pork was not accepted in Russia). All these elements complete the picture of a fluctuating relationship, in which full confidence has never fully been found because Romanian history is marked by so much suffering caused by the Great Power in the East (Naumescu and Dungaciu 2015: 325–55).

Germany

At the beginning of the post-communist period, Romania was in the unhappy situation of having lost the most powerful factor binding it to Germany: the community of Saxons and Swabians, drastically diminished by departures during the regime of Nicolae Ceauşescu, continued to emigrate at an alarming pace during 1990–2. State-level relations must be understood from the perspective of multiple factors: Germany's interest in gradually creating a security area in its close vicinity, the priority being the Vişegrád Group countries; the need to give priority to deepening political and economic integration within the EU, while sparing British and French susceptibilities concerning possible German hegemonic intentions over CEE; and the wish to maintain good relations with Russia, with which Germany is in a close energy and trade interdependence.

During the early 1990s, Romanian–German relations did not carry a strong political weight, in the context of Germany's lack of interest regarding Romania. The main event was the signing, on 2 April 1992, of the Treaty between Romania and the Federal Republic of Germany concerning friendly cooperation and partnership in Europe, by which German reunification was recognized.

After 1996, Romania began a persistent campaign to attract Germany's support for its NATO accession. Foreign Affairs Minister Adrian Severin presented official excuses to Germany for the treatment applied to ethnic Germans during the communist period and the building of the former German Legation in Bucharest was also returned. Although President Emil Constantinescu had officially visited Germany even before the Madrid summit and had been cordially received by German officials, they did not strongly support Romania.

The Kosovo crisis represented the moment when the EU dramatically realized its structural weakness in the field of military security (Miskimmon 2007: 100–43). The political consolidation of South-East Europe also became a priority for Germany. This was the context in which Chancellor Gerhard Schroeder visited Romania in September 1999.

After the beginning of the EU accession negotiations, Romania established closer ties with Germany as a major political objective. On the occasion of the second visit to Romania of Chancellor Gerhard Schroeder in August 2004 a contract amounting to €650 million for securing borders was signed between the Romanian Government and the European Aeronautic Defence and Space Company (EADS). The signing of this contract was probably an additional reason why the German Chancellor declared public support for Romania's concluding of the EU negotiations in 2004 and the finalizing of the Accession Treaty in 2005.

Political relations at the highest level were supported by a dense network of other forms of economic and cultural bilateral cooperation. Germany did not show any interest in participating in the privatization of the Romanian economy's 'crown jewels': the banking and oil fields. An exception was the company E.ON Ruhrgas AG (in which the Russian company Gazprom has shares), which bought Distrigaz Nord and one of the eight electricity distribution companies.

Since the 2000s, Germany has become Romania's main trading partner; Romanian companies, as well as German companies with Romanian factories, have produced parts for large German companies, taking advantage of a cheap and skilled local labour force.

The Atlanticism manifested by Băsescu from the very beginning of his first mandate was tempered by the reality of European policy. Romanian–German political contacts became frequent after Romania's accession to NATO and the EU, the multilateral approach becoming predominant. Romania was a supporter of the economic austerity policies promoted by Germany within the EU, sometimes even against its own economic interests. Romania was among the first EU countries which ratified the EU Fiscal Compact (13 June 2012), by which Germany imposed a philosophy of balanced budgets and austerity policies.

The election of Klaus Iohannis, an ethnic German, to the highest position in the Romanian state has generated high hopes for the revival of bilateral relations. However, the state visit of the President of Romania to Germany in February 2015 was dominated by realism: Germany's political interests do not change depending on an individual, but are based on more complex calculations. From Berlin's perspective, Romania's accession to the Schengen Area should be a long process.

The level of bilateral political relations never reached the stage where they would have been bilaterally defined as 'strategic'. Within the German political environment there are psychological reservations towards Romania, ranging from the fact that Nazi Germany was 'betrayed' by Romania during the Second World War, followed by the emigration of ethnic Germans in exchange for financial compensation, to the Roma immigrants from German cities. As a consequence, Germany has used Community institutional mechanisms to fulfil its objectives concerning Romania, from the CVM in the field of justice to the repeated postponement of Romania's accession to the Schengen Area.

France

From Bucharest's perspective, the establishment of the modern Romanian state with France's support and the later international validation of Greater Romania with the support of Paris are fundamental elements at the basis of the French–Romanian relationship. Belonging to the family of neo-Latin nations is also a part of the essential identity of Romanian elites (Eliade 2000).

Bilateral French–Romanian relations must be understood in the context of French policy in CEE. François Mitterrand looked with reluctance at the revolutionary transformations in Eastern Europe. The interest of Paris was directed towards deepening the integration of the European Community, creating a new treaty (at Maastricht) which would establish the EU, a structure capable of being a competitor with the US. The French president continued to speak in September 1993 about 'developing countries' in CEE which, if they belonged to the EU, would cause great losses to the latter. This attitude was significantly different from that of Germany, which was a strong supporter of socio-political changes in the former communist space, especially in the Vişegrád countries (Deloche-Gaudez 2000: 53).

Jacques Chirac changed French strategy regarding Europe. The French president made several visits during 1996–7 to Poland, Hungary, the Czech Republic and Romania, by which he wanted to demonstrate French interest in CEE. Paris agreed with NATO enlargement in 1997 and 2002, as well as with EU enlargement, considering that the region could be an excellent economic outlet for French companies.

Among Romania's bilateral relations with the European Great Powers, those with France were the most intense. French and Romanian prime ministers and presidents made several mutual visits. Besides diplomatic statistics, some important elements must be highlighted. After the violent confrontations in 1990, Romania was quasi-isolated at the international level. It was François Mitterrand who took upon himself the mission of taking Bucharest out of 'diplomatic quarantine', being the first important Western official to visit Romania after the fall of the Ceauşescu regime, thus providing support to the administration that resulted from the 20 May 1990 elections. The legal consecration of the special relationship was accomplished by the signature, by Mitterrand and Iliescu, of the 'Treaty of friendly understanding and cooperation between Romania and the French Republic', which entered into force on 22 October 1992.

Chirac visited Bucharest in February 1997 in a special context: Romania had just experienced the first democratic change in power and Emil Constantinescu's administration had started a desperate race in order to be invited to join NATO. Again, the first Western head of state to visit Bucharest was the French president. In his speech in the Romanian Parliament, Chirac promised that France would be Romania's 'friendly advocate' within NATO, though it would be to no avail.

The Iraq War of 2003 gave rise to tensions in French–Romanian relations. The pro-US position of Poland, Romania and Bulgaria raised negative reactions in the most important European capitals. On 5 February 2003, ten CEE countries, all NATO candidates, among them Romania, signed the 'Call of the Ten' by which the US point of view was strengthened. The gesture irritated Chirac, who, on 17 February 2003, during the European Council, declared that the ten countries had 'missed a good opportunity to shut up'. The beginning of the Iraq War and Romania's military participation in the post-Saddam era generated tension in the political relations between Romania and France. In October 2003, Catherine Lalumière, vice-chair of the European Parliament, considered Romania a potential US 'Trojan horse', within the EU. However, Romania's pro-American position during the Iraq crisis did not affect the country's European path, as Paris supported the Romanian state in its European integration.

The first year of Băsescu's mandate brought an abrupt cooling of relations with France, in the context of his statement on the transatlantic axis thesis. Băsescu visited Paris in November 2005, in an attempt to repair bilateral relations and was received with little sympathy by Chirac. Mutual interests determined the normalization of relations, taking into account the fact that the Francophonie Summit was organized in Bucharest between 28 and 29 September 2006, the first such meeting organized in CEE.

After Romania's EU accession and Nicholas Sarkozy's electoral victory in France in 2007, bilateral relations resumed, as Bucharest's Atlanticism, stated by Băsescu, was partially consonant with that of the Élysée Palace. The result was a 'Common Declaration on establishing a Strategic Partnership between France and Romania', signed in Bucharest on 4 February 2008 by Presidents Băsescu and Sarkozy. Behind it was Băsescu's promise to offer French companies even more contracts with the Romanian state. The economic crisis left the bilateral arrangements unfulfilled, as public investment in Romania was drastically reduced. President Sarkozy, for his part, tried to bring Romania back into the French sphere of influence, in order to demonstrate that Paris remained a first-rank European political operator.

In 2010, a new crisis occurred in bilateral relations. Romania persistently requested accession to the Schengen Area, but in France there was an intense political and media campaign around the Roma issue, also motivated by the populist options of the French far right. Romania was considered to have the main responsibility for the westward migration of this historical ethnic minority. Opposition from Paris to Romania's and Bulgaria's accession to the Schengen Area, invoking problems in the fight against corruption and the issue of illegal migration, irritated Bucharest, while the term for applying full freedom of movement of persons, established for March 2011, was postponed *sine die*.

During the presidency of socialist François Hollande, the Romanian Social Democrat Prime Minister Victor Ponta attempted a revival of bilateral relations during a visit to Paris in February 2013. On that occasion a 'Roadmap' was adopted for putting into practice the Partnership provisions, both in the field of European affairs and at the level of sector-related bilateral cooperation.

The visit of Klaus Iohannis to Paris in February 2015 and his meeting with Hollande can be included in the long list of bilateral contacts that accompanied every political power change in both France and Romania.

Apart from the rhetorical romanticism concerning Romania's belonging to the Francophone community, Paris proved to be very pragmatic in its relations with Romania. The French–Romanian 'privileged relationship' also meant the acquisition by the Romanian state of three Airbus A310 aircraft in 1991 and four Airbus A318s in 2004. French companies participated in important privatizations in Romania. The car manufacturer Dacia was sold to Renault in 1999, becoming an authentic European success story. The Romanian Development Bank was privatized in favour of Société Générale in 1998, and a regional monopoly (Distrigaz Sud) in gas distribution was privatized in favour of GDF Suez in 2005. France also brought competitive companies in other fields, including telecommunications (Orange) and retailing (Carrefour).

The United Kingdom

British–Romanian relations were only partially resumed after 1989, following their deterioration at the end of the Ceaușescu regime. British political interest in Romania has tended to be more intense during various regional crises: the Crimean War (1853–6), the Oriental Crisis and the Russian–Turkish War (1878–9), the end of the Second World

War (1944–5), the Yugoslav Crisis (1999) and the Iraq War (2003). This can be explained by geopolitics: for London, Romania is a South-East European country which is important for the power equation within the area, but less so for the continental balance of power (Deletant 2005).

During the 1990s, London's interest in Romania was marginal, as British diplomacy was more preoccupied by the continental force ratio resulting from the interaction between France and Germany, and between Turkey and Greece, than by CEE. The most important political contact was Iliescu's visit to London in 1994, designed to attract British support for Romania's Euro-Atlantic integration.

The political level of British–Romanian relations significantly increased in the context of the 1999 Yugoslav Crisis and the involvement of the Anglo-American coalition. Romania's geostrategic value for managing the Western Balkans increased. Tony Blair visited Romania in May 1999, on which occasion he expressed London's support for Romania's integration into the Euro-Atlantic structures. The Labour leader promised British support for Romania to be invited to open EU accession negotiations at the Helsinki European Council in December 1999.

After the opening of accession negotiations with Romania, the Labour government in Britain was significantly involved in preparing the Romanian state for EU integration. On 7 March 2001 the action plan 'United Kingdom – Romania in Europe' was launched, turning in June 2003, on the occasion of Năstase's visit to London, into 'United Kingdom and Romania in Europe: a Strategic Partnership'. Improving British–Romanian relations after 2000 certainly had an ideological dimension. Năstase was invited in 2003 to the 'Progressive Governance' summit in London, which brought together most important left-wing leaders from all over the world (Abraham 2006b: 240).

The strongest form of strategic incentive for the UK to support the Romanian objective of NATO membership was the contract by which in 2003 the Romanian state bought two frigates from the British company BAE Systems, worth over US$180 million. Regarding the frigates, *The Guardian* newspaper published an investigation on 8 June 2006 which presented the hypothesis that a 'commission' amounting to £7 million had been paid by BAE Systems to business intermediaries. No investigation in Romania or the UK confirmed the alleged act of corruption in a judicial manner.

The British–Romanian partnership was rhetorically amplified by President Băsescu to the level of 'Axis'. The presidential initiative was not well received in London, as Tony Blair was more or less being accused in Paris and Berlin of wanting to block the European political project in order to keep the EU at the level of a mere greater market. Romania differed from the UK's vision of Europe, being closer to the French-German project of a stronger political and social integration of the Union.

In 2011 the 'Joint Declaration on the Intensification of the Strategic Partnership between Romania and the United Kingdom' was adopted, with the objectives of cooperating inside the EU and strengthening bilateral economic, social and cultural relations. Bilateral relations were dominated by common security interests, the UK being less involved in economic cooperation. Compared to Romania's relations with Germany,

British–Romanian trade relations were at best small, being significantly smaller than those between Italy and Romania. British companies and banks manifested only a secondary interest in the Romanian market.

'Romanians' were, after 2007, the subject of several negative campaigns in the British tabloid media, the major themes being the poor immigrant and the exoticism of Roma communities. It is not by chance that the UK was among the last EU countries which liberalized travel for Romanian citizens, and the lifting of labour market restrictions was accomplished only after energetic demands from the European Commission.

Undoubtedly, a symbolic element of bilateral relations is Prince Charles's interest in traditional Transylvanian villages. His purchase of some rural properties (after 1998) and his visits to Romania strengthened bilateral cultural relations, increasing British interest in a cultural and geographical space perceived to be interesting for its preservation of traditions and its natural environment.

China

China had been an important political partner of communist Romania, Ceauşescu's international policy being appreciated in Beijing. Immediately after the Revolution, bilateral relations were frozen, as democratic developments in Europe were not regarded with enthusiasm in Beijing.

Romania did not regard China as a Great Power which could offer credible security guarantees, but considered that a special political relationship, based on the foundations created during the communist period, could help it also in its relations with other important states (for example, Russia and the US). For its part, China wanted to preserve good relations with CEE countries, for which reason, when Romania was threatened with financial default under IMF pressure, it discretely provided Bucharest with a US$100 million loan, thus saving an old ally from collapse. In fact, Chinese premier Li Peng visited Romania in 1994, the first ex-communist country approached. President Jiang Zemin visited Romania, a country which he had often visited between 1970 and 1980, again in 1996.

The maximum intensity moment of Romanian–Chinese bilateral relations was the period 2002–4, when Prime Minister Năstase, at the height of the campaign for accession to the Euro-Atlantic institutions, undertook three visits to Beijing, during which collaboration contracts were signed in the economic, scientific and cultural fields. In 2003, while China was in quarantine determined by the spread of avian flu (SARS) epidemics, Năstase made a visit to Beijing, wishing to send the signal that China was a safe country. He was returning the favour China had given Romania during difficult times. In 2004, the president of China, Hu Jintao, arrived in Bucharest, on which occasion a Common Declaration was signed concerning the establishment of an Enhanced Partnership of Friendship and Cooperation. It was the strongest signal that Năstase could send that he wished for a foreign policy 'towards all the cardinal points'. In Năstase's view, NATO and EU membership were not incompatible with a close relationship with China.

The idea of reviving Romanian–Chinese relations, downgraded to a secondary level by Băsescu, a rigid Atlanticist, was resumed after 2012 by Prime Minister Ponta, who in 2013 actually proposed the adoption of a Strategic Partnership. The project, rejected by Băsescu, aimed at opening relations with China in order to attract as much investment as possible, in a context in which the interest of Western companies in developing large projects in Romania and their resources for this were limited. China repeatedly offered Romania generous proposals of financing great infrastructure projects, but these were blocked following informal requests from the European Commission and the IMF. Undoubtedly, the battle to dominate markets is also taking place in Romania and its political elites are not always capable of defending the interests of the country's modernization and development, even with Asian capital (Fox and Godement 2009: 45–51).

Regional policy

After the fall of the Iron Curtain the demons of the past were reawakened. Nationalism became once again the main ideological force throughout CEE. Inter-ethnic conflicts and old rivalries among nations came to the fore. Czechs and Slovaks split peacefully. Yugoslavia was fragmented during a decade of conflict whose wounds have not healed even in the present day. After Moldova and Ukraine became independent states, Romania no longer had Russia as a direct neighbour. Romania was again on the fault line between the West and the Russian world, in the proximity of the Muslim political and religious space.

Romania's regional policy was the result, often contradictory, of influences and pressures exercised by national public opinion, by the policies of other states in the vicinity, and by the diverse interests of Great Powers. Significant for the dynamic of Romania's regional policy is the very self-definition of the Romanian state in a regional context. While in 1990 Romania considered itself a 'Balkan state', reviving the interwar period, following Yugoslavia's break-up and the creation of the Vişegrád Group, Romanian diplomacy used the term 'Central European country' in the proximity of South-East Europe (Abraham 1999: 308–19). The Central European identity, considered to be much more prestigious than the Balkan one, was preserved until the achievement of NATO accession. After 2004, when Băsescu placed Romania on the 'Washington–London–Bucharest Axis', the Black Sea neighbourhood was favoured, as well as the potential of playing a part in the 'Wider Black Sea Region' (a US concept including the space between the Western Balkans and the Middle East) (Asmus 2006; Asmus, Dimitrov and Forbrig 2004). A key metaphor which Romania sought to capitalize on for its NATO and EU candidacy was the 'island of stability': as compared to the Balkans or to the region situated east of the Black Sea (the Caucasus area), the Romanian state truly represents a landmark of democratic consolidation.

Hungary

The key to Romania's regional policy lay in relations with Hungary, as its westward road also passed through Bucharest, and Romania's through Budapest. At the centre of bilateral relations was, for a very long time, the issue of identity and that of minorities.

Home and foreign policy were intrinsically related, not only by the rational element of state interest, but also by mythology, historical anxieties and fears.

The first stage was characterized by mutual suspicion. In Budapest, but also among Hungarian emigrant circles in the West, the hope that the 'Trianon Diktat' would be abolished was made public, with Greater Hungary once again becoming a real and not just an imagined entity. For example, during the electoral campaign of May 1990, József Antall declared that 'In my soul, I consider that I will be Prime Minister for 15 million Hungarians'. Hungarian conservative governments (Antall and Péter Boross from May 1990 to July 1994) led a predominantly symbolic policy, claiming that the rebirth of the Hungarian nation, recently freed from communism, could not be complete without the reunification, at least at a spiritual level, with Greater Hungary. Broad propaganda was undertaken for reopening discussions about the 'Trianon Diktat' (Kende 1995: 475–92). In Romania, a reactive nationalism developed against real or imaginary revisionist dangers. The March 1990 inter-ethnic conflicts in Târgu Mureş deepened mistrust between the Romanian majority and the Hungarian minority. Mutual confidence was at very low levels; Hungary's wish to block Romania's accession to the CoE was relevant, as this represented a decisive stage for Bucharest's exit from isolation. In the end, Budapest gave up, following pressure from Berlin.

Normalization of bilateral relations was achieved as a result of pressures from the US and the EU. As long as Hungary did not reconfirm its respect for border inviolability in Europe, specifically its borders with Slovakia and Romania, its chances of being accepted in NATO and the EU were poor. The situation was identical for Romania. The key moment was the EU summit at Essen in December 1994, which stated the need to achieve full normalization in relations with neighbouring countries. The socialist government of Gyula Horn gave up this revisionist rhetoric; the path to the resolution of regional problems was opening up.

Finalizing the Romanian–Hungarian agreement was for a long time blocked by the disagreement concerning Recommendation 1201 of the Council of Europe; the fear of the Romanian authorities was that its acceptance would be key to Hungary requesting territorial autonomy on ethnic criteria. After the unexpected signing of the Hungarian–Slovak treaty in March 1995, including Recommendation 1201, Romania found itself at risk of being considered a non-democratic state, and a potential source of tension in the area. Against this background, the authorities in Bucharest assumed the project of accomplishing the 'historical Romanian–Hungarian reconciliation'. In August 1995, Iliescu launched the idea of a 'historical reconciliation', following the French–German model. By doing so, Romanian politicians made acceptable to national public opinion the idea of signing an agreement with Hungary (Salat and Enache 2004). The 'Treaty of Understanding, Cooperation and Good Neighbourliness between Romania and the Republic of Hungary' signed in Timişoara, on 16 September 1996, was presented to Romanian public opinion as a step towards a common integration into NATO and the EU. In fact, within the text of the Treaty, at Article 7(1), the two parties expressed their agreement on mutual support concerning NATO, the EU and the Western European Union (WEU) (Abraham 2006b: 251–4; Vădean 2011: 47–89).

After overcoming the main political and psychological obstacle of reconfirming border inviolability, Romanian–Hungarian relations witnessed moments of oscillation, during which good neighbourliness alternated with political tension. Although Hungary was more advanced than Romania in Euro-Atlantic integration, in Budapest the issue of exercising a veto against the accession of the Romanian state was never truly considered. On 29 November 2002, the 'Declaration Regarding Cooperation and the Romanian–Hungarian Strategic Partnership for Europe During the 21st century' was signed between the social-democratic governments of Romania and Hungary, an initiative which had materialized during four common government sessions between 2005 and 2008.

The tense Romanian–Hungarian relations are correlated with the political ideology of the authorities in Budapest. FIDESZ, of a conservative-nationalist orientation, took upon itself the 'protection of the Hungarian nation' also beyond Hungary's borders. The adoption by the Viktór Orbán government of a law on the status of Hungarians in neighbouring countries in 2001, considered by the Hungarian leader 'a victory over Trianon', was rejected by the Năstase government because it was considered that it affected national sovereignty (Blokker and Kovacs 2015). The law was modified after the intervention of the European Commission and the CoE. In 2010, a new FIDESZ government adopted a law of dual citizenship. This was fundamentally different from the Romanian law of 1991/2006 on dual citizenship, as it was not limited to people who had had state citizenship at a particular point, or to their descendants, but applied to all speakers of Hungarian at intermediate level.

At the centre of Romanian–Hungarian disputes after 2007 were the ever-more persistent Hungarian demands for autonomy on ethnic criteria of areas mostly inhabited by ethnic Hungarians. Hungarian president László Sólyom spoke in October 2008, in the presence of Traian Băsescu, about the political autonomy of the area inhabited by the Szecklers in Mureş, Harghita and Covasna counties. The Hungarian president informed Romania that he was going to the 'Harghita self-government' (rather than 'local government') in order to celebrate the International Day of Hungarians, but he was refused landing rights at Târgu Mureş airport on 15 March 2009. Repeated declarations by FIDESZ leaders after 2010 regarding support for the unilateral secession of the Hungarian community in the Harghita and Covasna counties were considered by Bucharest to be actions of Hungarian domestic politics. Romania did not want to escalate tensions in bilateral relations, the more so as the UDMR either formed part of the Romanian government (2008–12; 2014) or offered conditional parliamentary support to the government (2012–13).

The main tendency after 1994 was to build a bilateral relationship that would not be centred exclusively on its ethnic component, but rather on the sub-regional cooperation project (Central European Initiative, CEFTA) and within NATO and the EU. Romania and Hungary are not authentic 'strategic partners', despite concluding a political agreement to this end, but they have not become 'irreconcilable enemies' again. As long as Hungary does not consider the issue of minorities as permanently closed, but wants instead to get various forms of territorial autonomy formulas on ethnic grounds for

Hungarians in Romania and Slovakia, there is the potential of new political tensions within CEE.

Republic of Moldova

The relationship between Romania and the Republic of Moldova has been the most important from the perspective of domestic policy, being complex, contradictory and marked by the emotional element of a common language, history and religion. In the context of the dissolution of the Soviet Union, the issue of unification with the area between the Prut and the Dniestr was approached at an unofficial level in Romania. From June 1990, after the Republic of Moldova's declaration of sovereignty, until 1994 there was a period of 'bridges of flowers' (it was considered that bridges over the river Prut rather unite than separate the Romanian nation), of predominantly emotional-symbolic relations, marked by the hope of state reunification (King 1999: 145–230). For example, at the beginning of 1991, when President Mircea Snegur visited Romania, there were voices among Romanian politicians demanding state reunification. During the Moscow *putsch* of August 1991, there were many calls in Romania for unity and solidarity with Moldovans and some political leaders even talked of a military intervention in order to ensure the restoration of Greater Romania.

Border change in Europe is not an issue that can be decided by only two countries; a broader international agreement is needed. It was obvious that, even if the USSR was shaken to its foundations, Moscow would not easily accept losing a territory which it had controlled for over half a century. Unification could not be carried out by repeating the events of 1917–18, when the Romanian army entered Chișinău, ensuring the pre-eminence and stability of pro-unionist forces. At the same time, Romania was more interested in preserving the status quo and could not afford to challenge the validity of the Paris Peace Treaty of 1947, which recognized its borders. Also, the US and the great Western powers were not very enthusiastic about the Soviet Union's dissolution, being primarily interested in stability rather than in applying the principle of peoples' self-determination. In this context, Romania became the main sponsor of Moldovan statehood, being the first country to recognize the Republic of Moldova, only a few hours after its declaration of state independence on 27 August 1991. Subsequently, visa-free movement was established across the Prut, with Romanian and Moldovan citizens being able to travel between the countries on the basis of their ID.

Starting in 1994, Chișinău increasingly sent signals concerning its abandonment of the option of unification with Romania. President Snegur organized the sociological poll 'Council with the People', according to which 90 per cent of citizens with the right to vote gave an affirmative answer to the question:

Are you in favour of Republic of Moldova's developing as an independent, unitary and indivisible state, within the borders existing at the date of its sovereignty proclamation, 23 June 1990, its promoting a policy of neutrality, its maintaining mutually profitable relations with all other countries, and its guaranteeing equal rights to all its citizens, according to the norms of international law?

Thus the idea of unification between the two states, following the German model, was abandoned because at least one of the partners had signalled an obvious lack of interest. In 1994, the Republic of Moldova ratified its accession to the Commonwealth of Independent States, a gesture which brought protest from the Romanian Parliament. Moreover, by the Constitution of 29 July 1994, the Republic of Moldova is declared to be a 'sovereign and independent, unitary and indivisible state' (art.1), having as its state language the 'Moldovan language'. This was a compromise formula, as pro-unionist forces wanted the proclamation of Romanian as the official state language and pro-Russians supported the imposition of Russian. Snegur also repudiated in November 1994 the formula of 'second Romanian state' (Enache and Cimpoieşu 2000).

In fact, we are dealing with the attempt of political elites to build a nation in a territory dominated ethnically by Romanians, but politically and economically by Russia. Russian political, economic and cultural influence was massive, as the young state's elites were educated in Moscow and not in Romania, and the feeling of belonging to the Romanian nation was hard to instil; in Chişinău, the marginal position of Bessarabia within interwar Greater Romania was exaggerated. The ideology of state building bore the name of 'Moldavianism', an ideological hybrid between definitions of national community specific to the nineteenth century and ideological formulas created by Stalinist propaganda (such as 'Romanian imperialism', 'Romanian fascism', and 'Romanian multinational state').

Bilateral Romanian–Moldovan relations were decisively marked by the political colour of governments in Chişinău. During periods with an obvious pro-Russian orientation (1994–8, 2001–9), especially while the government was led by the communist party, Romanian–Moldovan relations were often conflict-prone. Crises which emerged in Romanian–Moldovan relations were mainly determined by oscillations between a pro-European and a pro-Russian orientation of the Chişinău elites.

Between 1998 and 2001 an intense political dialogue was maintained between Romania and the Republic of Moldova, including three meetings of heads of state during 1998. The issue of a basic political treaty between the two countries was approached, and reference was also made to regulating the border problem. Chişinău refused to recognize the Metropolitan of Bessarabia, who is subordinated to the Romanian Orthodox Church, preferring to support an ecclesiastical structure subordinated to the Moscow Patriarchate.

After April 2001, the neo-communist and pro-Russian regime of Vladimir Voronin was in power in Chişinău, while in Bucharest, the objectives of President Iliescu and the PSD government were NATO and EU accession. The basic political treaty with Romania was delayed, but, on 18 November 2001, the political treaty between Russia and the Republic of Moldova was signed. The period was marked by several cases of political and diplomatic chicanery (e.g. the mutual expulsion of diplomats). In an echo of Stalinist times, Voronin accused Romania of 'imperialism'. The introduction of compulsory Russian language study in schools in the Republic of Moldova in 2002, the textbook entitled *History of Moldova*, and the publication by Vasile Stati of a Moldovan–Romanian dictionary were all perceived in Romania as measures of denationalization, of destroying the identity of the Romanian population between the Prut and the Dniestr. The critical reaction from Bucharest was moderate, for fear of endangering NATO and EU accession (Şarov and Ojog 2009: 12–23). In the spirit of a pragmatic approach, according to which economic and cultural support was destined for the population and not the government in Chişinău, funds were allocated in 2001 to enable the issuing to Moldovan citizens of passports with a high degree of security (in order to allow movement within the EU), as well as rescheduling Moldova's debt to Romania, which amounted to US$25 million.

Băsescu thought he could transfer the concept of 'player-president' to the sphere of international relations, so he unexpectedly went to Chişinău on 21 January 2005, a short time before parliamentary elections in the Republic of Moldova, at a time when orange revolutions had triumphed in Ukraine and Romania. Băsescu's visit to Chişinău was a premeditated gesture of help for Voronin (as the Romanian leader confessed in October 2009), being part of a strategy of negotiating with the leader of the Moldovan communists, who was considered to be more predictable than the conceited leaders of the openly pro-European parties. The illusion of a pro-European orientation within the communist regime in Chişinău was quickly shattered, however, and attacks on Romania's 'imperialism' were resumed by Voronin, against the background of ever more numerous declarations made by Băsescu about the unification of the Romanian nation within the EU. The Romanian president declared, in July 2006, that Romania offered its neighbouring country the alternative of joining the EU together and that, although they remained the only European people still divided, reintegration would be achieved within the EU. Obviously, Voronin rejected such a project and the initiative of the Romanian President lacked the Western support that it would need in order to be feasible.

As Romania was preparing to become a part of the EU, in September 2006, the Citizenship Law was modified, facilitating the recovery of Romanian citizenship by those who had lost it in 1940 and their descendants. An influx of applications for recovery of citizenship followed (Panaite 2012). While until 2006 the Romanian state had approved recovery of citizenship for a relatively small number of people (under 100,000), thereafter there was a considerable increase in the number of approved requests (about 520,000 from 1991 until 2015). The change of strategy imposed by Băsescu in the area of restoring citizenship was meant to be a tool to compensate for the drawing of the EU's eastern border on the river Prut, but also to attract a new body of loyal voters, grateful for being accorded European citizenship. The citizenship policy was anticipated in 2005 by an exponential increase in the number of scholarships granted to young Moldovans for study in Romanian universities. From a few hundred scholarships awarded before 2004, their number increased to 4,000, but not all of them were taken up. Romania's strategy was obvious: prepare for symbolic unification within the EU by creating a critical mass of young people educated according to EU values.

The year 2009 was marked by new political and diplomatic tensions between Bucharest and Chişinău, culminating with the Ambassador of Romania in the Republic of Moldova Filip Teodorescu being declared *persona non grata*. The incident occurred in the context of April street protests in Chişinău against the communist party of Voronin. The leaders of the Moldovan communists accused Romania of orchestrating a *coup d'état*, an accusation strongly denied by Bucharest. The proof of Romania's plot was never presented by the political authorities in Chişinău.

The formation of an openly 'pro-European' government in Chişinău in September 2009, led by Vlad Filat brought a quick normalization of bilateral political relations; Romania wanted to be the Republic of Moldova's main advocate for EU accession. Romania's support was formalized by the 'Declaration for the Establishment of a Strategic Partnership Between Romania and the Republic of Moldova for the Republic of Moldova's European Integration' (signed in Bucharest on 27 April 2010), a political formula substituting for a basic treaty. In order to facilitate Bessarabia's European road towards the EU, following the suggestions of some Western countries (particularly Germany), the issue of regulating the border regime was also resolved by the Treaty of 8 November 2010.

The signing of Moldova's EU Association Agreement in Brussels on 27 June 2014 represented an historic moment for a second state with an ethnic Romanian majority, officially opening up the prospect of EU accession. The liberalization of the visa regime for the Republic of Moldova's citizens in the EU (since 28 April 2014), a measure taken in the context of Russia's aggression in Ukraine, also reduced pressure on the Romanian state for Bessarabians to recover their citizenship.

The Republic of Moldova's accession to the European Union is de facto conditioned by solving the Transnistrian issue, an important issue on the agenda of Romanian diplomacy, not only in bilateral relations with Chişinău, but also at a broader Euro-Atlantic level. The experience of Russian elites in empire management was visible in the period of the USSR's dissolution, in the creation of conflicts in important areas, by means of which Moscow wanted to control its close neighbours. So-called frozen conflicts were born in Abkhazia, South Ossetia, Nagorno-Karabakh and Transnistria (Sussex 2012).

The re-launch of the Transnistrian issue was achieved following the proclamation, on 2 September 1990, of the Soviet Socialist Transnistrian Moldovan Republic. On 25 August 1991, this entity declared its independence. The event happened only two days before the independence of the Republic of Moldova, including Transnistria, was proclaimed in Chişinău. The military conflict began on 3 March 1992. The Republic of Moldova, which did not have its own army but only police units, had to face numerically superior and better-equipped forces. The decisive role in this conflict was played by the Russian 14th Army, which supported the separatist leader in Tiraspol, Igor Smirnov. The military conflict in itself was short-lived, ending after the Convention signed by Russian President Boris Yeltsin and his Moldovan counterpart Mircea Snegur on 21 July 1992. By this agreement a Unified Control Commission was established, made up of representatives of Chişinău, Tiraspol, the Russian Federation and the Organization for Security and Co-operation in Europe (OSCE), which was in charge of holding the effective control over the security area, and over places where violent conflicts occurred. The Commission's task was to identify and solve potential conflicts. The Commission was to function by consensus, which provided Russia with major leverage to influence decisions. For this reason, Moldova could not obtain the elimination of Transnistrian armed forces which remained (contrary to the 1992 Agreement) within the security area that was theoretically under the exclusive control of peace-keeping forces.

Initially, Romania was involved in negotiating this conflict, but it lost its role of mediator during 1992, after the establishment of a five-sided negotiation mechanism, made up of the Russian Federation, Ukraine, the OSCE, Moldova and Transnistria (Barabaroșie and Nantoi 2004; Dungaciu 2005). Romania permanently supported the integrity of the Moldovan state, including Transnistria's belonging to the Republic of Moldova.

After Romania's elimination from the ranks of the Transnistrian issue negotiator-states, the only instrument that Romanian diplomacy could use to contribute to solving this problem was, for a long time, the OSCE. This international organization, which acts on the basis of consensus among member states (therefore giving Russia power of veto), did not manage to establish important steps for solving the problem, one way or another. The only major achievement of the OSCE was to get a commitment from Russia, on the occasion of the Istanbul summit of November 1999, to withdraw Russian troops from the east bank of the Dniestr until 2002. This commitment was not fulfilled and Transnistria, together with the 14th Army, became just another issue on the agenda of Russia's discussions with the US and the EU.

Romania's main strategy towards Transnistria was to try to internationalize the issue, first within the OSCE, then within the EU. The efforts of Romanian diplomacy were unsuccessful, no matter how much energy was consumed to this end or who was leading the Romanian state. The Romanian failure to solve the Transnistrian issue can be seen in another light by Russia's aggression against Ukraine starting in 2014: Romania could not solve the Transnistrian conflict because it does not have the resources to defeat a former global power with nuclear weapons capabilities. NATO and the EU could not prevent Ukraine's transformation into a huge frozen conflict, compared to which Transnistria is only a sub-regional and not a transatlantic issue.

Ukraine

Ukraine has inherited all its unsolved issues from the former Soviet Union, being the beneficiary of the consequences of the Ribbentrop–Molotov Pact. From the dissolution of the USSR onwards, it became obvious that the US was interested in building a truly independent Ukraine, which could serve as a buffer zone against Russia (Brzezinski 1997: 57–122). For its part, Moscow tried to keep Ukraine within its sphere of influence and control. Ukraine is structurally divided between pro-Russians and nationalistic Ukrainians, between the western part, less developed and with an important Greek-Catholic religious community, and the eastern part, more industrialized but also more traditional and Orthodox. These structural divisions were exploited by Russia during the military aggression which started in Ukraine in 2014.

Romania was among the first countries to recognize Ukraine as an independent state. The establishment of diplomatic relations, on 1 February 1992, was immediately followed by the opening of a Romanian embassy in Kiev, replacing the Romanian Consulate General which had functioned in the Ukrainian capital since 1971.

Until 1997, bilateral relations were characterized by a barely dissimulated hostility, as Ukraine restricted the rights of its Romanian community, even if Bucharest did not officially raise the issue of northern Bukovina being returned although this was called for by several political parties and opinion leaders. According to the census of 2001, there were about 410,000 Romanians (including Moldovans) in Ukraine, making them the third largest ethnic minority in terms of numbers. Bucharest's constant approach was to support Kiev's granting of the same rights enjoyed by minorities in Romania, equivalent to preservation of ethno-confessional and linguistic identity, without demanding exclusively political rights.

After the emergence of clear prospects of NATO and EU enlargement and the normalization of relations with Hungary, the diplomatic priority became Ukraine. With Romania hoping to get an invitation for NATO accession on the occasion of the Madrid summit, the Romanian and Ukrainian presidents signed a 'Treaty Concerning Relations of Good Neighbourliness and Cooperation between Romania and Ukraine' at Neptun on 2 June 1997. On that occasion the first official visit to Romania of President Leonid Kuchma took place. If the treaty with Hungary was considered the cornerstone for a 'historical reconciliation', the treaty with Ukraine divided Romanian society and the political class, with some people considering it an 'historical betrayal', as by recognizing Ukraine's borders the consequences of the Ribbentrop–Molotov Pact were de facto accepted.

By signing the treaty with Romania, Ukraine took an important step towards consolidating its statehood, as, at that moment, it did not have its borders directly recognized through bilateral agreements by several of its neighbours (Russia, the Republic of Moldova and Romania). The strategy which was the basis of the Romanian negotiators' position was to include in the text of the treaty issues upon which an agreement had been reached and to leave for the future those where there was still disagreement. The treaty provides for the conclusion of a bilateral agreement to clarify the regime of state borders and for the demarcation of the Black Sea continental shelf, as well as for joint support concerning the position adopted by the International Court of Justice on this issue (art. 2, paragraph 2). By signing the treaty, Romania (art. 2) recognized the inviolability of Ukraine's borders, so that a territorial dispute between them could not take place unless the agreement was denounced. The Ukrainian side accepted the inclusion in the treaty of the CoE's Recommendation 1201 concerning human rights, referring to rights of national minorities, with the reservation that this did not amount to a right to territorial autonomy on ethnic grounds (this was also the interpretation offered by Romania in its basic treaty with Hungary).

On 17 June 2003, the 'Treaty Concerning the Romanian–Ukrainian State Border Regime and Mutual Assistance on Border Matters' was signed, entering into force, following the exchange of ratification instruments, at Mamaia on 27 May 2004. However, bilateral negotiations regarding the Agreement concerning demarcation of the continental shelf and exclusive economic areas of Romania and Ukraine in the Black Sea, taking place between 1998 and 2004, did not lead to concrete results; the text of this document was not agreed upon. Thus, on 16 September 2004, Romania sent to the International Court of Justice in The Hague a request to initiate procedures for a resolution of the issue concerning demarcation of the continental shelf and exclusive economic areas of Romania and Ukraine in the Black Sea. The resolution of The Hague Court was issued on 3 February 2009: Romania was assigned an area of 9,700 square kilometres of the continental shelf, amounting to 79.34 per cent of the 12,000 square kilometres which it had claimed (Aurescu 2014: 11–23).

Bilateral relations between Kiev and Bucharest were influenced by the international political situation. Attempts to improve Romania's relations with Russia after 2000 and changes emerging in relations between the Great Powers after 11 September 2001 also brought about a warming of relations between Bucharest and Kiev. The relationship between Romania and Ukraine must also be understood from the perspective of Kiev's oscillations between Moscow and Brussels. When the pro-European orientation became predominant, Ukraine adopted cooperative behaviour. However, when Moscow's influence became stronger, this also meant adopting restrictive policies towards minorities.

The agenda of bilateral relations also included some other issues. In 2004 a moment of worsening bilateral relations came up; in the context of electoral campaigning Ukraine decided to adopt a position of strength towards Romania, by reopening the Bystroye Canal through the Danube Delta, as part of a broader project aiming to create a separate waterway on the Kiliya Branch. Despite diplomatic protests and the negative reaction of environmentalist movements and the international media, the reopened Bystroye Canal, providing Ukraine with a direct waterway from the Danube to the Black Sea, was inaugurated by Ukrainian president Leonid Kuchma on 26 August 2004.

After the changes of power in Bucharest and Kiev, following the orange revolution of 2004, Viktor Yushchenko and Băsescu proposed a reset of bilateral policy, for the purpose of building a pro-American bloc around the Black Sea, together with Georgia. Băsescu associated Romania with Ukraine and the other countries in the area in a political structure (the Community of Democratic Option), which was clearly oriented against Russia's influence in countries in the region. Romania was in fact a marginal partner in this structure, as it could not become a real alternative to Russia. The orange revolution in Kiev collapsed after the March 2006 parliamentary elections, won by the Party of the Regions of pro-Russian politician Viktor Yanukovych. Romania was forced to give up the unfortunate ideologization of its bilateral relations with Ukraine, and to adopt a realistic strategy of cooperation with NATO and the EU for the democratization of the region.

Romania was not involved with Sweden and Poland in the establishment of the 2009 Eastern Partnership initiative concerning EU relations with Armenia, Azerbaijan, Belarus, Georgia, the Republic of Moldova and Ukraine. In fact, for the same non-EU countries, Romania aspired to play the role of catalyst through the Black Sea Synergy initiative in 2008. Intense diplomacy undertaken by Romania in the Black Sea area after 2004 had as its main objective the ensuring of energy corridors by which to avoid dependence on Russia. Romania assumed a secondary role in Eastern Partnership activities, its main commitment being to support the Republic of Moldova and only secondarily Ukraine (Ionescu 2013). In Bucharest, the issue of Ukraine was realistically considered to have a Euro-Atlantic dimension and Romania, either alone or together with Poland, did not have the necessary resources to completely remove Kiev from Moscow's sphere of interest.

In the context of Russia's aggression against Ukraine in 2014, Romania maintained its position on the Euro-Atlantic orientation of its north-eastern neighbour, considering that changing borders by violent means cannot be accepted.

The ex-Yugoslav space

After the fall of the communist regime, Yugoslavia seemed to be the most important regional ally of Romania. There has been a tradition of Romanian–Yugoslav (mainly Serbian) cooperation since the Middle Ages and, during the interwar period, the two countries joined in the Little Entente and the Balkan Pact (1934), in the so-called 'anti-revisionist front' established as a reaction to Hungary's territorial claims. Conflicts between Romanians and Serbs were insignificant, with the exception of the 1919 confrontation over the Banat. The Romanians' and Serbs' belonging to Orthodoxy was an additional binding factor for the existence of non-conflictual relations at state level.

Yugoslavia's violent break-up raised concern in Bucharest, but the attitude of diplomacy was dominated by realism and openness to state relations with successor states. Croatia and Slovenia proclaimed their independence on 25 June 1991 and Romania recognized this fact on 18 January 1992. Diplomatic relations between Romania and the Republic of Macedonia were established in 1992; relations with Bosnia and Herzegovina were established in 1996 and with Montenegro in 2006. Romania did not recognize the independence of Kosovo, starting from the premise this could legitimize separatism on ethnic grounds. Romania's position towards Kosovo was similar to that of certain other EU countries: Spain, Greece, Slovakia and Cyprus (Keil and Bernhard 2014: 6).

Romania's main strategy towards the ex-Yugoslav space was to support its integration into the Euro-Atlantic structures, as a main instrument for the stabilization and democratization of the region. Romania considered that the most efficient means of preventing Serbia's transformation into Russia's bridgehead in the Balkans was supporting its progress towards EU accession.

There were changes of emphasis in Romania's regional policy, with the advancement of the NATO and EU enlargement processes and also with Russia's resurrection in the area. At the beginning of the 1990s, Romania acted in the logic of interwar foreign policy, of looking for regional allies who would offer support in the event of new Hungarian interventionist initiatives. To this end, Romanian support for Belgrade was not only political but also economic. In spite of UN Security Council Resolution 713 of 25 September 1991, establishing a military embargo against Yugoslavia, extended to the economic field by another resolution on 30 May 1992, over 1,000 wagons of diesel and gasoline were sent through the Jimbolia border railway station in 1994–5, without the formal consent of the customs authorities. These activities were protected by *Serviciul Român de Informații* (SRI – the Romanian Intelligence Service) officers, following the orders of SRI Director Virgil Măgureanu, and part of the proceeds were used to finance the PDSR, as they went into the accounts of some businessmen close to the regime. However, there is no public evidence concerning the use of money from smuggling by institutions of the Romanian state.

The regime change that took place in Romania in 1996 also led to changes in Romanian–Yugoslav relations. The new regime in Romania wanted to avoid political contacts with a regime ostracized by the West and strongly challenged from within. Emil Constantinescu perceived himself as a regional leader, who had to assume the role of democratizing the region by supporting anti-Milošević forces within Yugoslavia. The turning point of Romanian–Yugoslav relations was the Kosovo war of 1999. The inter-ethnic conflict in the immediate neighbourhood of Romania polarized the Romanian political scene. President Constantinescu supported NATO intervention in Yugoslavia, considering it 'necessary and legitimate', risking a conflict with Russia but offering the US a show of loyalty with the prospect of NATO accession.

Slobodan Milošević's removal from power, followed by his extradition to the International Criminal Tribunal in The Hague on 28 June 2001, opened the road towards Yugoslavia's democratization. In the new context in which the Romanian–Yugoslav relationship could not create suspicions in the West, bilateral political and economic relations saw a re-launch after 2001 (Abraham 2006b: 301–10). Romania assumed the role of advocate for the integration of the whole ex-Yugoslav space into the EU, considering that this would soon heal the wounds of war and that it would have in its vicinity a democratically consolidated and economically prosperous region.

A sensitive problem was that of the Romanian-speaking minority in the ex-Yugoslav space, called Vlachs, whose official number is approximately 35,000 people, according to the 2011 census (unofficially, Vlach associations speak of about 350,000 people in the Timok Valley). Serbia was for a long time reticent about recognizing the cultural rights of the Vlachs, who speak a dialect of Romanian. Using a gesture by which it wanted to draw the attention of its neighbour, in March 2012 Romania opposed for a short time the opening of Serbia's EU accession negotiations, leading to protests from Germany and Sweden. The situation was quickly unblocked by European Commission promises to monitor respect for minority rights.

Bulgaria

Whether they wanted to or not, Romania and Bulgaria continued their common historical destiny after 1989. The two countries do not have territorial disputes, as the issue of the Quadrilateral (Durostor and Caliacra counties were part of Romania after the Second Balkan War in 1913 and regained by Bulgaria in 1940) has not been raised by the Romanian state.

Romanian–Bulgarian relations did not become conflictual but nor did they reach the highest potential. The main legal document regulating bilateral relations is the 'Treaty of

Friendship, Collaboration and Good Neighbourly Relations', signed on 27 January 1992, which came to replace legal documents from the communist period. On the basis of this treaty, numerous economic and trade agreements were signed for the mutual promotion and protection of investments, avoidance of double taxation, industry, energy, transport, agriculture and ecology.

The main aspect which has to be underlined is the competition between the political and intellectual elites in Romania and Bulgaria; there is a mutual perception of superiority-inferiority. Although during the Euro-Atlantic accession process there were moments in which the two countries wanted to separate from one another, ultimately reason prevailed and mutual support was chosen. The Calafat–Vidin Bridge over the Danube, built according to an agreement reached in 2000, was ultimately inaugurated only in June 2013 after several postponements. The issue of the Bulgarian nuclear power plant at Kozloduy, situated on the right bank of the Danube, was also on the agenda of bilateral relations, as the energy complex represented an environmental hazard due to its old Soviet reactors.

CHAPTER 13
THE RULE OF LAW

The notion of 'rule of law' witnessed a spectacular international spread after 1970, as a key concept of the political mythology related to the universality of human rights. The 'rule of law' topic was, initially, an instrument for fighting communism. It subsequently became one of the favourite US and EU methods for promoting political globalization (Magen, Risse and McFaul 2009). The integration of the post-communist space into NATO and the EU was achieved by using the 'rule of law' criterion (Sadurski, Czarnota and Krygier 2006). This concept became a legitimizing or marginalizing instrument, both in home and foreign affairs, being as it was, synonymous with 'democracy' (Maravall and Przeworski 2003). The teleology of modernization and democratization in a global context identified causal correlations not only between international security and the rule of law (Zifcak 2005), but also between socio-economic development and the institutionalization of the rule of law (Dam 2006). Much to the surprise of non-critical 'rule of law' ideologists, it regressed even among EU countries such as Hungary after 2010 (Blokker 2013; Bugarič 2014; Von Bogdandy 2013). The optimistic-naïve vision concerning citizens' irreversible attachment to liberal democracy, in any context, regardless of cost, was countered by the democratic deficit existing in some European countries.

The rule of law involves the supremacy of legal standards, but this definition must not be fetishized, the best example being the fiction of 'socialist legality', by which individual rights were restrained under communism. The correlation between legality–effectiveness–legitimacy is defining for the rule of law, as individuals' rights and liberties have priority over 'raison d'état' or fictional communities (for example, social classes); general interests represented by the state must be legitimate.

The establishment and consolidation of the rule of law in Romania was a gradual, non-final, contradictory process, marked by an apparent consensus subsumed to Euro-Atlantic integration. It was the result of conflict and collaboration among three categories of factors and actors: foreign conditionality, starting with accession to the CoE and ending with the European Commission's surveillance by means of the CVM; action of local actors, be they public institutions in the field of justice and integrity policies or non-governmental organizations politically or financially supported by Washington or Brussels; societal pressure, in the context of party competition for the political legitimacy that could be obtained by supporting, at least rhetorically, the fight against corruption. It is difficult to accomplish a clear separation between the rule of law as a façade and the in-depth societal internationalization of democratic values. A final conclusion concerning the functioning of the rule of law would be premature.

The judicial system

The transformation of communist justice from an instrument for applying the party-state vision on society into a public service capable of ensuring the rule of law was difficult and costly. The creation of Justice as a distinct state power emancipated from the influence of executive power and various interest groups within society was achieved by the gradual accumulation of legal procedures and customs. The Constitution offers the guarantee of judges' independence: 'subject only to the law', they are also irremovable, and their eventual sanctioning falls within competency of *Consiliul Superior al Magistraturii* (CSM – the Superior Council of Magistracy). This was consolidated following the revision of the Constitution in 2003, being defined as the institution which 'shall guarantee the independence of justice'. The CSM, as a collegiate organ comprising judges, prosecutors and civil society representatives, acquired the major role in recruiting, promoting and sanctioning judges and prosecutors.

According to the Constitution, 'Justice shall be administered by the High Court of Cassation and Justice, and the other courts of law set up by the law' (art.126, align.1). The defence of public interest in the field of criminal law is achieved through the Public Ministry, and 'Public prosecutors shall carry out their activity in accordance with the principle of legality, impartiality and hierarchical control, under the authority of the Minister of Justice', (art.132, align.1). However, unlike judges, prosecutors are not irremovable.

The courts of first instance have a general jurisdiction *rationae materiae*. A decision rendered at the level of courts of first instance may be challenged in appeal at the next court level. The means of judicial review regulated by law are: first instance, appeal and second appeal (*recurs*).

The Ministry of Justice, as an organ of the executive power, has the task of ensuring the organization and management of justice as a public service. The budget of the courts is managed by the Ministry of Justice. The Minister of Justice cannot ask prosecutors to initiate or to stop criminal investigations and has no means of interfering in their activity. The Minister of Justice may only check the manner in which prosecutors fulfil their managerial duties, their working obligations and the manner of their working relationships with litigants.

Under the terms of the law concerning the status of magistrates (Law no. 303 of 2004) the confusion between prosecutors and judges already created by the 1991 Constitution was maintained; prosecutors were assimilated to magistrates, equal to judges, although they are defined by the ECtHR as 'agents of the executive power having a special status'. This ambiguity allowed the transformation of prosecutors into judges. According to CSM statistics, from 1991 to 2012, no fewer than 381 people turned from prosecutors into judges, 21 of them within the *Înalta Curte de Casație și Justiție* (ÎCCJ – High Court of Cassation and Justice). This meant the intrusion of the prosecutor mentality among judges, prioritizing arguments in favour of the prosecution and being less open to the arguments of the defence. In countries such as Italy and Greece, famous for their widespread corruption, prosecutors are also magistrates. The Italian case is classic for the perversion of the social role of justice, turning the prosecution service into a powerful political actor.

One of the major problems was the creation of an ethos concerning the job of magistrates that was adequate for a democratic society. Romania did not re-evaluate the professional competence of magistrates, or their contribution to the abuses of the communist regime; instead, it considered that they would adapt to democracy alongside society. As within any bureaucratic structure, professional solidarity functioned in a conservative manner. Making judges accountable for judicial errors and prosecutors for abuses is difficult, due to an opaque *esprit de corps*, also supported by the CSM's lack of initiative. Criminal punishments or administrative measures against judges and prosecutors, when they exist, are directed, with rare exceptions, to the minimal threshold (*Analiza funcțională a sectorului justiției* 2013: 88–9, 110–14). The perception among magistrates that they are 'little gods' who are not accountable, as they are not controlled by an institution outside the justice system, created the premise for the establishment of a superpower within the state, not included in the normal checks and balances between the executive and the legislative power. There is a growing perception that magistrates are increasingly turning into a caste, thus perverting the meaning of independent justice.

The liberalization of society brought a quick growth in the amount of litigation, often concerning property rights, as well as an increase in the criminal phenomenon. For example, in 1990, 0.59 million cases were heard in the courts of justice, increasing to 1.32 million in 1997 and 3.5 million in 2014. As a consequence, the judicial system witnessed a sharp increase in the number of staff: in 1990 there were 1,513 judges and fewer than 1,200 prosecutors; in 1997 there were 3,130 judges and 2,765 prosecutors, and by 2014 there were 4,706 judges and 2,902 prosecutors (CSM 2015: 38, 64).

Initially, the entry requirements for judges and prosecutors were low. People with flawed legal education were integrated into the system, including former employees of the repressive communist apparatus and PCR activists. Only in 1997 was access to the magistracy made conditional on training within the National Institute of Magistracy and then on a university degree, thus improving the professional quality of candidates.

In parallel with increasing the number of judges and prosecutors, a real boom in self-employed legal professionals took place: from under 3,000 lawyers in 1990 to almost 30,000 practicing lawyers in 2015. Notaries were fewer than 500 in 1990; by 2015 the Ministry of Justice had approved 2,593 jobs at national level. A continuously expanding profession is also that of bailiffs. In 2015, 815 bailiffs' offices were registered at the national level. General statistical data shows that the judicial system has sufficient human resources for civil law activities in Romania.

The Romanian prison system did not witness significantly positive changes compared to the communist period. The Romanian state was convicted by the ECtHR for 'unfit detention conditions, which breach human rights and dignity', although the number of prisons increased from thirty-two in 1990 to forty-six in 2014. The number of detainees recorded significant oscillations: from 26,010 in 1990 (two years after the

1988 amnesty), peaking at 52,149 in 1998, but decreasing to under 30,000 in 2015. Amnesties were granted in 1997 and 2002, but they only temporarily solved the issue of bringing detention conditions in line with CoE standards (Administrația Națională a Penitenciarelor 2011: 4).

The new social realities determined the adoption of new civil and criminal codes and also of new civil procedure and criminal procedure codes, from 2011 to 2014. Thus, the 1865 civil code, whose essential structure had been preserved during the communist regime, was eventually replaced, as was the former criminal code, which had been in force since 1969, although it had undergone important changes.

An important step for the justice system was the ratification of the European Convention on Human Rights in 1994, which allowed a more efficient fight against abuses. Only after the ECtHR 2003 decision in *Pantea* v. *Romania* was the right of the prosecutors to make arrests without the mandate of a judge abolished.

Citizens' mistrust of Romanian justice was emphasized by the frequency of appeals to an extraordinary institution, the ECtHR. Romanian litigants, unhappy with solutions of national courts, addressed 56,683 complaints from 1994 to 2014 (*Overview 1959–2014* 2015: 8). In a general evaluation, Romania accounted for 6.27 per cent of the total number of complaints filed at the ECtHR from 1959 to 2014, although the first complaints were settled in 1994. Finalized complaints from 1994 until 31 December 2014 obliged Romania to pay total costs of €55 million (*Hotărârile CEDO* 2015).

From the mid-1990s, the most prominent public issue related to justice was the fight against corruption. The phenomenon was inevitable in itself, as a form by which preferential property transfer was achieved and local capitalists emerged all over the post-communist space. Corruption became a political issue when several companies were deliberately bankrupted in order to be taken over very easily and people lost their jobs. Bitterness against the newly rich of the transition was all the greater as they displayed their wealth in the form of luxurious properties and expensive cars in the face of the poverty of the common people.

From the very beginning of his presidential mandate, President Constantinescu established the National Council of Action against Corruption and Organized Crime in 1997, with the purpose of correlating the activities of the police, prosecutors and intelligence units. However, its results were rather modest. Under EU and US pressure, in 2002 the National Anticorruption Prosecution Office (PNA), which changed its name in 2005 to *Direcția Națională Anticorupție* (DNA – the National Anticorruption Directorate), was created. This structure, specialized in fighting high- and medium-level corruption, benefited from logistic and financial support from all governments. It was also supported politically by the European Commission, through the CVM reports (Coman 2009: 121–60). The SRI and other intelligence organisations were required by CSAȚ decisions (2006, 2007) to collaborate systematically with prosecutors in fighting corruption and organized crime. The most visible result of the DNA's activity was the conviction of eleven former ministers up to the end of 2015, to whom may be added other former MPs, mayors and even magistrates. Fighting high-level corruption saw certain progress, but this was not always achieved by a rigorous respect for human rights.

Corruption is a complex socio-political phenomenon, which cannot be countered just by using the instruments of criminal law; there is a need for deep institutional and cultural changes (Burduja 2015: 203–45). This was not always understood by Romania's international partners, who demanded punishment of the 'big fish', in a politico-judiciary ritual useful also for proving the efficiency of the Euro-bureaucracy (Mendelski 2012).

The activity of criminal justice was accompanied by a public display of investigations, a phenomenon called 'TV justice'. Initially, starting around 2000, TV justice was limited to spectacular police raids concerning criminal groups, the images being officially provided to TV stations. After 2005, in the context of the offensive against corruption, TV justice took other forms, with the media broadcasting information from ongoing criminal investigations, which should have been confidential. This information, including transcripts of private conversations, was offered by the DNA itself, sometimes even before defendants had officially found out the charges against them. Often TV stations were invited to the prosecutors' and police raids, in order to film the action. At the centre of this TV justice system was the DNA. The purpose of this media lynching, against which the CSM took no action, was on the one hand to satisfy the populist law-and-order expectations of the population and on the other hand to create immense public pressure upon judges, so that they would be afraid to reject the prosecutors' indictments. The benefit of doubt was de facto eliminated by the creation of a public perception of guilt, and defendants could hardly hope for a fair trial. The right to a defence or the image right of individuals was often violated, using the justification of the state policy of 'fighting corruption'. The right to a defence was often considered by prosecutors as an attack against the unfolding investigation.

The prototypic episode of the TV justice system was the 'Quality Trophy' case, in which the main incriminated person was former Prime Minister Năstase. He was accused of using, during the 2004 presidential campaign, some resources obtained as a result of a contest organized in 2003 by the State Inspectorate for Construction. The damage calculated by the DNA amounted to €1.48 million. The trial took place between 2009 and 2012, and was closely followed by the media. The DNA called 970 witnesses, while the main defendant, Adrian Năstase, was allowed to call only five. None of the witnesses heard by the court gave incriminating declarations about Năstase. The court of first instance decided to convict Năstase to two years in prison (30 January 2012). The decision of the appeal court on 20 June 2012 was pronounced two days before Năstase turned sixty-two. The motivation of the court of first instance explicitly stated that 'in this case there is no direct evidence that would incriminate the defendant', the sentence being based instead on 'logical-legal reasoning' (*Sentința penală no.176*: 117). Năstase was convicted on the grounds that, if the PSD had benefited from the resources of some private companies over the legal limit (electoral flyers and posters), the party's chairman could not have been unaware of this. Additionally, the judges stated that they had convicted Năstase because he 'embodied, at least in 2004' the corruption that had to be countered by justice (*Sentința penală no.176*: 132). The appeal court limited itself to finding that 'the actual situation, as it was established by the first instance, is fully covered by the given evidence' (*Decizia no.160*: 245).

The Constitutional Court and its controversies

Much like other states which returned to democracy after the fall of communism, Romania also included in its political system a Constitutional Court to balance relations between powers (Sadurski 2014). This was inspired by the French Constitutional Court, but without taking over all its competencies (Iacob 2005: 194). The Court is not part of the judicial system; it is a juridical-political institution, integrated into the political system.

The Court is made up of nine members appointed by the president of Romania, the Senate and the Chamber of Deputies, with a mandate of nine years. Constitutional judges do not have to be magistrates, but only people with a rich legal experience.

The Court judges a priori the constitutionality of laws before their enforcement and a posteriori, following notification from judicial courts. It oversees conformity to the procedure for electing the president of Romania and the appointment of an eventual interim in that office, giving consultative advice in the case of the suspension of the head of state. In the case of the Court's decisions on unconstitutionality, the laws or ordinances in question are legally null forty-five days after the publication of the decision in the Official Journal, with the unconstitutional dispositions being immediately suspended. However, the Court's decisions have no retroactive effect.

Following the revision of the Constitution in 2003, the Court's attributes were extended, by including the ability to solve 'legal constitutional conflicts between public authorities, at the request of the President of Romania, the president of one of the two Chambers, the Prime Minister or the President of the Superior Council of Magistracy' (art.146, letter e). The Court's decisions are binding; they can no longer be overturned in the Parliament with a two-thirds majority, as was the case according to the original 1991 Constitution.

The Court's activity can be clearly divided into two periods. Until 2005, the Court had a marginal role in the political system, being the place where parties or presidents sent their faithful as a reward for political services. The instatement of Băsescu's neo-caesarist regime meant the Court was involved in mediating political conflicts. The first notifications concerning the existence of a legal constitutional conflict between state institutions occurred with Băsescu's presidency. From 2005 to 2015 a total of thirty complaints were resolved. Presidents Iliescu and Constantinescu had used the procedure of challenging a law before promulgation only three times; Băsescu used it thirty-one times. During the period of Băsescu's mandates, the opposition parties sent 117 notifications to the Court, compared to only 96 between 1992 and 2004. The real purpose of this frequent appeal to the Court by politicians was not to verify conformity to constitutional principles, but to block inconvenient initiatives.

The moments of maximum political tension were the three initiatives of suspending Presidents Iliescu and Băsescu. Although the Court's advice is consultative, it is important from a political perspective. In 1994, the Court decided that President Iliescu had not breached the fundamental law. In any case, the PNȚCD initiative did not get the necessary votes in Parliament.

In 2007, the Court pronounced a favourable decision regarding Băsescu, but which was marked by ambiguity: 'The proposal of suspension from office concerning Mr. Traian Băsescu (...), refers to acts and facts of breaching the Constitution, committed during the exercise of his mandate, but which, by their content and consequences, cannot be qualified as serious and cannot support a suspension of the President of Romania from his office', (Official Journal no. 258 of 18 April 2007).

During President Băsescu's suspension in 2012, the Court avoided reaching a final conclusion, although it also noticed breaches of the Constitution: 'The fact that the President of Romania, by his political behaviour, publicly assumed the initiative of taking economic and social measures, before they were adopted by the Government, using the governmental responsibility procedure, can be regarded as an attempt to diminish the role and attributes of the Prime Minister', (Official Journal no. 456 of 06 July 2012). However, the Court did not say whether these facts justified a possible dismissal of Băsescu.

Entrusting the Court with increased powers in 2003, mainly by making the Parliament incapable of overturning decisions by a qualified majority, proved to be a mistake. Competing political factors wanted to gain control over the Court by imposing judges who would defend partisan interests. This led to embarrassing situations for democracy. For example, on 1 June 2010, Valer Dorneanu (PSD proposal) was elected as a Court judge, but the President of the Chamber of Deputies, Roberta Anastase (PDL) refused to validate the deputies' vote, claiming it was necessary to have the vote of an absolute majority. On 14 June 2010, the issue of appointing a Court judge was resumed in the Chamber of Deputies. Physical conflict broke out between PDL and PSD deputies. Long after midnight, after several interruptions and the PSD's attempt to stop the voting procedure, Professor Ştefan Minea, proposed by the PDL, was elected a member of the Constitutional Court.

The most controversial episode in the Court's activity is related to the procedure of validating the 29 July 2012 referendum for the dismissal of Traian Băsescu. The referendum turnout was 8,459,053, of whom 87.52 per cent (7.4 million) were in favour of the dismissal. The overwhelming result against Băsescu created a new political reality, opening a national and international battle concerning the validation of the referendum. The key issue was the quorum level according to which the referendum should be validated. The Election Office announced that a presence of 46.24 per cent of the total electorate was insufficient for the validation of the referendum. However, lawyers and politicians alike stated that the quorum should be evaluated according to the permanent electoral lists of citizens with permanent residence in Romania, in which case the referendum was valid and Băsescu would be dismissed. The Court initially decided to postpone the decision to validate the referendum, asking the government to provide real data concerning citizens voting within the country, as it was noticed that the permanent lists also included people who were deceased. On 6 August 2012, a so-called 'erratum' was sent to the Ministry of Interior, concerning the Court's demand that the votes of Romanians abroad also be included in the quorum. This clarification decision, essential for the validation of the referendum, was taken without consulting all the Court's members; it was not taken during a session of the Constitutional Court, but by informal consultations. Three of the judges challenged the decision of their colleagues, both by an appeal, arguing that the quorum was established only in relation to citizens having their residence in Romania, and because they had not been informed about the decision. The 'erratum' was the work of the same judge, Minea, for whom MPs from Băsescu's coalition had fought until late into the night in 2010. As a consequence of the Court's demand, the Ministry of Interior sent the same data as those initially used by the Electoral Office and Băsescu remained in office (Radu and Buti 2013: 142–73). The episode revealed how deeply the Court was politicized.

The Court contributed to the presidentialization of the political regime after 2005, creating ambiguities in the relationships between institutions. For example, by Decision no. 98 of February 2008, the Court endowed the President of the Republic with a power of veto against the first, but only the first, proposal for appointment as a minister. In practice, a second proposal can be worse than the first, but in this case the president can only act upon the prime minister's decision. If we follow the logic of separation, checks and balance between state powers, the president should have no veto powers at all concerning the composition of the government, as the prime minister should be able to build the team he wants, and the cabinet is accountable only to the Parliament.

The Court's activity was dominated by an awareness of its power, turning it into a legislative superpower which escaped the fundamental logic of mutual checks and balances. For example, in 2010, in the context of austerity measures, the Court did not accept the recalculation of magistrates' pensions to align them with the contributory principle. For the other socio-professional categories benefiting from occupational pensions (military, diplomats, pilots, etc.) the Court agreed with the recalculation of pensions.

At the same time, the Court has often played a positive role in democratizing Romanian society. For example, it rejected the proposal of the Boc government to change electoral legislation, which would have allowed parliamentary elections to be organized simultaneously with local elections (January 2012). Another case is clarification on teaching religion in schools, concerning the obligation on parents to give written consent. It also adopted a liberal attitude towards the issue of data storage in electronic communication, rejecting several laws which were intended to regulate this sensitive issue for human rights.

The Court acted as a conservative institution, however, in limiting the competencies of 'integrity institutions'. Even if these decisions were disputed by civil society (Popescu 2008), as they limit the efficiency of transitional justice, submitting National Integrity Agency and *Consiliul Naţional pentru Studierea Arhivelor Securităţii* (CNSAS – the National Council for the Study of the *Securitate* Archives) decisions to the filter of justice offers citizens a greater chance to defend their rights and reputations.

The Ombudsman

The process of political and institutional synchronization with a democratic Europe involved the creation of an institutional network by which citizens could control the political system. Inspired by the 'ombudsman' in the Nordic countries, the 1991 Constitution established the Romanian version, literally meaning 'attorney of the people'. Although it is an institution provided by Constitution, the Romanian Ombudsman began to work only in 1997, when the law establishing the organization and functioning of the institution was adopted. Similarly to the EU Ombudsman, the essential role of the Romanian institution is to defend the rights and freedoms of citizens in their relationships with public institutions and authorities, as a result of petitions from those affected or on the Ombudsman's own initiative.

The Ombudsman is autonomous from any other public authority, but does not substitute for them, and is appointed by the Parliament with a five-year mandate. The institution went through a restructuring process, starting with the training of specialized staff and the clarification of administrative competencies, before its areas of activity (rights of disadvantaged people, family rights, abuses of public institutions, etc.) were fully established. During its first year, the institution received 1,168 complaints; their number increased to 5,400 in 2003, reaching almost 10,000 in 2012, at the height of its activity. One should not, however, assume that all of these have been resolved, as a good part are not within the areas of competence of the Ombudsman. The petitions registered concern sensitive fields, often related to property restitution, free access to justice and freedom of information (Avocatul Poporului 2015).

The Ombudsman was confronted with excessive politicization during periods where presidents and governments came from different parties (2007–8; 2012–15), as various political actors called for exceptions of unconstitutionality to be raised regarding the government's emergency ordinances or laws adopted by Parliament. The most significant example of the involvement of the institution in political conflicts was the dismissal by the Parliament on 3 July 2012 of Ombudsman Gheorghe Iancu, who was close to the PDL, in the context of Băsescu's second suspension. The objective of replacing Gheorghe Iancu with Valer Dorneanu (a former PSD MP) was to prevent possible appeals to the Constitutional Court by the Ombudsman concerning legislation meant to facilitate Băsescu's dismissal.

Born during the dawn of Romanian democracy, the Ombudsman remains a promise of the hope that the problems of those without power will, ultimately, be solved by a slow and often self-sufficient administration (Hossu and Carp 2013).

The National Integrity Agency

In the context of Romania's EU membership and of Brussels' persistent monitoring of the CVM, the National Integrity Agency was established in 2007 with the purpose of fighting corruption with administrative tools. Its functioning mechanism is the following: ministers, MPs and other public servants must fill in detailed annual statements of their assets and interests, which can be checked by the Agency, on its own initiative or on request. If the Agency notices the existence of a state of incompatibility or conflict of interest, its findings then have to be validated in court. The outcome may be a penalty under criminal law (for conflict of interest) or being barred from holding a public office for three years. Wealth which is proven to have been accumulated illicitly can be confiscated.

The creation of the institution in charge of the integrity policies concerning public officials was received with reticence within the political environment, but it was tacitly accepted as an externally imposed condition in exchange for EU membership. The hostility was all the greater as this institutional model was unique among the EU member states, until the creation of a similar structure in France in 2013. The contribution of integrity policies to the democratization of Romanian society is difficult to evaluate. The apparent fortunes and interests of politicians and other public servants have become transparent, but it is highly likely that the degree of sophistication in hiding fortunes acquired by dubious means has simultaneously increased. No fortune of a high-ranking official has been confiscated as a result of the Agency's activities; the main results have been the exposure of conflicts of interest regarding MPs and local mayors and councillors, as a result of which several hundred people have been barred from holding public office.

Decommunization by exposing the *Securitate*

After the end of the Cold War, the democratization of former communist societies (their departure from social institutions and customs specific to a totalitarian regime) was achieved following a recipe which included the acknowledgement of former collaborators with the political police (Stan 2013: 84–110). Uncovering the *Securitate* was a significant objective, as it was noticed that some of the officers and collaborators of the former communist secret police had now turned into prosperous businessmen (Oprea 2004).

The failure to introduce lustration initiatives and to punish the guilty for crimes committed within the Romanian concentration camp system from 1945 to 1964 reduced the scope of decommunization policies to the institution that was least defensible, due to its negative image, the *Securitate*. There were multiple initiatives to expose *Securitate* officers and collaborators, but they were successful only in December 1999, when Romania was preparing to begin EU accession negotiations and when the prospect of NATO accession had become achievable. The opening of the *Securitate* archives and the removal from the intelligence services of officers compromised during the communist period was considered, at the level of the Romanian state leadership, a necessary 'sacrifice' for the country's accession to the EU and NATO. The establishment of the CNSAS was an informal condition requested of Romania to fulfil all the political criteria necessary for EU and NATO membership. Thus Romania was aligning itself with the politics of memory in Germany, the Czech Republic and Poland. The political role of the CNSAS was even from the beginning to facilitate public acknowledgement of each person's past in relation to the *Securitate*'s activity. *Securitate* officers and collaborators did not lose their jobs and are not excluded from public life by administrative tools. Disclosure of the communist past is essentially a moral action. Unlike in Germany, where a person's collaboration with the STASI (secret police agency of the former German Democratic Republic) is revealed only to their employer, in Romania the general public can find out about a relationship between the *Securitate* and individuals. These are displayed, where appropriate, on the website of CNSAS.

The activity of exposing the *Securitate* acquired some weight after the massive transfer of the former political police archives to the CNSAS in 2005–6. The CNSAS has over 26 kilometres of archives; the number of files remaining in the custody of the intelligence services – those considered to concern national security – being constantly reduced.

The elementary form of politics of memory related to *Securitate* activity consists in allowing Romanian citizens, or citizens of EU and NATO member states who used to be Romanian citizens, access to their own files. The right of access to one's own file is granted to the file holder or to their relatives to the fourth degree. From 2000 until 2015, over 42,000 people applied for access to their files, according to official reports of the CNSAS.

Summing up the result of CNSAS activity from 2000 to 2015, we find that, in the course of research carried out by the institution, over 2,800 people were found to have undertaken political police activities, including *Securitate* employees and collaborators (informers or people offering their homes for conspiratorial meetings of officers with informers) alike. People viewing their own files found out the identity of about 7,000 officers or informers who had conveyed data or participated in the surveillance or investigation of *Securitate* victims.

The impact on society of exposing the *Securitate* and its collaborators is hard to evaluate. From the very beginning of the transition period nostalgia towards communism emerged, a phenomenon increased by economic and social hardships and also by the discrediting of political parties. As an argument for the reduced importance of the communist past, Traian Băsescu was twice elected president of Romania, despite controversies regarding his relations with the *Securitate*. Some former *Securitate* collaborators succeeded in being elected to Parliament. However, one must not conclude that the whole of Romanian society is insensible to the issue of collaboration with the *Securitate*. There is a certain concern about this subject among urban elites: having belonged to or collaborated with the *Securitate* is generally regarded as a matter of social stigma (Abraham 2014: 142–64).

The army and the intelligence structures

The army emerged from communism with the perceived aura of having been close to the people against Nicolae Ceaușescu, having suffered together with the citizens, while the *Securitate* had a privileged status. The army was associated with patriotism and with a mostly positive form of socialization (people used to say that 'the army makes you a man'). Turning it from a popular to a professional force, in order to be compatible with NATO, was a difficult and costly process.

The Romanian army does not have a tradition of political involvement, as respect for the constitutional order is widespread among officers. The change to civilian control, starting in 1994 (with Defence Minister Gheorghe Tinca) did not generate a negative reaction. Indeed, it was the army who intervened in 1999 to stop the last mineriad of Miron Cozma, who was threatening to endanger the stability of the Romanian state (Watts 2001: 612).

With a view to becoming compatible with NATO standards in the area of military organization, the Romanian army gradually reduced its manpower. Military service was compulsory until 2007. In 1990 there were 320,000 officers and 230,000 active soldiers. By 2000, the number of officers had drastically reduced to 180,000, and after NATO accession, they had further reduced to 100,000 officers. From 2007, the army's manpower stabilized at 90,000 (75,000 military and 15,000 civilians). The reduction of military manpower was achieved by massive retirement among officers and military technicians. Even if the process was accomplished by offering financial compensation, former military personnel had to adapt to the realities of the market economy and to the precariousness of their new civilian condition.

In order to be able to participate in international missions under the UN or NATO mandate, the army was endowed with Western weaponry. The government acquired two frigates from the UK, four C-130B Hercules transport planes from the US, and twelve F16 fighters from Portugal. However, compared to the Ukraine or Russia, Romania's army is numerically inferior, with less efficient weaponry. The fundamental premise of the Romanian state was that it would not have to defend itself alone in the case of eastern military aggression, but would have help from its NATO allies.

The ghost of the *Securitate* haunted the political imaginary of the young Romanian democracy and preoccupied decision-makers from Western states, who wanted the immediate retirement or exposure of all 'moles', considering this was their right as the Cold War victors. The retirement of *Securitate* spies was considered a 'loyalty test' towards accession into the Euro-Atlantic institutions (Watts 2004: 17–21).

The dissolution of the *Securitate* by CFSN Decree no. 33 of 30 December 1989, after its subordination to the army on 26 December, was the decision by which the post-communist regime wanted to solve a serious perception issue, according to which the casualties of the Revolution had been victims of the *Securitate*. Iulian Vlad, the last *Securitate* head, was arrested and sentenced following a show trial, for 'favouring genocide'; he was subsequently released in 1994 (Deletant 2004: 504).

The strategy of the Romanian state for establishing new intelligence structures which would offer the necessary expertise to decision-makers was to create smaller institutions that would not be reminiscent of the *Securitate*. On 8 February 1990, the Foreign Intelligence Centre (CIE) was re-organized and turned into the SIE, led until 1992 by Mihai Caraman, who had distinguished himself by spying on NATO.

On 26 March 1990, immediately after the inter-ethnic conflict in Târgu Mureş, the SRI was created. It specialized in collecting information concerning national security. Its first director was a former *Securitate* officer, Virgil Măgureanu, who had been marginalized in 1989 as a result of his opposition towards the unipersonal regime of Nicolae Ceauşescu.

As early as 1990-1, the Interior Ministry, the Ministry of Defence and the Justice Ministry each created intelligence structures, directly subordinated to the Minister. In

1990, a protection structure for high-ranking officials was established, the Protection and Guard Service (SPP). Based on the structure of the 'R' special unit of the army, the Special Telecommunications Service (STS) was established in 1992, with the main objective of ensuring secure communication between public institutions in Romania, including their relations with the intelligence services.

According to the National Security Law no. 51 of 1991, all these structures are placed under the coordination of the CSAȚ. Within the supreme decisional forum concerning Romania's security policy (Law no. 39 of 1990), only the SRI and SIE were represented, while departmental services were represented by the ministers of the Interior, Defence and Justice.

The political coordination of intelligence institutions was accomplished by the President of Romania by means of his national security advisor. Traian Băsescu wanted to gain control over all the intelligence structures, so following a decision of the CSAȚ, the National Intelligence Community (CNI) was formed on 18 November 2005. Its main purpose was to bring the departmental structures, which were subordinated to the government, under the Presidency's control. The CNI, a structure within the CSAȚ, brought a welcome integration of the results of intelligence activity, turning the president into the 'best informed person', as Băsescu liked to consider himself.

The ministries' intelligence structures went through frequent reorganizations, the most important being the dissolution in 2006 of the Anticorruption Intelligence and Protection Service (SIPA) functioning within the Ministry of Justice. There were at least two permanent departmental structures, at the Defence and Interior ministries, in addition to the SRI, SIE, SPP and STS. This situation triggered a less visible competition between institutions in the field of national security, manifested by a lack of cooperation and a desire to attract as many resources as possible for their own development. The exact number of employees in all the intelligence institutions is secret, but in 2010, former SRI director George Maior assumed the existence of 3,000 operative officers. Unconfirmed unofficial information speaks about the existence of about 12,000 employees, more than the *Securitate* ever had. The general budget of all the intelligence structures is public, the trend being for it to increase every year, regardless of the economic context, while sectors such as education and health have suffered serious cuts during crisis periods.

The increase in the budget of institutions with responsibilities in the field of national security can be explained in several ways. The competition between presidents and prime ministers led to each vying for the loyalty of services under their control by offering them important resources: the head of state – the SRI, SIE and SPP; and the head of government – structures in the Interior Ministry, army and justice system. Democratic control, exercised by the Parliament over the SRI and SIE, was not as effective and efficient, as MPs cannot enter into operational details, with the result that democratic supervision is rather formal (Matei 2014). While politicians and the civil leadership of the SRI and SIE change according to election results, the hierarchy of the intelligence services is made up military staff, who transcend government changes and who accumulate information about leaders and political parties, which is useful for ensuring promotion or preservation in key positions. The intelligence services noticed the fact that a pre-constitutional law of national security is more useful than new legislation that would increase the efficiency of democratic control. In 2006, Băsescu sent to Parliament a package of six national security laws drafted by the intelligence services, which were blocked in the context of his conflict with Prime Minister Tăriceanu.

The message that the intelligence services had made a complete break from the totalitarian state, becoming a real guardian of the constitutional order, was hardly credible; information emerged periodically, fuelling fear of a 'new *Securitate*'. Unauthorized secret surveillance and the illegal interception of correspondence are the main accusations against the intelligence services, together with partisan involvement in politics (Kieran and Deletant 2001: 231–51; Watts 2007). It was speculated that officers of the former *Securitate* were behind the mineriads of 1990–1. In 1995, two SRI officers were discovered while they were tracking journalists who had published articles critical of Ion Iliescu (*Monografia SRI* 2015: 118–19). In 2007, in the context of the referendum on the dismissal of Traian Băsescu, Mircea Geoană presented notes with the names of three judges in the Constitutional Court, whom he declared could be blackmailed for their supposed relations with the *Securitate*. Also in 2007, thirteen notes sent to Băsescu were published, which contained information about politicians who were opposed to him. In 2009, a court decision required the SRI to pay damages to businessman Dinu Patriciu for illegally intercepting his correspondence. In September 2014, Băsescu, in the context of the presidential election campaign, accused the PSD candidate, Victor Ponta, of having been an undercover SIE officer, but without bringing evidence to prove it. In January 2015, SRI Director George Maior acknowledged the existence of undercover officers in the mass media, a declaration which was followed by his resignation.

Such information and hints about the exercise of power by the intelligence services was balanced by the approval of Romania's Western partners, who praised the efficiency of its intelligence services in the fight against terrorism, cybernetic security and various forms of organized crime (Matei 2009).

CHAPTER 14
SOCIETY UNDER THE PRESSURE OF CHANGE

The political regime change at the end of 1989 triggered antagonistic, often violent, changes in the identity and action mechanisms of the Romanian nation. Society had to give up the paternalist-authoritarian mentality resulting from the agglutination of deep historical experiences with communist ideology and the practices of a dictatorial state. The nation was facing cultural challenges brought by globalization, in a context in which the state was hesitant to use its monopoly of legitimate violence in order to preserve the social order and the process of justice.

The sources of change in Romanian society are multiple. The first and most important is the very transition from a dictatorial to a pluralistic regime, in the context of free access to the mass media and the opening up of overseas travel. The promise of belonging to the Euro-Atlantic world generated an accelerated process of societal change, undertaken by state institutions. The 'forms' of a plural society were imposed upon the 'substance' of a stratified society with various degrees of modernity. Top-down democratization could not help but be partial, as pluralist socialization is a long-term process, which can only change with difficulty the most conservative structures of society. Ultimately, a third main source of change is simply the succession of generations. Those who were not raised during the communist regime claimed a new social status, legitimized by their lack of 'contamination' by the 'totalitarian mentality'. Institutional changes in Romania took place simultaneously with mutations in the sphere of values. Social anomie became the dominant phenomenon, manifesting in various forms, from public violence to flouting laws and formal rules. The widespread belief was that law and social order were compromised values, as they belonged to communism. Freedom was understood to offer limitless possibilities, individuals being convinced that state authority was too weak to enforce the law.

Money became the main implicit aspiration and social stratification criterion. Individualism, often with Darwinian overtones, spread among ever larger categories of the population. 'To be equal' became synonymous with being a 'loser', 'inadequate' or a 'sucker'. Civic equality lost its real social meaning for many citizens, as the state did not offer guarantees that they could be effective by following 'the spirit of the laws'. Semi-legal or illegal means were instead the guaranteed mechanisms for social achievement. Their use was not prohibited, as at the societal level it was not considered to be illegitimate. The expression 'others would do the same if they had the opportunity', referring to the use of illegal mechanisms to be socially successful, shows that, within Romanian society, the significant difference between citizens depended only on opportunity and not on adherence to significant sets of radically different values. Equality became quasi-synonymous with poverty, and inequality acquired a new type of legitimacy, that obtained by the force of daily practice.

The creation of a pluralist society with regard to social values had to overcome the obstacle of ethnocentrism among various ethno-confessional groups. Identity values based on belonging to a certain ethno-racially, historically and confessionally structured community are the strongest and most stable and the development of social conflicts on their basis was easily achieved during periods of social and economic crisis.

Simultaneously, a fierce fight against traditional mentalities was waged in order to achieve full gender equality. Deep-rooted traditional social practices and the perpetuation of an unequal hierarchical family model in society have preserved gender discrimination in Romania.

The most insidious obstacle to positive change of society is mistrust, both in the future and in others. Interpersonal confidence is undermined by a lack of predictability in applying laws and customary rules. Frequent political crises and economic fragility have raised a question mark even over the social contract between state and citizen. Mistrust is an extended social phenomenon which characterizes a society dominated by fears in which individuals are looking for individual and not collective solutions and the state is perceived as an obstacle to the pursuit of individual and collective happiness.

Run through the labyrinth: social and political violence

Romania's recent history has been marked by a chain of social and political violence which divided society. It has followed a political trail different from its Central European neighbours, which did not witness the use of mass violence for achieving or preserving political power. Romania witnessed a different destiny from the violence of the Yugoslav space, but with some resemblances to the Russian Federation, where mass mobilization for 'defence of democracy' was a method used several times at the beginning of the 1990s.

It can truly be said that dissolution of the communist regime not only brought freedom, but it also liberated the demons of collective violence in an anomic society. If during the communist regime political violence was fundamentally unidirectional, from state to society, after 1989's social anomie, a phenomenon characterizing the fall of the totalitarian regime was manifested by violent actions between various social, political or ethnic groups. During the first post-revolutionary years, the state, de-legitimized following fusion with the mass party under communism, de facto abandoned the monopoly of legitimate violence, which was occasionally transferred by power factors to certain social and political groups. Violent confrontation between various social and political groups was decisively favoured by a perception of the illegitimate character of any intervention from state structures (mainly the police) to regulate street conflicts.

The spectacular presence of masses in the public space, as the agent of removing the Ceaușescu regime, attributed legitimacy to their intervention in political conflicts within society. Mass violence was used in political competition by various political interest groups. The popular character of the Romanian revolution, in the sense of large-scale citizen participation in protest movements, determined the birth of revolutionary legitimacy, in which the mere fact of public support for a cause or political projection gave the impression that it was desirable (Abraham 2006a: 423).

Social and political violence re-emerged in 2012 in the context of implementing painful austerity measures, with various social and political groups being allied against the state, which discovered that it was the only guardian of legitimate violence, and which it even used against protesters.

The first two mineriads

After the violence and emotional impact of the revolution, Romanian society was marked, after a short time, by another series of street conflicts. The power structure created after the flight of Ceaușescu, the CFSN, wanted to maintain power after the envisaged free elections. On 23 January 1990, the CFSN decided (by 128 votes for, 8 against, 5 abstentions) that the Front would participate in the elections and that these would be postponed from April to 20 May (Ștefănescu 1995: 47–8). As a protest reaction, the traditional parties (PNȚCD, PNL, PSDR) organized a protest against the FSN's participation in the elections on 28 January. In parallel, a counter-manifestation was organized by the FSN, which was supported by workers from several Bucharest factories (Gheorghe and Huminic 1999: 25–35). The key slogans expressed by the two camps were: 'Those who stayed five years in Moscow cannot think like Bush'; 'We don't want neo-communism!'; 'Yesterday Ceaușescu, today Iliescu!' versus 'Death to intellectuals!'; 'Down with the sons of kulaks and Legionaries!' Partisan protesters from opposition parties attacked the government's headquarters demanding its resignation. The next day, as a result of the CFSN leadership's appeals through the mass media, over 5,000 miners from the Jiu Valley arrived in the capital, armed with bats and chains. The counter-manifestation organized by FSN supporters resulted in assaults at some parties' headquarters, starting with the PNȚCD and PNL. The lives of these parties' leaders was in danger, some being forced to seek shelter from the 'popular fury' (Prime Minister Petre Roman rescued Corneliu Coposu from the besieged PNȚCD headquarters in a tank).

Violence during the first mineriad had several effects: it consecrated the principle of political legitimacy based on crowds using violent behaviour; appealing to violence (attacking the government's headquarters) by the opposition had provoked fear among the Front's leadership about maintaining its power monopoly, so that the latter was divided by the creation of the CPUN (established de facto on 9 February 1990), formed on a parity basis (112 members of the CFSN, 112 of newly established groups and parties, 27 on behalf of national minorities); and it delayed the process of reconstructing state authority.

Dividing power by creating the CPUN was not, however, enough to calm the post-revolutionary agitation. On 18 February 1990, a new anti-government and anti-presidential demonstration took place in Bucharest. On the banners was written: 'Down with communism!', 'Down with the *Securitate*!', 'State power is maintained with the help of the *Securitate*!', 'We don't want communists, *Securitate* people and activists!'

A group of protesters forced their way into the government's headquarters. The weakness of the police defending the Victoria Palace, as well as the persistence of groups armed with crowbars, axes and bats, allowed the protesters to gain access to the government's headquarters. Within the building, acts of violence were committed. Members of the Cabinet were sought, but only the Deputy Prime Minister, Gelu Voican-Voiculescu, was found. The army re-established order. During the evening, about 4,000 miners from the Jiu Valley arrived. As the situation was already under the control of the police, they expressed in harsh terms their disapproval at the events in Bucharest and promised to come back whenever such events occurred again (Rus 2007: 59–67).

The first two mineriads indicated the trust of a socio-professional group in the force of legitimacy acquired in defence of government, as well as the weakness of state institutions, of its police (who had to deal with a trust deficit as a result of their role as pillars of the totalitarian state, as well as their uncertain position during the removal of the Ceauşescu regime). At the same time, the miners created an *esprit de corps* in defence of 'revolutionary gains', based on the idea of the role they had played in opposing the Ceauşescu regime by organizing the Jiu Valley strike in August 1977. Among the Jiu Valley miners' community a messianic current developed, accompanied by a perception of themselves as having played an exceptional role, which was to be rewarded by society through the government's acceptance of any of their wage, trade union or even political demands. This kind of psychological state was reactivated on the occasion of the mineriads that followed during the 1990s, creating the motivational support allowing solidarity following the appeals of the 'morning star of coal', Miron Cozma, for them to participate in new violent actions.

The inter-ethnic violence in Târgu Mureş

In a fluid geopolitical context, in which Romania's neighbours, the USSR and Yugoslavia, were confronted with visible tendencies towards state disintegration, Romanian society witnessed the emergence of inter-ethnic conflicts. Since the removal of Nicolae Ceauşescu, disputes between ethnic Romanians and Hungarians had emerged in Transylvania around the issues of education in the minority language and the cultural and political rights of the Hungarian community (Gallagher 1995: 76–98; Judea 1991). Some cultural and political formations were established according to ethnic criteria: the UDMR and the Romanian Hearth Union. As a result of signals concerning inter-ethnic tensions, at the end of January 1990, Ion Iliescu, the president of the CFSN, called upon Transylvanians to remain calm and to avoid confrontations (Iliescu 1995: 202).

On 9 March 1990, a strike of students from the Medical-Pharmaceutical Institute of Târgu Mureş took place, demanding a complete separation of education according to the language used, Romanian or Hungarian. On 15 March, Hungarians celebrated the Hungarian Revolution of 1848. Due to memories of confrontation between Romania and Hungary in the last years of communism, the Romanian population was very sensitive to the national issues. At the same time, however, Hungarians hoped to 'change the Trianon diktat', by restoring Greater Hungary. During the celebration of the 1848 Revolution, wreaths with the Hungarian flag were laid. In Sovata, the statue of Nicolae Bălcescu came down, and in Târgu Mureş the statue of Avram Iancu was desecrated several times. Manifestations and counter-manifestations of Romanians and Hungarians followed, which degenerated into violent acts of an unusual brutality for peace time, culminating on 20 March. The city conflict was also attended by inhabitants of neighbouring areas, Romanians and Hungarians alike. Overcome by the situation, the police did not manage to stop the conflict between rival ethnic groups (Gallagher 2004: 105). An Orthodox church was set on fire and the headquarters of political parties were destroyed. During the evening of 20 March, the army intervened, eventually managing to stabilize the situation, but only after large-scale direct confrontations had taken place. On 21 March, a governmental delegation arrived in Târgu Mureş, and, together with the local authorities, it finally calmed the situation (Stroschein 2012: 111). According to official figures the violence resulted in five dead (two ethnic Romanians and three ethnic Hungarians) and 278 wounded (190 ethnic Romanians and 88 ethnic Hungarians).

There are two interpretations concerning the bloody events of Târgu Mureş: the first, which places responsibility upon Hungarian extremist forces, profiting from worsening relations between Romania and Hungary to try to destabilize the political situation, with a view to achieving the autonomy of Transylvania; the second emphasizes the involvement of the former *Securitate*, which is considered to have used inter-ethnic conflicts to regain institutional legality and legitimacy. The Romanian Intelligence Service was established soon afterwards on 26 March 1990. In fact, both interpretations are based on conspiracy theories, of the 'foreign enemy' and of 'occult interests'. It is certain that Hungary did want a reopening of the border issue and former *Securitate* officers were waiting for an occasion to justify the re-establishment of an intelligence structure into which they were to reintegrate. However, the presence of approximately 30,000 ethnic Romanians and Hungarians at the demonstrations and street conflicts can be understood, on the one hand, as a form of rebirth of national feelings and, on the other hand, as a form of post-dictatorial social anomie. Rebuilding inter–ethnic confidence was a difficult but successful process, facilitated by the desire for affiliation with the Euro-Atlantic world (Cernat 2012: 30–1).

University Square

The divisions in Romanian society deepened during the first free elections, on 20 May 1990. The FSN had on its side revolutionary legitimacy and control of state administration, and the historical parties stated that they were the only ones with democratic legitimacy. In the hope of blaming the FSN, the historical parties and their allies from the embryonic civil society considered that a strategy based on street rallies would have a positive electoral effect. On 22 April the electoral rally of PNŢCD took place, during which were shouted a few of the slogans which would be repeated in the following days: 'Iliescu, don't divide the country!'; 'Proclamation of Timişoara, law for all the country'; '16–22, who shot at us?'; 'Iliescu don't forget, the youth don't want you'; 'Iliescu for us is Ceauşescu II'; 'Ceauşescu don't be sad, Iliescu is communist'; 'Iliescu don't forget, we vote for you in Moscow'; 'The true result of the Revolution – Proclamation of Timişoara'; 'Don't be afraid, communism is falling' (Cesereanu 2003: 272–300). After the end of the electoral rally, a few of the participants, but also other curious onlookers, occupied University Square, blocking traffic. On the morning of 24 April 1990, police attempted to disperse the crowd and made some arrests. It was the attempt of state institutions to re-establish legal order. But the latter's credibility deficit and the suspicion of collective guilt about law enforcement during the communist period meant that they failed to disperse the protest.

The problem of the University Square protests was quickly debated within the CPUN, Ion Iliescu calling the people in the Square 'punks' ('*golani*'). He later retracted this statement, but the demonstration was taken over by protesters looking for a 'claim to fame'. The perimeter occupied by protesters received the name of '*Golănia*' or 'Communism-free Area'. The protesters' demands were: adoption of a lustration law, which was mainly aimed at Ion Iliescu; independence of public television and authorization of some independent radio and TV stations; finding out the truth about the Revolution; and prosecuting the forces of the police and the army who had participated in the repression of December 1989. The commission appointed by the CPUN to mediate the conflict could not appease the protesters, so the balcony of the Faculty of Geology became the platform from which personalities with (or claiming) an anti-communist past demanded the country's democratization. University Square was considered a 'communism-free area' (Rus 2007: 74–8), opposed to the FSN, which was considered to be the de facto continuator of the PCR. The protesters had a heterogeneous structure: young people who hoped for a radical split with the communist past, some curious people, but also dubious elements, who practised speculation and illicit trade, thus compromising the ideas about Romania's democratization which had formed the basis of the initial protest movement. The mixed composition of the demonstrators in the Square allowed the FSN to demonize the protest action, considering it a 'Legionary danger' (Iliescu 1994: 124–9). The historical parties did not embrace it formally, although they hoped to make major political gains from it.

The parliamentary and presidential elections of 20 May 1990, which were not affected by significant fraud, were won by Iliescu (85.07 per cent) and the FSN, with 66 per cent of the legally cast votes. Faced with the FSN's acquiring electoral legitimacy, the organizations present in the square (the 21 December Association, the Student League, the Independent Group for Democracy, the Architecture Students' Association) withdrew, following the suggestion of the Group for Social Dialogue. Within the public space of Bucharest there remained only the 16–21 December Association and the People's Alliance, two less organized structures with a radical-extremist programme, which did not recognize the result of the 20 May vote (Berindei et al. 1991: 12).

Iliescu and the FSN had acquired democratic legitimacy after the elections and the refusal of the few hundred protesters in the Square to accept the election result had a symbolic consequence rather than a political effect on the electorate. The FSN leaders were determined to end the protest movement, under the pretext of re-establishing order. On 11 June 1990, a meeting of the Petre Roman Cabinet took place, also attended by President Iliescu, in the course of which it was decided to break up the University Square demonstration. The police, army and SRI received orders to this effect. The action was carried out during the morning of 13 June, but violence broke out between protesters and law enforcement forces. The troops in charge of removing the protesters intervened brutally. The conflict spread to the occupation of the public television station, where there was some destruction of property and broadcasts were interrupted for several hours. Politically and socially heterogeneous groups, whose intentions and affiliations have not been fully clarified, set fire to police buses and several police cars. The headquarters of the capital's police, the Ministry of the Interior and the Romanian Intelligence Service were also attacked and set on fire. One interpretation of these violent acts is that they were the spontaneous actions of 'thugs', while another line of analysis holds that they were actually caused by the former *Securitate* (reincorporated into the SRI), to legitimize the intervention by force (Rus 2007: 79–87). The hypothesis that the violence was a set-up has never been confirmed, but there are still question marks concerning the loyalty of the intelligence services towards the democratic order. It is certain that Iliescu and some members of the Petre Roman government either coordinated, or at least were kept informed about, the actions of force undertaken by the army and the police. However, it cannot be proven beyond doubt that a set-up was planned to legitimize the elimination of political opponents by the miners.

Faced with a situation, in which the state could not efficiently exercise its legitimate authority monopoly (or in which a perception was created that this was the case), the previous model of public violence, in which the population is called to support the political leadership, was repeated. A government statement considers that 'we are talking about Legionary acts which have to be firmly stopped'. During the evening of 13 June 1990, President Iliescu issued a call through the radio and television channels:

It is obvious that we are faced with an organized attempt to forcibly overthrow, by unleashed violence, the leadership freely and democratically elected on 20 May 1990. We call on all citizens of the Capital, in the name of democracy won through free elections, to reject with all determination the irresponsible acts of violence and support the law enforcement agents in re-establishing the situation of law and order. We call upon all conscious and responsible forces to gather in front of the Government and Television buildings in order to stop the forceful attempts of these extremist groups, in order to defend our so hard-won democracy.

Constantinescu 1995: 42

The 13 June violence looked like the initial moments of the anti-communist revolution, when a state of anarchy was generalized. The emotional impact was increased by the interruption of a football match from the World Cup taking place in Italy to announce the attack on the television station. Order was re-established in Bucharest during the night of 13–14 June by military units.

Tension escalated with the arrival, on the morning of 14 June, of two trains carrying miners from the Jiu Valley (approximately 10,000 people), led by trade union leader Miron Cozma. From the balcony of the government building, President Ion Iliescu prompted them to go to University Square 'to clean up'. In fact, the arrival of the miners was not spontaneous, but took place with the political and administrative support of a part of the FSN leadership.

Groups of miners entered the University of Bucharest and the Institute of Architecture. Students who were caught were brutally beaten and laboratories and classrooms were devastated. 'Visits' of miners also took place at the headquarters of opposition parties (PNL, PNȚCD), at some of their leaders' homes and at the headquarters of some independent or political party newspapers and magazines. Some of these publications did not appear for several days (*România liberă, Cuvântul, Zig-zag, Viitorul, Baricada, Express*). There is speculation that the PNL and PNȚCD headquarters were attacked by common criminals or by 'specialized teams' belonging to the *Securitate,* used by those in power to compromise the opposition even before the miners' arrival in Bucharest (Rus 2007: 88–121).

The tragic balance sheet of the events of 13–15 June can be analysed on several levels. Atrocities were committed; innocent people were mistreated. At the miners' indication, numerous arrest were made, and Bucharest's citizens were searched in the streets. Official data indicate six dead, 560 wounded and 1,021 arrests, suggesting a situation in which fundamental human rights were violated.

The domestic and international political consequences of the repression of University Square were far-reaching. The US State Department suspended all economic non-humanitarian aid which could benefit Romania. The European Commission declared itself to be 'shocked and disappointed' at the violence used by the Romanian authorities against protesters and the Agreement with Romania was blocked. Accession to the CoE was postponed until 1993. Briefly, after the June 1990 mineriad, Romania was diplomatically isolated, leaving it vulnerable internationally; the difference between the Central European and Balkan states became more than obvious. International public opinion expressed its outrage at the horrors in Bucharest. Television stations and prominent newspapers all over the world broadcast news and reports about the Bucharest mineriad. The interpretation of the international media was that the University Square was a new 'Tiananmen'. Suspicions related to the 20 May elections were reiterated and the new leadership was considered by most of the Western media and governments to be 'neo-communist'.

Removal of the Petre Roman government

The fourth mineriad, between 24 and 28 September 1991, after which the Roman Cabinet was replaced with the Theodor Stolojan government, took place in a changed social and political context. The first significant social tensions occurred as a result of the application of measures to liberalize prices, as inflation accelerated (170 per cent in 1991). Within the FSN, the dissent between gradualists and radicals increased (a conflict which the media identified through the labels of 'conservatives' and 'reformists'), concerning several issues: the rhythm and direction of economic and social changes; governance responsibility; and distribution of power within the FSN.

From the very beginning of September 1991, social tensions resurfaced in the Jiu Valley, as a result of miners' demands about wages and their hard working conditions. By mid-September, tensions seemed to have been appeased, as during the Țebea festivities, in memory of Avram Iancu, (one of the leader of the Revolution from 1848-9 from Transylvania), Petre Roman met trade union leader Miron Cozma (Ștefănescu 1995: 162–9; Rus 2007: 170–87). Although the main wage demands were approved by the government, on 24 September 1991 miners from Vulcan, who were on strike, demanded that Prime Minister Petre Roman come to Petroșani in order to meet all trade union demands. He refused.

The miners' demand that the prime minister come to the Jiu Valley was considered a matter of prestige. But, even in late June 1990, Petre Roman had been careful not to be associated with their actions. He had no speeches for them nor had he thanked them for their support. The attitude of the Roman government towards the miners was influenced by the desire not to be associated with mineriads, to avoid expectations that he would reward them for their help. The ambiguity of Petre Roman's position towards the miners – he blamed them for the violence in 1990 – left the trade union leaders feeling betrayed by the politicians, especially by the prime minister (Pasti 1995: 267–9). Faced with the prime minister's refusal to respond to demands that could be interpreted as blackmail, Cozma announced his departure for Bucharest, but he was followed by only some of the miners (1,500–2,000) and by the main trade union leaders.

At Petroșani railway station, the miners demanded trains for the journey to Bucharest. When they were turned down, they destroyed the railway station, occupied a train and hijacked another two. On the trains requisitioned by miners on their way towards Bucharest was written: 'We want price freezing'; 'Down with the Roman Government!'; 'Down with Iliescu!'; 'Down with Iliescu and Roman!'; 'Iliescu and Roman, we want them to go underground'.

Upon reaching Bucharest on 25 September, miners led by Miron Cozma went to Victory Square, where they stopped in front of the government's building, demanding that Prime Minister Roman talk to them. The Victory Palace was attacked several times with petrol bombs. The assault on the government's building continued during the next day. The crisis situation was analysed in the CSAT, convened during the evening of 25 September, where measures for the intervention of police and army forces were discussed, as well as the establishment of a new government, 'of national concentration'.

Under the pressure of events, closed-door negotiations took place between representatives of the miners and the state leadership. Oliviu Gherman, vice-president of the Senate, met with four leaders of the miners, among them Miron Cozma. The latter said that, if by 12.00 pm an official press release announcing the resignation of the Roman government was not issued, 40,000 trade union members from the Pipera factory would join the miners in Victory Square. Under the threat of potential civil war, Alexandru Bârlădeanu, president of the Senate, announced the resignation of the Roman Cabinet on the national television station on 26 September.

After announcing the resignation of the Roman Cabinet, Miron Cozma asked the miners to go home because all their demands had been addressed. In spite of this, during the afternoon of the same day, miners entered the meeting hall of the Chamber of Deputies, without any resistance from law enforcement units, where they called for the resignation of Ion Iliescu and the fulfilment of all their demands.

The next day, 27 September, miners intended to attack the Cotroceni Palace in order to force Iliescu to resign, shouting 'Iliescu, you cannot kill all the miners!', but they were pushed back by the police guarding the official buildings. Simultaneously, consultations took place at the Cotroceni Palace with the representatives of the historical parties in order to set up a technocratic government, with an FSN majority. A meeting took place between Iliescu and a delegation of miners led by Cozma, who signed a declaration effectively ending the fourth mineriad.

The same day, a group of miners led by Cozma attended the PNȚCD Congress at the National Theatre, where they were acclaimed. With shouts of 'Down with Iliescu!' and 'Unity!', and the taking up of a collection to feed the miners, they were reconciled with the National-Peasantists.

The violence of this mineriad led to hospitalization of 455 people, of whom 50 needed treatment. Three people died in Bucharest (Andrei Frumuşanu, Aurica Crăiniceanu and Nicolae Lazăr) and one person (Enea Ionel) died in the town of Vulcan.

In the immediate aftermath of this mineriad, two partisan visions were constructed. A first interpretation was offered by Ion Iliescu, who declared that the 1991 mineriad had been 'spontaneous', but on the way it had degenerated and had taken on political connotations (Iliescu 1996: 449–595). On the other side, Petre Roman and Adrian Severin supported the thesis that the Roman government had not resigned during the evening of 25 December 1991, and not even after that: their handing of their mandate to the president had meant that they agreed to an extension of the political basis of the cabinet and not to a resignation. As such, the government could be said to have been replaced as a result of a '*putsch*', a '*coup d'état*' directed by 'conservative forces' joined by Ion Iliescu (Severin 1995: 369; Roman 1994: 156–7).

Later mineriads

Following the first four mineriads, the reputation of the miners, especially those of the Jiu Valley, suffered badly. Under the influence of the mass media and of the use made of the issue of mineriads during the 1996 elections, the Jiu Valley became an isolated area, thus increasing the vulnerabilities determined by its mono-industrial character. Mining had increasing costs and attempts to restructure the industry by the Victor Ciorbea government were received with hostility by the miners.

During the first days of 1999, rumours began to emerge in the mass media about preparations for a large strike, with Prime Minister Radu Vasile being invited to go to the

Jiu Valley, like Petre Roman in 1991. The miners' demands were excessive: US$10,000 and 2 hectares of land for each miner; later they would demand a monthly wage of US$500 until retirement.

Faced with the refusal of the Vasile government to answer such demands and after the miners' strike was ruled in court to be illegal, the fifth mineriad began (18–22 January 1999). The objective of the 10,000–15,000 miners was to get to Bucharest and to put state institutions under pressure, so that their demands would be fulfilled. The miners' 'march to Bucharest' began; the police barricades at the Jiu Gates were violently removed; violent confrontations took place in Costești, following which the police were defeated and hostages were taken from their ranks; acts of violence were committed. The slogans shouted by the miners were 'We want the PCR back!', 'Cozma – Vadim'. Cozma had already announced that the 'march to Bucharest' was a 'new revolution'.

The defeat of the police and gendarmes by miners took place in the context of serious deficiencies in military organization, suspicions of betrayal by some senior officers of the Ministry of the Interior and even the defection of the head of the intervention forces, General Gheorghe Lupu. The Minister of the Interior, Gavril Dejeu, overwhelmed by the situation, resigned and was replaced by Constantin Dudu Ionescu. The taking of gendarmes as hostages emphasized the defeatist attitude of the civilian political authorities at the head of institutions in charge of exercising legal state violence: the miners were encountered by gendarmes without firearms and ammunition.

The miners' victory over the police only highlighted the dissolution of state authority. While the miners' march towards Bucharest attracted the solidarity of discontented people in Oltenia, so that the event took on the appearance of an uprising, in Bucharest there was no coordination within the political leadership of the state. The interior minister did not consult with the prime minister; the presidential advisor for national defence, Dorin Marian, was out of the country; institutions were uncoordinated. Dilettantism and anxiety dominated state authorities.

Under the threat of the miners' entrance into Bucharest and of the achievement of a *coup d'état*, the constitutional order was saved by the reaction of state institutions and the desperate solidarity of civil society. During the night of 21–22 January 1999 the CSAȚ met, and announced that a state of emergency was to be enacted by default on 22 January.

The legitimacy of the state institutions' action was also supported by civil society. On 22 January, a 'march of solidarity' took place in Bucharest, attended by almost 50,000 people. A similar action also took place in Timișoara.

Under the pressure of the prospect of armed intervention against the miners as a result of the state of emergency, but also of Prime Minister Radu Vasile's decision to negotiate with the miners, an agreement was reached, also known as the 'peace of Cozia'. The miners were promised a good part of their social demands, and freedom from prosecution for the violence committed in Bumbești and Costești. This ended the fifth violent action, and the miners returned to the Jiu Valley with a winning air. The agreement between Radu Vasile and Miron Cozma on 22 January 1999 in Cozia meant the avoidance of a situation which could degenerate into civil war, but it also dealt a blow to the rule of law: the government negotiated with leaders of a strike that had been ruled in court to be illegal, with representatives of a group which had used violence against the lawful forces of the state. In fact, the resulting confusion following this agreement could be seen in less than a month, when a new mineriad took place (Rus 2007: 219–49).

The sixth mineriad, of 16–17 February 1999, like the first three in 1990, lacked the trade union pretext. Miners marched towards Bucharest, this time only numbering 1,500–2,000, in order to protest against the decision of the Supreme Court of Justice to sentence Miron Cozma to eighteen years in prison for the mineriad of 1991. In spite of the Ministry of the Interior's interdiction, forty buses carrying miners left the Jiu Valley to protest in Bucharest. A group of miners was, however, surrounded by police at Stoieneşti, where, after a fight, they dispersed. Miron Cozma and Romeo Beja, another trade union leader, were arrested on 17 February 1999 in Slatina, where they had hidden in fear of the police (Abraham 2006a: 442–7).

Following the sixth mineriad, the miners' trade union movement progressively declined and no trade union confederation ever sought again to fight against the state's legal order with violent means. Also, the state eventually exercised the monopoly on violence, giving a signal to citizens that arbitrary violence had no place in society.

Protests of January 2012

The state of social anomie had significant new manifestations in the context of the economic crisis. As there were to be parliamentary and presidential elections in 2008–9, the decision-makers did not want to adopt painful measures of macroeconomic consolidation, hoping that the crisis situation would be overcome without any major social and political cost. Budget expenses became difficult to sustain, with the result that some very harsh delayed austerity measures were taken in 2010. Because the Emil Boc government was widely considered illegitimate, as its parliamentary majority had been created as a result of inter-party migration and government–opposition parliamentary dialogue had broken down, numerous frustrations accumulated. In January 2012 important social protests emerged, the triggering factor being a draft bill introducing market economy rules in the field of health care. Within the major cities of Romania, massive street protests took place during January 2012, demanding the resignation of the president and the government together with the organization of early elections. The critical reaction of the mass media ultimately determined restraint in the massive use of force by the government; the police intervened in a limited manner in order to avoid large-scale destruction. Under the pressure of the street, the Boc government resigned on 6 February 2012, contributing to a temporary relief of the political situation (*Cum recâştigăm* 2012).

Non-governmental organizations

The state's domination over society did not end with the emergence of multiparty democracy; there was not yet a complete emancipation of society. Civil society, including in this formula all forms of association between state and family, was a major actor of democratization and its manifestations were numerous, diverse and often contradictory.

Civic activism

The unchaining of society from the tyranny of the Ceauşescu regime generated a huge enthusiasm for association in parties and non-governmental organizations. The genuine interest in civic activism synchronized with Western strategies for the democratization of the post-communist space by supporting civil society. From the very beginning of 1990, Romanian elites were encouraged to associate in order to contribute to their society's democratization. The US, the UK, Germany, Norway, the European Commission and private financiers such as George Soros allocated financial resources for the development of civil society. The democratization 'recipe' assumed a strengthening of civic structures, which would contribute to consolidating political pluralism. Interest in politics was predominant; the Group for Social Dialogue, which brought together a part of the intellectual elite, was established as early as 31 December 1989 (Adameşteanu 2014). It was followed by the Civic Alliance, the Pro Democracy Association, and the APADOR-Helsinki Committee. Most civic organizations turned into forms of contesting those in power, especially Ion Iliescu; confusion between the fight for democracy and partisan political interest was dominant. The election of Emil Constantinescu to the presidency and the CDR victory in the general elections of 1996 marked the end of civil society as it had been established at the beginning of the transition: elitist and radically anti-communist. The political and economic failures of the CDR government discredited the political activism of non-governmental organizations on behalf of 'civil society'; its leaders experienced the disillusionment of not being able to organize politics following moral principles (Puşca 2013). On its ruins a new generation of associations emerged, more prudent and sophisticated in promoting their political partisanship, such as the Romanian Academic Society, Transparency International Romania, the Centre for Independent Journalism, Freedom House, and the Centre for Legal Resources. Their favourite sources of financing were also foreign (European and American). After 2000, non-governmental organizations acquired an increasingly important role as public actors, as the consolidation of the non-governmental sector was an important desideratum for EU accession. The vision of politics also began to change, giving way to a rhetoric of 'state–civil society partnership'. A perception was created that non-governmental organizations defended interests of 'society' and political parties only those of their clientele. Thus, civic activists contributed to discrediting political parties. But the most visible organizations of the second generation were discredited, as they played the role of pseudo-parties associated with Băsescu, whose authoritarian behaviour they failed to censure, preferring instead to justify it in the name of the 'fight against corruption'.

Romania's EU accession also meant a dramatic decrease of funding for democratization, as it was considered that Romanian society was already democratized, and certain niche topics were favoured, such as: the fight against corruption; the Roma issue; environmental protection; and social exclusion (*Carta Albă* 2012). A third generation of non-governmental organizations emerged, many of them orientated towards street protest actions. Following the model of the Occupy movements in the West, protests were organized in the main cities in 2013 against the plans for gold mining in Roşia Montană. Protests were aimed at blocking the use of cyanide in mining and the destruction of historical heritage (gold mines from the time of the Roman Empire).

The spectrum of civic activism is not reduced to the political phenomenon, but is much broader: education; culture and the arts; the environment; sexual minorities' rights; combating domestic violence; children's rights; and social and cultural exclusion amongst others. According to the socio-demographic features of the population, a general model of activism can be outlined: men have a higher civic participation than women; militancy is weaker in rural areas compared to urban areas, and increases in the latter proportionally to the size of the city; the most reduced activism is until the age of twenty and after the age of sixty, increasing up to the age of forty, after which it shows a decrease, but with a smaller index than the previous increase (Bădescu, Sum and Uslaner 2004; *Percepţii privind activitatea ONG* 2013).

Trade unions

Trade union life was decisively influenced by changes in the structure of the economy. Not only was the number of employees reduced by half in 2015 compared to 1990, but their very structure changed. The result of creating a market economy was the inclusion of 80 per cent of the total employed population in private forms of organization. De-industrialization and an increase in the service-sector share of the economy translated into a drastic decrease of trade union membership. While during the first years of transition the level of trade union membership among employees was high, at over 90 per cent (7 million trade union members out of a total of 8 million employees), in the private sector trade union membership remained more reduced, gradually coming to be restricted to the public sector and some industrial sectors (metallurgy, energy), in which trade union organization continued out of inertia (Vasiliu 2000).

The history of the trade union movement was often linked, by invisible threads, with the political phenomenon. Trade unions fragmented at the beginning of the 1990s, with their leaders fighting for three main resources: attracting more employees in order to be representative; acquiring a larger part of the rich heritage of the former General Union of Romanian Trade Unions, made up of eighteen holiday resorts, hundreds of hotels, recreation facilities, restaurants, over fifty culture houses and significant amounts of cash (about US$300 million in 1990); and a privileged relationship with the political authorities in order to gain influence over privatization processes and the establishment of wage hierarchies (Abraham 2006a: 558–72).

After the initial stage of trade union fragmentation, the survival instinct of trade union elites led to an institutional cartelization and an informal agreement to preserve the status quo by ending infighting. A national representative trade union network was established, organized in a confederal structure: the National Confederation of Romanian Free Trade Unions – Brotherhood; the National Trade Union Bloc; the National Trade

Union Confederation – Cartel ALFA; the Confederation of Democratic Romanian Trade Unions; and the Meridian National Trade Union Confederation.

The weakening of the trade union movement resulted not only from the economic changes but also from the material enrichment process and the oligarchization of trade union structures. Changes in the central leadership of trade unions were few; the same leaders remained at the top for more than two decades (for example, Bogdan Hossu, Dumitru Costin and Ion Popescu). The real power of the trade union leaders was provided not so much by the recognition of legitimacy obtained through success in defending the interests of employees, as by the accumulation of impressive fortunes, which allowed them to block the natural rise of a new generation of trade union leaders. Emblematic is the case of Liviu Luca, long-term leader of the trade union of the rich Petrom energy company (privatized with OMV), who exhibited an opulent luxury, and was associated in various businesses with the mogul of the transition period, S.O. Vântu.

After the 2000s, trade union activity transferred its centre of gravity towards smaller trade unions, often in a single company and with limited objectives, no longer fighting for general changes of labour legislation. The main demand was increased wages.

Private Romanian and foreign companies often tried to stop the consolidation of the trade union movement in order to achieve bigger and quicker profits by maintaining low wages or on the basis of employees' extra work. Corporate social responsibility did not become an extended practice, being adopted only by some multinational companies which have such a policy at international level.

The relations of trade union leaders with the political parties were complex and contradictory. Trade union leaders were tempted to enrol in political parties, which were interested, for their part, in getting popular support as a result of 'player transfers'. Some former trade union leaders got important positions within important parties: Victor Ciorbea (PNȚCD) became prime minister (1996–8); Miron Mitrea (PSD), Minister of Transport (2000–4); and Marian Sârbu (PSD), Minister of Labour (2000–3). Numerous other trade union leaders became MPs, following institutional agreements with the PSD (2000 and 2004) or after deals with the PNL, ApR or PRM.

Trade union leaders were tempted to establish their own political parties. In 1992, a party of trade unions, the Social Solidarity Convention, gained only 0.32 per cent of the votes during parliamentary elections. The political experiment was resumed in 2004, with the creation of the National Democratic Bloc Party, which did not register for elections by itself, but under the umbrella of the PRM. Only seven trade union members became MPs, so the project of a political force supported by trade union confederations was abandoned. Trade unions also chose to collaborate with political parties by signing protocols during electoral years, but it is hard to estimate the electoral importance of trade unions.

The decline of the trade union movement is also revealed by the evolution of strikes. After 1989 in Romania there was no general strike covering the whole economy and public institutions, but only protests within specific companies or sectors (administration, education and health). Most of the street protests took place in the first decade of transition, with the climax in 1997–9, in the context of measures concerning privatization and the closure of factories and mines. The implementation of some harsh austerity measures in the public sector in 2010 was not followed by broad-based protest movements, but only by protests of some small trade unions in the fields of education, health and the police. The austerity policies were accepted rather resignedly, without the unions being able to organize a general strike.

Employers

Employers' associations re-emerged gradually, as the state turned from sole owner into regulator of the market. The establishment and activity of employers' associations, as a form of defending the economic, legal or technical interests of economic agents, began as early as 1990. In the beginning they followed the trade union model, being divided according to industrial fields or branches. A structure of the employers' organizations was established, which was dominated by two main institutions (the General Union of Romanian Industrialists 1903 and the Confederation of Romanian Employers) and two smaller organizations (the Romanian Industry Employers' Confederations (CONPIROM) and the National Confederation of Romanian Employers). These do not include the foreign shareholders present in Romania, and the main multinational companies prefer to deal directly with the government.

The employers' structures were revitalized by the establishment of the Economic and Social Committee at national level in 1997, followed by Romania being represented on the European Economic and Social Committee in 2007. The practice of social dialogue between government, trade unions and employers, although it had been institutionalized, often had a largely formal character, as the main fiscal-economic and industrial policies were influenced more by the IMF, the World Bank and the European Commission. The cause of the reduced influence of the national employers' organizations lay within the political system. Important decisions were influenced by businessmen following non-transparent relations with politicians, in exchange for electoral campaign finance. Public policies were often the result of private individual or group relationships between politicians and businessmen, not of three-way negotiations between government, employers and trade unions.

The increase of the private sector's share of the economy and of foreign capital in Romania also brought in a new actor: foreign investors' associations. The Foreign Investors Council represents the most important multinational companies in the Romanian economy. Some chambers of commerce were also very active in promoting international capital interests (e.g. Romanian-American (AmCham), Romanian-German, French-Romanian).

Mass media

For Romanians, one of the fundamental forms of freedom was the right to be free media consumers. The importance of media freedom was emphasized by the measures taken immediately after the removal of Nicolae Ceaușescu. On 22 December 1989, the National Salvation Front's 'Communication to the Country' stated that it had decided to 'take the newspapers, radio, television, from the hands of a despotic family to the hands of the people'. The revolutionary authorities annulled most of the communist legislation (including the media law of 1974) which limited fundamental human freedoms, such as the freedom of expression.

For the democratic state it was important to offer constitutional guarantees for freedom of expression. The Romanian Constitution (adopted in 1991 and revised in 2003) provides, at article 31, that 'A person's right of access to any information of public interest shall not be restricted.' On the basis of this principle, as well as 'freedom of expression of thoughts, opinions or beliefs' (art. 30, align. 1), the fundamental law guarantees media freedom and the right to publish. The constitutional text explicitly provides that 'Any censorship shall be prohibited,' and that 'No publication shall be suppressed.'

Institutional development

During the long Romanian transition towards democracy and capitalism, the process of creating a pluralist media has its own story, marked both by success and by resounding failure. The first significant phenomenon was the formal separation between the political authorities and the press; this was achieved by privatizing most of the communist media institutions. In order to be able to build a real base of journalistic independence, media people took all the necessary steps to take over ownership of the headquarters and editing equipment remaining from the communist era. In 1990–1, in spite of the desire of some FSN leaders to preserve state ownership of the media, most media institutions were privatized. (Self-)privatization of the mass media accelerated as a result of visible pressure from backstage negotiations between newspapers and the political authorities. A part of the pluralist mass media was thus born around the institutional core of the communist media. *Scânteia* (The Spark), the organ of the Communist Party Central Committee, became *Adevărul* (The Truth). *România liberă* (Free Romania), the former newspaper of the Front for Democracy and Socialist Unity, kept its name. *Scânteia tineretului* (The Spark of Youth) turned into *Tineretul liber* (Free Youth). The process was also similar in the case of local media, where county and regional newspapers were privatized in favour of journalists who had been working since the Ceaușescu regime (Petcu 2012).

The second important process for the development of a domestic media system was the emergence of a new media, of private initiative. The significant role played by television and radio during the anti-communist revolution had brought about a sudden increase in the audience and credibility of the mass media. Freedom of expression, curtailed for more than half a century, found its expression in a veritable media explosion. In 1990–1 there was a big increase in the number and diversity of media channels: by July 1991, there were already 1,600 titles (Frumușani and Saint-Jean 1992: 553–61). These figures can be explained by the fact that market access during the first two years after 1989 was fairly easy, with only relatively small sums needed for investment.

Foreign media investors also began to come to Romania (e.g. the Swiss group Ringier, which came to Romania in 1992). In 2003, the group bought the national daily newspaper *Evenimentul zilei* (The Event of the Day). Due to financial losses, it sold this, together with the economic weekly *Capital* to Bobby Păuncescu, a Romanian businessman, in 2010. Another investment experiment in Romania was the German group WAZ, which bought the newspaper *România liberă* in 2001. In 2010 the WAZ group sold half of its shares to local businessman Dan Adamescu, and the German group left Romania in the broader context of abandoning business in South-East Europe. The group had been accused by groups of oligarchs of distorting the media market. Ironically, Dan Adamescu himself proved to be corrupt; he was arrested and convicted in 2014 for bribing judges.

The most important international investment in the Romanian mass media was undertaken by Central European Media Enterprises (CME), a company founded in 1994 by the US businessman Ronald Lauder with the aim of operating in post-communist Europe. CME took over the television channel Pro TV, part of the Media Pro group created by Adrian Sârbu. It then bought most of the TV and radio stations of the Media Pro group, while Adrian Sârbu kept the most important news agency in Romania (Mediafax), which was founded in 1991. From its launch on 1 December 1995, Pro TV has become one of the most important television stations in Romania, with a major influence over its audience. The economic crisis has also affected CME in Romania; in 2014, Pro TV was reorganized, and a considerable number of its journalists were either fired or left to go to competing stations. Adrian Sârbu was arrested in 2015 for fiscal evasion within his media trust.

Turkish capital has been a significant presence in Romania since 2007, when the Doğan Holding chain created the television station Kanal D.

Foreign capital is also present in radio. Radio Contact, with Romanian and Belgian capital, and Europa FM, part of the Lagardere Active Radio International, are two examples of media institutions created by international initiatives.

In 2003, the National Audiovisual Council declared that electronic media outlets had to declare their shareholders (Abraham 2006a: 520). As far as the printed press is concerned, in the absence of a media law, there is no legal obligation for transparency and newspapers do not publicize the identity of their shareholders.

While the interest of foreign capital in the Romanian media sector was secondary, with the abovementioned exceptions, the development of the Romanian media is related to the establishment of national capitalism. The main feature of the Romanian media system is the fact that media shareholders are simultaneously related to other economic and/or political interests (Baya 2009).

At the beginning of the transition period, Romanian businessmen invested in the creation of national daily newspapers. For example, Dan Voiculescu, with business in trade, industry and agriculture, created *Jurnalul naţional* (The National Journal) in 1993. George C. Păunescu, with investments in tourism and transport, created *Curierul naţional* (The National Courier) in 1995. Following the development of audiovisual media, the printed press was integrated into media trusts belonging to the same owners. After the 1996 political change and the acceleration of the rhythm of privatization of the economy, the influence of media owners increased and the mass media began to be used as a tool to gain economic privileges.

An important media group is Intact Media, owned by the family of Dan Voiculescu (former *Securitate* collaborator and director of one of the international trade companies of the *Securitate*, Crescent), which is made up of the generalist television station Antena 1, and since July 2005, the news station Antena 3, the daily newspapers *Jurnalul național* and *Gazeta sporturilor* (Sports Gazette), the radio station Romantic FM, and others. The owners of these media institutions feature in the list of the ten richest families in Romania. What singles out the Intact group is the fact that Voiculescu (even if he has assigned his share in the Grivco chain to other members of his family), was directly involved in politics, being president of the PUR between 1991 and 2005, and then honorary president of the PC, after the party's name change. The suspicion concerning Voiculescu is that he used his position as the owner of media channels in order to acquire political influence and thus to increase his fortune by receiving favourable treatment for other businesses he controlled directly or through intermediaries. It is well known that the main contribution of Voiculescu was to bring media support to any electoral alliance during this time. In 2014, the Intact group suffered a blow, as Voiculescu was sentenced to ten years in prison. The headquarters of Grivco and Antena TV were confiscated. The editorial activity of the Intact group did not stop, but its expansion was slowed down significantly.

The family of George C. Păunescu (a former *Securitate* officer) acquired several bank credits from the state banking institution Bancorex. These were never fully returned and were used for acquisitions in the hotel industry or in air transport (e.g. Dac Air). As well as the daily newspaper *Curierul național*, the Păunescu family also owned the television station B1 TV (created in 2001), before giving up half of their shares in the television station in favour of Sorin Oancea, a former shareholder of the Intact group.

One of the most spectacular stories is that of Sorin Ovidiu Vântu. Profiting from the support of former *Securitate* officers, Vântu (himself a former *Securitate* collaborator) created a pyramid scheme (the National Investment Fund), under the appearance of an investment fund. It went bankrupt in 2000, and the savings of 300,000 investers were lost. Vântu was also behind the Romanian Bank of Discount and the Bank of Investment and Development, both of which went bankrupt. Vântu considered that he could ensure his protection from justice through buying not only several radio stations and newspapers, but also a television station (Realitatea TV) at the end of 2003. Following massive investment, Vântu managed to create the first news station, a niche channel, but with high ratings among viewers interested in politics. The Realitatea-Cațavencu group, formed in 2006 after a takeover of the satirical magazine *Academia Cațavencu*, also included a television channel dedicated to the business environment (the Money Channel) and a news agency (NewsIn). The media owner became notorious for coordinating media campaigns against certain parties or personalities (such as Adrian Năstase and Traian Băsescu) and acted as if he was above the law. But the media group owned by Vântu incurred increasing financial losses, which could no longer be covered by advertising or capital injections from its owner. In 2010, despite his urban legend,

Vântu was arrested, and subsequently convicted first in 2012 and again in 2014 in a separate case. In this context, the media group quickly lost credibility and Realitatea TV, lacking financial resources, was abandoned by its media stars.

These problems indicated the vulnerability of media institutions, strengthening the suspicion that some journalists were in fact 'euro jukeboxes', according to the phrase of Traian Băsescu, and totally subordinated to the oligarchs.

In the context of Vântu's decline, a young oligarch emerged: Sebastian Ghiță. He became notorious by establishing an economic group (Asesoft) with several contracts with public institutions and companies (including the intelligence services) in the IT field. In 2012, he became a PSD MP. In 2010, he took over the management of Realitatea TV from Vântu, promising investments of €75 million. However, Ghiță did not manage to become owner of the Realitatea-Cațavencu group, so a year later he created his own news television station, România TV.

The transformation of the mass media into an instrument of political competition between various political and economic groups is illustrated by the proliferation of private news television stations, each having its own editorial agenda: Realitatea TV (2004), Antena 3 (2005), România TV (2011), B1 TV (2011) and Digi 24 (2012), the last of these being part of an Eastern European network of media content, internet and phone services distribution (RCS&RDS). From this flourishing media activity, it should not be imagined that Romania is the international motherland of news reporting, or that those television stations follow closely the CNN or EuroNews model. The so-called 'news' television stations have as their fundamental objective the production of partisan interpretations of political and social realities. Often, media channels are used to launch direct personal and business attacks on warring oligarchs.

The brothers Ioan and Viorel Micula have businesses in the food industry and tourism. The Micula brothers own the television stations Național TV, N24 and Favorit, the radio station Național FM and the daily newspaper *Realitatea Românească* (The Romanian Reality). The huge state debts incurred by companies owned by the Micula brothers have hindered their ascent to a national level. They have been prudent enough not to enter into the political games of Bucharest, so have avoided becoming direct targets in the power games of the public prosecutors.

The gallery of Romanian oligarchs also included Dinu Patriciu (who died in 2014), who bought from the state an important refinery (Petromidia), from which he created an oil company (Rompetrol). The latter was sold in two stages (2007 and 2009) to a company from Kazakhstan. Part of this money was used to buy *Adevărul*, one of the most popular daily newspapers. In an attempt to win political and economic influence, Dinu Patriciu invested massively in the media, but his losses kept increasing. In 2013, *Adevărul* was sold to another controversial businessman, Cristian Burci, who owns Prima TV, a generalist station with a national audience.

Accomplishing pluralism in the audiovisual field in Romania was no easy task. In 1990–1, the issue of creating a competing audiovisual market was directly related to the development of political democracy. Demands for the establishment of a private television station were supported by the political opposition, by a part of the FSN, by citizens, but also by international organizations (the CoE) and Western states. The Roman government even intended to support the establishment of a private television station with the help of Italian tycoon Silvio Berlusconi, an initiative which was sabotaged by Adrian Sârbu, who would later himself become a media tycoon, and by the controversial businessman George Constantin Păunescu (Severin 1995: 306–14). The PNŢCD candidate in the presidential elections of 1990, Ion Raţiu, also intended to establish a private television and radio station, but did not receive the necessary authorizations from the government.

At the beginning of the transition, the public television station was accused of political partisanship, of controversial media coverage of the 1990 and 1991 mineriads, and for the fact that its president was appointed by the president and not by Parliament. Until 1994, public television and radio stations were under governmental control. After the adoption of the law on the organization and functioning of public radio and television in 1994, they came under the control of Parliament; the composition of the board of directors was the result of the parliamentary political algorithm, completed by adding representatives of the government and of the president. The perception that public television was politicized resulted not only from the often visibly partisan editorial content of some programmes, but also from the interest of governmental majorities in ensuring political control; the mandates of the boards of directors were interrupted in order to form new majorities, congruent with those in Parliament.

The public radio station (Radio Romania), established in 1928, regained its credibility and audience during the post-revolutionary period, but it faced competition from private stations especially for the audience in urban areas (Marinescu 1999: 34–7). While pluralism in the field of radio broadcasting was easier to obtain, due to the fact that private stations (Radio Delta, Radio Contact, Fan Radio) began broadcasting even if they did not have all the necessary approvals, the establishment of the first private television station with national coverage was especially difficult. As a first step, in January 1992 the SOTI station began broadcasting in Bucharest for a limited amount of time, using the frequency of the second channel of the national television service (Drăgan 1993: 19). Afterwards, TV 5 Europe broadcast daily on its own frequency (usually between 8.00 pm and 1.30 am), and the second channel of the national television service retransmitted news broadcasts from the BBC World Service and Spanish television. The continued creation of a pluralistic electronic media was achieved by inserting local and independent television stations on the frequencies of the national television service during the electoral campaigns of 1992.

Internal and international pressures, the accumulation of domestic capital and the investments of some foreign businessmen ultimately brought about the emergence of private television stations with a national audience. Antena 1 began broadcasting in the autumn of 1993, Tele 7abc in 1994 and Pro TV in December 1995. These private stations began to be important competitors for public television from 1995 onwards.

The development of political pluralism also meant the emergence of the communication vectors of political parties: *Azi* (Today) belonged to the FSN, then to the PD; *Dimineaţa* (Morning) expressed the point of view of the PDSR (later PSD);

Dreptatea (Justice) was the official newspaper of the PNȚCD, *Viitorul* (The Future) of the PNL, *Socialistul* (The Socialist) of the PSM. The apologetic and propagandistic character of party newspapers could not give them enough credibility to be able to survive on the free market, so that most party newspapers continue to be published only with the efforts of party organizations and at a circulation level which did not confer any real influence.

Politicians watched with concern as the media became hostile to the authorities and party newspapers failed to gain a readership. The solution was to support existing newspapers or to establish their own, nominally having an undecided, 'independent' status, but partisan in content. *Curierul național* was strongly supported by the Roman government to become a media vector which would at least not be hostile to the government and through which the latter could better explain its political initiatives. The idea was amplified by the Văcăroiu government, who established the newspaper *Vocea României* (The Voice of Romania). This proved to be a media fiasco, as the governmental newspaper did not manage to counter the influence of the independent media. After the 1996 elections, the Ciorbea government considered it no longer needed a governmental newspaper, as it had won the elections with the help of the independent media, so *Vocea României* was abolished.

A special case is the magazine *România Mare* (Great Romania), an 'absolutely independent weekly newspaper'; its popularity facilitated the establishment of a political party with the same name on 20 June 1991. The genesis of the PRM reverses the customs of political life, by which the first to emerge is the party, which then builds a press organ. The PRM went on to establish its daily newspaper, *Tricolorul* (The Tricolour) in 2004; its role was to offer a specific vision to a captive electorate (Abraham 2006a: 510–11).

Following the model established by Vadim Tudor of the PRM, in 2010 Dan Diaconescu, the owner of the television station OTV, founded the PP-DD, a populist political structure which managed to gain over a million votes during the parliamentary elections of 2012. Diaconescu's television station had its broadcasting licence suspended in 2002 (following the broadcasting of shows with C.V. Tudor, during which xenophobic and extremist opinions were expressed), and this was cancelled in 2013 as a result of accumulated unpaid fines.

The failure of party media caused a change in relations between political parties and media institutions. Media aggressiveness was neutralized by using two methods: the first, used by politicians to avoid being involved in negative media campaigns, consisted of tacit agreements between candidates and the media, promising non-aggression in exchange for advertising business; the second involved politicians becoming media owners. This situation is frequent at local level, often being cross-party.

The institutional development of mass media was influenced by the creation, in 1992, of *Consiliul Național al Audiovizualului* (CNA – the National Audiovisual Council). The Council oversees the licensing of radio and television broadcasting, drafts broadcasting regulations, and intervenes for the removal of restrictive competition practices.

In 1995–6, the Council was accused of being a partisan institution towards those then in power, an allegation supported by the fact that, in September 1995, the CNA had required public television to cease broadcasting a programme in Romanian produced by the BBC, *Săptămâna la zi* (The Week Up-to-Date) (Gross 1999: 112). Afterwards, opposition parties made a habit of criticizing the Council for allowing public radio and television stations to favour parties in power with more frequent and partisan coverage.

An important decision of the CNA in 2004 was the establishment of the rule of 'three parts' when presenting political activities. According to these regulations, the executive power, the parliamentary majority and the political opposition must each enjoy a third of the total space dedicated to political news.

The price and distribution of paper gave rise to abuses on the part of the state authorities at the beginning of the 1990s. Following the privatization of the paper mills, media institutions escaped from this form of political pressure (Coman and Gross 2012).

The initial look of the Romanian media, strongly politicized and partisan, dominated by opinions and not by information, ultimately affected its audience: the circulation of the daily newspaper *Adevărul* stood at 1,537,000 copies in March 1990, decreasing to 600,000 in December 1991, and further dropping to 200,000 in October 1992. *România liberă* sold 1,490,000 copies in March 1990, dropping to only 200,000 in October 1992.

The crisis of confidence affecting the Romanian media in the mid-1990s was augmented by harsher economic conditions (increasing costs of utilities, paper and distribution). In their fight for survival, newspapers adopted different strategies, but one of the common elements of those who managed to remain in the market was a gradual transfer to information, investigation and analysis media. The second grand strategy of adapting to a competing market was tabloidization (initially with *Evenimentul zilei*, then *Libertatea*), promoting a mostly commercial media cultivating sensational news and aiming to attract attention for marketing reasons than providing information or creating opinions and raising awareness (Coman 2003: 78–89).

As a result, circulation was more stable by the end of the 1990s, with the most important daily newspapers having a circulation of between 150,000 and 200,000 copies. After 2000, in the context of a new emerging wave of central daily newspapers but also of a more diversified local media, newspaper circulation dropped below 100,000 copies per issue. These numbers were exceeded only in the case of promotional campaigns (e.g. *Jurnalul Național*) which were also supported by audiovisual media. After the promotional campaigns ended, circulation decreased, which demonstrates that the interest of media consumers is conservative, increasing only if they are offered direct material incentives (cars, mobile phones, free subscriptions, etc.).

The emergence of news television and, especially, the spread of internet access (including tablets and smartphones) led to a real fall of newspaper circulation after 2004–5. Publications such as *Cotidianul* (The Daily) and *Gândul* (The Thought) abandoned the paper format altogether and became websites. Publications which continued to publish a paper version sold at best 15,000 copies in 2015, and their website content is permanently renewed to preserve its attractiveness. The attempt to create loyalty among readers by offering content exclusively through subscriptions was not successful, so the revenues of online newspapers are obtained by posting ads on their websites. The quick development of communication networks of the Web 2.0 generation contributed to decreasing interest in the mass media, as individuals can now select and personalize the media content they consume.

The democratization of Romanian society was related to the achievement of media pluralism and the spread of cable television networks. Since 1995, this sector has systematically expanded, first in big cities, then in smaller towns, and ultimately in rural areas. In 2003, the penetration rate of cable television services in urban areas was almost 80 per cent, while in rural areas it was about 17 per cent. A decade later, at the end of 2013, the penetration rate of pay-per-view retransmission of television programmes provided at national level was 85 per cent, with the highest increase taking place in rural areas (*Piaţa serviciilor de comunicaţii* 2013: 57–66).

The national television station remained the only one that maintained its coverage over the entire territory of Romania, regardless of the expansion of cable and satellite transmission networks. Its market share had decreased with the emergence of private stations and the spread of the cable distribution system. After 1996, the public television station retained a market share of almost 40 per cent, but this can be explained by the fact that it was the only station that could be received in rural areas. Pro TV reached very high market shares (25–30 per cent) between 1996 and 1999, and dominated the urban audience. After this period, the competition in urban areas was balanced by Antena 1 (the two channels have market shares of approximately 25 per cent each). After 2001, the market share of the public television station was stable for a few years at about 35 per cent, mostly from rural areas. Afterwards, this share dramatically shrank, with the spread of cable networks and the increase in the number of satellite transmission receivers in the countryside.

For 2015, according to data resulting from audience research, the top ten television stations had a cumulative market share of over 60 per cent at national level. The top ten is dominated by five generalist channels (including Pro TV, Antena 1 and Kanal D), together with the first public television (TVR 1). Romanian news channels, the most influential in shaping political opinion, had an annual average of about 15 per cent of the national audience. To these national stations may be added a significant number of regional or local stations, either local studios of national stations or purely local channels.

Since 2000, the Romanian mass media has undergone a structural crisis in the broader context of the global decline of print media, the increasing influence of television, and the rapid spread of the internet. The media is competing to shape opinions within society with the dense and anomic network of communication tools belonging to the Web 2.0 era.

Ecclesiastical institutions

Religious life witnessed a rebirth after the fall of communism; freedom of conscience was guaranteed by the Constitution. The state assumed the position of guarantor of confessional pluralism, as 'any forms, means, acts or actions of religious enmity' were forbidden (art. 29, align. 4 of the Constitution).

Applying the principle of state neutrality in relation to religious denominations, a consequence of the affirmation of Romania as a secular state, was difficult. The state officially recognizes the existence of eighteen denominations and confessions, equal before the law and the public authorities, but the real influence of ecclesiastical institutions is determined both by their demographic share of believers and by the historical role of each denomination.

Denominations have an extended organizational network, according to the number of their adherents and their tradition, and have considerable autonomy, in order to guarantee confessional pluralism. The BOR, representing over 86 per cent of the country's population, had, in 1990, 12,389 ecclesiastical units (parishes, branches, monasteries, etc.), which decreased to 11,730 in 1994 (Tănase 2008: 150), before increasing again to 14,648 in 2014 (*Statul și cultele religioase* 2014: 91). The BRC, representing almost 5 per cent of the population, is organized in six dioceses, comprising 647 parishes, together with some tens of congregations, monasteries, schools and publishing houses. The BGC, representing less than 1 per cent of the population, is organized into five dioceses, with 760 parishes (*Statul și cultele religioase* 2014: 97). The third most numerous confession, Calvinism (3.5 per cent), represented by the Reformed Church, has two dioceses, including 780 parishes and 140 affiliated organizations. Among non-traditional Protestant denominations, the most numerous are Pentecostals (1 per cent of the population), with 1,343 churches and 7,879 affiliated organizations. The Christian Baptist Church of Romania includes about 1,800 churches in all regions of the country, territorially organized around communities. Romania also has fifty Muslim communities and twenty affiliated organizations, mainly situated in Dobrogea. The few adherents of the Jewish faith are organized in seventy-eight communities and councils.

In 2014, 18,436 places of worship of legally recognized confessions were registered, out of which the BOR held 12,971 (70.4 per cent), BRC 1,114 (6 per cent), and the Reformed Church 962 (5.2 per cent). For all these buildings the religious denominations do not pay taxes, which is an important facility granted by the state.

The state's relation to legally recognized confessions is intermediated by the Secretariat of State for Religions, which is usually either part of the Ministry of Culture or an autonomous structure directly subordinated to the prime minister. The state annually allocates some amounts of money to each recognized confession to pay their personnel and for the construction or restoration of places of worship. Between 1990 and 2014, religious confessions received a total of 3.4 billion *lei* (about US$1 billion) from the state budget, including 2.3 billion *lei* for salaries and the rest for buildings (*Statul și cultele religioase* 2014: 151). The largest share of the money, according to the demographic principle, was received by the BOR.

In 2013, the state partially financed (at least 65 per cent of the salary) 15,227 clergy posts (priests, deacons, etc.) and 1,272 leadership posts (others than those assimilated to positions of high public office: for example, the BOR Patriarch and the BGC Archbishop are equally paid, having an allowance comparable to that of the president of Romania and the prime minister).

Religious effervescence, partially authentic and partially a new form of post-communist social conformism, manifested itself in an increase in the number of new churches. The BOR and non-traditional Protestant denominations (Pentecostal, Baptist) were in competition for building new places of worship: the Orthodox built over 2,000 and the Pentecostals, Baptists and others, several hundred. The BOR justified the new churches by the fact that the old buildings were insufficient for the number of believers but it also wanted to show in this way that it was the main ecclesiastical institution. The non-traditional Protestant denominations, persecuted during the communist regime, undertook persistent campaigns of religious proselytizing. With the help of newer and older adherents new places of worship were built all over the country.

The BOR has committed to an older but very costly project: the Cathedral for the Nation's Salvation in Bucharest, a building meant to represent, in the opinion of Orthodox bishops, the 'symbol of the Romanian soul'. With its gigantic dimensions (120 metres long, 70 metres wide and 120 metres high), placed near the huge former House of the People (now the Parliament building), having the objective of receiving 5,000 people, this architectural project launched in the midst of economic crisis in 2010 is predicted eventually to cost at least €200 million.

Religious buildings were built with contributions both from believers and from public funds, often obtained thanks to partisan support offered to certain political parties or leaders. The frenzy of building churches contrasts with the closing of schools and the appalling state of many of the buildings in which hospitals are functioning. On average, after 1989, for each new school constructed, five new churches were built. The situation could be explained by the fact that for a long time the legislation did not allow donations for state schools and hospitals. Also, citizens were more receptive to the priests' demands because they considered that building new schools and hospitals was the state's duty while churches belong to communities of believers. Donations to churches became a social custom as an exercise of the 'recovery' of religious freedoms.

Another important issue for ecclesiastical institutions was the recovery of property lost during the communist period. The hardest situation was in the case of the BGC, abolished in 1948, whose properties had either been taken into public ownership or been transferred into the possession of the BOR. Naturally, with the re-establishment of the BGC, it reclaimed its property. The 1990s were marked by intense disputes, some of which were violent, between Greek-Catholics and Orthodox in Transylvania. The situation was not easy to solve, as after 1989, the community of Greek-Catholics was appreciably smaller than in 1948. The automatic retrocession of all buildings would have created situations in which churches remained empty for lack of believers, or had very few adherents within a larger Orthodox community. Up until 2014, the BGC filed 6,723 retrocession requests, of which only 1,110 were resolved. Over 80 per cent of BGC buildings remained under the ownership of the BOR, which claimed that they belonged to the local communities and not to the ecclesiastical structures subordinated to the Vatican. In 1998, a BOR–BGC commission was established to seek an amicable settlement of the property issue, but it failed to find a final solution. In order to settle the differences between the Orthodox and the Greek-Catholics, the state partially supported the building of over 310 new Greek-Catholic churches (*Statul și cultele religioase* 2014: 74–9).

The retrocession of all properties confiscated by the communist regime, especially of those other than churches, has not yet been finalized. The BOR has filed 2,215 requests, of which 994 have been resolved; the BRC, 1,203 requests, with 617 resolved; the Jewish communities (through the *Caritatea* Foundation), 1,918 requests up until 2014, with only 751 resolved. The backlog of the Romanian state in solving the property issue must be understood in the specific context. Romania is the only former communist country which adopted the principle of *restitutio in integrum*, also concerning ecclesiastic institutions' properties. The main backlogs concern properties which are not places of worship but buildings in which public institutions, such as hospitals, schools and kindergartens, are functioning today.

Confessional education witnessed a quick expansion in all denominations. The BOR has eleven theology faculties within the public education system, the BRC has one, the BGC two and the Reformed Church two. At the elementary and secondary levels, religion was integrated among subjects which had to be studied in public schools, each confession being able to opt for its own form of religion (Stan and Turcescu 2007: 155–64). Religion classes are not compulsory; pupils can choose not to attend with the agreement of their parents or tutors. In November 2014, the Constitutional Court ruled that the automatic enrolment of pupils in religious classes breaches the right to freedom of conscience. Therefore, the burden is on parents who wish their children to study religion in school to fill in an application to this end. In 2015, applications for study of religion in schools amounted to 90 per cent of all pupils, which indicates, on one hand, the extent of social conformism concerning attitudes towards religion, and, on the other hand, the affirmation of secular options in society.

Ecclesiastical institutions programmatically assumed support for conservative-traditionalist options within society. The rigid, dogmatically legitimized attitude towards the issues of abortion or sexual freedom (homosexuality), in the context of the adoption of some virulent public positions, has contributed to preserving the distance between progressive intellectual elites and the hierarchy of the main denominations (Conovici 2009). The public moralizing discourse of the high ecclesiastical hierarchy was often countered by the media with reports of widespread mercantile practices among priests, more specifically cases of venality in appointments. Most of these concerned the BOR.

Both the Orthodox and the Roman Catholic hierarchy had an ambiguous attitude towards the issue of collaboration with the *Securitate*. The political police had created collaborator networks among clergymen and uncovering the past would have stained not only the credibility of ordinary priests but also of leading figures in the clergy.

In the relation of religious cults with political parties and state power we may note some essential elements. The main religious operator, the BOR, set out as early as 1990 to maintain neutrality towards political parties. However, despite several decisions of the Synod, priests became involved in electoral campaigns, not only as supporters in the shadows but even as candidates. Bishop Calinic Argatu was elected MP for Argeş county on the FSN list in May 1990, although he afterwards withdrew; the abbot of Plumbuita monastery, Simeon Tatu, was elected Senator for Bucharest in 1990, remaining in office until he died in 1998; Ilie Sârbu, a theologian by profession, was Minister of Agriculture in the Năstase and Boc governments (Stan and Turcescu 2007: 122–7). In 2004, the BOR Synod forbade the involvement of priests as candidates in electoral campaigns. In spite of this, the BOR hierarchy, led by Patriarch Daniel himself, has had a partisan involvement in politics, in exchange receiving governmental subsidies to build new churches and increased allocations from the state budget.

The Catholics also adopted formal decisions to preserve political neutrality; in reality, however, they supported parties which promoted the restitution of properties confiscated by the communist regime (e.g. PNŢCD, UDMR). The Reformed Church was a preferred channel of the UDMR for mobilizing their electorate and for sending messages during electoral campaigns. Nor did non-traditional Protestant denominations refuse collaboration proposals from political parties. For example, the Baptist pastor Petre Dugulescu was a PNŢCD MP; his son, also a Baptist pastor, became a PDL MP from 2008 to 2012.

Policies towards ethnic minorities

The new contract between state and society accomplished by the Revolution and the democratic Constitution of 1991 also included the sensitive subject of inter-ethnic relations. Following the French model, Romania introduced the concept of non-ethnic citizenship, based on the liberal principle of equality among citizens (the civic nation). Romanian society is undoubtedly multicultural (*România – o Europă în miniatură* 2005), if we take into account its ethno-confessional composition, but this reality has not translated into concepts with constitutional value. According to the fundamental law, 'Romania is the common and indivisible homeland of all its citizens, without any discrimination on account of race, nationality, ethnic origin, language, religion, sex, opinion, political adherence, property or social origin' (art. 4, par. 2).

The entirety of state policies towards ethno-confessional minorities are the result of a complex multi-level game: the dynamic of the phenomenon of nationalism, in its electoral dimension, in political life (Cinpoeş 2010); international demands, turning into conditions of Euro-Atlantic integration (Gallagher 1999); Romania's neighbourhood relations (King 2010: 164–7); and transformations in Romanian social and political life (Chiriac 2005).

The main tendency was to integrate minorities, in order not to transform ethno-confessional differences into insurmountable obstacles for an open society (Salat 2008). Of course, reciprocal trust is not completely achieved, as the majority considers that the preservation of the ethno-cultural identity of minorities can affect the very idea of a national state, while minorities have revived their ethnocentric discourse, rejecting integration policies, and considering that the state wants their assimilation.

The first issue that Romania solved was that of the minorities' political representation. From as early as 1990, minorities benefited from favourable conditions, so that even if they did not reach the electoral threshold (3 per cent until 2000, 5 per cent thereafter), they could still send one representative to Parliament (King and Marian 2012: 566–72). Following the general elections on 20 May 1990, twelve minorities benefited from reserved places in the first post-communist parliament. Apart from these twelve places, the UDMR was represented by forty-one senators and deputies, elected by the normal procedure and not to reserved places. Starting in 2000, eighteen ethnic groups are represented in Parliament, on the basis of a special mandate, not including the Hungarians. The minimum number of votes that a representative of a minority ethnic group must receive is reduced to about 1,000.

The initial impulse for creating institutions specializing in the issue of minorities was offered by Romania's CoE accession negotiations. The Council for National Minorities was established, with the status of a governmental advisory body and composed of organizations with parliamentary representation. In 1997, a Department for the Protection of National Minorities (DPMN) was established within the government, headed by a minister-delegate attached to the prime minister, in order to thus send out a political message concerning its importance in the hierarchy of governmental priorities. From the very beginning, its structure also included a National Office for the Social Integration of the Roma. In 2003, the DPMN was transformed into the Department for Interethnic Relations, under the direct coordination of the Prime Minister. In the autumn of 2007, an Institute for the Study of National Minority Issues began functioning in Cluj-Napoca, financed from public funds.

Romania adopted the main international documents in the field of minority protection: these include the Framework Convention for the Protection of National Minorities (1995) and the European Charter for Regional or Minority Languages (1995).

All Romanian governments rejected the idea of territorial autonomy according to ethnic criteria, in spite of repeated demands of the UDMR and other political organizations of the Hungarian community. However, the cultural autonomy of minorities is a reality in Romania; theatres, magazines and cultural institutions of minorities are financially supported from governmental funds.

A measure with a high symbolic impact was that of bilingual or multilingual signs in localities where minorities represent at least 20 per cent of the population (according to Law no. 215 of 2001). The most important political debates took place in Cluj-Napoca, where the number of Hungarians does not reach 20 per cent, but according to the policy of a local alliance between the UDMR and local parties, signs in Romanian and Hungarian ('Kolozsvár') were placed at the city entrances, then removed but re-installed following a court decision.

Initially, the issue of minority rights was built around the Hungarian community, which had the necessary elites to systematically promote its own agenda. Liberalization of travel in the EU meant the emergence of a truly European issue, that of the ethnic Roma. Protests took place in Italy and France against beggars and the delinquency of some Roma; the Bucharest government came under international pressure. In 2004, the

257

National Roma Agency was created. Special governmental institutions created for minority issues were headed by minority ethnics. In the same spirit of integrating minorities, within police departments and city halls special offices for members of minorities were created, aimed especially at the Roma community.

The national strategies for Roma inclusion (which started in 2001) concern access to education and jobs, eliminating racial discrimination, and accommodation. However, Roma integration plans, financed both from the national and the EU budget, cannot overcome their ethnic specificity, the traditional migration of tribally organized communities and also the pre-eminence of informal rules over legal norms (Zamfir and Preda 2002). Roma integration is difficult not only in a relatively poor country such as Romania, but also in the rich countries of Western Europe (Schneeweis 2012).

At the centre of multicultural policies in Romania are language rights. Minorities now have access to education in their mother tongue (mainly in Hungarian and German) from primary school to university level. The mother tongue can be used both in justice and with public authorities (in oral or written form). It is also used in the public space, including the audiovisual field, through special programmes on the public radio and television stations.

At the centre of disputes concerning language rights was the Babeş-Bolyai University of Cluj-Napoca. In 1995, the university adopted a Charter by which it was reorganized along three study sections (Romanian, Hungarian, German), according to the historical and cultural structure of Transylvania. The UDMR repeatedly demanded the establishment of a Hungarian state university, to be achieved by dividing up the Cluj institution, but this was not accepted by the Romanian government. In 1998–9, a solution was reached concerning a multicultural bilingual university, in Hungarian and German, to be called the Petőfi-Schiller University, but it was not established (Stroschein 2012: 172–4). Instead, in 2001, the Sapientia University was established, mainly financed by Hungary.

In 2011, the UDMR also demanded the de facto division of the University of Medicine and Pharmacy in Târgu Mureş by creating new programmes of education exclusively in Hungarian. The government decision issued by the Ungureanu Cabinet approving the segregation was annulled in court in 2012. In fact, separate universities using the Hungarian language represent a sort of 'ethno-business' practiced by the UDMR, as multicultural universities in Transylvania cover the need for educational training of the Hungarian community.

Inter-ethnic relations were not only dominated by harmony and good understanding; there were also moments of conflict (Cernat 2012). Undoubtedly, the most important inter-ethnic conflict took place in Târgu Mureş in March 1990. There were also conflicts between the Roma community and other ethnic groups (thirty-five in the 1990s). On 20 September 1993, a conflict broke out between ethnic Romanians and ethnic Roma at Hădăreni in Mureş County. After the killing of an ethnic Romanian, further conflicts developed, during which another four people were killed, fourteen houses were destroyed by fire, and another four were partially destroyed. In 1991, at Plăieşii de Sus (Harghita County) a member of the Roma minority was killed by ethnic Hungarians, and twenty-eight Roma houses were set on fire. Near Bucharest (at Bolintin Deal and Ogrezeni) in 1991, dozens of Roma houses were set on fire, in the context of repeated burglaries and other crimes. In rural areas there were a number of arson attacks on Roma houses, a violent action meant to chase away Roma families. Setting Roma houses on fire is an extreme form of segregation, but inter-ethnic intolerance also takes other forms. For example, in Baia Mare the city hall built a wall in 2011 (under the excuse of hiding garbage) along a street separating the Roma community from the rest of the city, but without actually restraining the Roma's freedom of circulation. Tolerance towards ethnic Roma is lower in rural areas, but a widespread negative perception of the Roma can be found in various forms throughout Romanian society (Fosztó 2009).

Ethnic Romanians are in a minority in some areas which are inhabited by a Hungarian majority (Harghita, Covasna). The main issue of inter-ethnic relations is the desire of some Hungarian nationalist groups to create a 'purely' Hungarian area in the so-called 'Szeckler Land', which the UDMR and the other ethnic Hungarian parties want to turn into the subject of territorial autonomy, possibly involving the federalization of Romania.

Culture, art and sport

State withdrawal from the economy in the context of the transition to a market economy was manifested in the cultural, artistic and sports fields. If, during the communist period, the state had assumed the role of political patron of culture, arts and sport, by often generously financing these areas, after 1989, culture and sport became peripheral fields, to which significant financial resources were no longer allocated. What is significant is that within Romanian governments between 1990 and 2015, the office of culture minister was occupied by twenty people, among whom the most influential political leader was Kelemen Hunor, president of the UDMR. Sport did not benefit from a stable governmental portfolio, being included in the ministries of education or youth. Using the phrase 'transition hardships' to justify the poverty of allocated public resources, lay hidden the institutional marginalization of the cultural-artistic and sports sectors (Radu 2011). Lower political interest in culture can be explained by the fact that direct electoral benefits are insignificant for any government party, as people working in these fields are hard to enlist politically, and the transfer of symbolic resources from sports people, artists and intellectuals towards politicians is limited.

Lack of political interest in culture and the arts is synchronized with the major social tendency of positively valuing activities and professions which bring quick and substantial financial benefits. The social position of intellectuals and artists was on a systemic periphery, as public interest was directed predominantly towards businessmen, politicians and sports stars. In these conditions, mass culture, the older communist project, gave way to a culture of elites for elites. Selling cultural creations only rarely ensures a living wage, the consequence being a reorientation of a considerable number of intellectuals towards professions which provide significant income (law, the financial sector, medicine, etc.).

Mass sport, which had been practised during the communist period as a form of social mobilization, became, after 1989, an ever-more restricted social phenomenon, while high-performance sport served as a privileged social platform for youth from poor families.

Social practices reveal a relatively low level of consumption of cultural products and services. Reading books and going to the philharmonic or the theatre are relatively uncommon, while going to the cinema and sporting events are considerably more popular. Television, internet and radio are the main sources of cultural consumption in Romanian society. Of course cultural consumption varies according to place of residence, age and education (human capital). Despite prejudice, sociological research emphasized the existence of a market for varied cultural consumption in rural areas, not only in big cities. The main problem of the rural areas is poor infrastructure. The most significant differences among cultural preferences are not between urban and rural, but between various regions of Romania (*Barometrul de consum cultural* 2014, 2015).

Another significant phenomenon was the decentralization of cultural policies, with the transfer of cultural facilities to local authorities (city halls and county councils), the privatization of sports facilities and institutions of artistic creation. The significant restriction of government influence over the cultural sector, as a consequence of budgetary allocation and the transfer of competencies towards local authorities had its positive consequences, especially the abolition of the ideological monopoly. At a local level, cultural policies depended on the limited resources of city halls and county councils. It was also noticed that certain local political leaders, of various political orientations and ethnic origins, were tempted to politicize local cultural institutions, in order to make them tools for the perpetuation and amplification of their power. Following a neo-feudal model, county political leaders also assumed the role of 'cultural patrons', requiring their 'clients' (museums, libraries, folk music groups, etc.) to pay a political 'tribute' in exchange for decent financing. Thus, cultural policies remained a national project, but were hijacked by a neo-feudal logic in their application.

Culture, art and even sport became enrolled in the ideological matrix of transition, in which two main currents competed, divided by different visions over three issues. The first is that of the relationship with the communist regime. Those who declared themselves to be partisans of a total break with the recent past defined themselves as 'anti-communists', while the others, who were nostalgic for some elements they considered positive, or even for the communist regime as a whole, were identified as 'neo-communists' or 'past-ridden'. The second issue revolved around national identity. A theme developed of minimizing the importance of national identity, considering that patriotism is similar to nationalism, and regarding the 'Europeanization' of the nation as an identity alternative. The opposite current was that of the 'autochthonists' (Ifrim 2013; Marino 2005), who supported the preservation of national identity, seeing it as being threatened by globalization and 'Europeanization'. The third issue, closely linked with the first two, concerned the relationship between state and market and especially the influence of the state over culture, arts and sport. 'Europeanist anti-communists' rejected state involvement in the economy, supporting the objective and positive character of the 'free market'. The idea of the state as a producer of 'cultural goods' was supported not only by the inertial 'autochthonous neo-communist' current but also by progressive left-wing intellectuals, who considered that the state has a duty to produce public goods in fields in which the market distorts society and that culture, arts and sports should benefit from abundant public resources (Matei 2004).

Culture

The enthusiasm created by the hope of a new beginning dominated the cultural and artistic world during the first part of the 1990s. The Romanian Academy became once more the main cultural-scholarly institution, identified by law as 'the highest scientific and cultural forum, reuniting highly knowledgeable personalities from Romanian science, technology, education, culture and arts, representing the nation's creative spirituality.' As early as 1990, the process of bringing various institutes under the Romania Academy's authority subordinated to ministries or governmental structures began, in parallel with the establishment of new institutions. The Romanian Academy came to include fourteen sections, three branches – in Cluj-Napoca, Iași and Timișoara – and sixty scholarly research institutes and centres in various fields. In 2001, a new headquarters for the Romanian Academy library was inaugurated in Bucharest, housing numerous collections of rare books, manuscripts and prints, along with a rich collection of contemporary publications.

The Romanian Academy, often accused of conservative behaviour, programmatically took on the role of being a traditional institution, which preserves the most important values of national culture and scholarship. Under the Academy's aegis several volumes of the *Treatise on the History of the Romanians* (vols. 5–10) were published, as well as dictionaries of Romanian language and critical editions of the most important Romanian writers' works. These 'fundamental works' represent one of the main contribution of the Romanian Academy to the progress of Romanian culture.

A preoccupation with promoting Romanian culture and arts in the world was not abandoned after the Revolution; in 1990, the Romanian Cultural Foundation was created, with its own publishing house, and this structure was transformed in 2003 into the Romanian Cultural Institute (ICR). In collaboration with the Ministry of Foreign Affairs, the ICR manages seventeen cultural centres and one branch centre abroad. The budgetary resources provided to the ICR gradually increased, reaching a stable annual budget of €10 million after 2008. Its main projects concerned the translation of Romanian authors, art exhibitions, concerts, theatre performances, and the provision of facilities for learning the Romanian language.

The Romanian state privatized most spaces where bookshops used to exist, resulting in a reduction of their numbers and a shrinking of their size. The number of publishing houses exploded after 1989, but only 500 were active on the market. One of the largest publishing houses, Humanitas, was established following the privatization of the former political publishing house of the PCR. Publishers from the communist period were replaced by new private publishers.

The main victim of transition in the cultural field was the country's built and archaeological heritage, not as a result of the state's destructive will, but due to a cumulative lack of interest on the part of the public authorities, lack of economic resources and the desire of individuals to build as and where they wanted. Several buildings classed as historic monuments were demolished or left in ruins; where restorations were made, the requirement to preserve the original character of the monument was not respected (Administraţia Prezidenţială 2009a). Undoubtedly, the largest discussion was generated by the intention to reopen the gold mine at Roşia Montană, which would have endangered existence of old mines from the time of the Roman Empire. Only broad-based public protests have postponed *sine die* any development.

In spite of decreasing budget resources allocated to culture after 1989, some important institutions were built or renovated. The National Library in Bucharest was provided with modern premises in 2012. The university libraries of Bucharest and Cluj-Napoca were renovated and endowed with computers and books. A National Museum of Contemporary Art was built in 2004 and the Village Museum in Bucharest was extended. On the other hand, the structure of the National History Museum building was not fully consolidated, with the result that only a few of its sixty rooms could be opened. Thus, a valuable part of the country's museum heritage was not accessible to the public.

Apart from governmental cultural policies and the state of cultural infrastructure, another issue was the diverse and often profoundly conflicting world of culture. The oldest and most prestigious professional association in the country is the Writers' Union of Romania. This has branches at national level and produces its own publications, meant to support the promotion of Romanian writers (*România literară*, *Convorbiri literare*, *Apostrof* and others).

Romanian literary circles were marked by bitter ideological disputes centred on the communist past and differing attitudes towards it. Often, it was considered that the body of literature created during the communist period was a 'ballast' which had to be abandoned. The spirit of the time was marked by the production of anti-communist biographies, often fictional, or exaggerating the importance of minor acts of dissidence. The favourite concept was 'resistance through culture', a concept which in fact hides the daily complicity with the communist regime that was necessary for survival.

Several writers assumed the role of 'ideological leaders' from the position of 'public intellectuals', their main instrument being polemical essays. Poetry was marginalized, as it was considered 'anachronistic' in a society animated by hedonistic-mercantile ideals. Historical works and novels were the literary genres most often published. The most important novelty was the proliferation of political prison memoirs. Representative of this literary genre is *Jurnalul fericirii* (The Journal of Happiness) by Nicolae Steinhardt. This was published in 1991, in several editions, with an impressive circulation.

Historiography developed institutionally after 1989, with an increase in the number of research institutes, faculties and historians. The communist past was at the focus of many works of historiography, being the most dynamic field (Abraham 2013: 164–90). Sociology was re-established as an academic discipline and several research institutes, mostly private, contributed to a better knowledge of Romanian society. Romanian philosophy lived on in the heritage of Lucian Blaga, Constantin Rădulescu-Motru and Emil Cioran, without producing a new thinker of international scope.

Performing and visual arts

The world of the performing arts manifested the same dominant features of precariousness, fragility and exacerbated individualism as the rest of cultural activity. The main artistic event organized by the Romanian state is the George Enescu International Festival, dedicated to classical music. The event, inaugurated in 1958, continued after the fall of communism, with eleven festivals organized from 1991 to 2015.

The main cities, which are also university centres, also have their own theatres and opera houses. The Romanian Athenaeum is the main architectural symbol for the Romanian performing arts. The main investment of the Romanian state was the complete renovation of the Caragiale National Theatre at a cost of €70 million.

Copyright and creative rights were regulated by a law appropriate to a pluralist society in 1996. Respect for it was a gradual process however, the main obstacle being individuals regarding non-material creations as not being covered by property rights. Reproduction of music, movies and books without respecting copyright was for a long time a widespread social practice, though this reduced once the law was more strictly enforced. The Romanian art market is only emerging, including only a few thousand regular and occasional clients, with revenues of about €30 million in 2015. The development of the local art market, especially for contemporary art, was related to an increase in the degree of sophistication of the new Romanian capitalists; they invested in art as a way of protecting their fortunes, but they also used it to launder money. Customers for art also include people from the leadership of multinationals, interested in possible 'bargains'.

The most spectacular international ascent concerned Romanian movies, represented by a series of young directors. The Romanian motion industry saw rivalries and conflicts between directors who had been active since the communist period, the emblematic figure being Sergiu Nicolaescu, and 'new wave' directors (Cristian Mungiu, Corneliu Porumboiu, Călin Peter Netzer) who came to the fore by criticizing the communist past or the transition period. Among the movies which received important prizes at competitions in Cannes or Berlin, we may recall, among others: *4 luni, 3 săptămâni și 2 zile* (4 Months, 3 Weeks and 2 Days), *Poziția copilului* (Child's Pose) and *După dealuri* (Beyond the Hills) (Nasta 2013). Without programmatically assuming Romania's negative exceptionality, directors who achieved international recognition were not always appreciated by the Romanian public; themes which attracted the appreciation of specialized juries were the suffering caused by a dysfunctional medical system, the dramas of an absurd Ceaușescu regime or the anomic and caricature-like world of post-communism (Andreescu 2013).

The glory of Romanian classical music was provided by sopranos like Mariana Nicolescu, Angela Gheorghiu and Nelly Mircioiu, who had the opportunity to sing on the world's most important stages. Artists promoting national folk themes, such as

Gheorghe Zamfir (panpipe) and Dumitru Fărcaş (taragot) also won international acclaim. Cultural globalization through music was also manifested by concerts from international artists: Michael Jackson (1992, 1996), Madonna (2009), Scorpions (2013), Elton John (2010) and Luciano Pavarotti (1999).

Romanian folk arts (on the whole) did not succumb, however, to the assault of international music and art, but instead attempted to adapt to consumers' tastes. Together with the revival of religious events, interest was also restored in traditions and folk culture, with younger generations being interested in preserving the past.

Sport

Sports activity fully reflects the contradictions and conflicts of a Romanian society in search of stability and internal balance. School sport, the most widespread sports phenomenon, went through a crisis simultaneously with the entire educational system. Investments in sports facilities were limited; the situation was better where local authorities managed to attract governmental support or private resources. The sports facilities of former state enterprises decayed and many of them were even demolished. The most extended programme of sports infrastructure investments was that of the Năstase government, which built 400 sports halls in schools all over the country from 2002 to 2004.

The most important sports infrastructure investment was the building of the National Arena, with a capacity of 55,000, at a high price (€234 million); it hosted the UEFA Europa League final in 2012. It was followed by the Cluj Arena, with a capacity of 30,000, which cost €45 million. Other investments in stadiums of lesser capacity were made in Ploieşti and Piatra Neamţ. Most of the stadiums, sports halls and pools capable of hosting international sports events were built in the 1960s and 1970s.

The most popular sport was football, which represents a social phenomenon in its own right for the emotions it triggers. The exit from communism also brought high expectations, as in 1989 when Steaua Bucharest played in its second European Cup final, having won its first in 1986 in Seville, while the national team qualified for the 1990 World Cup in Italy. Qualification for a World Cup quarter-final match followed in 1994, after which the decline of Romanian football generated veritable social depressions, as success was increasingly rare (*Istoria fotbalului românesc* Vol. II 2011). Football successes were associated with the 'golden generation' raised during the 1980s, whose main exponents were Hagi (Real Madrid), Popescu (Barcelona) and Petrescu (Chelsea).

Football turned into the showcase of ugly Romanian capitalism. The football clubs of departmental structures (Steaua – the army; Dinamo – the Interior Ministry) were privatized, along with other football clubs which had belonged to state enterprises or to local authorities. The main football investors were interested in immediate profits from selling players and in gaining celebrity which they could use in the interests of their other businesses. The caricature symbol of Romanian capitalism in its sports dimension was George Becali, a former shepherd who became the owner of the most popular football team (Steaua Bucharest, supported by over 40 per cent of Romanian football fans), the leader of a populist party (the PNG), a candidate for Romania's presidency and a PNL MP, before eventually being sentenced to three years in prison for fraudulent real estate business. Becali is the most exotic figure out of a vast gallery of beneficiaries of the transition who wanted to promote other interests through football, but who eventually ended up in prison for various fraud. Others are: George Copos of Rapid Bucharest; Marian Iancu of Politehnica Timişoara; George Bucşaru of Unirea Urziceni; and Dan Adamescu of Oţelul Galaţi.

Investments in football academies were few, the interest of the owners being to sell players to the West as quickly as possible and import cheap players from Africa and South America. Romanian football inevitably entered a period of crisis, emphasized by failures both at club level and of the national team. The main football success after 2000 was Steaua's qualification for the UEFA Cup semi-finals (2005–6).

The most spectacular international results were obtained by Romania in gymnastics, mainly for women. After Nadia Comăneci, several other Olympic champions followed: Lavinia Miloşovici, Simona Amânar and Cătălina Ponor. From the 1976 Summer Olympics until the London Olympics of 2012, the Romanian women's artistic gymnastics team each time came in the top three, winning sixteen Olympic gold medals, besides successes in numerous other World and European championships. The main credit for this goes to Octavian Bellu, the coach of the women's artistic gymnastics team. Another sport in which Romania managed to preserve its Olympic success is women's rowing, with several Olympic titles obtained in Atlanta, Sydney, Athens and Beijing.

Despite spectacular results in a few sports (gymnastics, rowing, athletics, fencing) the overall tendency has been a decline in Romanian sporting performances. During the 1984 Los Angeles Olympics, Romania won 53 medals. Thereafter their number drastically decreased: Barcelona (1992) – 18; Atlanta (1996) – 20; Sydney (2000) – 26; Beijing (2008) – 8; London (2012) – 9. The decline in results in the most important international competitions is a prominent sign of a profound crisis within Romanian society in the context of socio-economic and political changes. Public investment in high-performance sports has been reduced and national competitions without a national television audience do not attract advertising revenue. High-performance sport survived by virtue of tradition rather than following governmental programmes to support the sports movement.

CHAPTER 15
THE ECONOMY

Romania emerged from communism with an apparently favourable economic situation. Following payment of its foreign debt at the end of 1989, Romania had reserves of US$1.8 billion in convertible currencies, though these were quickly exhausted for population consumption (Murgescu 2010: 466). The first important event was the unfolding of the COMECON economic system, which led to an imbalance in the national economy. There followed a succession of economic changes: privatization of state companies and the abandoning of centralized planning management; the establishment of domestic capitalism and the difficult accumulation of capital; de-industrialization and major changes in the land property structure; a significant increase in foreign investment after 2000; the elimination of protectionist barriers and asymmetric integration into the single European market; structural dependence on international financial capital and, consequently, limitation of the government's economic policy tools.

We can identify three main stages in economic life. The first (1990–2001) was 'economic transition', marked by the introduction of market economy mechanisms and institutions, the attempt to restructure the agro-industrial sector, and the privatization of the economy. The main macroeconomic parameters indicate a decrease in national wealth, hyperinflation (1991–4), devaluation of the national currency (the *leu*) and high unemployment rates. In 1993, VAT was introduced, an important measure for the market economy. This first stage also witnessed two recessions (1990–2; 1997–9), during which national wealth significantly decreased.

The second stage was 'integration into globalization flows' (2001–8), in the context of Eastern Europe's NATO and EU accession. Important foreign capital flows entered the economy, a context in which privatization was carried out in strategic fields (banks, industry). National wealth quickly increased, with GDP tripling from 2001 to 2008, simultaneously with a significant decrease in inflation. Unemployment also decreased, in the context of the temporary migration to the West of over 2.5 million Romanians, in search of better paid jobs. In 2005 a flat-rate income tax of 16 per cent was introduced for individuals and companies, favouring an excessive increase of consumption and a dangerous growth in the trade deficit (Dăianu and Murgescu 2013: 6).

The international financial crisis of 2008 also brought Romania's economy into crisis, the effects of which were felt until 2015. After an abrupt fall in GDP in 2009 (–7.1 per cent), the economy recovered with difficulty, paying for the frenzy of consumer debt of 2005–8 and for the bursting of the speculative real estate bubble. Inflation was controlled through austerity policies and unemployment did not escalate only because the labour force found outlets in the West.

Table 15.1 Main macroeconomic indicators (1990–2015)

Year	GDP (volume, billions euro)	GDP (growth rate)	Balance of international trade (volume, millions US dollars/euro)**	Inflation (%)	Unemployment (%)
1990	35.7	−5.6	−3,427	5.1	−(5*)
1991	25.1	−12.9	−1,528	170.2	3
1992	15.1	−8.7	−1,896	210.4	8.2
1993	22.6	1.5	−1,629	256.1	10.4
1994	25.3	3.9	−958	136.7	10.9
1995	27.4	7.1	−2,368	32.3	9.5
1996	28.2	3.9	−3,350	38.8	6.6
1997	31.3	−6.0	−2,849	154.8	8.9
1998	37.4	−4.8	−3,538	59.1	10.4
1999	33.5	−1.1	−1,887	45.8	11.8
2000	40.3	2.1	−2,688	45.7	10.5
2001	44.9	5.7	−4,661	34.5	8.8
2002	48.5	5.0	−4,206	22.5	8.4
2003	52.6	5.5	−5,587	15.3	7.4
2004	60.8	8.4	−7,346	11.9	6.3
2005	79.5	4.2	−10,313	9.0	5.9
2006	97.7	8.1	−14,896	6.56	5.2
2007	123.7	6.9	−21,773	4.84	4.1
2008	139.7	8.5	−23,515	7.85	4.4
2009	118.2	−7.1	−9,869	5.59	7.8
2010	124.4	−0.8	−9,509	6.09	6.87
2011	131.3	1.1	−9,660	5.79	5.12
2012	132	0.6	−9,634	3.33	5.59
2013	140.6	3.4	−5,707	3.98	5.85
2014	149.5	2.8	−6,046	1.07	5.29
2015	159.4	3.7	−8,370	−0.6	5.12

Notes: * Estimated, no official figures. ** 1990–2000 – million US dollars; 2001–2015 – million euro.

Source: Own processing using data of the National Bank of Romania and the National Statistics Institute.

The issue of property

The fundamental issue for the transition from a command economy to a market economy was property. Nationalizations carried out at the beginning of communism and the nationalization of land and forests not only left behind psychological trauma, but created a huge economic problem after the fall of the dictatorship. An automatic return to the property structure previous to the communist regime, even if it was demanded by some who were nostalgic for the interwar period, was no longer possible: towns and villages had expanded and retrocession of all properties was not possible; nationalized enterprises had undergone various changes during four decades; nationalized houses and apartments were inhabited by people, who could not simply be thrown out. In addition, several new state-owned factories and other productive capacities had been created during the communist regime. What should happen to these?

The easiest issue to solve was that of housing which had been built under the communist regime and leased at low rent. By Decree-law no. 61 of 1990, as well as other regulations, it was established that dwellings built by the state would be sold to the tenants on favourable terms. Suddenly, a new extended category of home owners was born. Law no. 112 of 1995 partially regulated the issue of houses confiscated by the communist regime. These were given back to the former owners, even if there were tenants in them. However, some protection measures for tenants who could not buy their homes, because they were claimed by former owners, were also established. Former owners could be compensated at a maximum level of 40 per cent of the value of the property. Lawsuits filed by former owners against the Romanian state, which was increasingly convicted by the ECtHR over this issue, made the search for a solution essential. Law no. 10 of 2001 established a relative balance in terms of house restitution, including compensation methods for former owners. A real restoration was achieved by Law no. 247 of 2005; it adopted the radical solution of full restitution (*restitutio in integrum*) not only of houses, but also of industrial properties, lands and forests to their former owners. Where this was not possible, compensation was awarded at the market value. A new structure, *Fondul Proprietatea* (Property Fund) was created to deal with the restitution issue. Through it, those owners who could not receive their property in kind were compensated by shares in the most important public companies. In fact, this compensation turned into a form of masked privatization, whose main beneficiaries were not the former owners or their heirs, but various national and international companies or profiteers with connections in high political circles.

As far as land is concerned, Law no. 18 of 1991 allowed the recovery of a good part of small and medium-sized properties, and Law no. 1 of 2000 extended the restitution limit to 50 hectares. In 2005, as has already been mentioned, any limit concerning the area of land and forest that could be claimed was eliminated.

The process of property restitution was marked by corruption and abuses. Various properties were seized using false documents, an action often contested by those who considered themselves the rightful owners. The justice system was assaulted by property disputes, which were often difficult to solve. Illegal restitutions also took place with regard to forest resources. Out of the 3 million hectares which were restored up until 2012, 0.56 million hectares were wrongfully transferred to their new owners (Curtea de Conturi 2013: 16).

While the Central European countries solved the issue of property restitution at the beginning of transition, by means of limited restitution and compensation, Romania failed to do so. The result was an inflation of restitution regulations, which hampered the solution of this problem. The cost of compensation increased and entering into the restitution labyrinth slowed down economic development. If the property issue had been solved at the beginning of transition, Romania's economic development would have been much quicker.

The main issue for the economy was the introduction of state-owned enterprises into an economic framework specific to a market economy. The dominant approach, inspired by neo-liberalism, was that the form of ownership was more important than the manner of leadership. The widespread perception was that 'the state was a bad manager', the only solution being privatization.

The first step was to establish two categories of economic actors: trading companies, which had state capital and could be privatized, and autonomous administrations (*regii autonome*), which, although small in number, had an important share of the economy. Only after 1997 could the autonomous administrations be privatized (Welch 2008: 206).

Romania experienced privatization by selling shares to employees in the case of a small number of companies (MEBO – Management Employee Buy Out). In 1995 an acceleration of privatization was attempted by offering the whole adult population some nominal privatization coupons, which could not be traded initially, in order to avoid a speculative capital accumulation. The value of these coupons had to cover 30 per cent of the state enterprise's joint stock. However, the value of these coupons decreased and citizens' gains were minimal (Pop 2006: 88–98).

The rhythm of privatization was reduced until 1996 and was mainly concerned with the sale of small and medium-sized enterprises. In 1997, the rhythm increased, using the direct selling method of trading companies. Starting in 1999, following successive agreements with the World Bank, the number of small and medium-sized enterprises which were privatized or liquidated also grew rapidly. The most important companies were sold by international auction to 'strategic investors'. Around the year 2000, private companies held over half of joint stocks in the economy and state property was systematically reduced. In 2002, new privatization legislation was introduced, which established new sale conditions (preserving a minimum of jobs, refurbishment, environmental protection, etc.). This decreased the price of companies sold by the state, but the continuation of economic activity had to be ensured. By the time of EU accession, the most important companies had been privatized but the state still owned an important part of the private companies' joint stocks. The most important state companies remained those in the field of rail transport, aviation and energy, which successive governments did not want to privatize.

Summary information shows that Romania had an inappropriate approach concerning the property issue. After privatizing more than 7,700 enterprises, the Romanian state only accrued €7 billion and only a small part of these were destined for economic development. Less than a quarter of the privatized companies have survived in the economy. Compensation in money for nationalized properties amounted to €5.5 billion, out of which €4 billion was through the Property Fund. Some 10,500 buildings were returned, amounting to around €2 billion. In 2015 compensation backlogs were estimated to be around €5 billion, on the basis of citizens' demands.

Liberal-neoconservative ideology triumphed and state property was reduced to minority dimensions, its economic role becoming insignificant. The de-nationalization of the economy at any price did not just bring benefits, but also important costs, as the following sections will show.

Agriculture

The situation of agriculture was decisively determined by changes in the ownership structure. Immediately after 1989, Romania witnessed civil fury against collective forms, which were considered to be illegitimate and generators of poverty. Law no. 18 of 1991 concerning land property established a mechanism of limited property restitution, a real new agrarian reform. The 1991 de-collectivization was continued by the process of property restitution until the mid-2000s.

The dismantling of CAPs was not counterbalanced by efficient mechanisms to ensure continuity in the use of modern technical means (tractors, seeders, fertilizers, etc.), or by keeping the land in forms of association within the context of restoring ownership rights, as happened in Hungary. IAS farms were bankrupted step by step and often privatized for insignificant sums.

The main phenomenon in the ownership structure was polarization, while the agricultural area in use decreased: from 13.93 million hectares in 2002 to 13.3 million hectares in 2010. In 2010 there were 3.82 million family farms (decreasing from 4.4 million in 2002), occupying 7.44 million hectares (compared to 7.74 million hectares in 2002). The average holding in 2010 was only 1.95 hectares, the smallest in the EU. The number of holdings registered as companies was 30,000 in 2010 (increasing from 21,000 in 2002) covering 5.85 million hectares (decreasing from 6.2 million in 2002). The average farm size was 190 hectares (*Recensământul general agricol* 2011: 25). Out of the total agricultural area, commercial farms larger than 500 hectares occupied around 2.9 million hectares (less than a quarter). Family farms between 10 and 50 hectares used a million hectares, and those between 50 and 100 hectares another 0.45 million hectares. Small households up to one hectare totalled in 2010 over 5 million hectares and subsistence holdings with a maximum of 10 hectares, another 3 million hectares (Otiman 2012: 346).

Changes in ownership structure led to chain effects. In 1989 Romania had an irrigation infrastructure for 3.1 million hectares; only a decade later it covered just half that area

(Ministerul Agriculturii 2009: 1–5). Not only was the irrigation structure destroyed but the use of the surviving part was affected by high operating costs and lack of organization. Only 8–10 per cent of the irrigation potential was systematically used after the 2000s. Agricultural production began to depend overwhelmingly on weather conditions: if it rained at the proper times, Romania had a good agricultural year; if there was drought or flooding, production decreased.

The return to the logic of subsistence agriculture and the ageing of the village population led to a decrease in the worked agricultural surface, with natural pastures being abandoned and orchards and vineyards diminishing (Turnock 2007). The number of livestock also decreased with the dismantling of the big collective farms from the communist period (Otiman 2012: 340). This was only partially compensated for by private farms of medium and small size. Vegetable crops shrank with the privatization of IAS farms. Imported vegetables and fruit became more profitable for hypermarkets, and domestic producers encountered major difficulties in accessing the market.

The elimination of customs barriers in relation to the EU represented a real shock for agriculture. Production of milk, beef and pork decreased after Romania's EU accession, while imports increased (Administrația Prezidențială 2013: 51–4). Reduced investment in food industries resulted in Romania becoming a net exporter of agricultural produce and a net importer of food products. Much like any developing country, Romania exports raw or primarily processed products and imports highly processed products, which have a greater added value.

Agricultural capital shortage also limited the purchasing of agricultural machinery (Administrația Prezidențială 2013: 17). At the location of the former Tractorul plant in Brașov, which used to employ 25,000 people and produced 50,000 tractors in 1990, a hypermarket was built. At the location of the Semănătoarea agricultural machinery plant in Bucharest, an office block was built. Small farmers imported second-hand agricultural machinery from the West and big farms purchased it from abroad. The price of fertilizer became prohibitive due to the high price of energy. In such conditions, agricultural productivity remained at a reduced level, with its contribution to GDP decreasing from 20 per cent in 1991 to 4.4 per cent in 2014, although it employed approximately a third of the country's labour force.

Romania's agricultural potential is enough to provide food for a population of at least 40 million, but it has not yet been capitalized. The deep cause of agriculture's failure in the context of the market economy is the almost mystical relation between Romanians and their land property. As owners, although most of them are condemned to subsistence agriculture, Romanians are very reluctant to give up their land, considering that it offers them an ultimate safety net in case of new cataclysms of history.

Industry, construction and mining

The most important phenomenon taking place within Romania's economy after the fall of communism was de-industrialization. If in 1990, about 45 per cent of the 8.15 million employees worked in industry and construction, by 2015, out of 4.58 million employees only 30 per cent still worked in these sectors. Romanian de-industrialization was different from Western changes as a result of the post-industrial revolution. Romanian industry was not delocalized but had largely disappeared. Industrial decay was 'harder than a war' (Belli 2000), being the main cause of Romania's structural foreign deficits (Fota 2011: 21–119).

In 1990 a good deal of Romanian industry was technologically obsolete, as after 1980, investment had been drastically reduced. The disappearance of the COMECON was the first shock, as traditional relations with partner companies in the former Soviet camp immediately unravelled. From a barter type of relationship, there was a transition to hard currency (US dollars and German marks). Romanian companies, lacking capital, did not have enough financial resources to buy new technology in order to compete with cheap quality products. The industrial technocracy was more interested in preserving its status, trying to maintain a governmental production subsidies system (mainly through cheap electricity and gas). The government did not possess enough resources to grant the subsidies that were persistently demanded by the technocratic lobby, and the big industrial sites were in crisis. Nor were Romanian companies attracting foreign capital, due to negative perceptions of Romania. Foreign direct investments in the first decade of transition exceeded US$1 billion per year only in 1997. Until 1997, governments were fearful of foreign capital; the dominant idea was to support national capital.

Some parts of industry vanished because it was simply uncompetitive. For example, in 1990 Romania produced colour TV sets and radio-cassette players, but they were inferior to those from Sony or Panasonic; consumers preferred branded products. Industry was also restructured in order to become more competitive or as a result of introducing more efficient equipment. Another cause of de-industrialization was the interest of the technocracy in getting rich as a result of privatization. Several companies were intentionally bankrupted by their directors so that they could be bought for ridiculously low prices. The speculative purchasing of various companies also involved various foreign entrepreneurs, who were interested only in selling companies for scrap and using the land for real estate speculation. This was possible because the institutions in charge of privatization were inefficient and/or corrupt. EU accession and the elimination of any protectionist barriers deepened the decline of Romanian industry (Trif 2008), which was incapable of standing up to competition in the single market.

The symbols of de-industrialization are the ruins of factories in town centres or on the periphery as brownfield sites. Many mono-industrial areas went into profound crisis as a result of industrial decline. The steel industry and producers of industrial equipment suffered major adjustments. Light industry (textiles, leather works) was reshuffled and continued with *lohn* production. The food industry suffered massive contraction. The energy sector together with petrochemicals significantly shrank. The main success story was the car industry, both with the takeover of Dacia by Renault and Daewoo (former Oltcit) by Ford, and with the development of an active sector of car parts for the main European car manufacturers.

The industrial construction sector, infrastructure and housing dramatically decreased during the 1990s, witnessing a quick comeback starting in the 2000s. Industrial decay was also emphasized by the loss of some economic partners from the Middle East, Asia and Africa, and orders from these areas became insignificant for the Romanian economy. For example, before 1989, Romania exported tractors to Egypt, India and Iran, but these markets were lost. The same happened with the production of oilfield equipment, which had previously been exported to the Middle East.

Energy (coal) and non-energy (construction materials and metals) mining was drastically reduced. Metal mining (copper, gold) almost disappeared, being considered polluting. Coal mining in the Jiu Valley and the Gorj Basin witnessed a systematic decline; mines were gradually closed, in spite of numerous social protests and massive subsidies granted by the government.

In spite of the predominantly negative balance of the economic changes, Romania also witnessed the emergence of post-industrial economy areas (Thomas, Pop and Brătianu 2013); the IT industry sector (mainly software) was one of the main prestigious areas of growth.

Transport, post and telecommunications

The transport situation was influenced by socio-economic changes. Decreasing industrial production affected both freight and passenger traffic. The railways went into crisis as industry produced less and less. Long trains transporting coal, cereals or industrial products gradually disappeared. Commuter traffic by rail towards industrial centres decayed, being replaced by road traffic. The relatively dense railway network of about 13,000 kilometres, of which almost 4,000 kilometres were electrified, became increasingly hard to maintain; the consequence was a decrease in traffic speed and the closing of low traffic lines. Of the 153,000 freight and passenger cars and 4,400 locomotives in 1990, 40,000 cars and 1,700 locomotives were left in 2015. The national railway company (CFR) had accumulated debts of almost US$5 billion by 1998 and, following a demand from the World Bank in that year, was divided into five different companies. Railway traffic could not be recovered; out of a quarter of a million employees, by 2015 only around 50,000 remained. Private railway companies also emerged, especially in freight traffic and for short passenger routes.

An authentic boom concerned road traffic, with the total number reaching five million by 2015. Having a car became a sign of status in society. Truck and bus transport was preferred for its flexibility, although it is less safe and ecologically sound than railway transport. The increase in the number of cars was not accompanied by a similar development of infrastructure. In 2015 Romania had less than 700 kilometres of motorway (under 1 per cent of the total road system), as well as a dense network of secondary and tertiary roads: of about 52,000 kilometres, from a total 85,362 kilometres.

In the field of air travel, Romania barely managed to preserve a state company (Tarom), which purchased Airbus and Boeing aircraft after 1990. Trying to preserve its profitability, Tarom cancelled its transcontinental routes in favour of regional and domestic ones.

The most important setback concerned maritime commercial transport. The Black Sea port of Constanța is an important gateway towards Europe. In 1990, Romania had 311 sea- and river-going commercial transport ships. From 1993 a fleet privatization strategy was adopted; a few years later Romania had no sea-going ships under its own flag.

In 1991, the state-owned post and telephony services were organized in separate companies. The post remained under state control, but gradually national or international courier companies (such as DHL) emerged as competitors in the market. In 1998 a controversial privatization of the telephony company Romtelecom by the Greek state company OTE took place. After the emergence of mobile phones, the Romanian market matured as a result of competition between the multinational companies Orange, Vodafone and Telekom (which took over Romtelecom).

Trade, services and tourism

At the beginning of the transition, trade and services accounted for about 10 per cent of Romanian employees, so that the growth of the tertiary sector was necessary both because it was the main global economic trend and because in Romania this sector had been underdeveloped. Following a quick expansion, by 2015 trade and services contained more than half of the total number of employees.

The tertiary sector expanded because only a small amount of capital was needed (for example for trade). The development of small family businesses was often the only alternative for those losing their jobs in industry. In its turn, foreign capital reaching Romania was mainly invested in trade and services, where immediate gains could be obtained, and less in industry and agriculture, which needed greater and riskier investments. The symbol of the economy was no longer tall factory chimneys but hypermarkets, positioned at the centre of cities, not on the periphery as in Western Europe. Developed by local or foreign entrepreneurs, shopping malls became the place of worship of the new religion, consumerism. The big retailing chains (Carrefour, Metro, Billa and Lidl) occupied a dominant position in the market, contributing to the bankruptcy of small family businesses. Retail networks often adopted positions of strength towards local producers in negotiating prices but cartel agreements could rarely be proven and punished by the Competition Council.

Tourism witnessed significant changes. Great tourist resorts decayed because the decrease in the number of employees, especially in industry and mining, left them without clients. Tourism was quickly privatized for the benefit of the new domestic capitalists. Not all of them had the ability and financial resources to develop businesses. The symbol of failure in tourism is demonstrated by the Băile Herculane health resort, which fell into decay after its privatization in 2001. Mountaineering immediately developed, the Prahova Valley (Carpathians) being the main area of interest. The Black Sea remained the favourite destination for domestic consumers, with the resort of Mamaia being the main attraction. Ecotourism, religious tourism and rural tourism represented new forms, attempting to capitalize on particular consumer preference niches. Danube Delta tourism developed and became an exclusivist attraction at international level.

Banking sector

The transition from the Soviet single-bank system specific to the centralized economy began in 1990, following the creation of a Western type of system on two levels. The first level was represented by the central bank, the BNR, which issued currency and supervised banking activities, currency policies and inflation control. Commercial activities were transferred to a newly established bank, *Banca Comercială Română* (Romanian Commercial Bank – BCR), and sector banks were transformed into commercial banks: for foreign trade (Bancorex), agriculture (*Banca Agricolă*) and investments – *Banca Română de Dezvoltare* (BRD – Romanian Development Bank), while the population's savings were held at CEC. Mugur Isărescu became BNR governor in September 1990; under his administration the institution strengthened its role in the country's monetary policies (Caracota 2011: 24–9).

Private banks also emerged. The most dynamic of them, *Banca Dacia Felix*, went bankrupt in 1995, following fraud (Barisitz 2008: 46). During the same year Fortuna Commercial Bank was eliminated from the market due to suspicions of fraud. In order to restore citizens' trust in the banking sector, in 1996 a Deposit Guarantee Fund was created, which offered limited compensation.

At the beginning of the 1990s the banking sector was dominated by state-owned banks, used by governments for financing economic activities. In 1997 the Ciorbea government was forced to capitalize Bancorex and *Banca Agricolă* with almost US$1 billion in order to keep them functional. Bancorex offered credits that could not be recovered, both to state companies and to companies with political support. Following a World Bank demand, Bancorex was declared bankrupt in 1999. Valid credits were taken over by BCR, and bank properties and insolvent loans were assumed by the state. The most important bank bankruptcy was due both to fraud and to the massive devaluation of the national currency against international currencies in 1997 (debtors could not cover their credits taken in foreign currency).

In the context of the obvious fragility of the national banking system, it was privatized with foreign capital. In 1998, banks with predominantly Romanian capital amounted to 70 per cent of the total banking capital. Following privatization and the advent of new banks to the market, the share of national capital was substantially reduced. In 1998, BRD was privatized by the Vasile government in favour of Group Société Générale from France. Bancpost was privatized in 1998, and was bought by EFG Eurobank Greece. In 1999 the privatization of *Banca Agricolă* was initiated, in favour of Austria's Raiffeisen Zentralbank. The jewel of the national banking system, BCR, was eventually awarded to Erste Bank from Austria in 2005 for €3.75 billion (Barisitz 2008: 113). The system of commercial banks with Romanian capital was reduced to CEC and a minuscule investment bank (EximBank). By the end of 2013, the share of foreign capital amounted to 90 per cent, but following some regroupings in 2014 Romanian banking capital reached 20 per cent. The minority position of domestic capital is the consequence of the presence of several international banks such as ING Bank (Netherlands), Unicredit (Italy), Alpha Bank and the National Bank of Greece. The main banking actor with domestic capital became *Banca Transilvania*, established in 1993 in Cluj-Napoca.

Relations with the World Bank and IMF

In September 1991, Romania reopened relations with the World Bank. Up until the middle of 2015 Romania borrowed US$7.55 billion from the World Bank, for programmes concerning the privatization of the economy, health and education reform, consolidation of the business environment, and justice. The relationship with the World Bank was important not only due to the amounts borrowed, but also for the expertise used by Romania during its transition towards a market economy.

The dynamics of economic life were strongly influenced by Romania's relations with the IMF. From 1991 to 2015 Romania signed ten agreements, of which three were precautionary (with the possibility of taking money only in emergency cases) in 2004, 2011 and 2013. The biggest loan was contracted by Romania in 2009, amounting to €12.95 billion. The five agreements from 1991 to 1999 were not finalized as Romania (government and BNR) failed to fulfil all assumed obligations. The only agreement for which Romania took the entire loan from the IMF was signed by the Năstase government in 2001 and finalized in 2003.

Agreements with the IMF involved a temporary renunciation of sovereignty and applying the Fund's economic rules in exchange for loans with smaller direct costs than those from other banks. The relationship with the IMF became a warranty certificate for the solvency of the Romanian state in relations with international creditors.

At the centre of disputes were the consequences of applying IMF conditions to the economy. The main critique brought against the IMF concerned the implementation of 'shock therapy' in the economy, through hasty privatization or company closures, suppressing all price control and trade barriers. Countries applying the IMF textbook rules suffered quick economic recession marked by decreasing industrial production and a burst of inflation. Such a diagnosis fits Romania's agreement with the IMF signed in 1997. After the failure of the first three agreements, in 1997, Romania committed itself to broad economic restructuring in exchange for US$410 million. The shock therapy proposed by the IMF was not realistic in the evaluation of consequences: the GDP fall foreseen by the IMF was 2.2 per cent, while in reality it was 6 per cent in 1997, and inflation did not stop at 90 per cent, but instead reached 154.8 per cent (Popescu 2002: 169–70). The agreement was not finalized, because the assumed restructuring measures did not receive political support from the Ciorbea government, due to their high social costs.

The year 1999 was critical in relations with the IMF, as Romania was in danger of defaulting. The IMF suggested that the Romanian authorities declare a default and roll over the debt. Standard & Poor's and CNN stated in March 1999 that Romania was defaulting together with three other countries (Ecuador, Pakistan and Ukraine). In fact Romania avoided bankruptcy because it managed to get money from quick privatizations and French President Jacques Chirac spoke in its favour with the IMF director of the time, Michel Camdessus. Deutsche Bank and the Chinese government also offered discreet support (US$100 million from Beijing). Afterwards, as a result of support given during the Kosovo war, the Anglo-Americans supported Romania politically. The IMF concluded a new agreement with Romania in 1999, but the most important step was the negotiation with the World Bank of a massive privatization programme (Private Sector Adjustment Loan – PSAL I). By signing PSAL, Romania undertook to privatize or close the forty largest loss-making state-owned enterprises and a further 600 medium-sized enterprises. On the basis of the 1999 agreement with the World Bank and of a new agreement signed by the Isărescu government in 2000 (PSAL II), Romania's most important industrial capacities were either privatized or closed, including collapsing entities in the banking sector.

A second crisis moment during which the IMF and World Bank intervened as 'firemen' was in 2009–10. In 2008, the international crisis which started in the US also came to Romania via financial channels. The pro-cyclical fiscal policy of the Tăriceanu government proved to be an error, its main effect being a quick rise of consumption based on debt. Diminishing financing lines of Western banks for Romanian subsidiaries deepened the economic crisis (Ban and Gabor 2014: 12). The Boc government asked for the support of the IMF, the World Bank, the European Commission, the EBRD (European Bank for Reconstruction and Development) and the EIB (European Investment Bank). A total loan of €19.95 billion resulted, out of which €12.95 billion were contracted with the IMF. The loan agreement was doubled by IMF involvement in achieving an agreement in Vienna in 2009, by which the main nine foreign banks undertook to maintain financing for their subsidiaries in Romania (Stănescu 2014: 310–15). The IMF loan was mainly used to cover some state debts to banks which signed the agreement.

In spite of the 2009 loan agreement, the economy was in crisis and public spending could not be sustained. The IMF proposed an increase in taxes and fees, as well as measures for making the labour market more flexible in order to revive the economy. The Boc government, under the direction of President Băsescu, adopted another strategy: cuts in individual income and a freeze on hiring in the public sector. Paradoxically, the harshest austerity measures were not taken following IMF requests, but as a result of a domestic political decision. Romania got over the peak of the crisis by sacrificing an important share of the population; the relationship with the IMF and World Bank helped to preserve credibility on the international financial markets. The main cost covered by Romania for its relationship with the IMF was the slow rhythm of economic development and the domination of foreign capital in essential sectors: banks, industry and energy.

Physiognomy of Romanian capitalism

Historically, the term 'capitalism' aroused suspicion among Romanians, who associated the notion with inequality and exploitation of the majority by a rapacious minority, as communist propaganda had stated. Gradually, social support for a market economy increased and social inequalities were accepted as a given (Tufiş 2012: 269).

The private capital accumulation process in the context of economic de-nationalization and the establishment of market economy institutions led to the emergence of a *sui generis* form of capitalism, different from the Anglo-Saxon or Rhenish models. Often, there was talk of 'East-European capitalism', without clarifying whether it was a species in itself or a form of gradual transition towards the social capitalism of Western Europe. The main dilemma was how a capitalist system could be built without a group of capitalists (Eyal, Szelenyi and Townsley 2000; Stoica 2004: 239–52).

After the fall of communism a broad category of small entrepreneurs quickly formed. It was supported and encouraged by the Văcăroiu government's policies, through fiscal facilities, crediting and a slow privatization rhythm which allowed for the accumulation of national capital. The newly rich also emerged (labelled 'cardboard billionaires' by the media) as a consequence of privileged relations with political parties. The state-owned banking system financed the establishment of a group of domestic entrepreneurs, at the cost of weakening banks, which were no longer capable of recovering all credits. Romanian capitalists were not only involved in trade, small industry and agriculture, but had also timidly ventured into the financial-banking area. The increase of the rhythm of privatization in 1997 favoured the strengthening of domestic capital, but the new Romanian propertied class were strongly dependent on state subsidies and contracts and a tolerance of non-payment of taxes and fees. A decade after the fall of communism, a small stratum of very rich people had become consolidated, with businesses in industry, energy, transport and mass media. Great capitalists emerged as a result of privileged relations with political leaders, using the relational capital inherited from the communist regime. Some hundreds of thousands of successful entrepreneurs also emerged, who were not dependent on governmental orders or subsidies, especially in trade, small industry, tourism and IT.

The country's accession to the EU and NATO brought interest on the part of foreign capital, mainly European. For Romanian capitalists, Euro-Atlantic integration was bad news, as they had to confront foreign capital, which used political instruments (EU accession negotiations) to separate business from politics on behalf of a 'functional market economy' (Cernat 2006). Although Romanian capitalists tried to participate in the privatization of the most important national companies (for example, Petrom), they were too weak and lacked political support. Western companies occupied key positions in the economy and the consolidation of domestic capitalists was stopped. Lacking the support of the state, which had to drastically limit preferential policies, national capitalists became the favourite target of anti-corruption campaigns. Without the financial and logistic amplitude of Russian oligarchs, the main Romanian entrepreneurs limited their expansion to the Balkan area as access to the European single market was very difficult

(Pasti 2006: 307–416). The main issue for Romanian capitalism was the absence of financial resources, which were difficult to accumulate in a short time. Foreign banks in Romania were interested neither in financing local capitalists nor in great industrial investments. After EU accession, local entrepreneurs had to capitulate to international capital, whose interests began to prevail within governmental policies simultaneously with the 2008 economic crisis (Dăianu 2015).

EU accession represented an opportunity for economic development. Within the 2007–13 multi-annual budget, which could be spent until 2015, Romania was allocated €19 billion of structural and cohesion funds. Romania's total contribution to the EU budget was €12.3 billion from 2007 to 2015. Due to administrative weakness, bureaucracy and companies' lack of co-financing funding, Romania's absorption rate was below 70 per cent and nearly €6 billion of structural and cohesion funds (EU budget 2007–13) were lost. In spite of this loss, Romania's balance is positive, as total European funds (pre-accession and 2007–13 EU budget) amounted to almost €32.5 billion.

The development of oligarchic capitalism in Romania was slowed down by EU accession. Instead of a national class of capitalists, multinational companies prevailed, and took over the essential positions in the economy after privatization. Lacking governmental support, which was blocked by the European Commission's neo-liberal policies, national capital was forced to cooperate with international capital, and accept its domination. Foreign capital was localized around big cities; domestic capital sought out less developed areas. This physiognomy of Romanian capitalism substantially affected the substance of the welfare state, with working relations being decided in favour of companies which maximized their gains through low wages (Ban 2014). The 2008 economic crisis resulted in a strengthening of the influence of trans-national companies and banks; national capitalists were forced to adopt survival strategies rather than development plans. Faced with a deeply economically polarized society, inequality and the perception of missed chances, youth and professional elites looked for personal success in better paid jobs in Western Europe, thus diminishing the chances of consolidating the middle class and entrepreneurs. Romanian capitalism is far from the 'Romanian dream' of prosperity and freedom in Europe.

PART III
SOCIAL AND DEMOGRAPHIC TRENDS

It is not by chance that the social and demographic processes in the history of Romania are approached here in a distinct chapter and in a unified manner. A mechanical correlation between the social and demographic dynamics and the succession of political regimes is not the best choice, as developments within society have a high degree of inertia and can only be truly understood over the historical long- and medium-term. Nor is it by chance that this section is placed at the end of the book, as, after the presentation of the political, economic, social and cultural history, the reader will find out how these historical phenomena and processes influenced the social and demographic trends of the Romanian nation. The Second World War, the agricultural industrialization and collectivization policies, the pro-birth policy of the Ceausescu regime, and, last but not least, the effects of the transition to a market economy, influenced the social and demographic dynamics, which are an accurate historical measure for the sum of political, social and economic processes in Romania. The demographic behaviour of the individuals who form the nation is the result of multiple factors, including: the political and the socio-economic situation; the sense of belonging to an ethnic community and a religious group; accelerated urbanization; cultural changes and changes in gender relations; the nature of birth control policies (supporting birth control or, on the contrary, forcing families to procreate); and social mobility.

The main source of information for our analysis are the censuses of 1930 (*Recensământul general* 1938–40), 1948 (Golopenția and Georgescu 1948), 1956 (*Recensământul 1956* 1959), 1966 (*Recensământul 1966* 1969–70), 1977 (*Recensământul 1977* 1980–1), 1992 (*Recensământul 1992* 1994–5), 2002 (*Recensământul 2002* 2003) and 2011 (*Recensământul 2011* 2011). A synthesis of information from a part of the censuses can be found in various works in the field (Alexandrescu 2007; Ghețău 2012; Mureșan 1999; Trebici 1991). The eight social and demographic surveys mentioned above provide sources of information for an in-depth analysis of Romanian society.

CHAPTER 16
SOCIAL AND DEMOGRAPHIC TRENDS

Main demographic data

At the end of the First World War, Romania was in a favourable position, as, by the application of the principle of self-determination of nations, the territories in which ethnic Romanians were the majority population were united into a unitary state structure, with the support of the *Entente* powers. Following the union between Bessarabia (27 March/9 April 1918), Bukovina (28 November 1918), Transylvania (1 December 1918) and the Old Kingdom, the new state increased its territory from 137,903 square kilometres to 295,049 square kilometres (Mureşan 1999: 49). Its population also increased significantly, from 7.8 million in 1916 to a little over 18 million people in 1930. Furthermore, the census of 1930 proved that Romania accounted for 4.5 per cent of the population of Europe. With territories that had once belonged to the Tsarist Empire (Bessarabia) and the Austro-Hungarian Empire (Bukovina and Transylvania), Greater Romania had a diverse ethnic structure. Romanians were the main ethnic group (71.9 per cent), followed by Hungarians (7.9 per cent), Germans (4.1 per cent), Jews (4 per cent), Ukrainians and Ruthenes (3.2 per cent), Russians (2.3 per cent), Bulgarians (2 per cent), Gypsies (1.5 per cent) and others.

The loss of territories in 1940 to the Soviet Union and Bulgaria had a significant impact on the Romanian population. According to the data of the 1948 census, the total population of Romania was 15.87 million people and the total area was 238,391 square kilometres. As compared to the 1930 census and considering the same places (the equivalent area), there was an increase in the total population of Romania by 1.59 million (for all the war casualties and population movements during and after the war – the deportations of Germans to the USSR, and the emigration of Jews to Palestine).

The general data indicate two main trends: an increase in the population during the communist period, with 23,151,564 people registered on 1 July 1989 (an increase of more than 7 million people after the Second World War); and after the fall of communism, a decrease and ageing process, as proved by the 2011 census which registered 20,121,641 people, two million less than in 1989.

The density of the Romanian population varied significantly between 1930 and 2011, with 61 inhabitants per square kilometre in 1930, 66.8 in 1948, 73.6 in 1956, 80.4 in 1966, 90.8 in 1977, 95.7 in 1992, 90.2 in 2002, and 80 in 2011. Romania is far less densely populated than countries such as the UK, France or the Netherlands; however its density values compare with those of countries like Spain, Austria, Ukraine or Bulgaria.

The main trend in the Romanian society of the twentieth century, just as in other emerging countries, was an increase in the percentage of the population living in urban areas. While in 1930, 20.2 per cent of the population lived in the towns and cities of Romania, the 1948 census showed a percentage of 23.4 per cent, which almost doubled over three decades, to reach 54.3 per cent in 1992. After the fall of communism, the percentage of urban population decreased – but not significantly, with 54 per cent registered in the 2011 census. These statistical data show that the main urbanization phase occurred during the communist regime. The main determinant of the increase in the urban population was migration from rural to urban areas, first as a result of the agricultural collectivization process, and then as a result of rapid industrialization (Murgescu 2010: 348–52; Ronnas 1984: 198–213). A significant natural growth between 1948 and 1966, due to the decrease in mortality in urban areas, also adds to these determinants (Mureşan 1999: 102).

Urbanization meant both an increase in the population living in existing urban communities, and a change of status by which some rural communes became towns. In 1930, 142 localities in Romania ranked as towns, with an increasing trend: 1948 – 152; 1956 – 171; 1966 – 183; 1977 – 236; 1992 – 260; 2002 – 265; and 2015 – 320. It is important to mention a significant administrative change that took place in 1968, namely the lowering of the population threshold necessary for a locality to be ranked as a town, from 20,000 people to 10,000. In 2001 (by Law no. 351), the population threshold necessary in order for a place to be ranked as a town was further lowered to 5,000 people.

Beside the general statistical aspects, several other explanations may be added: the increase in the number of towns was achieved by the transformation of larger communes into smaller towns, many of them being industrial centres; after the end of the collectivization process in 1962, there was an increase in the number of cities, as they were the main beneficiaries of internal migration: Bucharest, Braşov, Cluj-Napoca, Constanţa, Craiova, Iaşi, Sibiu, Timişoara and others. The only city with more than one million inhabitants is Bucharest. After 1996, in the context of accelerated privatization measures, the prevailing form of internal migration was from urban to rural areas. For instance, while in 1992 Romania had eight cities with more than 300,000 inhabitants, ten years later their number was six, with only three cities reaching that threshold in 2011 (Bucharest, Cluj-Napoca and Timişoara). Industrial towns such as Galaţi, Craiova and Oradea lost about 20 per cent of their population between the censuses of 2002 and 2011, in the context of the general decrease of the Romanian population; after 1990, the most dramatic decrease in the urban population due to de-industrialization occurred in towns with less than 100,000 inhabitants (the population decreased by a quarter between 2002 and 2011 in towns such as Oneşti, Lupeni, Vaslui, Bârlad and Piatra Neamţ). The population of these towns either migrated to the EU, or settled in villages and started living at the pace of a subsistence economy; the increase in the urban population is not equivalent to the urbanization of that population (in terms of lifestyle), as part of the urban population preserves many rural customs (such as animal breeding in rural-urban areas – i.e. areas of transition between urban and rural areas).

The general European demographic features concerning sex composition are also valid for Romania, since women have always outnumbered men, in an average ratio of 51:49 per cent.

Romania has an ethnic structure specific to European national states. The main ethnic group is that of the Romanians, who speak a Romance language. In the Greater Romania of 1930, Romanians represented 71.9 per cent of the total population, while if we look only at the area equivalent to post-Second World War Romania, the percentage of Romanians increased in 1930 to 77.9 per cent. In the January 1948 census, Romanians represented 85.7 per cent, and their share increased to almost 90 per cent of the total population in the 2002 census. Romanians are the majority ethnic group over the entire territory of the Romanian state except for two counties (Covasna and Harghita), where Hungarians are the majority group. People of other ethnicities and belonging to other religious groups live together with the Romanians.

Hungarians are the main minority group. They speak a Finno-Ugric language and are located mostly in Transylvania and Banat, particularly in the south-eastern part of Transylvania. At the beginning of the communist period, there were 1.5 million Hungarians and in 1977 an increase of 200,000 people was recorded. Romania's return to democracy and, consequently, to freedom of movement in Europe, has led to the decrease of the Hungarian population, with 1.22 million Hungarians registered in the 2011 census (6.5 per cent of the total population who declared their ethnicity).

Germans are the second historical minority group in Romania. They belong to several cultural groups, the most important of which are the Transylvanian Saxons and the Danube and Banat Swabians. Together, in 1930, they represented 4.1 per cent (745,421 people) of the total population of Greater Romania. In the 1956 census, which included the stable German population after the tragedies of the Second World War and deportations to the Soviet Union, 384,708 people were registered. From the beginning of the 1960s, the German community in Romania constantly decreased, as the leaders of the communist regime allowed emigration to the Federal Republic of Germany in exchange for certain economic, financial and diplomatic advantages. After 1989, attracted by the dream of a Western life, the ethnic Germans migrated massively to Germany, so that only 36,042 people were registered in the 2011 census. Those Germans who have remained in Romania form an ageing community, with an average age higher than that of other ethnic and religious groups.

Jews are the third historical ethnical and religious group living in Romania. They represented 4 per cent of the population of Greater Romania (728,115 people), with percentages above the national average in Bessarabia (7.2 per cent), Bukovina (10.8 per cent) and Crişana–Maramureş (6.4 per cent). As a result of the loss of Bessarabia and Northern Bucovina (including the town of Chernivtsi, with its important Jewish community) and the Holocaust created by Romania and Hungary, and after the migratory waves to Israel, only 138,795 Jews were registered in 1948. Their numbers kept falling as a result of migration to Israel and Western countries, with 10,000 people in 1992, and a community of approximately 3,200 in 2011.

Slavs (Russians, Ruthenes, Ukrainians, Serbians, Croats, Slovenians, Bulgarians and Poles) numbered 1.5 million people in 1930. However, this is not a true ethnic and cultural community, as the main feature connecting them is their belonging to the extended family of Slavic peoples, whereas both their languages and their religions set them apart (the Russians and Ukrainians are Orthodox, while the Slovaks are Roman Catholic and Lutheran). In 1930, the Ruthenes/Ukrainians represented one-third of the population living in Bukovina and 11.8 per cent of the population living in Bessarabia, whereas Russians represented 10 per cent of the population in Bessarabia. Bulgarians represented one-quarter of the population of Dobrogea. After the territorial changes in 1940 and the movements of population during and after the Second World War, the share of the Slavic group decreased significantly. Ukrainians are a group living in the north of Romania, in areas near the Ukrainian border. The highest number of Ukrainians was registered in the 1992 census (65,472 people); this community was also affected by the demographic decline of Romania after 1989. Unlike the Germans, who preferred to emigrate massively, Ukrainians stayed in Romania, as the Soviet Union (and, afterwards, Ukraine) were not attractive for immigrants. The Lipovan Russians are a community of less than 25,000 people (in the 2011 census), living mainly in Dobrogea.

The Mongol–Turkic–Turanic family is represented in Romania by smaller communities of Turks and Tatars. In 2011, these two ethnic groups comprised approximately 50,000 people, living mostly in Dobrogea.

A special community is that of the Gypsies, who are first mentioned in documents dating from the fourteenth century, and were set free from slavery in the mid-nineteenth century. The registration of Gypsies in censuses has proved difficult, as part of this racial community assume other identities (Romanian, or even Hungarian in Transylvania), which are perceived as having a higher social status. While the 1948 census showed a total of 53,425 Roma people, their number increased to 227,398 in 1977 and 535,140 in 2002, to exceed 600,000 in 2011. The growth of the Roma population cannot be explained only by its increased birth rate, as we must also take into account the abovementioned issue of assuming an ethnical and cultural identity that is perceived to be less prestigious (Achim 2004b: 212–18).

Another important social and demographic factor are those belonging to a religious group. It is difficult to make a detailed quantitative analysis here, because there are no official records in the censuses organized during the communist period (Gog and Herțeliu 2012: 341–3). However, if we take as a reference point the 1930 census, we can estimate the dynamics of the main religious groups. The majority religious group is Orthodox which had 72 per cent of Romanian citizens in 1930. Not all Orthodox people are Romanian, as they also include Ukrainians, Russians and Serbs, within their various churches. After the fall of communism, the Christian Orthodox group comprises more than 80 per cent of Romanian citizens. The second important religious group in Romania is the Catholic one, with its two branches, Roman and Greek-Catholic. The Greek-Catholics are ethnic Romanians from Transylvania, and during the years of Greater Romania they represented 7.9 per cent of the population. Due to the dissolution of the BGC in 1948, the Greek-Catholics disappeared from the official statistics. After 1989, despite the legal re-creation of the BGC, the number of its believers has never exceeded 1 per cent of Romania's population. The Roman Catholics are mainly of Hungarian ethnicity, but also include Romanians and Germans. In 1930, the Roman Catholics formed 6.8 per cent of Greater Romania's population. In the 1992 census, Roman Catholics accounted for 5.1 per cent of those who declared their religion, but their percentage had decreased by 2011 to 4.6 per cent.

The analysis of the denominational dynamics in Romania shows a dramatic decrease in the numbers of followers of the Jewish faith and Lutherans, at the same time as the decrease in the numbers of the Jewish and German ethnic populations due to emigration.

The ethnic and religious picture of Romania shows the dynamics of three categories of religious groups: those that are stagnating or are suffering due to demographic decline (Orthodox, Roman Catholic, Reformed, Muslim); those that are in a massive decline following political and administrative decisions (Greek-Catholic) or due to emigration (Jewish and Lutheran); and those that have increased significantly (the most important non-traditional Protestant denominations: Pentecostal and Baptist).

The category of agnostics or atheists has always had low percentages in Romania, as compared to other European states, with the highest value registered in the 2011 census: almost 40,000 people (0.2 per cent).

The correlation between ethnic and religious dynamics shows the deeply conservative nature of Romanian society, both in the twentieth century and in the first decades of the third millennium. Denominational and ethnic trends correlate, and renouncing a religion is relatively rare (usually occurring as a result of marriage). The main change among the religious groups has been from the Orthodox Church to the non-traditional Protestant denominations. With less than 1 per cent of the population identifying themselves as atheist or agnostic, Romania is one of the few remaining countries in which religion has a great influence. Belonging to a religion is not just a personal option; it is also an important feature of social conformity. Citizens formally assume belonging to a certain religious group (usually that of their family) for fear of being stigmatized. This religious fervour becomes apparent during the main Christian holidays (Easter and Christmas). Religious proselytizing, more visible in the case of the non-traditional Protestant denominations, has had limited success. Transgression of ethnic and religious boundaries (such as 'Romanian = Orthodox', 'Hungarian = Reformed') only occurs at a low-scale level, as ethnic and religious identity is a powerful instrument for social and cultural integration.

Secondary social and demographic information

The demographic transition theory comprises numerous demographic parameters to explain the long- and medium-term trends in a society. The demographic transition is the crossing from one stable regime of high fertility and mortality rates to another stable regime characterized by lower fertility and mortality rates (Mureşan 2006: 266–7).

Table 16.1 Romania's population by residence and sex composition (1930–2011)

	1930	1948	1956	1966	1977	1992	2002	2011
Total population	18,057,028* 14,280,729**	15,872,624	17,489,450	19,103,161	21,559,910	22,810,035	21,680,974	20,121,641
Urban area (%)	3,651,039 (20.2%)	3,713,139 (23.4%)	5,474,264 (31.3%)	7,305,714 (38.2%)	9,395,729 (43.6%)	12,391,819 (54.3%)	11,435,080 (52.7%)	10,858,790 (54%)
Rural area (%)	14,405,989 (79.8%)	12,159,485 (76.6%)	12,015,186 (68.7%)	11,797,449 (61.8%)	12,164,181 (52.4%)	10,418,216 (45.7%)	10,245,894 (47.2%)	9,262,851 (46%)
Male (%)	8,886,883 (49.2%)	7,671,569 (48.3%)	8,503,420 (48.6%)	9,351,075 (49%)	10,626,055 (49.3%)	11,213,763 (49.2%)	10,568,741 (48.7%)	9,788,577 (48.6%)
Female (%)	9,170,195 (50.8%)	8,201,055 (51.7%)	8,986,030 (51.4%)	9,752,086 (51%)	10,933,855 (50.7%)	11,596,272 (50.8%)	11,112,233 (51.3%)	10,333,064 (51.4%)

Note: *Total population of Greater Romania; **Romania's population calculated for the territory in 1948.

Source: processing of official data from the Romanian censuses.

Table 16.2 Ethnic composition of Romania's population (1930–2011)

	1930*	1948	1956	1966	1977	1992	2002	2011
Total population	14,280,729	15,872,624	17,489,450	19,103,161	21,559,910	22,810,035	21,680,974	20,121,641**
Romanians (%)	11,118,170 (77.9%)	13,597,613 (85.7%)	14,996,114 (85.7%)	16,746,510 (87.7%)	18,999,565 (88.1%)	20,408,542 (89.5%)	19,399,597 (89.5%)	16,792,868 (88.9%)
Hungarians (%)	1,423,459 (10%)	1,499,851 (9.4%)	1,587,675 (9.1%)	1,619,592 (8.5%)	1,713,928 (7.9%)	1,624,959 (7.1%)	1,431,807 (6.6%)	1,227,623 (6.5%)
Germans (%)	633,488 (4.4%)	343,913 (2.2%)	384,708 (2.2%)	382,595 (2%)	359,109 (1.7%)	119,462 (0.5%)	59,764 (0.3%)	36,042 (0.2%)
Jews (%)	451,892 (3.2%)	138,795 (0.9%)	146,264 (0.8%)	42,888 (0.2%)	24,667 (0.1%)	8,955 (0.04%)	5,785 (0.03%)	3,271 (0.02%)
Gypsies (%)	242,656 (1.7%)	53,425 (0.3%)	104,216 (0.6%)	64,197 (0.3%)	227,398 (1.1%)	401,087 (1.8%)	535,140 (2.5%)	621,573 (3.3%)
Ukrainians (%)	45,375 (0.3%)	37,582 (0.2%)	60,479 (0.3%)	54,705 (0.3%)	55,510 (0.3%)	65,472 (0.3%)	61,098 (0.3%)	50,920 (0.3%)
Lipovan Russians (%)	50,725 (0.4%)	39,332 (0.2%)	38,731 (0.2%)	39,483 (0.2%)	32,696 (0.2%)	38,606 (0.2%)	35,791 (0.2%)	23,487 (0.1%)
Turks (%)	26,080 (0.2%)	28,782 (0.2%)	14,329 (0.1%)	18,040 (0.1%)	23,422 (0.1%)	29,832 (0.1%)	32,098 (0.1%)	27,698 (0.1%)
Tatars (%)	15,580 (0.1%)	–***	20,469 (0.1%)	22,151 (0.1%)	23,369 (0.1%)	24,569 (0.1%)	23,935 (0.1%)	20,282 (0.1%)
Other minorities/people who did not declare their ethnicity (%)	272,804 (1.9%)	133,331 (0.8%)	136,465 (0.8%)	113,000 (0.6%)	100,246 (0.5%)	88,551 (0.4%)	95,959 (0.4%)	1,317,877 (6.5%)

Note: *The census data corresponds to the current territory of Romania; **The information concerning ethnicity was available for the census in 2011 for 18,884,800 people who declared their ethnicity; and the percentages were calculated based on that number; ***Turks and Tatars, taken together.

Source: processing of official data from the Romanian censuses.

Table 16.3 Romania's population by religious groups (1930–2011)

	1930*	1992	2002	2011
Total population	18,057,028	22,810,035	21,680,974	20,121,641***
Orthodox (%)	13,108,227 (72.6%)	19,802,389 (86.8%)	18,817,975 (86.8%)	16,307,004 (86.5%)
Roman Catholic (%)	1,234,151 (6.8%)	1,161,942 (5.1%)	1,026,429 (4.7%)	870,774 (4.6%)
Greek-Catholic (%)	1,427,391 (7.9%)	223,327 (1%)	191,556 (0.9%)	150,593 (0.8%)
Reformed (Calvinist) (%)	710,706 (3.9%)	802,454 (3.5%)	701,077 (3.2%)	600,932 (3.2%)
Lutheran (%)	398,759 (2.2%)	21,221 (0.1%)	27,112 (0.1%)	20,168 (0.1%)
Unitarian (%)	69,257 (0.4%)	76,708 (0.3%)	66,944 (0.3%)	57,686 (0.3%)
Baptist (%)	60,562 (0.3%)	109,462 (0.5%)	126,639 (0.6%)	112,850 (0.6%)
Pentecostal (%)	–**	220,824 (1%)	324,462 (1.5%)	362,314 (1.9%)
Jewish (%)	756,930 (4.2%)	9,670 (0.04%)	6,057 (0.03%)	3,519 (0.02%)
Muslim (%)	185,486 (1%)	55,928 (0.2%)	67,257 (0.3%)	64,337 (0.3%)
No religion – atheist (%)	6,604 (0.04%)	34,645 (0.2%)	21,349 (0.1%)	39,660 (0.2%)
Other religious groups/people who did not declare their religion, of total population (%)	98,955 (0.5%)	301,135 (1.3%)	310,174 (1.4%)	1,535,323 (7.6%)

Note: *The census data are for the territory of Greater Romania; **A religious group that was recorded in the 'and others' category. ***In the census of 2011, 18,861,900 people declared their religious group and the percentage for each group was calculated based on that number.

Source: processing of official data from the Romanian censuses.

The demographic transition started in the Kingdom of Romania around the 1870s (in Transylvania, it had started several decades earlier), with a significant decrease in mortality, and around the 1890s, fertility also started to decrease. The demographic transition lasted approximately 120 years and passed through several stages, from

1870 to 1991, a period in which mortality decreased from 35 per thousand to 11 per thousand, and fertility from 44 per thousand to 11 per thousand (*Evoluția mortalității* 2013: 8–11).

Fertility dynamics are a key element for demographic analysis. The period after the Second World War can be divided into several distinct stages. In the period between 1947 and 1955, fertility rates were high (23.4 live births per thousand inhabitants in 1947; 25.6 live births per thousand inhabitants in 1955), because, after the war, new families were created and existing ones procreated in circumstances of peace and relative stability. In 1955, abortion became legal in the Soviet Union (in the wake of the de-Stalinization measures) and, starting with 1956, the birth rate decreased significantly in Romania to reach a record low in 1966 (14.3 per thousand), as the country legalized abortion in 1957. The decrease in fertility in Romania was the consequence of several factors including the liberalization of abortion, resumption and completion of the agricultural collectivization process which deeply affected the rural world, pushing women towards industry and services and, subsequently, the increasing pace of urbanization.

In 1966, the communist regime adopted a pro-birth policy, forbidding abortion and discouraging divorce. In 1967, fertility increased abruptly to 27.4 per thousand, and then gradually decreased to reach 18 per thousand in 1980. Until the fall of communism, fertility varied between 14 and 18 per thousand. The restrictive pro-birth policy was a failure and its implementation led to many tragedies and an increase in infant mortality.

The transition period after 1989 had major effects on fertility, which decreased to 13.6 per thousand in 1990, reaching a historical minimum level in 2011, of just 9.2 per thousand. The decrease in the fertility rate after 1989 can be explained by many factors such as the disappearance of repressive legislation in the field of abortion, the general insecurity caused by the economic and social transformation, the migration of the fertile female population to Western European countries in search of better-paid jobs, female emancipation and the participation of women in economic activities outside their households, and the increase in the duration of studies.

Fertility was lower in urban areas, except in the periods between 1979 and 1985 and between 2009 and 2011, when fertility was higher than in rural areas. Here, the prevailing model was that of a family with two or more children. In larger towns, with more than 100,000 inhabitants, families prefer one or two children. The changes in fertility are correlated with a rise in the age at which women give birth to their first child, thus reducing the fecundity period. Fertility is also inversely correlated with the level of urbanization: it tends to be higher in areas with a higher proportion of rural communities in which the percentage of younger people in the population is above the national average. The trend changed after 2000, with the migration of the younger population from poor areas to larger towns and cities which offered greater job opportunities.

Closely connected to fertility are the dynamics of marriage. Between 1949 and 1958, they varied between 10 and 12 marriages for every thousand inhabitants, then decreased below 10 per thousand, to reach less than 7 per thousand after 1994 (*Evoluția natalității*

2012: 11–5). In the Romanian demographic pattern, the first birth usually occurs immediately after marriage, which shows that the institution of marriage is a powerful instrument for the social integration of individuals. Marriage also has a big impact on fertility. In the communist period, more than 95 per cent of children were born to married parents. Then, during the transition period, the Romanian family changed. The number of divorces grew rapidly and, consequently, the average duration of a marriage decreased (for instance 12 years for ethnic Romanians, 13 years for ethnic Hungarians). Also, the number of children born outside marriages grew, the highest rate being among young mothers living in rural areas.

The synthetic measure of fertility provides complex information on family models in society, the values of individuals and the level of social optimism. The mortality level, another important demographic parameter, comprises information on the quality of the social systems, the healthcare system and social stress in a historical period. Mortality had the following dynamics: between 1947 and 1954 it decreased abruptly from 22 per thousand to 11.5 per thousand; after 1960, the downward trend continued, with values between 8.1 per thousand and 9.2 per thousand; between 1970 and 1979 it was less than 10 per thousand people, while after 1991 it grew to more than 11 per thousand, with a peak of 12.4 per thousand in 2002. With a rate of 12 per thousand, Romania is among the European countries with high mortality rates.

Mortality is not evenly distributed by age or by territory. Male mortality is constantly higher than female mortality, even from birth. The 'male excess death rate' is present both in towns and in rural communities. The mortality of the rural population grew at a constant pace (from 9.2 per thousand in 1960 to 14.3 per thousand in 2012), as a consequence of the ageing process and scarcity of healthcare services in the countryside. However, mortality in urban areas grew from 7.7 per thousand in 1960 to 10.1 per thousand in 2012 (*Evoluția mortalității* 2013: 12–14). Mortality is above the national average in less urbanized areas with a higher percentage of elderly population. The main causes of mortality are circulatory diseases, tumours, and respiratory and digestive diseases.

The decrease in mortality after the Second World War, following the rapid expansion of healthcare services, the increase in the quality of life and the discovery of new drugs, was an important success for Romanian society. Just like other societies, Romania overcame the stage when the main source of mortality was represented by infectious diseases. The demographic statistics indicate significant differences between men and women, but with a systematic upward trend for both. Life expectancy dynamics by sexes are as follows: 1956 – 65 years for women, 61.5 years for men; between 1970 and 1972 – 70.9 years for women, 66.3 years for men; between 1989 and 1991 – 73.1 years for women, 66.6 years for men; between 2003 and 2005 – 75.5 years for women, 68.2 years for men; and between 2009 and 2011 – 77.5 years for women, 70.1 years for men. In urban areas, life expectancy is one to two years higher than in rural areas, for both sexes. At the European level, Romania has one of the lowest life expectancies (*Evoluția mortalității* 2013: 35–42). These significant differences in life expectancy depending on sex indicate the hierarchically unequal nature of the traditional Romanian family. The man leads the family; he is the main provider, the woman's role being that of managing the household and, implicitly, of raising and educating children. Social stress affects men more, women being more resilient and adapting better to long periods of social change. A possible explanation for men's lower life expectancy may be the consumption of alcohol and tobacco, which is higher in men than in women. Loneliness in old age is better managed by women, who succeed better than men in coping with the loss of a life partner.

The population growth rate (calculated as the difference between the number of live births and the number of deaths in a defined period) is a critical measure for a nation. The growth rate of Romania's population was positive during the entire communist period, with higher values in the periods with high fertility (1947–55; 1967–80). The year 1992 saw the appearance of a negative natural increase (–0.2 per thousand), which reached a peak value in 2002 (–2.7 per thousand). The negative natural increase after the fall of communism was determined by a combination between the decrease in fertility and the increase in mortality, as well as a high rate of emigration (Simion 2004: 45–53).

Population ageing is a complex demographic phenomenon that has reached worrying levels in Europe during recent decades. The ageing process consists in an increase in the percentage of the population over 60 to 65 years old and a decrease in the population aged between birth and 14 years of age. Romania's main demographic trends show the scale of the ageing process. In 1930 the population aged fifteen and younger represented one-third of the total population, whereas the population aged above 59 was only 7.4 per cent. In the context of the demographic transition, the percentage of people aged between birth and 14 constantly decreased: 28.9 per cent in 1948; 27.5 per cent in 1956; 26 per cent in 1966; 25.4 per cent in 1977; 22.7 per cent in 1992; 17.61 per cent in 2002; to reach 15.85 per cent in 2011. The percentage of people aged 60 and older gradually increased: 9.3 per cent in 1948; 9.9 per cent in 1956; 12.3 per cent in 1966; 14.4 per cent in 1977; 16.4 per cent in 1992; 19.33 per cent in 2002; to reach 22.3 per cent in the 2011 census.

The downward trend in the infant population, as a consequence of the decrease in fertility and the increase in life expectancy, which has led to the increase in the percentage of old people, is a vicious demographic process due to the imbalances it creates. If the percentages of old people and children were balanced (1:1), Romanian society would easily succeed in solving its demographic challenges. The rapid ageing dynamics of the Romanian population have alarmed demographers and other social scientists (talking about the 'demographic winter'), who have drawn attention to the dangers facing the pension system, the health system and the workforce market for the future (2030–50), as a result of population ageing (Ghețău 2007 and 2012). The situation is worsened by the constant decrease in the labour employment rate and the number of employees after 1990, so that the social security systems are faced with the risk of being able to provide only a survival allowance to the inactive population.

The education level of a society is a primary measure for the evaluation of a nation in terms of its human capital. Education is, undoubtedly, a critical factor of social mobility. By education, individuals are able to progress socially because, in modern societies, social mobility provides opportunities to those who have acquired a minimum level of education. The primary measure for the educational level of a society is its literacy level. The 1930 census showed a literacy level of 57.3 per cent for Greater Romania, which varied depending on residence area, gender and historical region. Among men, 69.2 per cent were literate, while literacy was at a much lower level (45.5 per cent) among women. The literacy level was 51.3 per cent in the rural environment, while in towns (where one-fifth of the population lived), 77.3 per cent of the inhabitants could read and write. The historical region with the smallest number of people who could read and write was Bessarabia (38.1 per cent), followed by Oltenia (49.5 per cent) and Dobrogea (52.9 per cent). The provinces with the highest numbers of literate people were also those with the highest level of urbanization: Transylvania (68.3 per cent) and Banat (72 per cent). At the beginning of the communist regime in 1948, illiteracy was still an important issue in Romania, the percentage of illiterates being 23.1 per cent, with the same differences among regions, between urban and rural areas and between men and women. Following an important political and administrative effort of the communist regime, the percentage of people able to read and write grew rapidly, and illiteracy was eradicated in 1956. The PCR considered the issue solved, so that the official statistics do not contain any information on the literacy level. Certainly, illiterate people continued to exist during the communist regime; however illiteracy was no longer a mass phenomenon as it had been reduced to the level of marginal categories, particularly among Roma communities.

Illiteracy returned after 1990 as an officially recognized statistical reality. To some extent, the figures reveal a reality that had existed before the fall of communism, as well as being a negative phenomenon of the transition period. In 2011, the population census indicated almost a quarter of a million Romanian citizens (1.36 per cent of the stable population aged ten and older) were unable to write, and were, at the most, only able to read. In fact, this indicated progress, since the illiteracy level had been 2.6 per cent in 2002, and 3.1 per cent in 1992.

The demographic pattern of literacy evaluated in 1930 has continued to exist after 1990. Women living in the rural areas of Muntenia, Oltenia and southern Moldavia have the highest risk of illiteracy. Poor levels of literacy in Romania after 1990 is significantly correlated with ethnicity, the highest percentage being among the Roma, as this ethnic and cultural community has no proper tradition of integration in the school system (Tarnovschi 2012: 18). Poverty and social exclusion are the second cause of the occurrence of illiteracy in present-day Romanian society. In fact, the current subsequent negative phenomenon is that of functional illiteracy (people who go to school but are unable to read and write well enough to fulfil the needs of ordinary life). The prospects for complete elimination of illiteracy from Romanian society are not very optimistic, as the recent economic crisis (2008–12) has amplified social exclusion and caused an increase in the phenomena of inequality, which negatively impacts the education system.

Migration

One important fact to mention is that Romania has never been the destination country for significant international migratory flows, either during communism or after its fall.

It is only since Romania started negotiations for joining the EU and became a Member State, that the numbers of people wanting to settle there for political reasons or seeking political asylum have increased. For instance, in 2011, 57,000 foreigners had legal stay status in Romania (Suditu et al. 2013: 137). Since 2000, Romania has become a transit country for illegal migration from the Republic of Moldova, Turkey, China, the Middle East and North Africa. The situation of Romania is in obvious contrast with that of Southern Europe (Italy, Spain) and north-western Europe (Germany, France, the Netherlands and the UK), which are under pressure from international migration flows.

During the communist period, internal mobility – mainly determined by social and economic processes – consisted in the flow of migration from rural to urban areas. A series of sub-stages can be identified: between 1951 and 1953, the predominant migration was from rural to urban areas, due to rapid industrialization; after Stalin's death, until 1958, migration to towns decreased, because the pace of agricultural collectivization slowed down; the villagers' migration towards towns was resumed after 1960, with increased levels after 1971, as a result of rapid industrialization (Sandu 1984: 93); after 1980, migration towards the big cities was stopped by the closing of the cities to new-comers. Following the adoption of mandatory placement of university graduates, a significant demographic trend developed – that of migration from urban to rural areas.

Internal migration resumed after 1989, in the context of the annulment of legislation forbidding settlement in large cities. Until 1996, migration from rural to urban areas represented the predominant mobility flow, but this subsequently reversed, going from towns to villages (Suditu et al. 2013: 83–5). The population that returns is mainly adult and elderly. Young people are still, after 1996, part of the rural to urban flow and their destination is cities with more than 200,000 inhabitants, which are also academic and business centres. One characteristic of internal mobility in Romania after 1989 is that men migrate more than women, both from urban to rural areas and vice-versa.

Remigration from the urban to the rural environment (that is the return to the countryside of people who previously migrated to towns) after 1990 can be explained as follows: a part of the retired population withdraw to villages in the context of the retrocession of land; the cost of living in towns is no longer affordable for families affected by unemployment and/or retirement, so the subsistence economy of the rural environment becomes a solution for categories affected by the transition to the market economy; the scarcity of new houses in the 1990s is solved by leaving one's home to one's children and grandchildren – parents/grandparents withdraw to a more affordable place with a lower cost of living in the countryside.

Commuting is an underlying phenomenon of internal migration. The imbalance between the supply of accessible homes in the urban environment and the demand of labour for industry during the communist regime led to the daily movement of large numbers of people. Commuting supported the development of road and railway transport, but its main effects are at the level of lifestyle. Through coming into contact with town- and city-life, individuals transfer urban customs and practices to the rural world (for instance, better hygiene). However, it is also true that the presence in urban life of individuals deeply connected to rural life confers a colourful style, full of contrasts, to towns.

International migration is a dramatic process for a nation if it takes place on a large scale, since the departure for good or for a long period of a part of the individuals who form a country's population weakens the nation's biological resources. Migration affects the medium- to highly-qualified workforce. Also, a nation's capacity for internal change decreases, as migration involves people who are strongly motivated to improve their social status.

During the communist period, Romania experienced the mass emigration of two historical ethnic and religious communities: the Germans and the Jews. Almost half a million Romanian citizens (230,000 of German ethnicity and 200,000 Jews) left Romania legally, based on agreements with the Federal Republic of Germany and Israel (Horváth 2012: 200). The attraction of life in democratic countries and the wish to reunite their families explains the massive exodus of Germans and Jews, who were once a constituent part of the Romanian nation.

After the fall of the Iron Curtain, the migration processes accelerated. In the first three years, the German minority that remained in Romania departed to reunite with their families or in search of a better life in a prosperous society. So did the Jews, who departed for Israel or the US. Between 1990 and 1991 tens of thousands of Hungarians left for Hungary, many of them never to return to Romania. Also in the first years of the democratic regime, hundreds of thousands of ethnic Romanians migrated, requesting the right to work in Germany or France (Ulrich et al. 2011: 22–3). During the first phase (1990–5) of Romanian citizens' international mobility, the migration rate was 3 per thousand inhabitants. The main destination countries were Israel, Germany, Hungary, Turkey and Italy.

Starting with 1996, a new phase of international migration of Romanian citizens began, due to academic scholarships for students and immigration of varying legality for work purposes. The main destination countries were the Western European countries mentioned above, as well as Spain, the US and Canada. The migration rate increased to 7 per thousand (Stoicovici 2012: 433–4).

The visa waiver for Romanians who wanted to travel within the EU starting from 1 January 2002 triggered a new wave of emigration, which thus reached a rate of 28 per thousand. The main country of destination was Italy (40 per cent of the total emigration for work purposes), followed by Spain (18 per cent) and Israel (6 per cent).

With Romania's accession to the EU, the migration of Romanians in search of jobs in Europe has continued and has increased, with 458,000 people registered for 2007. The purpose of this migration has been the search for jobs, and the main destination countries in 2012 were Italy (46 per cent), Spain (34 per cent), Germany (7 per cent), and the UK (6 per cent) (*Migrația internațională* 2014: 4, 16).

The massive migration to Western Europe after 2001 is equivalent to the large-scale migration of Polish people to Western countries, in the same context of the liberalization of movement or EU membership. Romanians and Poles have found an important source of prosperity in the money sent to their countries by those who have left to work in the West. The Romanian migrants send an important part of their savings to their families in their home country, in order to ensure their subsistence. One of the negative effects of the emigration of the active population is experienced by children who are left in the care of their grandparents or other close relatives if both parents have left to work abroad. The children of the 'deserted' or 'home alone' generation are paying the psychological cost of separation from their parents, with an increased risk of suffering psychological traumas.

An important mutation took place after 2007 as regards emigration. The right to work granted to Romanian citizens in several EU Member States for certain highly specialized jobs (engineers, IT specialists, doctors) opened the legal path towards a migration of the highly qualified. The 'brain drain' phenomenon started to affect Romania, with the most visible situation being that of physicians. According to the Romanian College of Physicians (a professional association), during the period between 2007 and 2014, 16,500 professional certificates were issued to be used abroad for work purposes. This is a significant number, if we consider that, in 2015, the total number of physicians in Romania was around 55,000. The long-term or permanent migration of doctors puts the already challenged Romanian medical system into a situation of crisis, because the number of highly-qualified medical staff is decreasing even more.

It is also important to state that emigration since 2002 has taken the form of temporary residence abroad without giving up Romanian citizenship (Sandu 2006). The outbreak of the economic crisis in Europe in 2008 has led, on the one hand, to a reduction in emigration to Western Europe and, on the other, to the return of some of those who had left during Europe's boom years (Stoiciu 2011). Besides, starting with 2011, a balance has been reached between those leaving for Western countries in search of a job and those who return to their families in Romania. The great unknown for Romania is how many of its 2.5 to 3 million citizens working abroad in 2015 (in Italy, Spain, Germany and the UK) will return to the country, to help balance the demographic deficit. The worst case scenario is that they remain in their countries of residence and bring their families to join them, thus worsening the demographic problems of Romania.

At the end of this section, it is important to state that Romania, by its demographic trends after 1989, follows the general evolutions in CEE, as a result of demographic decline and the ageing process. The second important statement concerns the transformations occurring within families: the transition from the traditional family, with many children and unequal relations between the spouses, to the modern family, with one or two children and a relation of equality between the parents. A third important observation is that macro-economic changes did not determine immediate mutations in the demographic behaviour of Romania's population. An increase or decrease in the nation's wealth (its GDP) does not automatically explain its demographic evolution. For instance, the decrease in fertility after 1960 occurred despite GDP growth, whereas the record negative natural increase in 2002 occurred during a period of economic development. Macro-economic dynamics are set against a background in which other explanatory factors exist. The political decision adopted in 1966 to ban abortion illustrates the important role played by non-natural decisions in the dynamics of the demographic processes. Also, starting in 2003, political measures have been taken to increase fertility (up to two years of paid parenthood leave), which has led to an increase in the number of births among employed women (the political purpose being to create a populous middle class, able to ensure society's stability). To summarize, after the Second World War, Romania's demographic history has witnessed two moments of rupture. The first occurred in 1966, following the communist party's decision to impose a pro-birth policy. The second, immediately after the fall of communism, consisted in the decrease in fertility and the progressive increase in mortality. The Romanian scenario reconfirms the fact that social and demographic trends are the result of a plurality of factors: social, political, economic and cultural. Demographic policies may have long-term results if action is taken not only to increase fertility, as happened during the communist period, but also to develop the educational and health systems and, equally important, the predominant values of society. Finding a balance between all these factors has proved difficult in Romania, irrespective of the political regime.

CONCLUSIONS

The main continuity element in the history of Romania is the feeling of geopolitical insecurity, derived from its position of being a Central European country in the neighbourhood of the Balkans and the Black Sea. Situated in a fragile and unstable geopolitical area, at the crossroads of the Russian, German, Turkish and, more recently, US vectors, Romania's elite constantly tried to ensure the security of its borders by avoiding a simultaneous conflict with two Great Powers. The unravelling of Greater Romania took place as a result of a temporary Soviet–German alliance in 1939–40. During the Second World War, Romania became closer to Nazi Germany in the hope of regaining northern Transylvania from Horthy's Hungary and Bessarabia and northern Bukovina from Stalin's Soviet Union, and thus entered the war on the Axis side. When the political elite became conscious of the danger of being occupied by the Soviet Union and losing northern Transylvania indefinitely, the Ion Antonescu regime was removed, and the German path was abandoned. In the course of a single day Romania reorientated itself towards the United Nations and, implicitly, towards Moscow. After the end of the war, Bucharest politicians renounced the Romanian claim on Bessarabia and northern Bukovina to reduce the risk of hostility from Stalin; the stake at the 1946 Peace Conference thus became a full recovery of northern Transylvania.

During the Cold War, especially from the 1960s, Romania envisaged playing the intermediary role between antagonistic blocs, repeatedly adopting singular positions within the Soviet camp (for example, refusing to participate in the invasion of Czechoslovakia in 1968).

At the moment of the unravelling of the communist bloc, Bucharest decision-makers were prudent in reaffirming the project of unification with Bessarabia (the Republic of Moldova), as they knew the initiative had neither US nor German backing nor the support of other European powers, least of all Russia's agreement. Additionally, the resurgence of Hungarian revisionism, with the objective of cancelling the Treaty of Trianon (1920), and the outbreak of the Yugoslav conflicts reinstated the issue of border security for the Romanian political elite. The consequence was a natural emergence of a quasi-consensus over the need for NATO and EU membership. Accession to these structures was mythologized, and they were considered the solution not only for security risks but also for social and economic issues. After NATO accession in 2004 and EU integration in 2007 it was noticed belatedly that Euro-Atlantic integration was only a means for modernizing the country and not an end in itself.

The project of restoring Greater Romania was never totally forgotten, even if it has never become a priority on the political and diplomatic agenda after 1990. The hope of a good number of Romanian elites is to accomplish a Greater Romania within the EU, following the Republic of Moldova's accession to European institutions.

The feeling of geopolitical fragility, deeply instilled in the Romanians' collective mentality, was also transferred to the state's political organization. Almost instinctively, Romanians are supporters of authoritarian leaders, as long as they are perceived as patriots. The countenance and functioning of the political system are influenced by the perception of insecurity which they consider can he compensated for by entrusting power to authoritarian and paternalist leaders. Communist dictators Gheorghe Gheorghiu-Dej and Nicolae Ceauşescu managed to attract real popular sympathy, the latter being truly disliked only after 1980, when be subjected the population to cold, hunger and humiliation. After the fall of communism, the presidents who managed to gain at least two mandates by popular election were Ion Iliescu and Traian Băsescu, both political characters inclined towards authoritarian leadership. President Băsescu was popular until 2010, when he unilaterally decided to adopt the harshest austerity measures in the EU. Much like Nicolae Ceauşescu, he fell out of favour when he called on the nation to accept sacrifices on behalf of incomprehensible objectives. Having achieved the office of President of Romania as a result of accidental circumstances, Professor Emil Constantinescu proved to be too weak and hesitant and lost public trust; he gave up the idea of standing for a second mandate.

Romanians' cultural preference for authoritarian (and powerful) political leaders is deeply rooted in political and administrative institutions. It is well known that not all East European communist parties were equally rigid and centralized, and that a certain degree of internal autonomy was allowed, for example, by the Hungarian and Polish communists. The PCR was dictatorial not only for ideological reasons, but also because the arbitrary exercise of power was not opposed from within. After the fall of the communist regime, the most successful Romanian political parties were those associated with the image of authoritarian-paternalist leaders (Iliescu and Băsescu).

The predominant influence of the feeling of insecurity in Romania's history can also be understood by its attitude towards the Great Powers: Russia is very little appreciated by Romanians, while the US (considered a provider of security) is among the most valued countries. Russia's aggression against Ukraine in 2014 and its defiance of the rules of international law have confirmed not only the weakness of European leaders but also the historical fears of Romanians regarding the Russian threat.

The base of a country's power lies in its very demographics. Romania's population steadily increased during the twentieth century, the main tendency being an increase in the share of the ethnic Romanian element. The policy of the Ceauşescu regime distorted natural trends, and preempted a demographic crisis. The latter occurred around the 2000s, as a result of the combination between decreasing birth rates and an intensification of emigration processes. Population ageing is a manifestation of the demographic crisis. As a consequence, the social and health insurance systems are already under extreme pressure, which is predicted to become critical during the 2030s.

Complex societal processes can be illustrated by the collocation of 'two Romanias', which emphasizes the different development rhythms and the contradictory and irregular character of modernization. Romania is not a unique or exceptional case, but it reflects European societies that began the modernization race later. After the annulment of significant wealth differences through nationalization and collectivization, the communist regime set as its strategic objective the creation of a 'single Romania', by reducing regional disparities (mainly between west and east) and gaps between urban and rural areas. The communist social engineering project was centralized and enforced by the instruments of a dictatorial state. After 1989 the 'single Romania' project was mainly assumed by progressive (social democratic) forces, which added to the previous two dimensions a third: reducing social polarization by fiscal instruments. Liberal and conservative political forces did not acquiesce in the idea of social engineering undertaken by the state, starting from the premise that society is self-regulating and individuals must be left (according to a neo-Darwinian logic) to fight for survival and wealth, without any regulating state intervention.

The historical, traditional 'first Romania', predominates at rural level. It is characterized, in its main features, by conservatism, above-average religious belief, poverty, illiteracy, and limited access to the health system and modern means of information. It is poor, marginalized and ignored.

'The second Romania' is the creation of successive waves of modernization. It is located predominantly, but not exclusively, in urban areas. Life expectancy in this Romania is higher, life is better, access to the health system and mass media is easier. It is, however, an ideologically fragmented, multi-level Romania, being often frustrated and unstable in its electoral behaviour. It is not a more virtuous Romania; it is just different, luckier by virtue of its historical destiny.

Between the 'two Romanias' are several grey areas, in which features of the two are eclectically and incoherently intermingled. This is an 'atypical Romania' of social neurosis, in which individuals are searching for their identity and purpose; their lives are often consumed by this search.

There is also 'another Romania' of those outside its borders, made up of Romanian-speakers in the Republic of Moldova, Ukraine and Serbia, and Romanians born in the country but who have left for economic or political reasons. It is also a 'bipolar Romania', divided between those who have accumulated an immense frustration, as they could not find a purpose within the country's borders or were forced to leave, and the other part, in the East, unhappy with the fact that those borders stubbornly remain just as they were after the Paris Peace Treaty of 1947.

Tensions and rifts between these multiple and contradictory Romanias are not only the substance of the nation's dynamics but also the cause of political conflicts and, often, of the situation of anomie. The Romanian nation is at the same time an organic community based on relative uniformity of biological features, language and religion, but also an imagined one, the result of the activities of elites, who envisaged national unity by describing a tragic and glorious past, populated by characters who had supposedly fought ever since the Middle Ages for the ideal of national unity. In spite of historians' recent steps towards exposing the mythologized history of the Romanian nation, at popular level the 'Heroes' are vibrant characters who have their own reality in social memory.

At the economic level, Romania tried to overcome its status as an agrarian country and to become an industrial-agrarian nation. During the communist regime, a broad process of industrialization and subsequent urbanization took place. Industrialization was carried out at a forced pace, by a high rate of investments, being ideologically motivated (the defeat of the capitalist system). Trying to develop as many industrial sectors as possible, Nicolae Ceaușescu ended up wasting national resources. The economic collapse of Romanian communism was due to inefficient use of resources and technological backwardness compared to the West; it was also the result of fully repaying the country's foreign debt at an accelerated pace. After 1989, Romania's economy saw an emphatic decline. The dissolution of COMECON led to the collapse of the traditional foreign markets of Romanian industries. The transition from a command economy to a market economy was not a simple institutional-administrative process, but was the path by which in Romania, as in the rest of post-communist countries, a new 'primitive capital accumulation' took place. Strategic sectors (the banking system, energy, or key plants of heavy industry) were privatized by means of foreign capital, which became predominant in Romania's economy. Railway infrastructure quickly decayed for lack of state investment. There has been little motorway construction and the lack of an extended modern road network still hinders economic development.

The rural population went through the drama of quasi-total collectivization from 1949 to 1962. The main benefit of collectivization was the rationalization of agricultural land and the introduction of modern equipment. Extensive areas were drained and irrigated. After 1989, land was restored to its former owners, the consequence being a new fragmentation of farms and a return to subsistence agriculture, which had been widespread during the interwar period. The area of agricultural land remaining uncultivated quickly increased and a significant part of the irrigation system was destroyed. The agrarian issue is far from being solved in Romania, the main backlogs being an unsuitable property structure for a competitive agriculture within the EU and the lack of capital for agribusiness.

The communist social engineering project, which aimed at a quick increase in the resources allocated for education and health, for the purpose of their national spread, created until 1980 the appearance of escape from the pre-modernity trap. The debility of the social state, which remained at the level of constitutional desire and ideological project after 1989, threw the educational and health systems into a profound crisis. Deep economic polarization created by often fraudulent capital accumulation is visible in the existence of some private education and health institutions in big cities, which can offer high quality services, and of an underfinanced public sector, undermined by corruption and lack of interest.

As regards collective mentalities, it is difficult to identify a dominant tendency. The gender and sexual revolutions, which took place in the West during the 1960s and 1970s, occurred in Romania only after the fall of communism, as during the communist regime liberalization of manners was considered to be against 'socialist morality'. After 1989, one can witness a certain resurgence of individualism, because the perspective of prosperity and consumerist behaviour was suddenly opened up. The race after quick and primitive capital accumulation was glorified by the mass media in the name of 'free competition' and liberation from communism. Goods (cars, houses, jewels) do not have a utility value, but confer social prestige. The proliferation of supermarkets and shopping malls is not so much the consequence of the rationalizing of trading habits according to need, but reflects the hedonistic ideals of both the newly rich and the poor. Differences are only quantitative and not qualitative: while the newly rich possess the necessary resources to acquire an opulent prosperity, the poor can only dream about it and aspire to it. If 'moguls', 'oligarchs' and even the middle class are unhappy with the hedonist lifestyle which they can practise, the marginalized are systematically frustrated by the fact that the lifestyle and social security enjoyed by the victors of the transition is inaccessible to them. The post-communist world gradually became dominated by mistrust and frustration. The poorer strata cannot understand and accept the mechanisms of redistributing the nation's wealth, considering them to be not only non-transparent but blatantly fraudulent, while the 'winners', the new elites, want recognition of their status. As the losers of the transition seek refuge in collective protection mechanisms, the winners of the transition towards capitalism glorify themselves (at the same time looking for legitimacy) through radical individualism or even through economic libertarianism.

The strongest impetus for the proliferation of individualism in CEE was provided by the perception according to which any form of collectivism would belong to a past era. The idea of solidarity was thus discredited as a societal value and a social Darwinism was promoted, according to which the internal functioning of nations would follow the law of the jungle, the strongest and fittest being entitled to win. The social elevator was changed in order to be of use first of all to the individual and then to collective entities. Moral and political cynicism, which is seen as a sign of social intelligence, is the mechanism by which radical individualism is legitimized. In the conditions of anomie specific to a change of social system, individualism was considered the surest method for survival and/or prosperity, as collective mechanisms (state, communities) are not considered to be credible in providing assumed objectives (social security, the supply of goods and qualitative public service in a sufficient quantity).

Romania's cultural life is a product of elites for elites. The eradication of illiteracy during the communist period and the emergence of functional illiteracy after 1989 are important realities of Romania's socio-cultural life. In the communist era, cultural creation was decisively marked by socialist realism, especially during the first two decades, and thereafter by a national vein which often turned into nationalism (see the case of protochronism). After the fall of communism, the whole of cultural life consolidated its peripheral location within society, in the context of a lack of budget resources and of citizens' inclination towards individual economic accumulation. With regard to theme, cultural creation after 1989 was dominated by the issue of communist inheritance and the social anomy of the transition period. The mass media saw an explosive development after the fall of communism, influencing both consumer behaviour and the attitude of individuals towards civic participation. The media turned into a power instrument for the new post-communist oligarchy.

At the end of this incursion into Romania's recent history, the presentation of a single conclusion is risky. Romania's recent history, regarded from a broader perspective, contributes to understanding the huge puzzle of humanity, in which the Romanian nation takes its place as a particular case which can also be evaluated from the perspective of its singularity and of its common features with other European nations. This book is, in essence, just a modest attempt to understand the complexity of the history of humankind, through a case study: Romania, a country of Central and Eastern Europe, part of the Euro-Atlantic world.

MINI-BIOGRAPHIES

Antonescu, Ion (1882–1946). Career officer, *Conducător* (Leader) of Romania between September 1940 and August 1944. Under his leadership, Romania entered the war alongside the Axis Powers. After his removal from state leadership, he was arrested and sentenced to death for war crimes.

Apostol, Gheorghe (1913–2010). Communist political leader, First Secretary of the PMR for a short period of time (1954–5). Seen as a potential competitor, Apostol was removed by Ceaușescu from the top of the PCR in 1969.

Băsescu, Traian (b. 1951). Social democratic, then neo-conservative, politician, President of Romania (2004–14). During his first mandate, Romania joined the EU.

Blaga, Lucian (1895–1961). Philosopher, poet and playwright, the most important creator of a philosophical system in Romanian culture. During his lifetime, Blaga was censored by the communist regime, but was later accepted as an important thinker of the twentieth century.

Bodnăraș, Emil (1904–76). Communist politician and army officer. He held important political and administrative functions during the leadership of Gheorghiu-Dej, and had a considerable influence as a result of his direct relations with the Soviet secret services.

Brâncuși, Constantin (1876–1957). World-famous Romanian sculptor. Living in exile in France, Brâncuși was initially challenged by communist ideologists, but was later accepted by the regime because of his international recognition.

Carol II, King of Romania (1893–1953). Sovereign of the Kingdom of Romania (1930–40). He undermined the democratic regime by imposing his personal dictatorship in 1938, and bears a considerable share of responsibility for the crisis of the Romanian state in 1940. He died in exile in Portugal.

Ceaușescu, Nicolae (1918–89). Communist politician. He took over the leadership of the PCR in 1965, and after 1974 combined this with the office of President of the Republic. He tried to lead a skilful foreign policy but failed and ended up in international isolation. Domestically, after a stage of liberalization and prosperity, he imposed a severe level of control over society and living conditions deteriorated dramatically. Overthrown from power in December 1989, he was sentenced to death by shooting, together with his wife, Elena.

Comăneci, Nadia (b. 1961). Gymnast. She achieved the first score of 10 in the Summer Olympic Games (Montreal, 1976), and she won five Olympic gold medals during her career.

Constantinescu, Emil (b. 1939). Christian democratic politician, President of Romania (1996–2000). During his mandate, Romania was invited to start EU accession negotiations.

Coposu, Corneliu (1914–95). National-Peasant politician. He was a political prisoner for seventeen years during the communist regime. As chairman of the PNȚCD (1990–5), he played an important role in Romania's democratization.

Drăghici, Alexandru (1913–93). Communist politician. He held important political and administrative offices during the leadership of Gheorghiu-Dej, and was the main coordinator of the communist repression undertaken by the *Securitate*. He was banished from the power circle by Ceauşescu in 1968.

Enescu, George (1881–1955). Composer. He was a well-known personality at international level. In 1946, he left Romania for good, choosing to live in exile in Paris.

Gheorghiu-Dej, Gheorghe (1901–65). Communist politician, leader of the party for two decades and Prime Minister of Romania (1952–5). Under his leadership, Romania was communized and satellized. He bears the responsibility for crimes committed by the state against 'class enemies'. In 1964 he decided to liberate all political prisoners. A close follower of Stalinism, he coordinated the collectivization of agriculture and the process of industrialization. After 1960 he adopted a policy of autonomy towards the USSR.

Goma, Paul (b. 1935). Writer. He became an anti-communist dissident. After publicly expressing his adherence to Charter 77, he was arrested and forced to emigrate to France in 1977.

Groza, Petru (1884–1958). Left-wing politician who became an instrument of the communist takeover. He was prime minister of Romania between 1945 and 1952, then President of the Grand National Assembly Presidium, a position similar to that of head of state. He was head of government without being a PCR member, being accepted as a façade leader.

Hagi, Gheorghe (b. 1965). Football player and captain of Romania's national team. He played for Steaua Bucharest, Real Madrid, Barcelona and Galatasaray.

Iliescu, Ion (b. 1930). Left-wing politician, consecrated during the communist period, with an important role during the 1989 Revolution. He was President of Romania in 1989–96 and 2000–4. During his terms in office, Romania became a member of the CoE and NATO and finalized EU accession negotiations.

Isărescu, Mugur (b. 1949). Economist. Governor of the National Bank of Romania from 1990. He was Prime Minister of Romania between 1999 and 2000. He is a member of the Trilateral Commission.

Maniu, Iuliu (1873–1953). National-Peasant politician, leader of the PNȚ and prime minister of several governments during the interwar period. A strong defender of democracy, he became one of the most important opponents of communism. He was arrested in 1947 following a setup and sentenced to life imprisonment. He died in the Sighet penitentiary.

Markó, Béla (b. 1951). Ethnic Hungarian politician, he was President of the UDMR between 1993 and 2011, and minister in several cabinets. He made an important contribution towards settling the minorities issue in Romania.

Maurer, Ion Gheorghe (1902–2000). Communist politician and lawyer. He held important political and administrative offices. As prime minister of Romania between 1961 and 1974, he supported Ceaușescu in consolidating his power. He was one of the authors of Romania's policy of autonomy within the Soviet bloc.

Michael I, King of Romania (b. 1921). Sovereign of the Kingdom of Romania (1927–30, 1940–7), he made an essential contribution towards removing Romania from the war against the United Nations. He unsuccessfully tried to stop the sovietization of Romania. He was removed from power after the Cold War intensified in 1947. After 1989 he did not have the necessary support to return as head of state.

Năstase, Adrian (b. 1950). Social democratic politician and leader of the PSD, Prime Minister of Romania between 2000 and 2004. During his mandate, Romania joined NATO and finalized its EU accession negotiations.

Nicolaescu, Sergiu (1930–2013). Director and actor. He produced fifty-four movies, which were very popular in Romania and abroad. The most well-known of them deal with episodes in the history of the Romanian people.

Paraschiv, Vasile (1928–2011). A mechanical worker, he wanted to establish a free trade union in 1979, but was investigated by the *Securitate* and placed under house arrest.

Patzaichin, Ivan (b. 1949). Canoeist. He won four gold medals at the Summer Olympics of 1968, 1972, 1980 and 1984.

Pauker, Ana (1893–1960). Communist politician, who held important political and administrative functions (including that of Foreign Minister) during the leadership of Gheorghiu-Dej. She was removed from the leadership in 1952.

Popescu-Tăriceanu, Călin (b. 1952). Liberal politician and PNL leader, Prime Minister of Romania between 2004 and 2008. During his mandate, Romania joined the EU (2007).

Roman, Petre (b. 1946). Social democratic, then liberal, politician. One of the leaders of the 1989 Revolution, he became leader of the FSN. He took the first measures for democratization and the transition to market economy.

Sadoveanu, Mihail (1880–1961). Prolific writer and collaborator of the communist regime. He published novels in the social realism style.

Văcăroiu, Nicolae (b. 1943). Economist. A former member of the communist technocracy, he was prime minister of Romania between 1992 and 1996. His time in office was characterized by a stagnation in the democratization of Romanian society.

BIBLIOGRAPHY

Abraham, F. (1999). 'Discursul politic despre Europa Centrală. Studiu de caz: Ion Iliescu', *Analele Universității din Oradea. Seria Drept*, VII, 308–19.

Abraham, F. (2006a). *România de la comunism la capitalism (1989–2004). Sistemul politic.* Bucharest: Tritonic.

Abraham, F. (2006b). *Transformarea României (1989–2006). Rolul factorilor externi.* Bucharest: INST.

Abraham, F. (2007). 'Social-democratizarea stângii românești. Studiu de caz: Partidul Social Democrat', V. Ciobanu and S. Radu eds., *Partide politice și minorități naționale din România în secolul XX.* Vol. II. Sibiu: Techno Media, 236–52.

Abraham, F. (2013). *Provocări epistemologice ale totalitarismului: o metodologie a studiului regimurilor comuniste.* Bucharest: Editura Muzeului Național al Literaturii Române.

Abraham, F. (2014). 'A colabora și a pedepsi. Democrație și justiție de tranziție în România', *Arhivele totalitarismului*, 84–85(3–4), 142–64.

Achim, V. ed. (2004a). *Documente privind deportarea țiganilor în Transnistria.* Vol. I–II. Bucharest: Editura Enciclopedică.

Achim, V. (2004b). *The Roma in Romanian history.* Budapest: Central European University Press.

Achim, V. (2010). 'Încercarea romilor din România de a obține statutul de naționalitate conlocuitoare (1948–1949)', *Revista istorică*, 21(5–6), 449–65.

Achim, V. ed. (2013). *Politica regimului Antonescu față de cultele neoprotestante. Documente.* Iași: Polirom.

Adameșteanu, G. (2014). *Anii romantici.* Iași: Polirom.

Administrația Națională a Penitenciarelor (2011). Document de politică publică privind îmbunătățirea condițiilor de detenție. Bucharest.

Administrația Prezidențială (2008). Raportul Comisiei prezidențiale pentru analiza și elaborarea politicilor din domeniul sănătății publice din România. Bucharest.

Administrația Prezidențială (2009a). Raportul Comisiei prezidențiale pentru patrimoniul construit, siturile istorice și naturale. Bucharest.

Administrația Prezidențială (2009b). Riscuri și inechități sociale în România. Bucharest.

Administrația Prezidențială (2013). Cadrul național strategic pentru dezvoltarea durabilă a sectorului agroalimentar și a spațiului rural românesc în perioada 2014–2020 – 2030. Cadrul strategic național rural. Bucharest.

Alexandrescu, I. (2007). *Recensămintele României. Mica enciclopedie.* Bucharest: Meronia.

Allin S. and P. Mladovsky eds. (2008). 'Romania: Health system review', *Health Systems in Transition*, 10(3), 1–172.

Analiza funcțională a sectorului justiției din România (2013). Bucharest: Guvernul României-Banca Mondială.

Analiza funcțională a sectorului sănătate în România (2012). Bucharest: Banca Mondială. Regiunea Europa și Asia Centrală.

Ancel, J. (2012). *The History of the Holocaust in Romania.* Lincoln: University of Nebraska Press.

Andreescu, F. (2013). *From Communism to Capitalism: Nation and State in Romanian Cultural Production.* New York: Palgrave Macmillan.

Andreescu, G. (2003). *Extremismul de dreapta în România.* Cluj-Napoca: Editura CRDE.

Andreescu, M.M. and I. Bucur (2009). *Revoluția română în București (21 decembrie 1989–8 februarie 1990).* Cluj-Napoca: Mega.

Andrei, Ş. et al. (2011). *I se spunea Machiavelli. Ştefan Andrei în dialog cu Lavinia Betea*. Bucharest: Adevărul Holding.

Andriescu, M. and S. Gherghina (2012). 'Discursul identitar maghiar în România postcomunistă', *Sfera politicii*, 20(5), 93–105.

Anton, M. (2007). *Ieşirea din cerc. Politica externă a regimului Gheorghiu-Dej*. Bucharest: INST.

Anton, M. (2013). 'Planificarea postbelică britanică pentru o nouă Europă central-răsăriteană (1940–1945)', N. Ecobescu ed., *România. Supravieţuire şi afirmare prin diplomaţie în anii Războiului Rece*. Vol. I. Bucharest: Fundaţia Europeană Titulescu, 43–75.

Anton, M. and I. Chiper (2002). *Instaurarea regimului Ceauşescu. Continuitate şi ruptură în relaţiile româno-sovietice*. Bucharest: INST.

Apostu, O. et al. (2015). *Analiza sistemului de învăţământ preuniversitar din România din perspectiva unor indicatori statistici. Politici educaţionale bazate pe date*. Bucharest: Editura Universitară.

Arsene, M. (1997). *Un tablou uriaş arde. Dosar 'Braşov, 15 noiembrie 1987'*. Vol. I–II. Braşov: Erasman.

Asmus, R. (2002). *Opening NATO's Door. How the Alliance Remade Itself for a New Era*. New York: Columbia University Press.

Asmus, R.D. ed. (2006). *Next Steps in Forging a Euroatlantic.Strategy for the Wider Black Sea*. Washington: German Marshall Fund of the United States.

Asmus, R.D., D. Dimitrov and J. Forbrig (2004). *A new Euro-Atlantic strategy for the Black Sea region*. Washington: German Marshall Fund of the United States.

Aurescu, B. ed. (2014). *Romania and the International Court of Justice*. Bucharest: Hamangiu.

Autoritatea Electorală Permanentă (2013). *Evoluţia reprezentării femeilor în Parlamentul României*. Bucharest.

Avocatul Poporului (2015). *Avocatul Poporului. Raport de activitate pentru anul 2014*. Bucharest.

Axenciuc, V. (2012). *Produsul Intern Brut al României (1862-2000). Serii statistice seculare şi argumente metodologice*. Vol. I. Bucharest: Editura Economică.

Bădescu, G., P. Sum and E.M. Uslaner (2004). 'Civil Society Development and Democratic Values in Romania and Moldova', *East European Politics and Societies*, 18(2), 316–41.

Ban, C. (2012). 'Sovereign Debt, Austerity, and Regime Change: The Case of Nicolae Ceausescu's Romania', *East European Politics and Societies and Cultures*, 26(4), 743–76.

Ban, C. (2014). *Dependenţă şi dezvoltare. Economia politică a capitalismului românesc*. Cluj-Napoca: Tact.

Ban, C. and D. Gabor (2014). *Recalibrarea înţelepciunii convenţionale: o analiză aprofundată a relaţiilor dintre România şi FMI*. Bucharest: Friedrich Ebert Foundation.

Banu, F. (2004). *Asalt asupra economiei României: de la Solagra la SOVROM (1936–1956)*. Bucharest: Nemira.

Banu, F. (2009). 'O critică a izvoarelor privind numărul victimelor regimului comunist', *Arhivele totalitarismului*, 17(1–2), 77–100.

Barabaroşie, A. and O. Nantoi eds. (2004). *Aspects of the Transnistrian Conflict*. Chişinău: Institutul de Politici Publice.

Barbu, D. (1999). *Republica absentă. Politică şi societate în România postcomunistă*. Bucharest: Nemira.

Bărbulescu, E. ed. (2009). *Documente privind politica sanitară în România (1948–1964)*. Cluj-Napoca: Editura Mega.

Barisitz, S. (2008). *Banking in Central and Eastern Europe 1980-2006*. London: Routledge.

Barometrul de consum cultural. Cultura şi noile tehnologii, între sedentarism şi activism cultural (2014). Bucharest: Institutul Naţional pentru Cercetare şi Formare Culturală.

Barometrul de consum cultural 2014. Cultura, între global şi local (2015). Bucharest: Institutul Naţional pentru Cercetare şi Formare Culturală.

Baya, A. (2009). *The Concentration of Media Ownership in Romania*. Iaşi: Institutul European.

Bibliography

Belli, N. (2000). *Tranziția – mai grea decât un război. România 1990–2000.* Bucharest: Expert.

Berindei, M., A. Combes and A. Planche (1991). *România, cartea albă. 13–15 iunie 1990.* Bucharest: Humanitas.

Betea, L. (1997). *Alexandru Bârlădeanu despre Dej, Ceaușescu și Iliescu: convorbiri.* Bucharest: Evenimentul Românesc.

Betea, L. (2011). *Lucrețiu Pătrășcanu. Moartea unui lider comunist.* Bucharest: Curtea Veche.

Betea, L. et al. (2012). *Lungul drum spre nicăieri. Germanii din România deportați în URSS.* Târgoviște: Cetatea de Scaun.

Blokker, P. (2013). *New Democracies in Crisis? A Comparative Constitutional Study of the Czech Republic, Hungary, Poland, Romania and Slovakia.* Oxon: Routledge.

Blokker, P. and K. Kovacs (2015). 'Unilateral Expansionism: Hungarian Citizenship and Franchise Politics and their Effects on the Hungarian-Romanian Relations', E. Baseska and D. Kochenov eds, *Good Neighbourliness in the European Legal Context.* Nijhoff: Brill, 136–159.

Boda, I. (1999). *Cinci ani la Cotroceni.* Bucharest: Evenimentul Românesc.

Boia, L. (2001). *Romania: Borderland of Europe.* London: Reaktion Books.

Bold, E. and I. Seftiuc (1998). *Pactul Ribbentrop-Molotov.* Iași: Institutul European.

Bosomitu, Ș. and M. Burcea eds. (2012). *Specterele lui Dej. Incursiuni în biografia și regimul unui dictator.* Iași: Polirom.

Bottoni, S. (2010). *Transilvania roșie. Comunismul român și problema națională (1944–1965).* Cluj-Napoca: Kriterion.

Brătescu, L. ed. (2014). *Conservatorismul românesc. Origini, evoluții, perspective.* Iași: Editura Universității 'Alexandru Ioan Cuza' din Iași.

Brown, A. (2009). *The Rise and Fall of Communism.* New York: HarperCollins.

Brucan, S. (2004). *Profeții despre trecut și despre viitor.* Iași: Polirom.

Brzezinski, Z. (1997). *The Grand Chessboard: American Primacy and Its Geostrategic Imperatives.* New York: Basic.

Bucur, I. (2012). *Cartea represiunii 1989.* Bucharest: Editura IRRD.

Bucur, I. (2014). *Anul 1990: partide, ideologii și mobilizare politică.* Bucharest: Editura IRRD.

Buga, V. (2012). 'Partidul Comunist Român', D. Cătănuș ed., *România 1945–1989. Enciclopedia regimului comunist. Instituții de partid, de stat, obștești și cooperatiste.* Bucharest: INST, 402–69.

Buga, V. (2013). *Pe muchie de cuțit. Relațiile româno-sovietice (1965–1989).* Bucharest: INST.

Buga, V. and I. Chifu (2003). *România – Rusia: intrarea în normalitate.* Bucharest: NATO House.

Bugarič, B. (2014). 'Protecting Democracy and the Rule of Law in the European Union: The Hungarian Challenge', *LSE 'Europe in Question' Discussion Paper Series,* 79. London: LSE.

Burakowski, A. (2011). *Dictatura lui Nicolae Ceaușescu (1965–1989). Geniul Carpaților.* Iași: Polirom.

Burduja, S.I. (2015). *Între speranță și deziluzie. Democrație și anticorupție în România postcomunistă.* Bucharest: Humanitas Digital.

Buti, D. and A. Radu eds. (2015). *România între 'lucrul bine făcut' și 'Marea Unire'.* Bucharest: Pro Universitaria.

Buzatu, G. (2003). *România și Marile Puteri (1939–1947).* Bucharest: Editura Enciclopedică.

Calafeteanu, I. ed. (2003). *Istoria politicii externe românești în date.* Bucharest: Editura Enciclopedică.

Căliman, C. (2000). *Istoria filmului românesc (1897–2000).* Bucharest: Editura Fundația Culturală Română.

Caracota, C.R. (2011). *Sistemul bancar din România: realizări și perspective.* Bucharest: Editura Universitară.

Cârneci, M. (2013). *Artele plastice în România (1945–1989). Cu o addenda 1990–2010.* Iași: Polirom.

Carta Albă a sectorului ONG din România (2012). Bucharest: FDSC.

Case, H. (2009). *Between States. The Transylvanian Question and the European Idea during World War II*. Stanford: Stanford University Press.

Caşu, I. (2000). *Politica naţională în Moldova Sovietică (1944–1989)*. Chişinău: Cartdidact.

Cătănuş, A.M. (2014). *Vocaţia libertăţii. Forme de disidenţă în România anilor 1970–1980*. Bucharest: INST.

Cătănuş, D. (2011). *Tot mai departe de Moscova . . . Politica externă a României în contextul conflictului sovieto-chinez (1956–1965)*. Bucharest: INST.

Cătănuş, D. and G. Neacşu (1998). 'Componenţa PCR în perioada 1945–1970. Evaluări statistice', *Arhivele totalitarismului*, 21(4), 154–71.

Ceauşescu, N. (1971). *Propuneri de măsuri pentru îmbunătăţirea activităţii politico-ideologice, de educare marxist-leninistă a membrilor de partid, a tuturor oamenilor muncii*. Bucharest: Editura Politică.

Ceauşescu, N. (1978). *Politica internaţională a României de pace, prietenie şi colaborare internaţională cu toate popoarele*. Bucharest: Editura Politică.

Cernat, L. (2006). *Europeanization Varieties of Capitalism and Economic Performance in Central and Eastern Europe*. Basingstoke: Palgrave Macmillan.

Cernat, V. (2012). 'Ethnic Conflict and Reconciliation in Post-Communist Romania', O. Simić et al. eds., *Peace Psychology in the Balkans: Dealing with a Violent Past while Building Peace*. London: Springer, 17–34.

Cesereanu, R. (2003). *Imaginarul violent al românilor*. Bucharest: Humanitas.

Cesereanu, R. (2004). *Decembrie '89. Deconstrucţia unei revoluţii*. Iaşi: Polirom.

Chiper, I., F. Constantiniu and A. Pop (1993). *Sovietizarea României: perceptii anglo-americane (1944–1947)*. Bucharest: Iconica.

Chiriac, M. (2005). *Provocările diversităţii. Politici publice privind minorităţile naţionale şi religioase în România*. Cluj-Napoca: CRDE.

Chivu-Duţa, C. (2007). *Cultele din România între prigonire şi colaborare*. Iaşi: Polirom.

Cinpoeş, R. (2010). *Nationalism and Identity in Romania: A History of Extreme Politics from the Birth of the State to EU Accession*. London: I.B. Tauris.

Cioroianu, A. (2004). *Ce Ceausescu qui hante les Roumains: le mythe, les représentations et le culte du Dirigeant dans la Roumanie communiste*. Bucharest: Curtea Veche.

Cioroianu, A. (2005). *Pe umerii lui Marx. O introducere în istoria comunismului românesc*. Bucharest: Curtea Veche.

Ciucă, M.C. et al. eds. (1997–2008). *Stenogramele şedinţelor Consiliului de Miniştri: guvernarea Ion Antonescu*. Vol. I–XI. Bucharest: Arhivele Naţionale ale României.

Ciuceanu, R. et al. eds. (1997). *Misiunile lui A.I. Vâşinski în România. Din istoria relatiilor româno-sovietice (1944–1946). Documente secrete*. Bucharest: INST.

Cojoc, M. (2014). *The Totalitarian Experiments in Romania: The Danube–Black Sea Canal (1949–1953)*. Palermo: Italian Academic Publishing.

Coman, I. and P. Gross (2012). 'Uncommonly Common or Truly Exceptional? An Alternative to the Political System–Based Explanation of the Romanian Mass Media', *The International Journal of Press/Politics*, 17(4), 457–79.

Coman, M. (2003). *Mass-media în România post-comunistă*. Iaşi: Polirom.

Coman, R. (2009). *Réformer la justice dans un pays post-communiste: Le cas de la Roumanie*. Brussels: Editions de l'Université.

Conovici, I. (2009). *Biserica Ortodoxă Română în postcomunism: între stat şi societatea civilă*. Cluj-Napoca: Eikon.

CSM (2015). *Consiliul Superior al Magistraturii. Raport privind starea justiţiei 2014*. Bucharest.

Constantinescu, E. (2002). *Timpul dărâmării, timpul zidirii. Cărţile schimbării*. Vol. I–IV. Bucharest: Universalia.

Constantinescu, M. (1995). *Piaţa Universităţii – cine a trişat?* Bucharest: Convexus-2000.

Bibliography

Constantinescu, N.N. ed. (2000). *Istoria economică a României (1939–1989)*. Vol. II. Bucharest: Editura Economică.

Constantiniu, F. (1997). *Doi ori doi fac şaisprezece: a început Războiul Rece în România?* Bucharest: Eurosong & Book.

Constantiniu, F. (2001). *PCR, Pătrăşcanu şi Transilvania (1945–1946)*. Bucharest: Editura Enciclopedică.

Constantiniu, F. (2010). *O istorie sinceră a poporului român*. Bucharest: Univers Enciclopedic Gold.

Constantiniu, F. and I. Schipor (1995). *Trecerea Nistrului. 1941: o decizie controversată*. Bucharest: Albatros.

Constantiniu, L. (2010). *Uniunea Sovietică între obsesia securității şi insecurității*. Bucharest: Corint.

Convenția de armistițiu între guvernul român, pe de o parte, şi guvernele Uniunii Sovietice, Regatului Unit şi Statele Unite ale Americii, pe de altă parte (1944). Official Journal no. 219, 22 September.

Constituția Republicii Populare Române (1948). Official Journal, no. 87, 13 April.

Constituția Republicii Populare Române (1952). Official Journal, no. 1, 27 September.

Constituția Republicii Socialiste România (1965). Official Journal, no. 1, 21 August.

Copilaş, E. (2015). *Națiunea socialistă. Politica identității în Epoca de Aur*. Iaşi: Polirom.

Corneanu, C. (2007). *Sub povara marilor decizii. România şi geopolitica marilor puteri (1941–1945)*. Bucharest: Scripta.

Costache, B. (2012). *Activitatea României în Consiliul de Ajutor Economic Reciproc (1949–1974)*. Bucharest: INST.

Crăcană, I. (2015). *Dreptul în slujba puterii. Justiția în regimul comunist din România (1944–1958)*. Bucharest: INST.

Cum recâştigăm democrația în România? Analiza protestelor publice (2012). Bucharest: Institutul 'Ovidiu Şincai'.

Curtea de Conturi (2013). *Sinteza Raportului de audit privind 'Situația patrimonială a fondului forestier din România, în perioada 1990–2012'*. Bucharest.

Dăianu, D. (2015). *Marele impas în Europa. Ce poate face România?* Iaşi: Polirom.

Dăianu, D. and B. Murgescu (2013). *Încotro se îndreaptă capitalismul românesc. O pledoarie pentru reforme, instituții incluzive şi o Uniune Europeană mai funcțională*. Bucharest: Friedrich Ebert Foundation.

Dam, K.W. (2006). *The Law-Growth Nexus. The Rule of Law and Economic Development*. Washington D.C.: Brookings Institution Press.

de Waele, J. M. ed. (2003). *Partide politice şi democrație în Europa centrală şi de est*. Bucharest: Humanitas.

Decizia no.160. File no. 2470/1/2012, ÎCJC, 20 June 2012.

Declinul participării la vot în România (2009). Bucharest: Friedrich Ebert Foundation.

Deletant, D. (1999). *Communist Terror in Romania: Gheorghiu-Dej and the Police State (1948–1965)*. New York: St. Martin's Press.

Deletant, D. (2004). 'The Security Services since 1989: Turning over a New Leaf', H.F. Carey ed., *Romania since 1989. Politics, Economics, and Society*. Lanham: Lexington Books, 503–22.

Deletant, D. ed. (2005). *In and Out of Focus. Romania and Britain. Relations and Perspectives from 1930 to the Present*. Bucharest: British Council.

Deletant, D. (2006). *Hitler's Forgotten Ally. Ion Antonescu and His Regime. Romania 1940–44*. London: Palgrave Macmillan.

Deloche-Gaudez, F. (2000). 'La réaction de la France à l'élargissement à l'Est de l'Union européenne' in *L'Europe centrale et orientale. Dix ans de transformations (1989–1999)*. Paris: La documentation Française.

Denca, S.S. (2013). 'Romania: A Black Sea Atlanticist', M. Baun and D. Marek eds., *The New Member States and the European Union: Foreign Policy and Europeanization*. London: Routledge, 175–89.

Diaconescu, I. (2003). *După revoluție*. Bucharest: Nemira.

Diaconescu, I. (2012). *Scriitori în arhivele CNSAS. Intelectuali urmăriți informativ, arestați, condamnați, uciși în detenție (1946–1989). Studii însoțite de anexe selectate din arhivele CNSAS*. Bucharest: Fundația Academica Civică.

Dima, C. (2009). 'Conflictul intraexecutiv în regimul semiprezidențial românesc. Primul-Ministru Călin Popescu Tăriceanu *versus* Președintele Traian Băsescu', *Sfera politicii*, 139, 44–54.

Djuvara, N. (2012). *Misterul telegramei de la Stockholm din 23 august 1944 și unele amănunte aproape de necrezut din preajma dramaticei noastre capitulări*. Bucharest: Humanitas.

Dobre, F. ed. (2003). *Bande, bandiți și eroi. Grupurile de rezistență și Securitatea (1948–1968)*. Bucharest: Editura Enciclopedică.

Dobre, F., F. Banu, L. Banu and L. Stancu eds. (2011). *Acțiunea, Recuperarea'. Securitatea și emigrarea germanilor din România (1962–1989)*. Bucharest: Editura Enciclopedică.

Dobrescu, P. (1997). *Iliescu contra Iliescu. Analiză din interior a campaniei electorale*. Bucharest: Editura Diogene.

Dobrincu, D. and C. Iordachi eds. (2009). *Transforming peasants, property and power: the collectivization of agriculture in Romania (1949–1962)*. Budapest: Central European University Press.

Dobrinescu, V.F. and I. Constantin (1995). *Basarabia în anii celui de-al Doilea Război Mondial*. Iași: Institutul European.

Documente privind Revoluția română din decembrie 1989. Activitatea Consiliului Provizoriu de Uniune Națională. Vol. I- III (2009). Cluj-Napoca: Editura Mega

Drăgan, I. (1993). *Comunicarea de masă și spațiul public în perioada de tranziție*. Bucharest: Academia Română.

Drăghicescu, D. (1996). *Din psihologia poporului român: introducere*. Bucharest: Albatros.

Drăgoescu, R. M. (2013). 'Transformări în sistemul de învățământ superior din România după 1990', *Revista Română de Statistică*, 3, 19–27.

du Bois, P. (2008). *Ceaușescu la putere. Anchetă asupra unei ascensiuni politice*. Bucharest: Humanitas.

Dumănescu, L. (2012). *Familia românească în comunism*. Cluj-Napoca: Presa Universitară Clujeană.

Dungaciu, D. (2005). *Moldova ante portas*. Bucharest: Tritonic.

După 20 de ani: opțiuni pentru România. Raportul social al ICCV (2010). Bucharest: Academia Română

Durandin, C. (2011). *Moartea Ceaușeștilor. Adevărul despre o lovitură de stat comunistă*. Bucharest: Humanitas.

Duțu, A. ed. (1999). *L'armee roumaine dans la Deuxieme Guerre Mondiale (1941–1945)*. Bucharest: Editions Militaires.

Duțu, A. (2000). *Între Wehrmacht și Armata Roșie. Relații de comandament româno-germane și româno-sovietice (1941–1945)*. Bucharest: Editura Enciclopedică.

Duțu, A. (2010). *Revoluția din decembrie 1989. Cronologie*. Craiova: Editura SITECH.

Edwards, R. (2006). *White Death: Russia's War on Finland (1939–40)*. London: Weidenfeld & Nicolson.

Eliade, P. (2000). *Influența franceză asupra spiritului public în România*. Bucharest: Humanitas.

Enache, M. and D. Cimpoieșu (2000). *Misiune diplomatică în Republica Moldova*. Polirom: Iași

Evoluția mortalității generale în România (2013). Bucharest: National Institute of Statistics.

Evoluția natalității și fertilității în România (2012). Bucharest: National Institute of Statistics.

Eyal, G., I. Szelenyi and E.R. Townsley (2000). *Making capitalism without capitalists: class formation and elite struggles in post-communist Central Europe*. London: Verso.

Bibliography

Fătu, M. et al. (1985). *Teroarea horthysto-fascistă în Nord-Vestul României: septembrie 1940–octombrie 1944*. Bucharest: Editura Politică.

Feldman, M. ed. (2008). *A Fascist Century. Essays by Roger Griffin*. New York: Palgrave Macmillan.

Fischer-Galati, S.A. (1991). *Twentieth century Rumania*. New York: Columbia University Press.

Florescu, Gh.I. and C.M. Spiridon eds. (2000). *Iași, 14 decembrie 1989, începutul Revoluției române?* Oradea: Cogito.

Fosztó, L. (2009). *Colecție de studii despre romii din România*. Cluj-Napoca: Kriterion.

Fota, D. (2011). *Reforma reformei românești*. Bucharest: Editura Universitară.

Fox, J. and F. Godement, (2009). *A Power Audit of EU-China Relations*. London: ECFR.

Frumușani, D. and A. Saint-Jean (1992). 'Une presse en transition: le cas de la Roumanie', *Canadian Journal of Communication*, 17(4), 553–61.

Gabanyi, A. (2003). *Cultul lui Ceaușescu*. Iași: Polirom.

Gaddis, J.L. (2009). *Războiul Rece*. Bucharest: Rao.

Gallagher, T. (1995). *Romania after Ceaușescu: the politics of intolerance*. Edinburgh: Edinburgh University Press.

Gallagher, T. (1999). 'The West and the Challenge to Ethnic Politics in Romania', *Security Dialogue*, 30(3), 293–04.

Gallagher, T. (2004/2005). *Furtul unei națiuni. România de la comunism încoace*. Bucharest: Humanitas / *Modern Romania: the end of communism, the failure of democratic reform, and the theft of a nation*. New York: New York University Press.

Gallagher, T. (2009/2010). *Romania and the European Union: how the weak vanquished the strong*. Manchester: Manchester University Press / *Deceniul pierdut al României. Mirajul integrării europene după anul 2000*. Bucharest: All.

Gardner, L.C. (1995). *Sferele de influență. Împărțirea Europei de către marile puteri la München și Ialta*. Bucharest: Elit.

Geoffrey, R. (2002). *Victory at Stalingrad. The battle that changed history*. London: Longman.

Georgescu, A.A. (2011). *Foreign Policy change. The case of Romania*. Saarbrücken: Lambert Academic Publishing.

Georgescu, V. (1990). *The Romanians: A History*. Ohio: Ohio State University Press.

Gheorghe, G. and A. Huminic (1999). 'Istoria mineriadelor din anii 1990–1991', *Sfera politicii*, 67, 25–35.

Gherghina, S. (2015). *Party Organization and Electoral Volatility in Central and Eastern Europe. Enhancing voter loyalty*. London: Routledge.

Gherghina, S. ed. (2011). *Voturi și politici. Dinamica partidelor românești în ultimele două decenii*. Iași: Institutul European.

Gherghina, S. and M. Chiru (2013). 'Taking the Short Route: Political Parties, Funding Regulations, and State Resources in Romania', *East European Politics and Societies and Cultures*, 27(1), 108–28.

Gherghina, S. and S. Mișcoiu eds. (2010). *Partide și personalități populiste în România postcomunistă*. Iași: Institutul European.

Gherghina, S. and S. Mișcoiu (2013). 'The Failure of Cohabitation: Explaining the 2007 and 2012 Institutional Crises in Romania', *East European Politics and Societies and Cultures*, 27, 668–84.

Ghețău, V. (2007). *Declinul demografic și viitorul populației României. O perspectivă din 2007 asupra populației României în secolul 21*. Bucharest: Alpha MDN.

Ghețău, V. (2012). *Drama noastră demografică*. Bucharest: Compania.

Gilberg, T. (1990). *Nationalism and Communism in Romania: the rise and fall of Ceausescu's personal dictatorship*. Boulder: Westview Press.

Gill, G. (2002). *Democracy and Post-communism: Political Change in the Post-communist World*. London: Routledge.

Gillet, O. (2001). *Religie și naționalism: ideologia Bisericii Ortodoxe Române sub regimul comunist*. Bucharest: Compania.

Giurescu, D.C. (1996). *Guvernarea Nicolae Rădescu*. Bucharest: All.

Giurescu, D.C. (2007). *Falsificatorii. Cum a câştigat Partidul Comunist alegerile din 1946?* Bucharest: Rao.

Giurescu, D.C. ed. (2013). *Istoria Românilor. Volumul X. România în anii 1948–1989*. Bucharest: Editura Enciclopedică.

Giurescu, D.C. (2015). *România în timpul lui Gheorghe Gheorghiu-Dej*. Bucharest: Univers Enciclopedic.

Giurescu, D.C. and S.A. Fischer-Galati eds. (1998). *Romania: a historic perspective*. New York: Columbia University Press.

Gog, S. and C. Herţeliu (2012). 'Religia în societatea românească', T. Rotariu and V. Voineagu, *Inerţie şi schimbare. Dimensiuni sociale ale tranziţiei în România*. Iaşi: Polirom, 335–60.

Golopenţia, A. and D.C. Georgescu (1948). *Populaţia Republicii Populare Române la 25 ianuarie 1948: rezultatele provizorii ale recensământului*. Bucharest: National Institute of Statistics.

Grad, C. (1998). *Al doilea arbitraj de la Viena*. Iaşi: Institutul European.

Grosescu, R. (2006). 'Conversia elitelor comuniste din România în perioada de tranziţie:1989–2000', *Anuarul Institutului de Investigare a Crimelor Comunismului în România*, 1, 229–54.

Gross, P. (1999). *Colosul cu picioare de lut: aspecte ale presei româneşti postcomuniste*. Iaşi: Polirom.

Harbutt, F.J. (2010). *Yalta 1945: Europe and America at the crossroads*. New York: Cambridge University Press.

Haynes, J. ed. (2012). *Routledge Handbook of Democratization*. New York: Routledge.

Heinen, A. (1999). *Legiunea 'Arhanghelului Mihail'. Mişcare socială şi organizaţie politică. O contribuţie la problema fascismului internaţional*. Bucharest: Humanitas.

Heinen, A. (2011). *România, Holocaustul şi logica violenţei*. Iaşi: Editura Universităţii 'Alexandru Ioan Cuza' din Iaşi.

Hillgruber, A. (2007). *Hitler, Regele Carol şi Mareşalul Antonescu. Relaţiile germano-române (1938–1944)*. Bucharest: Humanitas.

Hitchins, K. (2014). *A concise history of Romania*. Cambridge: Cambridge University Press.

Horváth, I. (2012). 'Migraţia internaţională a cetăţenilor români după 1989', T. Rotariu and V. Voineagu, *Inerţie şi schimbare. Dimensiuni sociale ale tranziţiei în România*. Iaşi: Polirom, 199–222.

Hossu, L.A. and R. Carp (2013). 'The Multifaceted Image of the Romanian Ombudsman', *Transylvanian Review of Administrative Sciences*, 40, 71–95.

Hotărârile CEDO în cauzele împotriva României 2014. Vol. X (2015). Bucharest: Editura Universitară.

Iacob, M.C. (2005) 'Examen comparativ al unor Curţi Constituţionale europene', *Analele Ştiinţifice ale Universităţii Al.I.Cuza Iaşi. Ştiinţe Juridice*, LI, 191–200.

Iaţu, C. ed. (2014). *Atlasul electoral al României: 1990–2009/ Atlas électoral de la Roumanie: 1990–2009/ Electoral Atlas of Romania: 1990–2009*. Iaşi: Editura Universităţii 'Alexandru Ioan Cuza' din Iaşi.

Ifrim, N. (2013). *Identitate culturală şi integrare europeană perspective critice asupra discursului identitar românesc în perioada postdecembristă*. Bucharest: Editura Muzeul Naţional al Literaturii Române.

Iliescu, I. (1994). *Revoluţie şi Reformă*. Bucharest: Editura Enciclopedică.

Iliescu, I. (1995). *Momente de istorie I. Documente, interviuri, comentarii-decembrie 1989–iunie 1990*. Bucharest: Editura Enciclopedică.

Iliescu, I. (1996). *Momente de istorie II. Documente, interviuri, comentarii-iunie 1990–septembrie 1991*. Bucharest: Editura Enciclopedică.

Iliescu, I. (2004). *Marele şoc din finalul unui secol scurt. Ion Iliescu în dialog cu Vladimir Tismăneanu. Despre comunism, postcomunism şi democraţi*. Bucharest: Editura Enciclopedică.

Bibliography

Iliescu, I. (2011). *Fragmente de viață și de istorie trăită*. Bucharest: Litera Internațional.

Inglot, T. (2008). *Welfare States in East Central Europe (1919–2004)*. Cambridge: Cambridge University Press.

Ioan-Franc, V. (2000). *Din lucrările Comisiei de la Snagov, martie-iunie 1995*. Bucharest: Centrul de Informare și Documentare Economică

Ioanid, R. (2006). *Holocaustul în România distrugerea evreilor s#t11 romilor sub regimul Antonescu (1940–1944)*. Bucharest: Hasefar.

Ioanid, R. (2015). *Securitatea și vânzarea evreilor. Istoria acordurilor secrete dintre România și Israel*. Iași: Polirom.

Ionescu, A. (2002). 'La resurgence d'un acteur politique en Roumanie. Le Parti National Paysan Chretien-Democrate', *Studia Politica. Romanian Political Science Review*, 2(1), 141–201.

Ionescu, I. (1964). *Communism in Rumania (1944–1962)*. London: Oxford University Press

Ionescu, M.E. ed. (2013). *The Eastern Partnership: The Road So Far*. Bucharest: Military Publishing House

Ionescu-Gură, N. (2004). 'Verificarea membrilor Partidului Muncitoresc Român', *Arhivele Securității*, Vol. 1. Bucharest: Nemira, 326–34.

Iordachi, C. and A. Bauerkämper (2014). *The collectivization of agriculture in communist Eastern Europe: comparison and entanglements*. Budapest: Central European University Press.

Istoria fotbalului românesc. Vol. II (2011). Bucharest: Federația Română de Fotbal.

Istoria României. Transilvania. Vol. II (1997). Cluj-Napoca: Editura George Barițiu.

Ivan, R. (2009). *La politique étrangère roumaine (1990–2006)*. Brussels: Editions de l'Université de Bruxelles.

Judea, I. (1991). *Târgu-Mureș. Cumpăna lui martie. Val și ură*. Târgu Mureș: Tipomur.

Katz, R.S. and P. Mair (1995). 'Changing Models of Party Organization and Party Democracy: The Emergence of the Cartel Party', *Party Politics*, 1(1), 5–28.

Katz, R.S. and P. Mair (2009). 'The Cartel Party Thesis: A Restatement', *Perspectives on Politics*, 7(4), 753–66.

Keil, S. and S. Bernhard eds. (2014). *The Foreign Policies of Post-Yugoslav States. From Yugoslavia to Europe*. London: Palgrave Macmillan.

Kende, P. (1995). 'The Trianon Syndrome: Hungarians and Their Neighbors', B.K. Király ed., *Lawful Revolution in Hungary (1989–94)*. New York: Columbia Univ. Press, 475–92.

Kieran, W. and D. Deletant (2001). *Security Intelligence Services in New Democracies. The Czech Republic, Slovakia and Romania*. London: Palgrave.

King, C. (1999). *The Moldovans: Romania, Russia, and the politics of culture*. Stanford: Hoover Institution Press.

King, C. (2010). *Extreme Politics. Nationalism, Violence, and the End of Eastern Europe*. Oxford: Oxford University Press.

King, R. (1980). *A History of the Romanian Communist Party*. Stanford: Stanford University Press.

King, R.F. and C.G. Marian (2012). 'Minority Representation and Reserved Legislative Seats in Romania', *East European Politics and Societies*, 26(3), 561–88.

Kissinger, H. (2008). *Diplomația*. Bucharest: All.

Kligman, G. (1998). *The Politics of Duplicity: Controlling Reproduction in Ceausescu's Romania*. Berkeley: University of California Press.

Kligman, G. and K. Verdery (2011). *Peasants under siege: the collectivization of Romanian agriculture (1949–1962)*. Princeton: Princeton University Press.

Komine, Y. (2008). *Secrecy in US Foreign Policy Nixon, Kissinger and the Rapprochement with China*. Aldershot: Ashgate.

Kunze, T. (2002). *Nicolae Ceaușescu. O biografie*. Bucharest: Vremea.

Labour Market Developments in Europe 2013 (2013). Brussels: European Commission (Directorate-General for Economic and Financial Affairs).

Lache, E.I. (2012). 'Preparativele URSS de război împotriva României în ajunul notelor ultimative ale lui V.M. Molotov din 26–27 iunie 1940', G. Buzatu ed., *Bătălia pentru Basarabia (1941–1944)*. Târgoviște: Mica Valahie, 9–22.

Lache, Ș. (2013). 'Tratatul de pace între puterile aliate și asociate și România: clauze injuste și împovărătoare', N. Ecobescu ed., *România. Supraviețuire și afirmare prin diplomație în anii Războiului Rece*. Vol. I. Bucharest: Fundația Europeană Titulescu, 231–65.

Larrabee, F.S. (2003). *NATO's Eastern Agenda in a New Strategic Era*. Santa Monica: Rand.

Lazardeux, S.G. (2015). *Cohabitation and Conflicting Politics in French Policymaking*. New York: Palgrave Macmillan.

Leuștean, L.N. (2008). *Orthodoxy and the Cold War: Religion and Political Power in Romania (1947–65)*. London: Palgrave Macmillan.

Levy, R. (2002). *Gloria și decăderea Anei Pauker*. Iași: Polirom.

Light, L. and D. Phinnemore eds. (2001). *Post-Communist Romania: Coming to Terms with Transition*. New York: Palgrave Macmillan.

Linz, J.J. and A. Stepan (1996). *Problems of Democratic Transition and Consolidation. Southern Europe, South America and Post-Communist Europe*. Baltimore: Johns Hopkins University Press.

Lup, A. (2014). *Agricultura socialistă a României (1949–1989). Mit și realitate*. Constanța: Ex Ponto.

Magen, A., T. Risse and M.A. McFaul eds. (2009). *Promoting Democracy and the Rule of Law American and European Strategies*. New York: Palgrave Macmillan.

Maravall, J.M. and A. Przeworski eds. (2003). *Democracy and the Rule of Law.* Cambridge: Cambridge University Press.

Marin, M. (2014). *Între prezent și trecut: cultul personalității lui Nicolae Ceaușescu și opinia publică românească*. Cluj-Napoca: Mega.

Marinescu, P. (1999). *Managementul instituțiilor de presă: teorie, practică și studii de caz*. Iași: Polirom.

Marino, A. (2005). *Pentru Europa. Integrarea României. Aspecte ideologice și culturale*. Iași: Polirom.

Mâță, D.C. (2011). *Relațiile franco-române în perioada 1964–1968. Dialog în anii destinderii*. Iași: Editura Universității 'Alexandru Ioan Cuza'.

Matei, F.C. (2009). 'The Challenges of Intelligence Sharing in Romania', *Intelligence and National Security*, 24(4), 574–85.

Matei, F.C. (2014). 'Balancing Democratic Civilian Control with Effectiveness of Intelligence in Romania: Lessons Learned and Best/Worst Practices Before and After NATO and EU Integration', *Intelligence and National Security*, 29(4), 619–37.

Matci, S.A. (2004). *Boierii minții. Intelectualii români între grupurile de prestigiu și piața liberă a ideilor*. Bucharest: Compania.

Matichescu, M. and O. Protsyk (2011). 'Political Recruitment in Romania: Continuity and Change', R.F. King and P.E. Sum eds., *Romania under Basescu: Aspirations, Achievements, and Frustrations during His First Presidential Term*. Lanham, MD: Lexington Books.

Mendelski, M. (2012). 'EU-Driven Judicial Reforms in Romania: A Success Story?', *East European Politics*, 28(1), 23–42.

Migrația internațională a României (2014). Bucharest: National Institute of Statistics.

Mihalache, F. and Alin Croitoru (2011). *Mediul rural românesc: evoluții și involuții. Schimbare socială și antreprenoriat*. Bucharest: Expert.

Milin, M. (2009). *Timișoara. 15–21 decembrie 1989*. Timișoara: Saol.

Ministerul Agriculturii, Pădurilor și Dezvoltării Rurale (2009). Proiect de reabilitare și reformă a irigațiilor. Analiza economică a sectorului de irigații.

Miskimmon, A. (2007). *Germany and the Common Foreign and Security Policy of the European Union. Between Europeanisation and National Adaptation*. New York: Palgrave Macmillan.

Møller, J. (2009). *Post-communist Regime Change. A comparative study*. London: Routledge.

Monografia SRI 1990-2015 (2015). Bucharest: Rao.

Morar, F. (2000). *Systemes electoraux et systemes de partis. La production electorale du systeme roumain de partis*. Bucharest: Editura Universității din București.

Moraru, C. (2008). *Politica externă a României (1958-1964)*. Bucharest: Editura Enciclopedică.

Müller, F. (2003). *Politică și istoriografie în România (1948-1964)*. Cluj-Napoca: Nereamia Napocae.

Muraru, A. ed. (2008). *Dicționarul penitenciarelor din România comunistă (1945-1967)*. Iași: Polirom.

Mureșan, C. (1999). *Evoluția demografică a României: tendințe vechi, schimbări recente, perspective (1870-2030)*. Cluj-Napoca: Presa Universitară Clujeană.

Mureșan C. (2006). 'Demographic bonus or malus in Romania', I. Pool, L.R. Wong and E. Vilquin eds., *Age-structural transitions: challenges for development*. Paris: Committee for International Cooperation in National Research in Demography, 259-88.

Mureșan, M. (1995). *Evoluții economice (1945-1990)*. Bucharest: Editura Economică.

Mureșan, M. (2012). 'Economia României în anii socialismului. Un model de dezvoltare de tip extensiv', Ș. Bosomitu and M. Burcea eds., *Specterele lui Dej. Incursiuni în biografia și regimul unui dictator*. Iași: Polirom, 247-74.

Murgescu, B. (2010). *România și Europa. Acumularea decalajelor economice (1500-2010)*. Iași: Polirom.

Murgescu, M.L. and B. Murgescu (2010). 'Tranziție, tranziții: conceptualizarea schimbării în cultura română', V. Neumann and A. Heinen eds., *Istoria României prin concepte. Perspective alternative asupra limbajelor social-politice*. Iași: Polirom, 419-46.

Nasta, D. (2013). *Contemorary Romanian Cinema: The History of an Unexpected Miracle*. New York: Wallflower Press.

Năstase, A. (2006-11). *România după Malta. 875 de zile la Externe*. Vol. I-X. Bucharest: Fundația Europeană Nicolae Titulescu.

Năstase, A. (2012). *Lumea, americanii și noi*. Bucharest: Tiparg.

Naumescu, V. and D. Dungaciu eds. (2015). *The European Union's Eastern Neighbourhood Today. Politics, Dynamics, Perspectives*. Cambridge: Cambridge Scholars Publishing.

Negrici, E. (2010). *Literatura română sub comunism (1948-1964)*. Vol. I. Bucharest: Cartea Românească.

Oliker, O., K. Crane, L.H. Schwartz and C. Yusupov (2009). *Russian Foreign Policy Sources and Implications*. Santa Monica: Rand Corporation.

Olteanu, C. (1999). *România, o voce distinctă în Tratatul de la Varșovia. Memorii. 1980-1985*. Bucharest: Aldo.

Olteanu, C. and A. Duțu (2014). *România: 36 de ani în Tratatul de la Varșovia*. Bucharest: Niculescu.

Olti, Á. and A. Gidó eds. (2009). *Minoritatea maghiară în perioada comunistă*. Cluj-Napoca: Kriterion.

Oprea, M. (2002). *Banalitatea răului. O istorie a Securității în documente (1949-1989)*. Iași: Polirom.

Oprea, M. (2004). *Moștenitorii Securității*. Bucharest: Humanitas.

Oprea, M. (2008). *Bastionul cruzimii. O istorie a Securității (1948-1964)*. Iași: Polirom.

Opriș, P. (2008). *România și Organizația Tratatului de la Varșovia (1955-1991)*. Bucharest: Editura Militară.

Oprișan, M. (1951). *Planurile cincinale staliniste, exemplu măreț în construirea socialismului în R.P.R.*. Bucharest: ARLUS.

Oșca, A. ed. (2009). *Revoluția română în Banat*. Bucharest: Editura IRRD.

Otiman, I.P. (2012). 'Structura agrară actuală a României – o mare (și nerezolvată) problemă socială și economică a țării', *Revista Română de Sociologie*, 13(5-6), 339-60.

Overview 1959–2014 (2015). Strasbourg: European Court of Human Rights.

Panaite, S. (2012). *Redobândirea cetățeniei române: o politică ce capătă viziune?* Bucharest: Fundația Soros România.

Pântea, C. (2008). 'The Ethno-Demographic Evolution of Moldavian Autonomous Soviet Socialist Republic', *Codrul Cosminului*, 14, 169–204.

Papadimitriou, D. and D. Phinnemore (2008). *Romania and the European Union. From marginalisation to membership.* London: Routledge.

Parlamentarismul în România: diagnoză și propuneri de reformă (2011). Bucharest: Institutul 'Ovidiu Șincai'.

Pașcu, I.M. (2014). *Bătălia pentru NATO. Raport personal.* Bucharest: Rao.

Pasti, V. (1995). *România în tranziție. Căderea în viitor.* Bucharest: Nemira.

Pasti, V. (2006). *Noul capitalism românesc.* Iași: Polirom

Pavel, D. and I. Huiu (2003). *'Nu putem reuși decât împreună'. O istorie analitică a Convenției Democratice (1989–2000).* Iași: Polirom.

PCR (1965). *Congresul al IX-lea al Partidului Comunist Român (19–24 iulie 1965).* Bucharest: Editura Politică.

PCR (1969). *Congresul al X-lea al Partidului Comunist Român (6–12 august 1969).* Bucharest: Editura Politică.

PCR (1975a). *Congresul al XI-lea al Partidului Comunist Român (25–28 noiembrie 1974).* Bucharest: Editura Politică.

PCR (1975b). *Programul Partidului Comunist Român de făurire a societății socialiste multilateral dezvoltate și înaintare a României spre comunism.* Bucharest: Editura Politică.

Percepția opiniei publice din România asupra politicii externe și a relațiilor internaționale (2005). Bucharest: Institutul de Politici Publice.

Percepții asupra sistemului medical din România (2010). Cluj-Napoca: IRES.

Percepții privind activitatea ONG în România (2013). Cluj-Napoca: IRES.

Petcu, A.N. ed. (2005). *Partidul, Securitatea și Cultele (1945–1989).* Bucharest: Nemira.

Petcu, M. ed. (2012). *Istoria jurnalismului din România în date. Enciclopedie cronologică.* Iași: Polirom.

Petre, Z. and C. Durandin (2008). *La Roumanie post 1989.* Paris: L'Harmattan

Petrescu, C. (2013). *From Robin Hood to Don Quixote. Resistance and Dissent in Communist Romania.* Bucharest: Editura Enciclopedică.

Petrescu, D. (2010). *Explaining Romanian Revolution of 1989. Culture, Structure, and Contingency.* Bucharest: Editura Enciclopedică.

Piața serviciilor de comunicații electronice din România: raport de date statistice 2013 (2014). Autoritatea Națională pentru Administrare și Reglementare în Comunicații.

Pintilescu, C. (2012). *Justiție militară și represiune politică în România communistă (1948–1956). Studiu de caz: activitatea Tribunalului Militar Cluj.* Cluj-Napoca: Presa Universitară Clujeană.

Pleșa, E. (2016). *Gheorghe Gheorghiu-Dej. Cultul personalității (1945–1965).* Târgoviște: Cetatea de Scaun.

PMR (1949). *Hotărârea Biroului Politic al CC al PMR asupra problemei stimulării și dezvoltării continue a culturii fizice și sportului.* Bucharest: Editura Partidului Muncitoresc Român.

PMR (1964). *Declarația cu privire la poziția Partidului Muncitoresc Român în problemele mișcării comuniste și muncitorești internaționale adoptată de Plenara lărgită a CC a PMR din aprilie 1964.* Bucharest: Editura Politică.

Poenaru, F. and C. Rogozanu eds. (2014). *Epoca Băsescu.* Cluj-Napoca: Tact.

Poguntke, T. and P. Webb eds. (2007). *The Presidentialization of Politics. A Comparative Study of Modern Democracies.* Oxford: Oxford University Press.

Pop, A. (2002). *Tentația tranziției. O istorie a prăbușirii comunismului în Europa de Est.* Bucharest: Corint.

Bibliography

Pop, L. (2006). *Democratising capitalism? The political economy of post-communist transformations in Romania, 1989–2001*. Manchester: Manchester University Press.

Popescu, C.L. (2008). 'Uzurparea de putere comisă de Curtea Constituțională în cazul cenzurii dispozițiilor legale privind deconspirarea poliției politice comuniste', *Noua Revistă de drepturile omului*, 4(1), 3–15.

Popescu, L. (2002). 'Where the Domestic Meets the International: the Role of the International Financial Institutions and the EU in Romania's Post-Communist Transformations', *The Romanian Journal of Society and Politics*, 2(2), 158–87.

Popescu, L. (2010). 'Europenization of Romanian Foreign Policy', *Romanian Journal of European Affairs*, 10(4), 50–65.

Portocală, R. (1991). *România – autopsia unei lovituri de stat. În țara în care a triumfat minciuna*. Timișoara: Editura Agora Timișoreană.

Preda, D. ed. (2000). *1989. Principiul dominoului. Prăbușirea regimurilor comuniste europene*. Bucharest: Editura Fundației Culturale Române.

Pricopie, R. et al. (2011). *Acces și echitate în învățământul superior din România. Dialog cu elevii și studenții*. Bucharest: Comunicare.ro.

Prizonieri de război români în Uniunea Sovietică. Documente (1941–1956) (2013). Bucharest: Monitorul Oficial.

Procacci, G. (1994). *The Cominform. Minutes of the three conferences 1947, 1948, 1949*. Milan: Feltrinelli.

Pușca, A. (2013). *Revolution, Democratic Transition and Disillusionment: The Case of Romania*. Manchester: Manchester University Press.

Pușcaș, V. (1995a). *Speranță și disperare. Negocieri româno-aliate (1943–1944)*. Bucharest: Litera.

Pușcaș, V. ed. (1995b). *Al doilea Război Mondial. Transilvania și aranjamentele europene (1940–1944)*. Cluj-Napoca: Centrul de Studii Transilvane.

Pușcaș, V. ed. (2000). *Central Europe since 1989*. Cluj-Napoca: Dacia.

Pușcaș, V. (2003–6). *Negociind cu Uniunea Europeană*. Vol. I–VI. Bucharest: Editura Economică.

Pușcaș, V. (2006a). *European Negotiations. A case study: Romania accession to the European Union*. Gorizia: International University Institute for European Studies.

Pușcaș, V. (2006b). *Sticks and carrots: regranting the most favored-nation status for Romania (US Congress, 1990–1996) / Bastoane și morcovi: reacordarea clauzei națiunii celei mai favorizate pentru România (Congresul SUA 1990–1996)*. Cluj-Napoca: Eikon.

Radosav, D. (2006). 'Rezistenta anticomunistă armată din România între istorie și memorie', R. Cesereanu ed., *Comunism și represiune în România. Istoria tematică a unui fraticid național*. Iași: Polirom, 82–107.

Radu, A. (2000). *Nevoia schimbării. Un deceniu de pluripartidism în România*. Bucharest: Editura 'Ion Cristoiu'.

Radu, A. (2009). *Un experiment politic românesc. Alianța 'Dreptate și Adevăr' PNL-PD*. Iași: Institutul European.

Radu, A. (2012). *Politica între proporționalism și majoritarism. Alegeri și sistem electoral în România postcomunistă*. Iași: Institutul European.

Radu A. and D. Buti (2013). '*Statul sunt eu!' O istorie a crizei politice din iulie-august 2012*. Bucharest: Monitorul Oficial.

Radu, R.N. (2011). *Instituții culturale în tranziție*. Bucharest: Nemira.

Rădulescu, A.M. (2011). 'Biserica Ortodoxă Română', O. Roske ed., *România: 1945–1989. Enciclopedia regimului communist. Represiunea*. Vol. I (A–E). Bucharest: INST, 194–204

Rădulescu, D.C. (2006). 'Învățământul românesc 1948–1989 – între derivă și recuperare instituțional-funcțională', *Calitatea vieții*, 17(3–4), 307–18

Rădulescu, D.C. and M.S. Stănculescu (2012). 'Oferta turistică din România: 1949–2010', *Calitatea vieții*, 23(4), 299–326.

Raport final. Comisia internațională pentru Studierea Holocaustului în România (2005). Iași: Polirom.

Răutu, L. (1949). 'Împotriva cosmopolitismului şi obiectivismului burghez în ştiinţele sociale', *Lupta de clasă*, 4, 52–83.

Recensământul general agricol 2010. Rezultate provizorii (2011). Bucharest: National Institute of Statistics.

Recensământul general al populaţiei României din 29 decemvrie 1930. Vol. I–VII; IX–X. (1938–40). Bucharest: Central Statistical Institute.

Recensământul populaţiei din 21 februarie 1956: rezultate generale (1959). Bucharest: Central Statistical Direction.

Recensământul populaţiei şi locuinţelor din martie 1966. Vol. I–III. (1969–70) Bucharest: Central Statistical Direction.

Recensământul populaţiei şi locuinţelor din 6 ianuarie 1977. Vol. I–III. (1980–1) Bucharest: Central Statistical Direction.

Recensământul populaţiei şi locuintelor din 7 ianuarie 1992. Vol. I–IV (1994–5). Bucharest: National Commission for Statistics.

Recensământul populaţiei şi locuinţelor din 18 martie 2002. Vol. I–III (2003). Bucharest: National Institute of Statistics.

Recensământul populaţiei şi locuinţelor 2011, http://www.recensamantromania.ro (accessed February 2016).

Rees, E.A. (2004). *The Nature of Stalin's Dictatorship. The Politburo (1924–1953)*. New York: Palgrave Macmillan.

Referendumul din 19 mai 2007, radiografia unei confruntări politice (2007). Bucharest: Institutul 'Ovidiu Şincai'.

Refugiaţii polonezi în România (1939–1947). Documente din Arhivele Naţionale ale României / Polscy uchodźcy w Rumunii (1939–1947). Dokumenty z Narodowych Archiwów Rumunii (2013). Vol. I–II. Bucharest-Warszawa: Instytut Pamięci Narodowej/Arhivele Naţionale ale României.

Retegan, M. (1998). *1968: Din primăvară până-n toamnă: schiţă de politică externă românească*. Bucharest: Rao.

Retegan, M. (2002). *Război politic în blocul comunist. Relaţii româno-sovietice în anii şaizeci.* Documente. Bucharest: Rao.

Rokkan, S. (2010). *Citizens, Elections, Parties: Approaches to the Comparative Study of the Processes of Development*. Colchester: ECPR Press.

Roman, P. (1994). *Libertatea ca datorie*. Cluj-Napoca: Dacia.

România – o Europă în miniatură. Scurtă prezentare a minorităţilor din România (2005). Bucharest: Departamentul pentru Relaţii Interetnice.

România la Conferinţa de Pace de la Paris. Vol. I (2007). Bucharest: Institutul Naţional pentru Memoria Exilului Românesc.

România la Conferinţa de Pace de la Paris. Vol. II (2011). Bucharest: Editura Enciclopedică.

Roncea, V. ed. (2005). *Axa. Noua Românie la Marea Neagră*. Bucharest: Ziua.

Ronnas, P. (1984). *Urbanization in Romania. A Geography of Social and Economic Change Since Independence*. Stockholm: Economic Research Institute.

Roper, S.D. (2000). *Romania: the unfinished revolution*. Amsterdam: Harwood Academic.

Rose, R. (2009). *Understanding Post-communist Transformation: A Bottom-Up Approach*. New York: Routledge.

Roske, O., F. Abraham and D. Cătănuş (2007). *Colectivizarea agriculturii în România. Cadrul legislativ (1949–1962)*. Bucharest: INST.

Rotman, L. (2004). *Evreii din România în perioada comunistă (1944–1965)*. Iaşi: Polirom.

Rus, A. (2007). *Mineriadele. Între manipulare politică şi solidaritate muncitorească*. Bucharest: Curtea Veche.

Rusu-Toderean, O. (1997–8). 'Mass-media şi opinia publică în campania României pentru integrarea în NATO', *Studia politica*, 42–43(1), 91–110.

Bibliography

Sadurski, W. (2014). *Rights Before Courts. A Study of Constitutional Courts in Postcommunist States of Central and Eastern Europe. Second Edition.* London: Springer.

Sadurski, W., A. Czarnota and M. Krygier eds. (2006). *Spreading Democracy and the Rule of Law? The Impact of EU Enlargement on the Rule of Law, Democracy and Constitutionalism in Post-Communist Legal Orders.* Dordrecht: Springer.

Săftoiu, A. (2015). *Cronică de Cotroceni.* Iași: Polirom.

Sălăgean, M. (2002). *Administrația sovietică în Nordul Transilvaniei (noiembrie 1944–martie 1945).* Cluj-Napoca: Centrul de Studii Transilvane.

Salat, L. ed. (2008). *Politici de integrare a minorităților naționale din România. Aspecte legale și instituționale într-o perspectivă comparată.* Cluj-Napoca: CRDE.

Salat, L. and S. Enache eds. (2004). *Relațiile româno-maghiare și modelul de reconciliere franco-german.* Cluj-Napoca: CRDE.

Sandu, D. (1984). *Fluxurile de migrație în România.* Bucharest: Editura Academiei Republicii Socialiste România.

Sandu, D. ed. (2006). *Locuirea temporară în străinătate. Migrația economică a românilor: 1990–2006.* Bucharest: The Foundation for an Open Society.

Șarov, I. and I. Ojog (2009). *Evoluția politicii externe a Republicii Moldova (1998–2008).* Chișinău: Cartdidact.

Sava, C. and C. Monac (2000). *Revoluția din decembrie 1989 percepută prin documentele vremii.* Bucharest: Editura Axioma Edit.

Schneeweis, A. (2012). 'If they really wanted to, they would: The press discourse of integration of the European Roma (1990–2006)', *The International Communication Gazette*, 74(7), 673–89.

Schonberg, K.K. (2009). *Constructing 21st Century U.S. Foreign Policy. Identity, Ideology, and America's World Role in a New Era.* New York: Palgrave Macmillan.

Scurtu, I. (1996). *România. Retragerea trupelor sovietice – 1958.* Bucharest: Editura Didactică and Pedagogică.

Scurtu, I. (2005). *Istoria contemporană a României (1918–2005).* Bucharest: Editura Fundației România de Mâine.

Scurtu, I. (2006). *Revoluția română din Decembrie 1989 în context internațional.* Bucharest: Editura Enciclopedică.

Scurtu, I. (2010a). *Istoria românilor de la Carol I la Nicolae Ceaușescu.* Târgoviște: Mica Valahie.

Scurtu, I. (2010b). *Istoria românilor în timpul celor patru regi. Mihai.* Vol. IV. Bucharest: Editura Enciclopedică.

Scurtu, I. (2014). *Tezaurul României de la Moscova.* Bucharest: Editura Enciclopedică.

Scurtu, I. and G. Buzatu (1999). *Istoria românilor în secolul XX (1918–1948).* Bucharest: Paideia.

Șeitan, M., M. Arteni and A. Nedu (2012). *Evoluția demografică pe termen lung și sustenabilitatea sistemului de pensii.* Bucharest: Editura Economică.

Sentința penală no.176. File no. 514/1/2009, ÎCJC, 30.01.2012.

Șercan, E. (2015). *Cultul secretului. Mecanismele cenzurii în presa comunistă.* Iași: Polirom.

Severin, A. (1995). *Lacrimile dimineții. Slăbiciunile guvernului Roman.* Bucharest: Scripta.

Seyom B. (2015). *Faces of Power: Constancy and Change in United States Foreign Policy from Truman to Obama. Third Edition.* New York: Columbia University Press.

Shafir, M. (1985). *Romania. Politics, economics, and society: political stagnation and simulated change.* Boulder: L. Rienner Publishers.

Siani-Davies, P. (2005/2006). *The Romanian revolution of December 1989.* Ithaca: Cornell University Press/*Revoluția română din decembrie 1989.* Bucharest: Humanitas.

Simion, A. (1996). *Dictatul de la Viena.* Bucharest: Albatros.

Simion, M. (2004). 'Profilul demografic al României', *Calitatea vieții*, 14(1–2), 44–58.

Șinca, F. (2014). *Martirii Poliției Române. Distrugerea poliției sub regimul comunist.* Bucharest: RCR Editorial.

Soare, S. (2010). 'The Romanian-Russian bilateral relationship in the aftermath of Romania's euroatlantic Integration', *Monitor Strategic,* 11(1–2), 93–121.

Solonari, V. (2009). *Purifying the Nation: Population Exchange and Ethnic Cleansing in Nazi-Allied Romania.* Washington: Woodrow Wilson Center Press.

Şperlea, F. (2003). *De la armata regală la armata populară: sovietizarea armatei române (1948–1955).* Bucharest: Editura Ziua.

Stahel, D. (2009). *Operation Barbarossa and Germany's Defeat in the East.* Cambridge: Cambridge University Press.

Stan, A. (2009). 'Conflictul dintre preşedinte şi premier. O analiză a instituţiei prezidenţiale din România (2004–2008)', *Sfera politicii*, 139, 37–43.

Stan, L. (2013). *Transitional Justice in Post-Communist Romania. The Politics of Memory.* Cambridge: Cambridge University Press

Stan, L. and L. Turcescu (2007). *Religion and Politics in Post-Communist Romania.* Oxford: Oxford University Press.

Stan, L. and D. Vancea (2015). 'House of Cards: The Presidency from Iliescu to Băsescu', L. Stan and D. Vancea eds., *Post-Communist Romania at Twenty-Five: Linking Past, Present, and Future.* Lanham, MD: Lexington Books, 193–18.

Stanef, M.R. (2013). 'Sistemul educaţional din România, disparităţi dintre mediul urban şi cel rural', *Economie teoretică şi aplicată*, 20(1), 83–93.

Stănescu, M. (2010). *Reeducarea în România comunistă (1945–1952).* Iaşi: Polirom.

Stănescu, I. (2014). *Puterea politică în România. De la comunism la noul capitalism (1989–2014).* Bucharest: Pro Universitaria.

Statul şi cultele religioase (2014). Bucharest: Secretariatul de Stat pentru Culte.

Ştefan, L. (2012). *Who Governs Romania? Profiles of Romanian Political Elites before and after 1989.* Bucharest: Editura ISPRI.

Ştefănescu, D. (1995). *Cinci ani din istoria României. O cronologie a evenimentelor decembrie 1989–decembrie 1994.* Bucharest: Editura Maşina de Scris.

Steinhardt, N. (1991). *Jurnalul fericirii.* Cluj-Napoca: Dacia.

Stoenescu, A.M. (2005). *Istoria loviturilor de stat în România.* Vol. IV, Second part. Bucharest: Rao.

Stoenescu, A.M. (2006). *Din culisele luptei pentru putere 1989–1990. Prima guvernare Petre Roman.* Bucharest: Rao.

Stoica, C.A. (2004). 'From Good Communists to Even Better Capitalists? Entrepreneurial Pathways in Post-Socialist Romania', *East European Politics and Societies*, 18(2), 236–77.

Stoiciu, V. ed. (2011). *Impactul crizei economice asupra migraţiei forţei de muncă româneşti.* Bucharest: Friedrich Ebert Foundation.

Stoicovici, M. (2012). 'România ca ţară de origine, de tranzit şi de destinaţie a migranţilor', *Revista Română de Sociologie*, 23(5–6), 429–43.

Stroschein, S. (2012). *Ethnic struggle, coexistence, and democratization in Eastern Europe.* Cambridge: Cambridge University Press.

Suditu, B.A. G. Prelipcean, D.C. Vardol and O.A. Stângaciu (2013). *Perspectivele politicii de migraţie în contextul demografic actual din România.* Bucharest: European Institute of Romania.

Sussex, M. (2012). *Conflict in the Former USSR.* Cambridge: Cambridge University Press.

Tănase, L.D. (2008). *Pluralisation religieuse et société en Roumanie.* Berna: Peter Lang.

Ţăranu, L. (2007). *România în Consiliul de Ajutor Economic Reciproc (1949–1965).* Bucharest: Editura Enciclopedică.

Ţârău, V. (2005). *Alegeri fără opţiune. Primele alegeri parlamentare din centrul şi estul Europei după încheierea celui de-al doilea război mondial.* Cluj-Napoca: Eikon.

Tarnovschi, D. ed. (2012). *Roma from Romania, Bulgaria, Italy and Spain between Social Inclusion and Migration: comparative study.* Constanţa: Editura Dobrogea.

Bibliography

Tatulici, M. ed. (1990). *Revoluția română în direct*. Vol. I. Bucharest: Televiziunea Română.

Thomas, A.R., N.A. Pop and C. Brătianu eds. (2013). *The Changing Business Landscape of Romania: Lessons for and from Transition Economies*. New York: Springer.

Tismăneanu, V. (2003). *Stalinism for all seasons: a political history of Romanian communism*. Berkeley: University of California Press.

Tismăneanu, V., D. Dobrincu and C. Vasile eds. (2007). *Raport final. Comisia Prezidențială pentru Analiza Dictaturii Comuniste din România*. Bucharest: Humanitas.

Tofan, L. (2013). *Șacalul Securității. Teroristul Carlos în solda spionajului românesc*. Iași: Polirom

Trașcă, O. (2001). 'Impactul problemei Transilvaniei asupra colaborării militare româno-germane (1941–1944)', *Anuarul Institutului de Istorie 'George Bariț'. Series Historica*, XL, 155–84.

Trașcă, O. (2013). *Relațiile politice și militare româno-germane (septembrie 1940–august 1944)*. Cluj-Napoca: Argonaut.

Trașcă, O. and A.M. Stan (2002). *Rebeliunea legionară în arhivele străine (germane, maghiare, franceze)*. Bucharest: Albatros.

Trebici, V. (1991). *Genocid și demografie*. Bucharest: Humanitas.

Trif, A. (2008). 'Opportunities and Challenges of EU Accession: Industrial Relations in Romania', *European Journal of Industrial Relations*, 14(4), 461–78.

Tucker, A. (2015). *The Legacies of Totalitarianism. A Theoretical Framework*. Cambridge: Cambridge University Press.

Tudor, A. and D. Cătănuș (2001). *O destalinizare ratată. Culisele cazului Miron Constantinescu – Iosif Chișinevschi (1956–1961)*. Bucharest: Elion.

Tufiș, C.D. (2012). *Learning Democracy and Market Economy in Post-Communist Romania*. Iași: Institutul European.

Tufiș, C.D. (2014). 'The not-so-curious case of low political participation in Romania', *Calitatea vieții*, 25 (3), 281–306.

Turnock, D. (1986). *The Romanian Economy in the Twentieth Century*. London: Croom Helm.

Turnock, D. (2007). *Aspects of Independent Romania's Economic History with Particular Reference to Transition for EU Accession*. Aldershot: Ashgate.

Ulrich, L., M. Bojincă, S. Stănciugelu and V. Mihăilă (2011). *Al patrulea val. Migrația creierelor pe ruta România-Occident*. Bucharest: Soros Romania Foundation.

Vădean, M.R. (2011). *Relațiile româno-ungare în contextul integrării în structurile europene și euro-atlantice*. Iași: Lumen.

Vălenaș, L. (2003). *Republica iresponsabililor. Convorbiri cu Victor Ciorbea*. Bucharest: Tritonic.

Văratic, V. (2000). *Preliminarii la raptul Basarabiei și Bucovinei (1938–1940)*. Bucharest: Libra.

Vasile, A. (2011). *Le cinéma roumain dans la période communiste. Représentations de l'histoire nationale*. Bucharest: Editura Universității București.

Vasile, C. (2003). *Între Vatican și Kremlin. Biserica Greco-Catolică în timpul regimului comunist*. Bucharest: Curtea Veche.

Vasile, C. (2011a). *Politicile culturale comuniste în timpul regimului Gheorghiu-Dej*. Bucharest: Humanitas.

Vasile, R. (2002). *Cursa pe contrasens: amintirile unui prim-ministru*. Bucharest: Humanitas.

Vasiliu, F. (2000). *Sindicate și sindicaliști. O analiză sociologică a reconstrucției sindicalismului în România*. Sibiu: Editura Universității 'Lucian Blaga'.

Veiga, F. (1995). *Istoria Gărzii de Fier (1919–1941). Mistica ultranaționalismului*. Bucharest: Humanitas.

Verdery, K. (1995). *National Ideology under Socialism: identity and cultural politics in Ceaușescu's Romania*. Berkeley: University of California Press.

Verenca, O. (2000). *Administrația civilă română în Transnistria (1941–1944)*. Bucharest: Vremea.

Verheijen, T. (2004). 'Romania', R. Elgie ed., *Semi-Presidentialism in Europe*. Oxford: Oxford University Press, 193–215.

Verona, S. (1992). *Military Occupation and Diplomacy. Soviet Troops in Romania (1944–1958)*. Durham and London: Duke University Press.

Vlăsceanu, L. and M.G. Hâncean (2014). *Modernitatea românească*. Piteşti: Paralela 45.

Vlăsceanu, L. et al. (2010). *Barometrul Calităţii – 2010. Starea calităţii în învăţământul superior din România*. Bucharest: Aracis.ro.

Voinea, L. and F. Mihăescu (2008). *Impactul cotei unice asupra inegalităţii în România*. Bucharest: Grupul de Economie Aplicată.

Von Bogdandy, A. ed. (2013) *Constitutional Crisis in the European Constitutional Area: Theory, Law and Politics in Hungary and Romania*. Oxford: Hart.

Vultur, S. (1997). *Istorie trăită – istorie povestită. Deportarea în Bărăgan (1951–1956)*. Timişoara: Amarcord.

Watts, L. (1993). *O Casandră a României. Ion Antonescu şi lupta pentru reformă*. Bucharest: Editura Fundaţiei Culturale Române.

Watts, L. (2001). 'Reform and Crisis in Romanian Civil-Military Relations 1989–1999', *Armed Forces & Society*, 27(4), 597–22.

Watts, L. (2004). 'Conflicting Paradigms, Dissimilar Contexts. Intelligence Reform in Europe's Emerging Democracies', *Studies in Intelligence*, 48(1), 19–25.

Watts, L. (2007). 'Control and Oversight of Security Intelligence in Romania', M. Caparini and H. Born, *Democratic Control of Intelligence Services: Containing Rogue Elephants*. Aldershot: Ashgate, 47–64.

Watts, L. (2010). *With friends like these . . . The Soviet Bloc's Clandestine War Against Romania*. Bucharest: Editura Militară.

Watts, L. (2013). *Cei dintâi vor fi cei din urmă. România şi sfârşitul Războiului Rece*. Bucharest: Rao.

Welch, D. (2008). 'Privatization in Romania from 1989 to 2007', I.W. Lieberman and D.J. Kopf eds., *Privatization in transition economies: the ongoing story*. Amsterdam: Elsevier.

Zamfir, C. and M. Preda eds. (2002). *Romii în România*. Bucharest: Expert.

Zamfir, C. ed. (1999). *Politici sociale în România*. Bucharest: Expert.

Zifcak, S. ed. (2005). *Globalisation and the Rule of Law*. London: Routledge.

INDEX

Index

Index

Index

Constitutional Court 155, 161, 168, 181, 220–3, 228, 256
Convorbiri literare 262
Copenhagen 184, 185
Coposu, C. 123, 146, 149, 161, 231, 306
Cornea, D. 71, 114
corruption 12, 122, 123, 126, 147, 150, 152–4, 156, 162, 163, 165, 185, 188, 191, 199, 200, 215, 217–19, 223, 242, 269, 279, 302
Coseşti 239, 240
Costin, D. 243
Costineşti 101
Cotidianul 252
Cotroceni Palace 181, 238
Council for National Minorities 257
Council of Ministers 34, 40, 48, 52, 80
county 16, 35, 53, 70, 81, 99, 102, 109, 110, 119, 131, 161, 169–71, 175, 246, 256, 259, 261
Court of Auditors 137, 161
Covasna 57, 204, 259, 285
Cozma, M. 226, 232, 236, 237, 238, 239, 240
CPSU 38, 39, 46, 48
CPUN 136, 141, 147, 231, 232, 234
Crăiniceanu, A. 238
Craiova 7, 82, 111, 284
Crescent 247
Creţu, C. 188
Crimea 180
Crimean War 200
Criminal Code 63, 72, 218
Criminal Procedure Code 63, 218
Crişana-Maramureş 285
Croatia 212
Croitoru, C. 138
CSAŢ 144, 148, 157, 181, 218, 227, 238, 239
CSM 137, 216, 217, 219, 220
CSP 40, 93, 94
Cuba 46, 108, 109
Cuban Missile Crisis 45
culture 52, 57, 75, 79, 80, 82, 84, 98, 111, 192, 242, 243, 254, 260–4, 305
CVM 186–8, 197, 215, 218, 223
Cyprus 185, 212
Czech Republic 117, 182, 183, 185, 190, 198, 224
Czechoslovakia 3, 22, 24, 28, 36, 41, 43, 45, 57, 59, 61, 71, 89, 107, 114, 192, 193, 299

Dac Air 247
Dacia 97, 199, 273
Daciada 55, 84
Daewoo 273
Danube 44, 211, 214, 285
Danube Delta 6, 211, 276
Danube–Black Sea Canal 37, 58, 67, 73, 99
Dăscălescu, C. 52, 110, 112
death penalty 115

decentralization 94, 158, 172, 175, 261
decommunization 224
de Gaulle, C. 59
Dejeu, G. 239
democracy 3, 23, 29, 31, 33, 34, 38, 106, 107, 117–23, 130, 132, 136, 145, 146, 154, 169, 178, 215, 217, 220, 221, 223, 226, 230, 234–6, 241, 245, 246, 249, 285, 306
demography
  fertility 57, 287, 290–3, 297, 298
  life expectancy 176, 292, 293, 301
  marriage 31, 287, 291, 292
  mortality 284, 287, 290–3, 298
  population 6, 8, 11, 12, 16, 17, 19, 20, 22, 26, 30, 37, 49, 51–4, 56–8, 68–70, 73, 74, 76, 78, 79, 82, 86, 87, 88, 91, 92, 96, 97, 98, 103, 104, 108, 110, 111, 121, 137, 151, 155, 170, 174, 175, 176, 179, 207, 219, 229, 233, 235, 242, 253, 254, 258, 267, 270, 272, 276, 278, 283–97, 300, 302
demolition 75, 86
Denmark 5
Department for Interethnic Relations 258
Department for the Protection of National Minorities 258
deportation 15–17, 42, 73, 89, 283, 285
d'Estaing, V. 60
de-Stalinization 38, 39, 97, 291
Diaconescu, D. 127, 251
dictatorship 3, 9–11, 15, 33, 50, 53, 64, 68, 76, 82, 108, 113, 147, 269, 305
Dimitriu, S. 150
Dinescu, M. 112, 114
Distrigaz Nord 197
Distrigaz Sud 199
DNA 218, 219
Dniester 6, 11, 12
Dobrogea 4, 7, 30, 72, 73, 92, 254, 286, 294
Doğan Holding 246
Doncea, C. 39
Dorneanu, V. 221, 223
Drăghici, A. 18, 19, 65, 306
Dubček, A. 59
Dudu Ionescu, C. 239
Dugulescu, P. 256
Durostor 7, 214

earthquake 75
Eastern Partnership 212
economat 92
economic crises 91, 127, 169
economy 19, 23, 30, 36, 40, 42, 44, 50, 58, 61, 75, 77, 91, 93–7, 100, 101, 103, 104, 113, 117, 118, 120, 121, 144, 145, 148, 150, 156, 160, 163–5, 176–8, 187, 190, 197, 226, 240, 242, 244, 245, 247, 260, 261, 267, 269, 270–81, 284, 295, 302, 307

329

Index

Index

Index

Index